Dynamics of Caste and Law

This monograph breaks new ground in understanding how caste and law relate in India's democratic order. Caste is a very visible phenomenon, often associated with politics, social inequality and discrimination. India's constitutional democracy has been remarkable for its goal of creating equality in the context of caste. Despite constitutional promises of equal opportunities for the lower castes and the outlawing of untouchability at the time of independence, reoccurring atrocities and inadequate implementation of law have called for rethinking and legal action.

Building on a post-foundational approach to critical explanation, this work provides an account of how Dalit experiences represent a starting point to analyse the dynamics of law and caste-based domination. Sociological terms invented by Bhimrao Ambedkar, an anti-caste leader of Dalits and a groundbreaking scholar, are incorporated to explain the enduring relevance of caste. In addition to case studies of Dalit movements, atrocities and caste politics, it is argued through detailed examination of court cases that law could be redirected to suit the members of dominant castes.

Making a clear departure from conventional disciplinary approaches, the book explains how caste-based oppression, public policy and the ontology of caste intersect. It will be of interest to students of South Asia studies and the social sciences more broadly. While contributing to new developments in poststructuralist social and political theory, political ethnography and historical institutionalism, the book has comparative relevance for discussions of democracy, law and racism.

Dag-Erik Berg is associate professor of political science at Molde University College, Norway. His research takes an interdisciplinary approach to study hegemony, governance and constitutional democracy in global perspective. Recent publications by him have examined the intersection of post-foundational political theory, social exclusion and law relating to India's Dalits.

SOUTH ASIA IN THE SOCIAL SCIENCES

South Asia has become a laboratory for devising new institutions and practices of modern social life. Forms of capitalist enterprise, providing welfare and social services, the public role of religion, the management of ethnic conflict, popular culture and mass democracy in the countries of the region have shown a marked divergence from known patterns in other parts of the world. South Asia is now being studied for its relevance to the general theoretical understanding of modernity itself.

South Asia in the Social Sciences will feature books that offer innovative research on contemporary South Asia. It will focus on the place of the region in the various global disciplines of the social sciences and highlight research that uses unconventional sources of information and novel research methods. While recognising that most current research is focused on the larger countries, the series will attempt to showcase research on the smaller countries of the region.

Other books in the series:

Government as Practice: Democratic Left in a Transforming India
Dwaipayan Bhattacharyya

Courting the People: Public Interest Litigation in Post-Emergency India
Anuj Bhuwania

Development after Statism: Industrial Firms and the Political Economy of South Asia
Adnan Naseemullah

Politics of the Poor: Negotiating Democracy in Contemporary India
Indrajit Roy

South Asian Governmentalities: Michel Foucault and the Question of Postcolonial Orderings
Stephen Legg and Deana Heath (eds.)

Nationalism, Development and Ethnic Conflict in Sri Lanka
Rajesh Venugopal

Adivasis and the State: Subalternity and Citizenship in India's Bhil Heartland
Alf Gunvald Nilsen

Maoist People's War and the Revolution of Everyday Life in Nepal
Ina Zharkevich

New Perspectives on Pakistan's Political Economy: State, Class and Social Change
Matthew McCartney and S. Akbar Zaidi (eds.)

Crafty Oligarchs, Savvy Voters: Democracy under Inequality in Rural Pakistan
Shandana Khan Mohmand

Dynamics of Caste and Law

Dalits, Oppression and Constitutional Democracy in India

Dag-Erik Berg

CAMBRIDGE
UNIVERSITY PRESS

CAMBRIDGE
UNIVERSITY PRESS

Shaftesbury Road, Cambridge CB2 8EA, United Kingdom

One Liberty Plaza, 20th Floor, New York, NY 10006, USA

477 Williamstown Road, Port Melbourne, VIC 3207, Australia

314–321, 3rd Floor, Plot 3, Splendor Forum, Jasola District Centre, New Delhi – 110025, India

103 Penang Road, #05–06/07, Visioncrest Commercial, Singapore 238467

Cambridge University Press is part of Cambridge University Press & Assessment, a department of the University of Cambridge.

We share the University's mission to contribute to society through the pursuit of education, learning and research at the highest international levels of excellence.

www.cambridge.org
Information on this title: www.cambridge.org/9781108489874

First published 2020

A catalogue record for this publication is available from the British Library

Library of Congress Cataloging-in-Publication data
Names: Berg, Dag-Erik, author.
Title: Dynamics of caste and law : Dalits, oppression and constitutional democracy in India / Dag-Erik Berg.
Description: New York : Cambridge University Press, 2019. | Includes bibliographical references and index.
Identifiers: LCCN 2019043619 | ISBN 9781108489874 (hardback)
Subjects: LCSH: Caste--Law and legislation--India. | Dalits--Legal status, laws, etc.--India. | Dalits--Abuse of--India. | Constitutional law--India. | Democracy--India.
Classification: LCC KNS513.3 .B47 2019 | DDC 342.5408/7--dc23
LC record available at https://lccn.loc.gov/2019043619

ISBN 978-1-108-48987-4 Hardback

Contents

Abbreviations

ABVP	Akhil Bharatiya Vidyarthi Parishad
AIIMS	All India Institute for Medical Sciences
ASA	Ambedkar Students' Association
BJP	Bharatiya Janata Party
FIR	first information report
IIT	Indian Institutes of Technology
NGO	non-governmental organization
OBC	Other Backward Classes
PoA Act	The Scheduled Castes and the Scheduled Tribes (Prevention of Atrocities) Act
PUCL	People's Union for Civil Liberties
RSS	Rashtriya Swayamsevak Sangh
SC	Scheduled Castes
ST	Scheduled Tribes
TDP	Telegu Desam Party
UPA	United Progressive Alliance – the coalition led by the Congress party since the general elections in 2004

Preface

India's democratic constitution offers a rare possibility to acquire insights into how a constitutional democracy deals with embedded inequalities. Caste is a central topic in this context, and the historically excluded 'untouchable' castes (Dalits) have, along with the tribal population (Adivasis), been at the centre of the ambitious policy of equal opportunity. The caste system, however, creates inequalities and exclusion and represents a source of challenges at the heart of the democratic project. In fact, the topic of this book – caste and law – has grown bigger, more global and politically charged, as I have been writing about it. It is as if this object of study has become more visible every day.

Caste-based exclusion compares to racism as a phenomenon that is aggravated by the rise of right-wing rhetoric and mobilization. The mobilization of Hindu nationalist groups since 2014 seems to have put India's constitutional democracy in a critical situation. But caste-based violence and abuse have been a troubling side of India's democracy throughout the postcolonial period. Caste is part of the everyday social order. Despite its current visibility in India and overseas, however, there is a great deal of confusion and mystification about this complex social system. Caste does not fit into pre-existing categories in law, politics or sociology. The social sciences were developed with the growth of the modern nation-state, and its many technical approaches have not been designed to address caste in South Asia.

A huge amount of writing has emerged on caste and Dalits. Yet this book is premised on the idea that there is much more to learn by bringing caste into the global conversation on social inequalities and exclusion in constitutional democracies, states and organizations. Social scientists must have the courage to use their understanding outside the strictures of disciplines' silos, since these are often mired in Eurocentrism, empiricism or theoretical deductions. This implies, among other things, that one needs to bring the study of caste outside the discipline of social anthropology. Caste represents a thought-provoking social system in which hegemony and inequality are systematically reproduced. This matters for law and democratic thought, and many concepts appear either out of date or inadequate to explain its significance.

I am pleased to have developed this book over quite a long time because this has had some advantages regarding making sense of complex materials and challenging questions concerning caste and law. I have benefitted not only from long-term data collection when new developments have occurred in the cases I have been concerned with, but I have also been able to benefit from new conceptual innovations in political and institutional theories that bolstered my engagement with the materials. For example, Ernesto Laclau has advanced his post-foundational approach in his approach to hegemony in his final book, published in 2014. He has been able to refine a novel approach to political ontology by revisiting Kant's concept of antagonism while skilfully manoeuvring between Heidegger, Marx and other thinkers. His mature approach to hegemony dovetailed with my work on Bhimrao Ambedkar – the leader of India's untouchables during the independence movement whose scholarship on caste makes significant contributions to an ontological turn in political theory. What is crucial, however, is that Ambedkar's scholarship offers a possibility of developing more productive questions about caste and law at the centre of India's democratic system. In the past decade, Ambedkar has become more acknowledged in Indian public and academic debates than he used to be. Today, India's diplomats in the United Nations in New York even organize discussions of Ambedkar's work with leading scholars and tweet comments and pictures to a global audience. Indeed, while Ambedkar is a contested and sometimes insulted symbol on the streets of India, it seems as if his statesmanship and scholarship offer novel visions involving Enlightenment ideals and democratic justice in India today.

Readers of this book will realize that caste is anything but a trivial phenomenon. In 2018, there have been noteworthy reminders about how caste and law matter for social and political dynamics in India and internationally. It has been discussed in non-discrimination law in the United Kingdom, for example. In India, the Supreme Court delivered two contentious judgments about legal protection for Dalits and Adivasis and temple entry for women in a temple in Sabarimala, Kerala. These examples involve notions of caste, 'untouchability' and law in India's constitutional democracy. While caste-based atrocities and legal protections are central themes in this book on caste and law in India's democracy, the question of women's social status is a relevant background factor. What was noteworthy about the events of 2018 was that seemingly ancient notions of purity and untouchability, once used to legitimize a hierarchical social order, gained prominence in national politics. The controversial book *The Laws of Manu*, which has been symbolically burned by successive Dalit movements because of the humiliating statements it makes, includes statements about how menstruating women also represent a source of pollution and says that they are not supposed to watch a priest eat. I recall the shock of a customer in a book shop in Chennai in the early 2000s when he noticed that I had collected a copy of this ancient book, *The Laws of Manu*. Indeed, it is one of the many paradoxes of India's constitutional state that a statue of Manu has been erected just outside the high court in a different part of the country, in the state of Rajasthan. While the statue has been disputed in court since it was erected in 1989, two Dalit women from Maharashtra decided to travel to Jaipur on 8 October 2018 where one of them ended up colouring the statue with black paint as a sign of protest against casteism and patriarchy.[1] No doubt the statue of Manu outside a high court does give rise to some questions about how law is applied in a country with one of the most innovative constitutions of liberal democracy in the postcolonial period. As I make clear in this book, however, the world's largest democracy involves a significant history of movements that have articulated rights and demands for dignity and freedom as well as struggles for power and position.

The goal of this book is to develop a new approach to explain caste-based domination and the intersections of caste and law in India's constitutional democracy. It is a test for the social sciences to provide fuller explanations of such an embedded phenomenon, not only because caste shapes millions of lives but also because it offers unique insights into the reproduction of social inequalities and dominance in constitutional democracies.

Notes

1 *Indian Express*, 'A Day in the Life of a Manu Statue in the Rajasthan High Court', 28 October 2018, accessed 10 July 2019, https://indianexpress.com/article/india/a-day-in-the-life-of-a-manu-statue-in-the-rajasthan-high-court-5421545.

Acknowledgements

I am grateful to every individual and institution that has made this book possible. I hope that those with whom I have discussed questions related to the topic of this book will consider it as a tribute to the time I have spent with them. This interaction has contributed to my thinking about this complex subject, even though I have not been able to mention everyone here or in the references (and some people have been anonymized). Although I used several other methods during my research, dialogue liberates thinking and understanding.

My work on this book has benefitted considerably from thought-provoking discussions with various academic audiences in Hyderabad, New Delhi, Oxford and Göttingen in addition to a number of colleagues, peers and friends. Before its new developments, the book was initially presented as my PhD thesis at the University of Bergen (UiB). I was a PhD candidate in the Department of Administration and Organization Theory, once characterized by its combination of abstract thought, studies of organizations and historical processes, but I was lucky in being able to explore the Department's novel approach in a new direction and to be advised by a multidisciplinary team of professors. As I moved away from the UiB, I had the good fortune of working with several individuals, teams and institutions that further enabled me to develop a genuine interdisciplinary approach in which I could combine political theory and empirical analysis. Jason Glynos from the University of Essex invited me to be associated with the Centre for Theoretical Studies in the Humanities and Social Sciences as a non-residential scholar, for which I remain grateful. A period as an assistant in David Mosse's project 'Caste Out of Development' at the School of Oriental and African Studies, London, offered a rare opportunity to learn from David's insights into development policy, organizations and caste in south India. It was a great pleasure to work with his team members S. Anandhi, Sundara Babu, Luisa Steur, Dominic Davidappa and Selvaraj. Professor of intercultural studies Line A. Ytrehus was a perfect boss at the time that I taught at NLA University College, Bergen.

The work on this book gained new momentum during a period of research and teaching at the Centre for Modern Indian Studies (CeMIS) at the University of Göttingen. Thanks to Professor Rupa Viswanath, I was able to participate in her research group Inequality and Diversity, from which I started a fruitful cooperation with Gajendran Ayyathurai. In fact, Gajendran not only helped me to more clearly identify how rationalities may be excluded through research and writing, but his cheerful nature and sustained support also became treasured aspects of this project. At CeMIS, I taught several graduate courses, including Caste and Governance, which gave me an opportunity to explore new ways of organizing my approach and readings while learning from discussions with the students. I am grateful for the unique interdisciplinary approach at CeMIS and its congenial and vibrant intellectual atmosphere, as well as for the many stimulating workshops and conferences on the Göttingen Campus.

Many ideas inspiring this book originated more than a decade ago, and most of the interviews and fieldwork were conducted from 2003 to 2010, although there was a supplementary trip later. As a graduate student in 2003, I met Korivi Vinay Kumar at the Centre for Dalit Studies (CDS), Hyderabad, then headed by Mallepalli Laxmaiah. Vinay explained the details of the Tsundur massacre in 1991, and the story created a lasting impression. At the CDS, I met Gaddam Krishna Reddy, Professor of political science at Osmania University, who later became a dear colleague and mentor until he sadly passed away. But I am grateful to have been in contact with Krishna's extended circle, from Ajay Gudavarthy at Jawaharlal Nehru University to his students Kumaraswamy Nagam, Rajesh Kota and Sudarshan Balaboina. Another of his PhD students, Sooriaprakash, also passed away too early.

While I have conducted fieldwork in several regions, Hyderabad has become my hub and intellectual home. I would like to thank academics at Osmania University and K. Satyanarayana at the English and Foreign Languages University, as well as Professor Prakash Sarangi at University of Hyderabad and K. C. Suri and K. Y. Ratnam at the Department of Political Science for their kind cooperation. Thanks to Vare Laxman and Ramesh Babu Para for accompanying me on the trips to Tsundur in 2008 and making them more worthwhile. Thanks also to Ram Babu Mallavarapu, Suresh and other students, Manohar for translations from Telugu, as well as to Suman Reddy, Kalpana Kannabiran, Amita Dhanda, Suresh Lelle, Sunkapaka Devaiah Madiga, P. Krupakar Madiga, P. Muthaiah, Manda Krishna Madiga, Sampangi Shanker, Gaddar and Charles Wesley. Thanks also to V. Nanda Gopal, D. Bhoopal and the staff at Sakshi for their time and help. I am grateful for the several extensive interviews I had with Bojja Tharakam and a memorable meal in his home before he passed away. Thanks also to Katti Padma Rao who, along with Tharakam, has been a senior Dalit leader in Andhra Pradesh. I was also fortunate to meet K. G. Kannabiran and K. Balagopal, two towering figures in the human rights movement in Andhra Pradesh, before they passed away. B. Chandrasekhar from Guntur was part of this remarkable civil rights movement. He was the special public prosecutor in Tsundur court and was extraordinarily generous in sharing his experience, insights and materials from the trial. He passed away too young. Thanks also to Nageswaram Rao, Tenali, Chukka Nagam Bhushanam and Jaladi Moses in Tsundur. Along with Ramesh Babu Para, I was invited to Moses' home and experienced the peaceful atmosphere there while learning more about his enduring struggle for justice after his father had been so brutally killed in 1991. It adds to a number of other meetings which have left lasting impressions.

Elsewhere in India, I wish to extend my gratitude to Meshram and Suryakant Waghmore in Mumbai and to several people in Tamil Nadu, especially Paul Panneer Selvam, Punitha Pandian and Christobadoss Gandhi in Chennai; Yesumarian and Marimuthu in Chengalpattu; Milton Vilveraj and the late Jayakaran Joseph in Vellore; and V. Bhaskaran, Anthony Raj, Kadirvelu, Mohan Labeer and Anbuselvam in Madurai. In Kerala, Dinesan Vadakkiniyil and Matthew Varghese supported my fieldwork, which involved meeting Sanal Mohan, Kaleswaram Raj, Sunny Kapicad, K. K. Kochu and other impressive individuals while learning about caste and law in this state. One of them was Professor Yesudasan, who later delivered a lecture at the Anveshi Research Centre for Women's Studies in Hyderabad; his lecture represents one of many examples of how knowledge is translated between regions, social movements and scholars. I am also grateful for a number of meetings with Sudhir Krishnaswamy, Jayna Kothari, Saravanan, S. Japhet and Gopal Karanth from Bangalore.

In Delhi, I am indebted to a range of people, including Upendra Baxi, Pratiksha Baxi, Rajeev Dhavan, P. P. Rao, S. K. Thorat, Jagpal Singh, John Dayal, Manoj Mitta, S. Anand, Rajasekhar Vundru, G. Srinivas, Chinna Rao, Avinash Kumar, Ajith Kanna, Nitin Ramesh, Vinay Sitapati and P. N. Malik from the Nordic Centre. P. S. Krishnan has shared his knowledge with me during extensive interviews. I also owe him my gratitude for the subsequent clarifications of technical questions concerning the Atrocities Act, as well as to as Ramesh Nathan and Rahul Singh from the National Campaign on Dalit Human Rights in Delhi.

Several friends have offered their support during the period that this book project has been in progress. Han Peng Ho, my contemporary at SOAS, offered to discuss multiple tasks with me after completing his studies at Columbia. Thanks also to Sumeet Mhaskar, Jayaseelan Raj, Umakant, Amarjit Singh and Murali Shanmugavelan for their friendship, help with primary or secondary sources and for their encouragement. Over the years, I have benefitted from support, discussions or cooperation with Thomas Hylland Eriksen, Leif Manger, Rochana Bajpai, Faisal Devji, Sumantra Bose, Gurharpal Singh, Surinder Jodhka, Sambaiah Gundimeda, Arild Engelsen Ruud, Pamela Price, Marc Galanter, Alexander Fisher, Claus Halberg, Randi Gressgård, Chittibabu Padavala, Nathaniel Roberts, Karin Klenke and the staff at CeMIS. Thanks to Kari Normo at the university library in Bergen for ensuring a decent supply of books during the final stage of the project.

In Hyderabad, my greatest debt goes to Augustine Bonam and Girija Augustine, who have so generously accommodated me and my family, created a sense of belonging and virtually adopted us into their family. My family, and especially my wife Mona, has become part of an unexpected journey that this project has involved. Her support has been decisive for my ability to complete this book. Our two daughters, Selma Marie and Rebekka, have grown up seeing my preoccupation with ‘philosophy books’ and Indian studies as a reason for my absent-mindedness while becoming old enough to realize that something important was taking shape. I am proud to have relied on the support from the ladies at home.

I have been fortunate regarding the comments received on this manuscript. I am grateful to Sumeet Mhaskar, T. Dharmaraj and Narendra Subramanian for their comments on the Introduction, to Eleanor Nesbit and Torjus Midtgarden for comments on Chapter 1 and to K. Y. Ratnam, G. Krishna Reddy and Priyadarshini Vijaisri for comments on an earlier version of Chapter 3. Gajendran Ayyathurai has read drafts and offered comments on the Introduction, Chapter 6 and the outline. Beverley Sykes helped me with an extra set of eyes during the final stage of writing the manuscript with her proficient copy-editing. Finally, I am grateful to the two anonymous reviewers from Cambridge University Press for their constructive comments on this manuscript and to the editorial team for their proficient work and for managing the process so well.

An earlier version of Chapter 3 appeared as ‘Karamchedu and the Dalit Subject in Andhra Pradesh’, *Contributions to Indian Sociology* 48, no. 3 (2014): 383–408. I thank Sage Publications for permission to include it in this book.

Introduction

On 20 March 2018, two judges from India's Supreme Court delivered a judgment that put the legal protection of the country's historical outcastes into question. Inspired by the power of judicial review, the judges modified one provision of the Scheduled Castes and the Scheduled Tribes (Prevention of Atrocities) Act (PoA Act), 1989. They concluded that police officers should arrest accused individuals only after investigations have been conducted rather than immediately after the alleged offence has occurred. They also argued that the Act had been misused.[1] Victims of caste-based violence are often in fear of approaching police stations, where officers could be more loyal to the perpetrators than to members of the victims' communities. The PoA Act has considerably improved legal protections for victims and has strict consequences for the accused persons. Therefore, the judgment of 20 March 2018 provoked reactions across India, resulting in a countrywide mobilization of oppressed groups, Dalits and Adivasis, many of whom travelled to New Delhi to protest against the Supreme Court's decision. The mobilization was such that the Hindu nationalist government started responding to their demands and eventually introduced a bill in parliament in August to restore the Act and its original provisions.[2] The decision to restore the Act proved to be contentious among the government's supporters, and some members of its vote bank took part in protests.[3] The PoA Act, 1989, has been contested since the early 1990s,[4] and the controversy regarding this piece of legislation reflects a larger theme – that caste and law are central to India's democratic practices.

India adopted a constitution in 1950 that included a sophisticated set of democratic rights, but caste-based oppression has endured since that time. Atrocities have occurred in the postcolonial Indian state at the same time as there has been a significant policy of equal opportunity, which has benefitted groups such as the untouchables (Dalits) and tribal people (Adivasis). This book practices political ethnography by combining case studies and historical sources to discuss what this paradox represents for law and Dalits and to conceptualize the relation between caste and law. Casteism has dehumanized certain groups who have contested its practices and distinctions. By considering the contemporary struggles against caste-based discrimination from a historical perspective, one can explain how laws have been created, institutionalized and changed as a response to questions that arise out of caste-based domination.

Caste-based discrimination in India and the mobilization of the castes formerly known as the untouchables have become visible in India and internationally, especially with the adoption of digital technologies in the new millennium that have enabled the rapid spread of information beyond the local context. The current designation for untouchables, Dalit, is more globally known than it was a decade ago. 'Dalit' is a political term, meaning oppressed. Deriving from Sanskrit, in which it means 'ground down' or 'reduced to pieces',[5] Dalit has become the self-chosen designation among the so-called untouchables who fight against their exclusion and humiliation in the traditional caste system.[6] Social media is one of several tools that makes the various forms of oppression that frequently affect groups such as India's Dalits more apparent today. In an interconnected world, the information is spread to audiences far away from the places in which they occur to national and international audiences. Violence against oppressed groups has become a clear threat in India since the Hindu nationalist government led by Narendra Modi assumed power in May 2014. But the general pattern described in this book, which goes beyond Modi's Hindu nationalist government, is that powerful groups gain leeway to exercise violence when their political leaders control institutions of law and order.[7]

While the current recognition of caste-based discrimination is noteworthy, each generation of social activists has experienced atrocities that have revealed questions of caste-based dominance in the Indian social order. Caste did not vanish when India adopted its democratic constitution in 1950, although it was declared that 'untouchability' was abolished. Caste undoubtedly changed during the postcolonial period, but the system of domination has become re-embedded and even more visible in Indian politics. Indeed, while caste is politicized, values of caste shape gender relations and subjugation in both rural and urban contexts. Many forms of exploitation gain public attention. But the story of the Dalits and the Indian state involves many cases in which Dalit activists have fought caste-based exclusion without attracting media attention.

This book looks at the contemporary struggles against caste-based discrimination from a historical perspective to illuminate how laws emerge, become institutionalized and change as a response to the questions of caste-based domination. To explain how caste and law evolve, I integrate social, political and ideological dimensions of caste in my analysis. The goal is not to simply report how individuals have used various opportunities throughout history, though.[8] Caste is a multidimensional social system, and casteism creates intense experiences. I argue that the dynamics of caste and law must account for an ontological drive to practise caste. And studying how caste and law evolve requires that each domain is properly understood.

The Constitution of India provides a solid framework for the world's largest democracy. In the constitution, equal opportunity policies are included in the part entitled Fundamental Rights, that is, among a list of rights of citizens. The explicit provision of equal opportunity in this part of the constitution creates a stable framework for policymaking, especially for the Scheduled Castes (SCs) and the Scheduled Tribes (STs) as these categories are integral to the constitution. But there is also a history of legal change and learning processes where the limits of equal opportunity policy and other legal provisions have been addressed. To identify these processes, one needs to step outside the legal framework to study caste-based dominance and, particularly, the excluded Dalits. Through case studies, this book examines the dynamics of caste and how Dalits and formal law relate to each other. My main empirical studies are from the Telugu-speaking states of Telangana and Andhra Pradesh in south India. Dalit movements in this region have responded to atrocities and struggled with the embedded problem of caste-based oppression in ways that make their history comparatively significant.

Dalits face a problem of enduring inequality and represent a democratic paradox. Officially classified as the 'Scheduled Castes', there were 201 million Dalits among India's total population of 1.2 billion inhabitants in 2011.[9] Their legal classification as SCs means that they are entitled to policies such as equal opportunity, referred to as 'reservation' (affirmative action), and other legal provisions. This has created a Dalit middle class. At the same time, most Dalits remain exploited in the agrarian structure and humiliated and often excluded in urban contexts. The contrast between formal equality and social inequality was highlighted by Bhimrao Ambedkar (1891–1956), the main leader of India's untouchables at the time when the constituent assembly adopted the constitution. In a speech on 25 November 1949, he stated, 'On the 26th of January 1950, we are going to enter into a life of contradictions. In politics we will have equality and in social and economic life we will have inequality.'[10] Despite its reflective style, this contrast is too schematic to characterize the Dalit situation today. Rather than accepting the wording 'life of contradictions', I will refer to what I call the 'mechanism of oppression in the Dalit situation'.

The mechanism of oppression refers to the paradox of how upward mobility among Dalits coexists with enduring atrocity. The concept provides a basis on which to reconceptualize the enduring problems of oppression found among Dalits today as well as the legal developments during the postcolonial period. It represents a theme whereby one can move beyond stalemates in postcolonial theory, where the study of caste was transformed into a question of category-making.[11] Category-making is significant, but I avoid universalizing this single dimension. Instead I will utilize, among other things, common-sense observations such as the mechanism of oppression to explain the dynamics of caste and law. I will also draw on Ambedkar's scholarship on caste as an embedded form of domination, which adds value to a post-foundational social and political theorical engagement with caste and law. Ambedkar's remarkable career, in which he moved from belonging to an untouchable caste to making contributions to the Constitution of India, makes him a symbol for the recognition of Dalits and constitutional commitments in India. His career, scholarship and symbolic value make him an essential component of attempts to conceptualize the relation between caste and law in India today.

Caste and Legal Developments since Colonialism

Caste involves questions of grading, inequalities, purity and religion, which make castes inherently unstable and dynamic identities. The term 'caste' is often used in two ways – as *varna* and *jati*. There are four graded *varna*s in Hindu theology,[12] while the untouchables are those without *varna* (*avarna*). But there are multiple *jati*s (sub-castes or the everyday caste) within each *varna*, and there are further subdivisions among those *jati*s. In public policymaking, however, caste is an enumerated group.[13]

Official entitlements for groups and electoral politics are important for the overall institutionalization of caste in the Indian state and Indian society.[14] On the one hand, caste loyalties matter because there is electoral competition among dominating castes. Such competition is a defining feature of the long-term rivalry between the 'forward castes', Reddys and Kammas in Andhra Pradesh, south India.[15] Caste is also prominent in the large north Indian state of Uttar Pradesh, where the Dalit party, the Bahujan Samaj Party (BSP), gained electoral success in the 1990s.[16] On the other hand, category-making has become part of competition regarding access to resources and positions that the state can provide. Even powerful castes, such as the Jats in north India, have demanded reserved seats in educational institutions and public employment as well. Group-based entitlements represent a legacy of policymaking in India, and colonial history provides the explanation for the beginnings of this type of process.

Historically, group-based entitlements gained force at the beginning of the twentieth century. In 1909, the colonial government introduced the Morley–Minto Reforms, which aimed to accommodate groups in the colonial government's decision-making processes.[17] These reforms involved new policies, such as creation of a separate electorate comprising Muslim voters. They were crafted by civil servants in the colonial administration to manage rising concerns among Muslims, who feared that they were losing power in relation to politically assertive Hindu groups.[18] There were regional group concessions prior to this date, but the Muslim demand at that time represented a first step towards a national-level policy of group-based entitlements for minorities. A separate Muslim electorate was permitted in 1909, but this policy was abandoned before independence.[19]

The institutionalization of caste can be traced back to the colonial government's decision to map and enumerate the Indian population. There were early attempts at enumerating the population at the beginning of the nineteenth century,[20] but the idea of conducting systematic censuses became prioritized after the Great Rebellion in 1857. The realization that the colonial government had too little systematic knowledge about the Indian population pushed the momentum for what the anthropologist Nicholas Dirks refers to as an 'ethnographic state'. Here, civil servants and colonial ethnographers were engaged in increasing imperial knowledge by mapping the population.[21] Meanwhile, the colonial administration was dominated by members of the Brahmin (priestly) castes, who imposed their religious point of view on the social order. The effect of this was a 'Brahminization' of Hindu law in the nineteenth century. It included the use of ancient texts in court cases, such as Manu's Code of Law, in which hierarchical customs of caste were justified as legitimate traditions.[22] Therefore, caste-based prejudices were aggravated at the same time as colonial ethnographers applied racial stereotypes from European science as they mapped the population.

The first census was conducted from 1871 to 1872, and a new census was conducted every tenth year after that. Data collection relied on notions of race (head, nose and skull forms), particularly in the census of 1901 led by the civil servant Herbert Risley.[23] It was also Risley who drafted the policies that were used to address the Muslim question a few years later, but these policies had a different origin.[24] In the Morley–Minto Reforms of 1909, the colonial government made concessions to Muslim representatives by enabling their community to elect its own representatives via separate electorates.

Led by the then Secretary of State for India, Edwin Montagu, the colonial government wanted to consult Indian representatives in 1917 about developing a constitution with more self-governance. They endorsed the policy of having separate electorates, and the idea of mutually exclusive religions became institutionalized in the colonial state.[25] Therefore, the concept of a separate electorate represented a policy solution that encouraged similar demands from other groups.[26] It was in this context of several political movements and policies that Ambedkar emerged as a representative for the untouchables in 1919. The untouchables represented a large cluster of castes, which was called the SCs in the Government of India Act, 1935. At the beginning of the twentieth century, however, the untouchable castes were known as the 'Depressed Classes'. This condescending designation recurred and was even used during the constituent assembly debates between 1946 and 1949, even though technically it had only been created for use during the initial period of drafting a constitution for India.

Ambedkar became a representative for the Depressed Classes on the Southborough Franchise Committee in 1919 after returning from studying in the USA, where he had graduated from Columbia University in 1916. Ambedkar's experience grew over the next decades, especially during the early 1930s, and he became a leading expert in the drafting of India's constitution from 1946 to 1949. His constitutional battle with Gandhi in the early 1930s has gained epic significance regarding his role as a national leader. While participating in the Round Table Conference in London in 1931, he ended up in a confrontation with Gandhi over the question of separate elections for the Depressed Classes. Ambedkar's experiences and his determination to address the problem of caste-based oppression make him an important symbol among contemporary Dalits in India. The phenomenon has been labelled Ambedkarization and constitutes a postcolonial trend, especially among middle-class and literate Dalits.[27]

Ambedkar's story corresponds to central dilemmas and aspirations among Dalits today who engage with questions of modernity and caste. His career was marked not only with upward mobility and successes but also with humiliation. The route Ambedkar took also explains the interface between the social level of Dalits and the level of public law. The mismatch between caste and equality remains a challenge for Dalit activists today. Although the term 'Dalit' was only popularized after the creation of the Dalit Panthers in 1971, the contemporary repertoire of activists and Dalit policies often point back to Ambedkar – his visions for emancipation and the constitutional entitlements that he contributed to framing. For example, the association of Dalits with Ambedkar has resulted in a replacement designation for the untouchables, 'Harijan', which means 'People of God'. The word 'Harijan' was adopted by Gandhi as part of his ideas concerning reforming Hinduism. The term was in frequent use several decades after independence, but it has been largely sidelined by the assertion of the Dalit identity and identifications with Ambedkar's life and vision. Gandhi has come to be seen as an adversary of the Dalit project of emancipation from caste-based oppression because his approach to social reforms involved paternalistic ideas about the untouchables being part of a divine natural order of caste.

Equal-opportunity policies (reservation) have been the main approach that has been used to alleviate poverty in the postcolonial Indian state; in fact, reservation has been more important than land reforms despite the latter's significance for redistribution of resources. Group-based quotas started early on in south India and the Madras Presidency. Here, the non-Brahmin movement made demands in the 1870s for ameliorative policies for the so-called backward classes, which at that time referred to a large cluster of castes comprising the untouchables and the lower castes known as Shudras. The constitutional settlements of 1935 and 1950 did not provide India-wide legislation for either of these groups. It was the SCs and STs who were defined, listed and entitled to equality of opportunity in the Constitution of India. While the term 'backward classes' was used in Madras in 1884 for underprivileged groups who deserve special treatment, it was officially adopted in Mysore in 1918 for what later became a policy to recruit non-Brahmin groups in public service.[28] But the constituent assembly did not define the backward classes as a national policy in any meaningful way and deferred this mysterious category to be clarified by a commission at a later date. This had a major relevance for north Indian politics, in which there were no reservation policies designed for the lower castes in the same way as in south India prior to independence.[29]

The concept of backward classes became contested in the postcolonial period, especially as it changed from the focus on class into a basic list of castes. Although regional states had leeway to use caste to designate those who were backward, the chairman of the first Backward Classes Commission from 1955 opposed specifying backwardness in terms of caste at the national level. This changed with the second Backward Classes Commission, the *Mandal Commission Report* in 1980, which proposed using caste as the main criteria for determining those who were to be officially classified as backward classes. The report assumed significance in the early 1990s. The report had been pending for a decade and had been controversial for sociological reasons: the data collection was viewed as wholly inadequate.[30] The commission had been initiated by the Janata Dal government on 21 March 1979.[31] Although the fragile Janata coalition collapsed before the report was completed in 1980, it had ensured that the Mandal Commission consisted of members from 'backward castes' who highlighted the ways in which caste was useful to identify the beneficiaries.[32]

The report was left aside until a new Janata Dal government returned to power under the leadership of Prime Minister V. P. Singh in 1989. The following year, his government introduced the *Mandal Commission Report*, resulting in what became 'quota politics'. The plan was to introduce reservation to up to 60 per cent in the public sector, including the Other Backward Classes (OBCs) as well as the SCs and STs. There are significant legal and sociological differences between these categories. Even though the large cluster of castes known as the OBCs differs from the SCs and STs, the debates and concepts regarding OBC reservation tend to colour the entire approach to group-based quotas.[33] Equal opportunity policy (reservation) generates various discourses of inequality, merit and stratification.

The reservation policy is significant for Dalits because their official status as SCs gives them entitlements that they may claim in everyday situations, such as in applications for jobs or admissions to schools. The federal and regional governments, moreover, have launched targeted development programmes and schemes for them.[34] Thus, by way of being officially registered as SCs, Dalits are entitled to special rights, protection under law and special concessions in terms of education, jobs and scholarships. More universal programmes such as a Mahatma Gandhi National Rural Employment Guarantee Act, 2005, by which poor and unemployed people are provided some minimum 'government work',[35] have added to these provisions.

The category of SCs reflects the fact that untouchability is a theme that is integral to India's constitutional framework. Ambedkar was a central actor during the process through which this category was introduced; it was officially adopted in 1935 and reaffirmed in India's constitution of 1950. It is often with explicit or implicit reference to the category of SCs that the contemporary Dalit identity gains its shape and direction. The official recognition as 'SCs' ensures several official provisions. Dalits fight against caste-based atrocities and enduring inequalities. While the term 'Scheduled Castes' is an official designation and an enumerated category, Dalit is a political concept that is malleable and cannot be reduced to the individuals who are officially enumerated as the SCs. Moreover, as the historian Rupa Viswanath underlines, the SCs category was given a theological definition during colonialism with the effect that Dalits, or the Depressed Classes, were classified as people who were Hindus. Since the Constitution of India defines the SCs as those who profess Hinduism, Sikhism and Buddhism, Dalits who have converted to Christianity or Islam are not entitled to the application of constitutional provisions.[36] The political decisions made in the interwar period have implications for politics and entitlements today. The story of Ambedkar does in any case relate to each concept – Dalit and the SCs – while exceeding them in a distinctive way.

Ambedkar's biography represents a story about a person who is central to the history and meaning of the constitutional term 'Scheduled Castes' at the same time as he is a source of inspiration for current Dalit politics. Ambedkar is a historical reference and a symbol – new facts are interpreted with reference to his role, experience and career. In practice, the Dalit approach evolves like a spiral in contemporary politics because new episodes and lessons are added to what Dalit rights and their struggles for recognition mean in practice. In general, the Dalit identity gains shape and momentum by claiming rights and dignity. Enlightenment values loom in this tradition, comprising novel starting points among anti-caste leaders in the mid-nineteenth century. The Constitution of India has incorporated the ideals of Enlightenment and democracy, providing a tangible framework of entitlements, rights and security. Movements often made their demands with specific reference to the constitutional state and provisions or decisions made by politicians or courts. There have been many leaders among Dalits before and after

Ambedkar, but his role in developing India's constitution makes his legacy and contribution integral to the movement.

While being recognized as SCs and citizens of India along with others, Dalits are still exploited and subject to the stigma of untouchability. Therefore, it is appropriate to characterize them as untouchable citizens.[37] This expression largely captures the 'life of contradictions' that Ambedkar described as existing between democratic principles and social oppression.[38] As a generic term, however, 'Dalit' refers to a heterogenous group that has inequalities and caste differences within it. Some Dalits are teachers and government officers, others are security guards and some are successful businesspersons.[39] But most Dalits are still manual workers and are often dependent on local strongmen, landowners or corporations. They could be regular agricultural labourers, bonded labourers in exploitative brick-kiln businesses in Punjab, north India, or seasonal labourers in the construction industries in Telangana or in the green agricultural fields of Andhra Pradesh.[40] The Constitution of India prohibited forced labour, but exploitation of labourers continued during the postcolonial period. In 1976, the central government tried to solve the problem by adopting an Act to abolish bonded labour.[41] Neoliberal developments since the 1990s have increased vulnerabilities among labourers, and many Dalits remain in a marginal workforce irrespective of the general economic development.[42] There are inequalities among Dalits and the many different castes among them. Legally, however, they represent one homogeneous population and are known as the SCs.

Politics of Category-Making and Identity

The use of generic categories in modern states and public administration has been criticized in postcolonial studies for excluding differences and creating new identities and racial conceptions. In his seminal book *Imagined Communities*, Benedict Anderson emphasizes the ways in which censuses created new identities in the former colonies and maps, contributed to cognitively imagine the nation as a unity.[43] In political science, the idea that categories are internally heterogeneous has been advanced by so-called constructivists. Dvora Yanow, for example, argues that hermeneutics will easily bring into view complexities that are otherwise bracketed in a category. As she underlines, one may unpack many things categorized in a generic category, such as in the word 'fruit'.[44] This is an old point, previously addressed by Aristotle in his categories of thought. There are, nonetheless, powerful political effects of category-making in modern statecraft. It has a more decisive role in generating politics and rearticulating stereotypes than conventional hermeneutical theory of knowledge suggests. In Foucault's governmentality perspective, for example, technology produces subjectivities and identities.

The constitutional category of the SCs has an India-wide relevance. Sociologically, this generic category brackets complexity and sub-caste fragmentation, since the SCs category is literally a list of castes considered to be the untouchables in the traditional caste system. It is premised on the same type of homogeneous identity that Partha Chatterjee highlights would exclude heterogeneous facts.[45] In practice, the SC category neither reflects sub-caste differences within it nor corresponds to class differences between or within its sub-castes. The exclusion of such internal differences has reinforced politics and identity formations among the SCs, and this has been aggravated by the fact that this is a constitutional category at the federal level. In other words, India has a multilevel form of governance in which a regional state can design a policy to address inequalities, but it does not have the constitutional authority to create new categories among the SCs. The constitutional category can only be amended by the Indian parliament at the national level.[46]

Given the inequalities among the SCs,[47] the central problem is that some gain education and middle-class status, whereas others do not. This tension is particularly prominent in Telangana and Andhra Pradesh, the two Telugu-speaking states in south India. Here, inequalities reinforce conflicts between sub-castes registered as the SCs. Castes associated with agricultural production, such as Malas, have gained more upward mobility than castes working with leather and in shoemaking, Madigas, and far more than the manual scavengers, Rellies. Inequalities create many questions and fragmentation of facts, policies and castes, and the promise of reservation remains contested among the SCs. Privatization of India's economy in 1991, furthermore, appears to have had a greater impact on the Madigas. Members of their caste earn their living by making traditional leather sandals – a product that cannot compete with cheaper plastic sandals made by large manufacturers. Many Dalits, and especially the Madigas, have become vulnerable to exploitation in private construction industries.[48] The unequal social and economic developments affect identity politics among Dalits. Rather than simply projecting a Dalit identity, for example, Madiga leaders have launched a movement in the region to boost their caste identity by adding Madiga to their name.[49] The Madiga identity has therefore been used affirmatively.[50] The affirmation of caste (in this case *jati*) identity has consolidated the Madiga movement's struggle to reform the reservation policies that apply to SCs.

A further challenge for group-based entitlements in India is that even groups traditionally known as very powerful castes have tried to ensure that their members become entitled to be part of those groups who can access officially designated quotas in educational institutions and state administration. The mobilization of dominant castes differs from the original goal of the Constitution of India of redressing social injustices and compensating for historical forms of oppression. Members of the Jat community in Haryana, a traditional landowning caste in north India, have resorted to violence and obstructed water supplies to the capital city, New Delhi, to make their demands heard. The mobilization of dominant castes shows how, as the political scientist Rajni Kothari once stated, caste 'gets politicised' and bolsters campaigns to consolidate or regain economic power.[51] The rationality of reservation policies will change if historically dominant castes such as the Jats in north India, the Patels in Gujarat and the Marathas in Maharashtra are nominated to reserved seats in the same manner that historically oppressed groups like the SCs, STs and OBCs have been. These examples of powerful groups utilizing their political and numerical leverage show how group-based entitlements become central to the politicization of caste.

Apart from the political struggles over access to public employment and education, the politics of category has become central to the rearticulating of stereotypes and social distinction. This was evident in controversies regarding access to higher education in 2006. At that time, there was considerable opposition to extending reservation in higher education to the OBCs. The fact that the term 'OBCs' mainly designates a large cluster of castes that includes affluent members certainly animated the debate. The word 'category' became important for reservation critics when they distinguished between those who are entitled to reserved seats and those who are competing in a 'general category'. Opponents of reservation used this distinction in 2006 to claim that candidates in General category are selected by merit, whereas appointment to reserved seats is based on caste. The asymmetry highlighted here between the meritorious and the reserved categories has been analysed by the sociologist Satish Deshpande, who argues that the term 'general category' projects an openness that does not explicitly refer to caste. The effect, he argues, is that privileged upper castes identify as casteless, which they contrast with categories of people who are identified by their caste and not by merit.[52] Focusing on merit makes caste distinction implicit while articulating it more effectively as an indispensable virtue for modern institutions. This is how, according to French sociologist Bourdieu, symbolic capital is converted into moral authority, power and positions.[53] Yet the focus on categories and how merit becomes an implicit symbolic capital of caste has its limitations if one wants to make sense of caste and its numerous dimensions.

Laws, Equality and Caste

The equal opportunity policy that was granted to the SCs and STs in the Constitution of India in 1950 is central to the wider approach to 'reservation' for disadvantaged groups in India. The country's reservation policies are perhaps among the most comprehensive approaches to equal opportunities or positive discrimination in the world. They are comparable to affirmative action in the USA.[54] Based on his readings of the deliberations of the founding fathers of India's constitution, law professor Marc Galanter characterized India's policies of equal opportunity as a type of 'compensatory discrimination' when he wrote his seminal book *Competing Equalities*.[55] He argued that the rationale of the reservation policies in the constitution was to create policies that compensated historical injustices. Yet Galanter's classic account is now out of date regarding legal developments. The concept of compensatory discrimination is also ambiguous as it refers more to injustices in the past than in the present.

The main legal development pertaining to the SCs is the creation of the PoA Act, 1989. This piece of legislation was a significant attempt to provide protection against abuse, attacks and violence. To understand the relation between law and caste, it is important to supplement studies of equal opportunity with a perspective that takes the protective measures offered by criminal law into account. By adopting the concept of compensatory discrimination or reservation alone, one may end up reproducing the benevolent rationality of the nationalist movement rather than explaining the implications that caste-based dominance has for legal developments. However, Galanter points to another dimension that has had lasting effects on this legal history, namely the role of religion in the early conceptualizations of equal opportunity policy in India.

The Constitution of India stipulates a procedure for identifying castes that can be classified as SCs. According to Article 341, it is the president who should specify these castes. The religious principle appears in subclause 3, where it is stated that a person classified as belonging to the SCs 'must *profess* to be either a Hindu or a Sikh'.[56] Since 1991, Dalit Buddhists have also been recognized as SC, but anyone who has converted to Christianity cannot be recognized as belonging to the SCs. The theological emphasis was confirmed early during the postcolonial period when a judge in 1957 dismissed the idea that there could be untouchability practices in a Jain temple in Bangalore. He argued that the victims, who claimed to have been excluded from the temple or interaction with members of the Jain community, were neither Hindus nor people who had been suffering because of their untouchability in the past.[57] The judge stressed that historical lineage and birth were essential for understanding untouchability than temporary discrimination in the present. These were deliberations at an early stage during the postcolonial period and before the significant development of cases and constitutional amendments. But the religious dimension has an enduring relevance for interpretations of law pertaining to the SCs. A Dalit Christian activist once called it a 'nonsecular' aspect of the constitution.[58] Religious identity matters not only for determining entitlements to reservation but also the legal approach to atrocities. For example, religion was relevant in discussions about whether the accused in the court case that took place after the massacre in Tsundur village in 1991 (see Chapter 4) could be tried under the PoA Act.

While aspects of inequality, discrimination and religion shape the legal approach to Dalits, one could also view the legal development during the postcolonial period as an expansion of an egalitarian project. The term 'reservation' is central to this egalitarian discourse. There has been a noteworthy development of the sections on Fundamental Rights in the constitution and, in particular, the articles concerning equality. Article 16, concerning equal opportunity, is an example of a legal regime in expansion. The long sequence of debates in the public arena, in parliament and in various courts has resulted in the creation of new constitutional amendments to enhance the scope of reservation. These amendments constitute changes in reservation policies for the SCs and STs as well as for the OBCs to ensure formal access to (or promotion in) educational institutions and government offices. The term 'reservation' is mentioned in the fourth subclause of Article 16. The use of this term follows from Article 16(1), which declares that there should be 'equality of opportunity in matters relating to employment and appointment'. The ensuing reservation debates have resulted in the creation of new subclauses in this Article, such as 16(4A) and 16(4B), as well as Article 15(4). As one leading constitutional lawyer claims, Articles 15 and 16 have become 'the most litigated clauses of the Indian Constitution'.[59] The amendments are the results of these recurring debates, which comprise discussions of court judgments and responses from politicians.

More than two decades ago, a distinguished sociologist, André Béteille, in an attempt to account for how social relations have changed, stated that equality was the prime value in the modern, postcolonial society. He explained that equality was a legitimate principle in public discussions and that there was no public defence of hierarchy in India.[60] Such an assumption could be further substantiated by pointing to how the constitution-makers decided to abolish and prohibit untouchability. But recent studies confirm that Béteille's account was overstated, since the endorsement of equality has been consistent with redescriptions of caste-based prejudice through a focus on merit.[61] In theory, equality and caste values are not necessarily contradictory. Louis Dumont's old anthropological argument was that equality was a value that made hierarchy more implicit and, therefore, more difficult to recognize.[62] In courts, moreover, the principle of equality generates noteworthy paradoxes. The principle of equality before the law has often been used to acquit persons accused of crimes under the PoA Act by citing a lack of evidence.[63]

In the past decade, it has become obvious that casteism is at play in urban contexts and in higher education.[64] In 2006, exclusion and bullying of Dalit students at the All India Institute of Medical Sciences in New Delhi intensified during the anti-reservation debates. Dalit students were locked in their rooms, and conflicts among students resulted in the creation of caste-based ghettos on campus.[65] In 2016, a significant controversy arose after the articulate Dalit student Rohith Vemula committed suicide at the University of Hyderabad, south India. While highlighting the plight of many Dalit students, this episode attracted interest in national politics after it became clear that Vemula had been excluded by the university administration at the request of members of the central government in New Delhi. Vemula's suicide provides insights into how the Hindu nationalist movement cooperates across several levels to curb dissenting voices in Indian academia.[66] But the larger historical trend during the postcolonial period is the recurrence of exclusion and caste-based violence, often as a response to articulate and upwardly mobile Dalits.

This dramatic trend during the postcolonial period involved several brutal incidents of caste-based violence, and cases that occurred in the prosperous agrarian regions during the 1960s represent a starting point. Such cases were decisive for the creation of the PoA Act, 1989. Since the PoA Act is under India's criminal code, it differs from the reservation policy. While both offer legal provisions and protection for the SCs, they resonate with different sociological topics and belong to different branches of law.

To understand the relation between caste and law, it would be useful to provide a new starting point outside the legal domain. The legal developments could be viewed as a response to the enduring trend in which the upward mobility of Dalits coexists with enduring atrocities against their community.[67] The coexistence of upward mobility and atrocity represents a political determination to maintain social order and subjugate Dalits. Thus, if the policies of equal opportunity have created upward mobility, the creation of the PoA Act is also a result of how upwardly mobile or assertive Dalits have been attacked. The Tsundur massacre, discussed in Chapter 4, reflects this phenomenon. In short, my proposition is that the Dalit situation can be accounted for by considering how upward mobility and atrocity coexist, so much so that this constitutes a mechanism explaining their overall situation.

A mechanism of oppression, where success and discrimination coexist, can be found among other oppressed groups, such as women, black people and Muslims. New forms of exclusion that emerged alongside upwardly mobile and assertive individuals motivated the civil rights movement in the USA. In any case, the mechanism of oppression provides a starting point for characterizing the Dalit situation. This common-sense observation provides a basis for making explanations of caste-based dominance more robust.

Caste, Race and International Law

While the study of Dalits and caste involves complex questions concerning hierarchy, inequality, exploitation, gender relations and exclusion, it is relevant to discuss them in relation to racism and human rights law. Postcolonial studies have not followed up this aspect of global politics as they have mainly focused on how category-making reifies caste as an identity.[68] This represents a stalemate and an incomplete global perspective, especially since the old question of whether caste and race can be compared has become part of transnational advocacy and politics.

In 2001, several non-governmental organizations, mainly associated with the National Campaign on Dalit Human Rights, participated in the World Conference against Racism (WCAR) in Durban, South Africa.[69] The Dalit participation opened up the possibility of critically reinterpreting caste-based discrimination as a problem of human rights violations in a context of the international approach to intolerance and racism. This shows how the concept of race has attained global significance concerning a moral re-evaluation of discrimination. The idea of race has a deeply laden history in India that is associated with colonialism. Referring to racism to criticize India has proved to be controversial for several reasons.

The Dalit attempts to internationalize the problem of caste-based discrimination at the WCAR in Durban in 2001 has been widely rejected as irrelevant to India and futile for dealing with the local problems. For the Indian government and political establishment, the rejection of race as a relevant concept for evaluating caste discrimination in India is a claim to sovereignty and a rejection of an international approach to evaluating matters of caste in India. India's answer to the United Nations human rights regime was to make a statement saying that it had already developed significant legislation on affirmative action as well as an array of other types of legislation to address the problems of the social exclusion of the SCs and STs in India.[70] The statement can be understood by noting how India's foreign policies have historically been dominated by the principle of non-intervention in sovereign states. At the grass-roots level, Dalit activists have also expressed their criticism, arguing that participating in this international conference did not improve the situation in India. During my conversation in 2014 with the late Bojja Tharakam, who was a senior movement leader in Hyderabad, he explained that the Durban conference had 'made no difference' to the movement or to the Dalit situation in India.[71]

The Durban conference, nevertheless, emerged as a starting point for addressing caste at an international level and in new jurisdictions overseas. Early labour migration to South Africa was celebrated by a south Indian anti-caste leader in 1913 for being a departure from caste-based oppression.[72] Recent history, however, shows how caste-based discrimination has been reproduced in the South Asian population outside India. The most significant development has occurred in the United Kingdom, where the British parliament discussed whether caste should be included in the Equality Act, 2010. The Labour leader Jeremy Corbyn is one of the politicians who has supported the inclusion of caste in British legislation on non-discrimination to support Dalit rights.[73] But the policy initiatives have triggered protests. The initial recognition of caste-based discrimination in the British parliament was weakened by the upper house, and it was objected that adopting the concept of caste in law would make it a 'permanent feature' in British society.[74] In 2017, moreover, a Conservative member of the British parliament hosted a representative of the National Council of Hindu Temples in the UK who argued that references to caste represent an attack on the Hindu religion.[75] In July 2018, the UK's Government Equalities Office concluded its consultation by claiming that caste was too controversial and difficult to define. It recommended that caste discrimination in the UK could be treated by existing provisions, such as those referring to 'ethnic origins' in the Equality Act, 2010.[76]

The idea that legislation about caste may serve to make caste a 'permanent feature' of society has a long history in the scholarly tradition. Sceptics include the fathers of the sociology of caste in India, such as G. S. Ghurye, his student M. N. Srinivas and, subsequently, Béteille, all of whom have felt that caste-based entitlements perpetuate caste rather than eliminating it. The French anthropologist Dumont characterized this scholarly ambivalence by arguing that Ghurye created a starting point for a sceptical approach that was erected on 'a certain fondness for Brahmanism' which tended to idealize the past.[77] One of Dumont's contributions was to make observations by Ghurye and the early scholarly literature more explicit, particularly by spelling out the claim that caste was being substantialized and transformed into segmented identities.[78] Dumont's main contribution, however, was to create an advanced approach to comparing hierarchy from a universal perspective, claiming that race was a Western concept whereas caste belonged to the Indian civilization. It is striking that the current Indian government has adopted a similar argument in its foreign policy to avoid international scrutiny of caste.[79] Although Dumont's argument resonates with the hegemonic articulation of caste, one of the main problems with his approach to caste is that his theory is based on viewing Brahmins and the untouchables as two extremes outside the caste system. This argument is based on French structuralism. It did not explain the historical changes in hegemonic articulations and how (as in Laclau's discussion of antagonism) one of the two antagonistic poles dominated and undermined the existence of the other.[80] In addition, Dumont did not have an empirical perspective to engage with the facts of oppression and state institutions, which is essential for understanding anti-caste movements in the democratic state.

The goal of this book is to step away from these old approaches, which are mired in an anthropological concern with difference, and to develop a new approach to caste. In fact, despite internal differences, seminal accounts of caste have been motivated by questions about the production of caste either in terms of hierarchy (Dumont) or power (Dirks). These approaches to 'the caste question' do not adequately explain how specific laws and forms of governance intersect with dimensions of caste, why atrocities are carried out or why Dalits mobilize in support of legal protection.

Outlining a Critical Explanation of Caste and Law

The relation between a complex problem of oppression and evolving public policies pertaining to the Dalits involves several interrelated processes, but there are limitations when applying several conceptual approaches to understand these processes. For example, political scientists are likely to discuss institutional continuity and change in terms of concepts such as 'path dependency' and 'critical junctures'. But these concepts do not explain how social complexities and changes matter for law and state institutions, nor do they illuminate the ability or reluctance to incorporate various social and cultural characteristics.[81] Path dependency is a concept that emphasizes linear developments and relatively autonomous institutional processes. The concept has its merits in a discussion about the constitutional trajectories in India in *longue durée*.[82] But path dependence does not explain how the official goals could be redirected to fit with the interests of powerful actors in society who are able to leverage state power.[83] In terms of theories of caste, moreover, the anthropological and postcolonial inclinations to study the 'caste question'[84] as an offshoot of colonial power has its shortcomings in discussions of law and social realities. In fact, the claim in postcolonial studies that category-making reifies identities resembles an approach 'from above' and is paradoxical given that caste is reproduced through marriage practices. Therefore, my aim is to engage with the Dalit situation to account for the relation between caste and law. But the dynamics of caste cannot be grasped using only one legal domain or concept. Indeed, caste is not only a multidimensional social system, there are also several dimensions of law with their own discourses; each of which resonates with specific dimensions of caste.

The approach that I develop in this book has been inspired by the political theorists Jason Glynos and David Howarth, who outlined the steps that should lead to a critical explanation. They underline how empirical research in social and political theories needs to characterize the object of study while using concepts to explain the problem.[85] Likewise, I utilize a common-sense observation to characterize the relation between the Dalit situation and law before engaging with conventional scholarly concepts. The theory of hegemony that Glynos and Howarth inherited from Ernesto Laclau's post-structuralist theory corresponds well with delineating different domains in the study of caste-based dominance and Ambedkar's thought. In my argument about caste-based dominance and law, I engage with three interrelated themes: the mechanism of oppression, the institutionalization of laws and the institutionalizing ideology. I discuss each of them in response to the following three questions.

The first question is, how can the legal response to the Dalit problem be characterized? I suggest that the legal developments reflect the mechanism of oppression in the Dalit situation, where upward mobility coexists with enduring atrocity. That is, the legal developments during the postcolonial period can be viewed as adjustments that, on the one hand, allow upward mobility to ameliorate embedded inequalities and, on the other hand, provide protection against caste-based atrocities. The concept of a mechanism of oppression is at the intersection of two types of conflict, violence and negotiation. While negotiation and argumentative practices reflect democratic practices, violence creates fear and resentment.

The mechanism of oppression of upward mobility and enduring atrocity could be viewed as a common-sense observation. I first encountered this account during my first fieldwork as a graduate student. I was told by Dalit activists that untouchability and enduring repression occur because 'upper castes' or 'caste Hindus'[86] would not tolerate Dalits gaining wealth, behaving in a sophisticated way or demanding their rights. I initially thought that this explanation was too elementary to gain scholarly attention, but I soon realized that this description was constantly repeated in various ways during interviews, in my reading of documents and the literature and, crucially, when I analysed cases of atrocities against Dalits. In practice, it resembles a collective narrative and assumption that had been developed around a common experience. It corresponds to common sense in Gramsci's perspective. Gramsci argues that unlike academics or priests from privileged classes, 'organic intellectuals' articulate and develop a shared narrative that resonates with the common experience of a group or social group: their expertise is organically linked to the lived reality of the social class in question.[87] Considering the mechanism as a perspective embedded in common sense in this sense offers a productive approach to analysing dominance. There are instances of how powerful Dalit mobilization has created greater scope for freedom and recognition, which show other social and political conditions than the mechanism of oppression does, but they do not eliminate its overall relevance.

In 2008, I met the Dalit leader and long-time activist late Bojja Tharakam in Hyderabad, and I asked him why Dalits in villages, such as those in Karamchedu in 1985, were attacked. The senior leader's resolute answer was that they were attacked because they belonged to untouchable castes and that only an untouchable would understand the meaning of that attack. Tharakam's source of inspiration was Ambedkar, whom he had briefly observed on a cold winter's night in Delhi in 1956. Unsurprisingly, Ambedkar deals with the scope for recognition in his scholarly writings. While he was a political leader and statesman, Ambedkar developed a sophisticated scholarship that has been neglected by academics in the same way that the work of the black academic W. E. B. Du Bois was silenced by academics in the USA.[88] In his work, Ambedkar explains why caste-based exclusion persists. From his perspective, caste is a system of 'graded inequality' in which the untouchables are supposed to remain 'nobodies' and where every touchable caste has an interest in avoiding being equal with them.[89] His argument highlights an ontological difference between touchables and untouchables. It also corresponds with the idea that Dalits should be 'taught a lesson', should remain submissive and should not assert their rights.

In the scholarly literature, the concept of a mechanism is discussed in several ways, many of which are unduly technical attempts to develop the sociological imagination. I largely follow Jon Elster's concept of causal mechanism as a frequently occurring and easily recognizable pattern, which often involves opposites. He identifies such opposites in proverbs, such as 'haste makes waste' versus 'he who hesitates is lost' or 'don't put all your eggs in one basket' versus 'Jack of all trades and master of none'.[90] This type of explanation differs from conventional procedures concerning deduction from general laws or those in which variables are identified and divided into independent and dependent ones; the former acting on the latter like one billiard ball hitting another. These conventional procedures in the social sciences are often based on theories that resemble a universal or general law, and the assumption of causality at such abstract levels is open for alternative explanations. Elster's causal mechanisms try to bring explanations to a lower level of abstractions and identify frequently occurring and recognizable patterns, which are explained by relying on accumulated wisdom often passed down over several generations.[91]

I leave the term 'causal' aside not only because it resembles a scientific metaphor but also because the concept of mechanism could be combined with a different conceptual approach. Readers may assume that the opposition between upward mobility and atrocity resembles a structuralist emphasis on binaries. It has become conventional wisdom to reject the use of binaries in structuralism because they tend to put less emphasis on the study of practices (Bourdieu) or hegemonic antagonisms (Laclau).[92] Although the concept of the mechanism of oppression is a common-sense explanation of reoccurring problems, it does not necessarily need to be associated with structuralism. Structuralism has the advantage of emphasizing historical continuities, which is partly why I once described the mechanism as a structural theme myself.[93]

In this book, I avoid the term 'structure' because – as with any essentially contested concept – it ends up being a source of confusion.[94] Conceptually, moreover, the 'mechanism of oppression in the Dalit situation' can be viewed as a reflection of an antagonism in an ontological sense. When Ambedkar highlights the distinction between 'touchables' and 'untouchables' and how the latter are kept at bay (see Chapter 1), he characterizes an antagonism in Laclau's sense as a concept of hegemony. Following Laclau's innovations in political theory, therefore, I advance Ambedkar's theory by arguing that this antagonism constitutes an ontology of caste.

The mechanism of oppression of upward mobility and enduring atrocity informs legal changes and involves different types of conflicts in the democratic state. While the data in this book point to persistent patterns of violence, there are other perspectives on democracy and caste. It has been argued by many authors that caste has become less hierarchical and that Dalits have a greater social and political prominence and therefore can negotiate and contribute to reaching agreements. This emphasis on everyday deliberative practices has been highlighted by James Manor, who claims that the power of rural hierarchy has declined.[95] In my view, Manor paints a rosy picture and tends to underplay facts of oppression, sidelining atrocities as something inexplicable and extreme. Yet his statement merits attention because democratic discussions and settlements do shape India's democracy. These practices can be conceptualized as 'agonistic democracy', which is a term designating dissent and how negotiation occurs in a democratic manner. The Greek term *agon* has been translated as strife, conflict or contest. Although the last word may conjure up an image of sports, the modern idea is to view *agonism* as a new conceptualization of struggles with power and institutions. The political theorist Chantal Mouffe has gained prominence for her contribution to agonistic democracy, though the tradition comprises many others, including Arendt and Foucault.[96] While I view agonism as a post-foundational approach to struggles with power, the term designates primarily one type of conflict – democratic negotiation or dissent.

The problem with caste-based domination is that conflicts could gain ontological significance and even involve violence to 'teach Dalits a lesson'. While agonism designates disagreements and not violence, casteism may quickly elicit antagonisms because of its systematic grading, ontological distinction and violence. Mouffe's overall approach is too schematic to account for what caste-based dominance implies. Instead, I engage with the concept of antagonism developed by Laclau[97] to better analyse how the ontological distinction between touchables and untouchables make Dalits subject to hostility and exclusion. In short, my starting point for characterizing the Dalit situation remains the mechanism of oppression, but I also consider the idea that ontological difference could transform agonistic conditions into hostile antagonisms and violence.

The second question is, what does the institutionalization of caste mean in the context of law? Historical institutionalism is a theory about how episodes and decisions made in the past determine present and future practices. The Constitution of India could be understood from this perspective as a central document from 1950 which has provided directions for policymaking in India for nearly seventy years. The implementation of reservation policies and debates largely follows a constitutional 'path'. The dispute between Gandhi and Ambedkar in the early 1930s led to a decision that granted reserved posts for the untouchables rather than a separate electorate for them. This settlement was the framework for the measures that were adopted in the Constitution of India, and it remains relevant for current policies.

But the state and the legal system are not simply coherent wholes, nor do developments only move forward in a linear fashion after laws are created. Laws generate different discourses within the state. Each law amplifies a specific social or cultural element, creating a discourse that elicits one dimension (often at the expense of another) in a multidimensional social system. For example, the policy of equal opportunity creates a discourse of social stratification, which resembles what Weber and Bourdieu refer to as status positions in society. This policy is not directly concerned with discrimination or violence. Likewise, the creation of the PoA Act, 1989, constitutes a discourse concerning protection from discrimination and violence. Each of these laws produce and reproduce their specific theme in the overall Dalit situation. Using concepts in institutional theory to analyse atrocity cases, I will explain that the active political manoeuvring often starts in an organization after a particular decision has been made or a particular event has occurred. At that stage, policies may be redirected and the official goals changed to comply with the interests of powerful actors.[98] In short, the institutionalization of caste in the context of law means, among other things, that there are continuities, paradoxical outcomes and individualizing discourses, but they do not define the totality of caste.

The final question when discussing caste is, why does it not vanish and sometimes even gains new impetus, whether it is intensified or politicized? The idea of caste could intensify in situations where there is a new mobilization or an emergence of new social behaviour because it is sustained by ontologically embedded belief in caste. Here, one needs to rethink the ideological dimension of caste. In doing so, one needs to distinguish more clearly between social, political and ideological dimensions of caste-based dominance. In Glynos and Howarth's contribution to critical explanations, they distinguish between three logics – social, political and fantasmatic.[99] The third logic – fantasmatic – explains how ideas or ideologies may have a grip on subjects or put an idea into practice. This concept, which differs from a range of other understandings of ideas, is developed using the psychoanalytical theory of Jacques Lacan. Glynos and Howarth explain that a fantasmatic logic gives extra force to individuals engaged in either social or political logic.[100] In my view, the term 'fantasmatic' is imprecise and unhelpful, but the explanation of an ideational drive in social and political action offers a useful tool for analysing casteism and Ambedkar's account of caste.

Ambedkar's perspective becomes a more compelling resource if one uses the psychoanalytical perspective in current political theory to analyse cases of caste-based dominance. For Ambedkar, belief in caste is a matter of sanctity, mentality and ontological reassurance. The conventional approach has been to discuss intensification of caste as a matter of politicization.[101] But the proposition that I develop is that caste relations may intensify when locally dominant castes are aligned with political power. The concept of dominant caste was defined in Srinivas' old village studies as a caste that 'preponderates' other castes by their numerical, economic and political strength and whose ritual status is 'not too low'.[102] What I highlight, however, is that dominant castes may be familiar with and have close connections with political power, and this increases their confidence in managing or colluding with state representatives, such as the police. Just as militant caste Hindus have felt emboldened to terrorize opponents and minorities after 2014, the constellation of political power and dominant castes is a frequent pattern in atrocity cases. It is common across the three key cases discussed in this book, Karamchedu (1985), Tsundur (1991) in coastal Andhra and the suicide of Rohith Vemula in Hyderabad (2016). In each of these cases, local power-holders are emboldened by connections to ruling politicians and push the limits to reinstitutionalize a ruling order.

This book differs from other discussions of the politicization and intensification of caste in two ways. First, the most prominent way of discussing caste has been to argue that caste is a useful tool for mobilizing political support and that caste has been politicized.[103] The rise of lower-caste politics in north India, particularly in the state of Uttar Pradesh, is a significant case that shows how caste has been central to gaining electoral power. In Uttar Pradesh, however, the main political parties include the lower-caste party Samajwadi Party (SP) and the Dalit party BSP, each of which has been ruling the state and competing with major parties such as the Hindu nationalist Bharatiya Janata Party (BJP) and the old Congress party. The electoral successes of the BSP are unique phenomena of the political mobilization of Dalits in India, and their central impetus has been to create more social justice for the impoverished Dalit population in the state. The role of caste for parties such as the BSP and SP has been so central that it created a widespread debate about the rise of lower castes and identity.[104] This occurred more prior to the rise to power of Modi's government, which added to the transformation of castes in power in Uttar Pradesh. In 2017, the controversial Hindu nationalist Yogi Adityanath became chief minister of the state. When he assumed power, he explained that while casteism was 'not fine', caste was good for the social order. Later, he declared that the members of his cabinet were vegetarians, thus affirming the upper caste Hindu identity.[105] Although electoral politics matters for how caste is reproduced in India's democracy, it is not my primary focus.

Second, the contextual and case-based approach to discussing the intensification of caste provides an important supplement to the postcolonial interpretation of caste that Dirks projects in his book *Castes of Mind*.[106] Dirks rightly emphasizes how colonial forms of knowledge made caste more central to social and political conduct. Using Foucault's ideas, he argues that discourses and epistemic regimes produced new subjectivities and details how the colonial government used a type of expertise and rationality to govern the population, which effectively produced a greater consciousness of caste. From this perspective, caste is produced by 'governmentality' by which consciousness of identities increase. While the Foucauldian approach has its merits, it is a mistake to apply his ideas to each issue relating to caste and social and political action.[107] His work did not address inequality and stratification as such.

It will be clear during the course of this book that I do apply Foucault's analytics, but I do so where I think Foucault's concepts are particularly fruitful, namely to explain how particular discourses are recognized and institutionalized.[108] I agree with leading scholars such as Chatterjee that antecedent factors and the rationalities of governing the population have contributed to the production of modern subjectivities;[109] indeed, caste has become central to modern statecraft. But the Foucauldian approach, in the sense of merely referring to the technologies of governing, does not lead to a comprehensive understanding of the intensity of caste. Rather than unduly focusing on how caste is produced through the technologies of governing a population or is intensified in a historical perspective, this book combines the study of the institutionalization of caste from a historical perspective with case studies that reveal casteism to be an intense experience. For Dalits, whose self-chosen designation means 'ground down', casteism represents a negation of their dignity and freedom.

To sum up, my aim is to provide a critical explanation of the relation between caste and law in which I characterize the social situation of Dalits, specify the meanings of institutions and laws and discuss why caste appears to be vital for social, political and economic developments in India.

Great Transformation, Frontier and the Re-embedding of Caste

Almost seventy-two years after India's independence, Dalits still face caste-based discrimination and a radical socio-economic disadvantage. Despite economic growth, globalization has re-embedded inequalities in the Indian economy and in its society. On the one hand, some studies have shown that Dalits have made material progress. According to a survey study in Uttar Pradesh villages, Dalits could afford basic amenities such as toothbrushes and vegetables to an extent that has meant that they feel their quality of life has improved.[110] On the other hand, as Corbridge and Harriss highlight in their book, *Reinventing India*,[111] liberalization of India's economy in 1990 consolidated elite power. New market-driven policies facilitated 'elite revolt' by asserting Hindu nationalism and avoiding transfers of power to new 'subaltern' classes. Nearly twenty years later, the militant Hindu nationalist movement has consolidated a political frontier that has emphasized a distinction between its own patriotism and 'anti-nationalists', which represents a forceful rearticulation of hegemony. Caste, however, represents a distinct and multidimensional form of domination in the democratic order.

The mechanism of oppression, which I advance in this book, could be viewed as part of a re-embedding of caste-based domination where the idea of 'teaching Dalits a lesson' is context-dependent. The mechanism corresponds to a pattern that has been identified in a quantitative study of caste-related crimes based on data from 415 districts in 18 large Indian states during the period from 2001 to 2010. In this study, economist Smriti Sharma found that crimes decrease when there is an increased gap in expenditures between lower and upper castes, whereas reduced inequality correlates with increased caste-based crimes.[112] While the findings strengthen general assumptions in this field of study, this book is not a study of correlations. Instead, the book traces the mechanism of oppression in the Dalit situation through case studies and political ethnography while explaining, among other things, how Ambedkar's concepts provide a productive opportunity to reconceptualize the relation between caste and law.

Overview of the Book

The following chapters examine the historical and conceptual framework of caste and law and the subsequent legal changes before tracing the relevant processes in revealing case studies. As a starting point, in Chapter 1, I will explain Ambedkar's career and his social and political thought while developing my analysis of how caste is produced and sustained through religious beliefs. Ambedkar's vision of a casteless society should be viewed in the context of a broader history of struggling against caste-based oppression, as an uphill struggle against Brahminism as well as against social and political dominance. He contributes to political theory, arguing in favour of freedom from caste-based domination in a discussion of how the social and political order is constituted. In addition, Chapter 1 includes a discussion of his participation in the process of developing a constitution at the beginning of the twentieth century. The drafting process culminated in substantial contributions from Ambedkar to designing a legal basis in 1950 for India to be a pioneering constitutional democracy.

In Chapter 2, I examine the legal developments from prohibiting untouchability at the time of independence to the creation of the PoA Act, 1989. I show how the problem of the social exclusion of untouchable castes has been subject to deliberations, changes and re-conceptualizations in the context of law. The initial approach used after India's independence was set aside. What occurred was a move away from the prohibition of untouchability in the framework of civil law (civil wrongs) and to re-conceptualize exclusion as a question of atrocity that should be prevented by developing a new approach under the criminal law. I focus on the discoursive break from a civil rights approach to a criminal law approach to oppression. The aim at the time of independence was to address the plight of the untouchables by granting them constitutional entitlements to access public space, especially temples and places of worship. Article 17, which abolishes untouchability and then tries to prohibit it, was the pillar of this approach. In the second chapter, I argue that access to public space was a concern that did not fully address the overall problem with oppression characterizing the Dalit situation. The ongoing atrocities against Dalits represented a trend that required different concepts and a legal approach to be applied. In other words, the model at the time of independence of granting access to public space was insufficient. The paradigm of civil law had clear limitations. The concept of untouchability lacked substance and definition. But a more critical fact was that atrocities were an enduring problem for Dalits and constitute a trend in India's modernity. Atrocities were not specifically about access to public space. I explain the history of massacres against Dalits during the postcolonial period and how this became a concern that eventually resulted in a completely new piece of legislation to prevent violence from occurring – the PoA Act, 1989.

In Chapter 3, I describe the history of Dalit mobilization in Andhra Pradesh in the mid-1980s, which gained momentum after the massacre of six Dalits in the wealthy village of Karamchedu in coastal Andhra. This history provides revealing insights into the re-embedding of caste relations in the agrarian economy. The massacre involved elements of both caste and class, and it shows how political power was decisive for organizing caste-related violence. Ideologically, the members of the movement that was created distinguished themselves from the Maoist movement by adhering to Ambedkarite ideology and addressing the Dalit problem specifically. Their demand for legal improvements was essential and shows how casteism was, in fact, integral to the mode of production in one of the successful agricultural areas benefitting from social, political and economic developments caused by the Green Revolution.[113]

In Chapter 4, I introduce a case that shows how upward mobility and assertion among Dalits could result in collective violence, organized by caste Hindus from several villages. I provide a detailed account of the massacre in Tsundur village in 1991. While the Karamchedu massacre occurred a few years prior to the PoA Act, 1989, the Tsundur massacre occurred after this law was created. According to a special provision under the Act, a special court could be organized in the village where the people involved lived. The Karamchedu and Tsundur massacres reveal processes whereby peasant castes have gained economic power and become dominant castes. Both events reflect how economic power may intensify the notion of caste. But the massacre in Tsundur gives a particularly clear indication of how the mechanism in the Dalit problem of upward mobility and atrocity may appear in practice.

In Chapter 5, I discuss how the official goal of providing legal protection and preventing atrocities could be changed in the institutional processes that took place after a particular incident. Institutions of law represent possibilities for powerful actors to change outcomes. I focus on atrocity cases in Andhra Pradesh and Maharashtra, particularly Tsundur and Khairlanji, which had rather different trajectories and experiences in court. In each case, there was a constant possibility that caste Hindus accused of carrying out organized violence might avoid punishment or effective court proceedings because of their ability to influence the court or prior processes. These cases indicate that courts and the legal system by no means guarantee effective use of the PoA Act. Instead, they suggest that the official legal goals are open to be redirected to other ends. Here, the power of dominant castes is crucial. The chapter uses concepts from historical institutionalism to explain how an official policy may be subject to goal conversions in practice.[114]

In Chapter 6, I discuss the institutionalization of caste in modern institutions and modern forms of governance. I focus on how caste is being re-embedded in India's social order and how it may become subject to various types of conflicts in modern institutions. Caste relations could be antagonistic, or they could be characterized by democratic recognition of disagreements. While earlier chapters focus on caste-related atrocities in the countryside, this chapter focuses on caste in more typically modern institutions, particularly those in higher education. Here, I discuss the conflicts by using the distinction between antagonism and agonism (strife) in democratic theory[115] while following up my discussion of how caste relations may involve two types of conflicts. In a political ontology characterized by an ontological drive to practise caste, there is only a small gap between antagonism and agonism and discrimination and negotiation.

Education is the key object of struggle and a location where caste relations become subject to various processes and types of conflict. I examine different struggles and how they either reflect various political decisions or represent separate struggles for social justice or power. I show how policies play out at different levels in the federal system. On the one hand, I demonstrate that higher education has become a crucial site for articulations of caste and power in the new millennium, both during Hindu nationalist governments and during the rule of the Congress party. This applies on the national level. On the other hand, I discuss various sub-caste struggles in different parts of India, comparing the radically different groups engaged in political campaigns to make the reservation policy correspond with the interests of their group. Here, I show that there are struggles among the underprivileged SCs as well as among very powerful dominant castes, known as 'forward castes', who aim to be officially classified as the OBCs. Although each of these groups negotiates in the political system for their cause, they face different barriers to legal change. The constitution is based on a framework that creates stability, and the scope for policymaking in regional states is specified and restricted. There is more path dependency in the constitutional framework in relation to the SCs (Dalits) than there is for the OBCs.

I conclude by summarizing my observations concerning how caste and law relate. After clarifying what I mean by providing a critical explanation in a post-foundationalist sense, I outline three themes and the main questions asked in this book. In institutional theory, organizations relate to their social and political environment and various histories. The study of caste and law, however, reflects much more; it includes an ontological desire for caste, power, legal choices and a system of governance that is both path dependent and vulnerable to exploitation in an area with enduring inequalities. More broadly, the discussion of caste and law shows how formal organizations in a constitutional democracy operate in a context of embedded inequalities, hegemony and exclusion.

Notes

1. *Dr. Subhash Kashinath Mahajan versus the State of Maharashtra and Anr.* (New Delhi: Supreme Court of India, 20 March 2018), accessed 4 April 2018, http://supremecourtofindia.nic.in/supremecourt/2017/22086/22086_2017_Judgement_20-Mar-2018.pdf.
2. Government of India, The Scheduled Castes and the Scheduled Tribes (Prevention of Atrocities) Amendment Bill, 2018, accessed 7 July 2019, https://www.prsindia.org/billtrack/scheduled-castes-and-scheduled-tribes-prevention-atrocities-amendment-bill-2018.
3. *Wire*, 'Shivraj Chouhan's Legally Untenable Promise on SC/ST Act Betrays BJP's Desperation in MP', 22 September 2018, accessed 8 Novemebr 2018, https://thewire.in/politics/shivraj-chouhan-madhya-pradesh-bjp-sc-st-act.
4. P. S. Krishnan, 'Scheduled Castes and Scheduled Tribes (Prevention of Atrocities) Amendment Act 2018: Justified by Constitutional Duty to Protect SCs and STs, but Does Not Pose Any Threat to Really Innocent Persons, Annexure-2', letter to chief minister, Madhya Pradesh, unpublished (26 September 2018), 11.

5. Oliver Mendelsohn and Marika Vicziany, *The Untouchables: Subordination, Poverty and the State in Modern India* (Cambridge: Cambridge University Press, 1998), 3–4; Anupama Rao, 'Who Is the Dalit? The Emergence of a New Political Subject', in *Claiming Power from Below: Dalits and the Subaltern Question in India*, ed. Manu Bhagavan and Anne Feldhaus (New Delhi: Oxford University Press, 2009), 11.
6. I will use Dalit as the common designation. But since this word was mainly popularized from the 1970s onwards, I use the 'untouchables' and 'Scheduled Castes' when referring to the period prior to independence. The untouchables were generally known in the colonial period as 'Pariahs', which referred to the Paraiyars or Parayars, a Dalit sub-caste from Tamil Nadu. The term 'Pariah' is an insulting designation. The term 'Dalits' has replaced many attributed names since the 1970s, and especially, since the 1990s, and using the term Dalit indicates awareness among those who use the term as a self-chosen designation. I will explain more about this terminology throughout the book.
7. For a similar argument, see Steven I. Wilkinson, 'Communal Riots in India', *Economic and Political Weekly* 40, nos. 44–45 (2005), doi:10.2307/4417364.
8. Sidney Tarrow, *Power in Movement: Social Movements and Contentious Politics* (Cambridge: Cambridge University Press, 2011).
9. Census Organization of India, *Scheduled Castes Population: Census 2011* (New Delhi: Ministry of Home Affairs, Government of India, 2011), accessed 5 November 2018, https://www.census2011.co.in/scheduled-castes.php. This number excludes converts to other religions, such as Christianity and Islam.
10. Constituent Assembly of India, 'Adoption of the Constitution', in *Dr. Babasaheb Ambedkar Writings and Speeches*, ed. Vasant Moon, vol. 13 (New Delhi: Dr. Ambedkar Foundation, 2014), 1216, accessed 7 November 2018, https://www.mea.gov.in/Images/attach/amb/Volume_13.pdf.
11. Nicholas B. Dirks, *Castes of Mind: Colonialism and the Making of Modern India* (Princeton, NJ: Princeton University Press, 2001).
12. The fourfold *varna* system comprises the Brahmins (priests), the Kshatriyas (rulers), the Vaishyas (traders) and the Shudras (servants).
13. Sudipta Kaviraj, 'The Imaginary Institution of India', in *Writings on South Asian History and Society*, ed. Partha Chatterjee and Gyanendra Pandey, Subaltern Studies, VII (New Delhi: Oxford University Press, 1992), 1–39.
14. Rochana Bajpai, *Debating Difference: Group Rights and Liberal Democracy in India* (New Delhi: Oxford University Press, 2011).
15. G. R. Reddy, 'The Politics of Accommodation: Caste, Class and Dominance in Andhra Pradesh', in *Dominance and State Power in Modern India*, ed. Francine R. Frankel and M. S. A. Rao, 2 vols. (Delhi: Oxford University Press, 1989), 268; M. N. Srinivas, 'Caste in Modern India', *The Journal of Asian Studies* 16, no. 4 (1957): 537–40.
16. Sudha Pai, *Dalit Assertion and the Unfinished Democratic Revolution: The Bahujan Samaj Party in Uttar Pradesh* (New Delhi: Sage Publications, 2002).
17. Edwin Samuel Montagu and Frederic John Napier Thesiger Chelmsford, *Report on Indian Constitutional Reforms*, East India (Constitutional Reforms), presented

to both houses of parliament by command of His Majesty (London: H. M. S. O., 1918), 6.

18. C. J. Fuller, 'Anthropologists and Viceroys: Colonial Knowledge and Policy Making in India, 1871–1911', *Modern Asian Studies* 50, no. 1 (2016), 257, doi:10.1017/S0026749X15000037; Marc Galanter, *Competing Equalities: Law and the Backward Classes in India* (Berkeley CA: University of California Press, 1984).
19. Rochana Bajpai, *Debating Difference*, 31–2, 51.
20. Bernard S. Cohn, *An Anthropologist among the Historians and Other Essays* (Delhi and Oxford: Oxford University Press, 1987), 231.
21. Dirks, *Castes of Mind*, chap. 10.
22. Lloyd I. Rudolph and Susanne Hoeber Rudolph, *The Modernity of Tradition: Political Development in India* (Bombay: Orient Longman, 1969), 274; D. A. Washbrook, 'Law, State and Agrarian Society in Colonial India', *Modern Asian Studies* 15, no. 3 (1981), 649–721.
23. Dirks, *Castes of Mind*, 212–27; Herbert Risley, *The People of India*, 2nd edn (New Delhi: Munshiram Manoharlal, 1991).
24. Fuller, 'Anthropologists and Viceroys', 257.
25. C. J. Fuller, 'Colonial Anthropology and the Decline of the Raj: Caste, Religion and Political Change in India in the Early Twentieth Century', *Journal of the Royal Asiatic Society* 26, no. 3 (2016): 475, doi:10.1017/S1356186315000486.
26. Francesca R. Jensenius, 'Mired in Reservations: The Path-Dependent History of Electoral Quotas in India', *The Journal of Asian Studies* 74, no. 1 (2015): 92, doi:10.1017/S0021911814002162.
27. Jagpal Singh, 'Ambedkarisation and Assertion of Dalit Identity: Socio-Cultural Protest in Meerut District of Western Uttar Pradesh', *Economic and Political Weekly* 33, no. 40 (1998): 2611–18, doi:10.2307/4407245.
28. P. Radhakrishnan, 'Backward Classes in Tamil Nadu 1872–1988', *Economic and Political Weekly* 25, no. 10 (1990): 512, accessed 26 February 2016, http://www.epw.in/journal/1990/10/special-articles/backward-classes-tamil-nadu-1872-1988.html; Dirks, *Castes of Mind*, 282; Galanter, *Competing Equalities*, 156.
29. Christophe Jaffrelot, *India's Silent Revolution: The Rise of the Lower Castes in North India* (London: Hurst, 2003).
30. P. Radakrishnan, 'Mandal Commission Report: A Sociological Critique', in *Caste: Its Twentieth Century Avatar*, ed. M. N. Srinivas (New Delhi: Penguin Books, 1996), 207.
31. Backward Classes Commission, *Reservations for Backward Classes. Mandal Commission Report of the Backward Classes Commission, 1980: Alongwith Introduction* (Delhi: Akalank Publications, 1991), i.
32. Jaffrelot, *India's Silent Revolution*, 320–1.
33. The evocative concept 'creamy layer' is one example. It was invented in 1975 to characterize an elite profiting from the institutional benefits of reservation at the expense of other, poorer sections in the same category. In 1992, it became a bureaucratic rule to omit affluent households from the OBCs. The creamy layer has not been applied to the SCs as a bureaucratic rule, but it has been discussed in

subsequent constitutional debates. See Rajeev Dhavan, *Reserved! How Parliament Debated Reservations 1995–2007* (New Delhi: Rupa & Co., 2008).

34. Dag-Erik Berg, 'Scheduled Castes Policies in Interstate Perspective: Constitutional Power, Argumentative Practices, and Governance in India', *India Review* 13, no. 3 (2014): 235–50, doi:10.1080/14736489.2014.937269.
35. David Mosse, 'Caste and Development: Contemporary Perspectives on a Structure of Discrimination and Advantage', *World Development* 110 (2018): 426, doi:10.1016/j.worlddev.2018.06.003.
36. Rupa Viswanath, 'Commissioning Representation: The Misra Report, Deliberation and the Government of the People in Modern India', *South Asia: Journal of South Asian Studies* 38, no. 3 (2015), 500–1, doi:10.1080/00856401.2015.1049773; Rupa Viswanath, *The Pariah Problem: Caste, Religion, and the Social in Modern India* (New York: Columbia University Press, 2014), 251.
37. Hugo Gorringe, *Untouchable Citizens: Dalit Movements and Democratization in Tamil Nadu* (New Delhi: Sage Publications, 2005).
38. Constituent Assembly of India, 'Adoption of the Constitution', 1216.
39. Devesh Kapur, Chandra Bhan Prasad, Lant Pritchett and D. Shyam Babu, 'Rethinking Inequality: Dalits in Uttar Pradesh in the Market Reform Era', *Economic and Political Weekly* 45, no. 35 (2010): 39–49; Devesh Kapur, D. Shyam Babu and Chandra Bhan Prasad, *Defying the Odds: The Rise of Dalit Entrepreneurs* (Gurgaon: Random House India, 2014).
40. Anti-Slavery International, 'Slavery in India's Brick Kilns & the Payment System Way Forward in the Fight for Fair Wages, Decent Work and Eradication of Slavery', September 2017, accessed 12 November 2017, http://www.antislavery.org/wp-content/uploads/2017/09/Slavery-In-Indias-Brick-Kilns-The-Payment-System.pdf; David Picherit, 'Rural Youth and Circulating Labour in South India: The Tortuous Paths towards Respect for Madigas', *Journal of Agrarian Change* 37, no. 43 (2018): 178–95, doi:10.1111/joac.12196.
41. S. R. Sankaran, 'Social Exclusion and Criminal Law', in *Challenging the Rule(s) of Law: Colonialism, Criminology and Human Rights in India*, ed. Kalpana Kannabirān and Ranbir Singh (Los Angeles and London: Sage Publications, 2008), 136; Ministry of Labour & Employment, The Bonded Labour System (Abolition) Act, 1976 (Act No. 19 of 1976), Ministry of Labour & Employment, Government of India, 9 February 1976, accessed 11 November 2017, http://labour.gov.in/sites/default/files/TheBondedLabourSystem(Abolition)Act1976.pdf.
42. Jayaseelan Raj, 'Alienated Enclaves: Economic Crisis and Neo-bondage in a South Indian Plantation Belt', *Forum for Development Studies* 40, no. 3 (2013): 465–90, doi:10.1080/08039410.2013.799098.
43. Benedict Anderson, *Imagined Communities: Reflections on the Origin and Spread of Nationalism* (London: Verso, 1991).
44. Examples of generic categories are 'fruit' and 'meat', which cover several items (such as bananas and oranges or beef and lamb, respectively); see Dvora Yanow, *Constructing 'Race' and 'Ethnicity' in America: Category-Making in Public Policy and Administration* (Armonk, NY: M. E. Sharpe, 2003)

45. Partha Chatterjee, *The Politics of the Governed: Reflections on Popular Politics in Most of the World* (New York: Columbia University Press, 2004), 4ff.
46. Supreme Court of India, *E.V. Chinnaiah v. State of Andhra Pradesh and Ors*, Civil Appeal No. 6758 of 2000, New Delhi, 5 November 2004, http://www.judis.openarchive.in/.
47. In 2018, there were sixty-one castes listed as SC in the state of Andhra Pradesh, fifty-nine in Telangana, seventy-six in Tamil Nadu, fifty-nine in Maharashtra and sixty-six in Uttar Pradesh. See Department of Social Justice and Empowerment, *List of Scheduled Castes* (New Delhi: Department of Social Justice and Empowerment, Government of India, 2018), accessed 11 November 2018, http://socialjustice.nic.in/UserView/index?mid=76750.
48. Picherit, 'Rural Youth and Circulating Labour in South India'.
49. Sambaiah Gundimeda, 'Dalits, Praja Rajyam Party and Caste Politics in Andhra Pradesh'. *Economic and Political Weekly* 44, no. 21 (2009): 50–8.
50. For further details, see Chapter 6.
51. Rajni Kothari, 'Introduction', in *Caste in Indian Politics*, ed. Rajni Kothari (New Delhi: Orient Longman, 1970), 20.
52. Satish Deshpande, 'Caste and Castelessness: Towards a Biography of the "General Category"', *Economic and Political Weekly* 48 (2013): 32–9, accessed 24 October 2015, http://www.epw.in/perspectives/caste-and-castelessness.html.
53. Pierre Bourdieu, *Distinction: A Social Critique of the Judgement of Taste* (London: Routledge & Kegan Paul, 1984), 291.
54. Thomas E. Weisskopf, *Affirmative Action in the United States and India: A Comparative Perspective* (London: Routledge, 2004).
55. Galanter, *Competing Equalities.*
56. Durga Das Basu, *Shorter Constitution of India*, 13th edn (Nagpur: Wadhwa and Company, 2001), 1559, emphasis in original. For an explanation of the origins of this theological norm that is used to determines the SC status, see Viswanath, *The Pariah Problem*, 251.
57. *Devarajiah vs B. Padmanna* (Karnataka High Court, 10 September 1957), http://indiankanoon.org/doc/337685/.
58. S. Lourduswamy, 'Christian or Hindu, a Dalit Is a Dalit, Reservation Is His Right', *Times of India*, 11 October 1998.
59. Dhavan, *Reserved!*, 8.
60. André Béteille, *Society and Politics in India: Essays in a Comparative Perspective* (London: Athlone Press, 1991), 206.
61. Surinder S. Jodhka and Katherine S. Newman, 'In the Name of Globalization: Meritocracy, Productivity, and the Hidden Language of Caste', in *Blocked by Caste: Economic Discrimination in Modern India*, ed. Sukhadeo Thorat and Katherine S. Newman (New Delhi: Oxford University Press, 2010), 52–87; Deshpande, 'Caste and Castelessness'; Ajantha Subramanian, 'Making Merit: The Indian Institutes of Technology and the Social Life of Caste', *Comparative Studies in Society and History* 57, no. 02 (2015): 291–322, doi:10.1017/S0010417515000043.

62. Louis Dumont, *Homo Hierarchicus: The Caste System and Its Implications* (Chicago: University of Chicago Press, 1980).
63. See Chapter 5; *Dr. Subhash Kashinath Mahajan versus the State of Maharashtra and Anr.*
64. Subramanian, 'Making Merit'; Deshpande, 'Caste and Castelessness'.
65. Sukhadeo Thorat, K. M. Shyamprasad and R. K. Srivastava, *Report of the Committee to Enquire into the Allegation of Differential Treatment of SC/ST Students in All India Institute of Medical Science, Delhi* (New Delhi: University Grant Commission, 2005); Charu S. Kasturi, 'Ghetto in Medical Hostel: Quota Students in AIIMS Allege Being Driven into a Corner', *Telegraph*, Calcutta, 5 July 2006, accessed 6 February 2018, https://www.telegraphindia.com/india/ghetto-in-medical-hostel-quota-students-in-aiims-allege-being-driven-into-a-corner/cid/785574.
66. Dag-Erik Berg, 'Hindu Nationalism and Caste Exclusion in Indian Universities', *openDemocracy*, 9 April 2016, accessed 23 May 2016, https://www.opendemocracy.net/openindia/dag-erik-berg/hindu-nationalism-and-caste-exclusion-in-indian-universities.
67. Dag-Erik Berg, 'Structural Mechanism, Law, and the Dalit Question in India', *Asian Journal of Law and Society* 2, no. 1 (2015): 21–33, doi:10.1017/als.2014.14.
68. Dirks, *Castes of Mind.*
69. Dag-Erik Berg, 'Race as a Political Frontier against Caste: WCAR, Dalits and India's Foreign Policy', *Journal of International Relations and Development* 21, no. 4 (2018): 990–1013, https://doi.org/10.1057/s41268-017-0091-3; Dag-Erik Berg, 'Sovereignties, the World Conference against Racism 2001 and the Formation of a Dalit Human Rights Campaign', in *Questions de Recherche/Research in Question*, no. 20 (Paris: Centre d'études et de recherches internationals, Sciences Po., 2007), https://www.sciencespo.fr/ceri/sites/sciencespo.fr.ceri/files/qdr20.pdf; Clifford Bob, '"Dalit Rights Are Human Rights": Caste Discrimination, International Activism, and the Construction of a New Human Rights Issue', *Human Rights Quarterly* 29, no. 1 (2007): 167–93; Eva-Maria Hardtmann, *The Dalit Movement in India: Local Practices, Global Connections* (New Delhi and Oxford: Oxford University Press, 2009); Sukhadeo Thorat and Umakant, eds., *Caste, Race and Discrimination: Discourses in International Context* (New Delhi: Indian Institute of Dalit Studies, 2004).
70. Soli J. Sorabjee, 'The Official Position', *Seminar - India*, no. 508 (2001), accessed 25 February 2016, http://www.india-seminar.com/2001/508/508%20soli%20j.%20sorabjee.htm.
71. Boja Tharakam, interview with the author, Hyderabad, 8 December 2014.
72. Gajendran Ayyathurai, 'Foundations of Anti-Caste Consciousness: Pandit Iyothee Thass, Tamil Buddhism, and the Marginalized in South India', unpublished PhD thesis, Columbia University, New York, 2011, p. 168.
73. *Economist*, 'Arguments over Caste Spread from India to Britain', 1 November 2015, accessed 17 November 2017, https://www.economist.com/blogs/erasmus/2015/11/hinduism-britain-and-caste.

74. Quoted in Arvind Sivaramakrishnan, 'Caste out by the Law', *Hindu*, 1 August 2013.
75. *Daily Mail*, 'Modi's India on Britain's Doorstep? An MP and a 'Hindutva' Charity Accused of Working together to "Push into the Long Grass" a Law to Protect British Dalits', 31 October 2017, accessed 5 February 2018, http://www.dailymail.co.uk/indiahome/indianews/article-5032729/National-Council-Hindu-Temples-working-repeal-caste.html.
76. Government Equalities Office, *Caste in Great Britain and Equality Law: A Public Consultation: Government Consultation Response* (London, 2018), 14, accessed 5 August 2018, https://assets.publishing.service.gov.uk/government/uploads/system/uploads/attachment_data/file/727790/Caste_in_Great_Britain_and_equality_law-consultation_response.pdf.
77. Dumont, *Homo Hierarchicus*, 220–2. Ironically, the allegation that studies of caste have been focused on the past has been used in a critique of Dumont too; see André Béteille, *Anti-Utopia: Essential Writings of André Béteille* (Oxford: Oxford University Press, 2005), pp. 85, 356.
78. Dumont, *Homo Hierarchicus*, 222.
79. Berg, 'Race as a Political Frontier against Caste'.
80. Ernesto Laclau, *The Rhetorical Foundations of Society* (London: Verso, 2014), 101.
81. Giovanni Capoccia, 'When Do Institutions "Bite"? Historical Institutionalism and the Politics of Institutional Change', *Comparative Political Studies* 49, no. 8 (2016): 1095–127, doi:10.1177/0010414015626449.
82. Jensenius, 'Mired in Reservations'.
83. Kathleen Thelen, 'How Institutions Evolve: Insights from Comparative Historical Analysis', in *Comparative Historical Analysis in the Social Sciences*, ed. James Mahoney and Dietrich Rueschemeyer, Cambridge Studies in Comparative Politics (Cambridge: Cambridge University Press, 2003).
84. Dirks, *Castes of Mind*.
85. Jason Glynos and David R. Howarth, *Logics of Critical Explanation in Social and Political Theory* (New York: Routledge, 2007).
86. The expression 'upper castes' is itself problematical and contested. I alternate between this and 'caste Hindus', although the latter does not convey the fact that casteism is practised in other religions such as Christianity and Islam.
87. Antonio Gramsci, *Selections from the Prison Notebooks of Antonio Gramsci* (London: Lawrence & Wishart Ltd, 1971), 5. For a discussion of Gramsci's complex concept of organic intellectuals, see Kate A. F. Crehan, *Gramsci's Common Sense: Inequality and Its Narratives* (Durham: Duke University Press Books, 2016), pp. 20, 28–33.
88. Aldon D. Morris, *The Scholar Denied: W.E.B. Du Bois and the Birth of Modern Sociology* (Oakland, CA: University of California Press, 2015); Upendra Baxi, 'Emancipation as Justice: Legacy and Vision of Dr Ambedkar', in *From Periphery to Centre Stage*, ed. K. C. Yadav (New Delhi: Manohar Publishers, 2000); Dag-Erik Berg, 'Foregrounding Contingency in Caste-Based Dominance: Ambedkar, Hegemony, and the Pariah Concept', *Philosophy & Social Criticism* 44, no. 8 (2018):

843–64, doi:10.1177/0191453717744007; Olivier Herrenschmidt, 'Ambedkar and the Hindu Social Order', in *Reconstructing the World: B. R. Ambedkar and Buddhism in India*, ed. Surendra Jondhale and Johannes Beltz, (New Delhi: Oxford University Press, 2004), 37–48.

89. B. R. Ambedkar, 'Untouchables or the Children of India's Ghetto', in *Dr. Babasaheb Ambedkar Writings and Speeches: Unpublished Writings*, ed. Vasant Moon, vol. 5 (Bombay: Education Department, Government of Maharashtra, 1989), 102.
90. Jon Elster, *Alchemies of the Mind: Rationality and the Emotions* (Cambridge: Cambridge University Press, 1999), 10–12.
91. Jon Elster, *Explaining Social Behavior: More Nuts and Bolts for the Social Sciences* (Cambridge: Cambridge University Press, 2007), 37.
92. Pierre Bourdieu, *Outline of a Theory of Practice* (Cambridge: Cambridge University Press, 1977); Laclau, *The Rhetorical Foundations of Society*, 101.
93. Berg, 'Structural Mechanism, Law, and the Dalit Question in India'. For a different and more empirical use of the term 'structural', see David Mosse, 'Caste and Development: Contemporary Perspectives on a Structure of Discrimination and Advantage', *World Development* 110 (2018): 422–36, doi:10.1016/j.worlddev.2018.06.003.
94. David R. Howarth, *Poststructuralism and After: Structure, Subjectivity, and Power* (Basingstoke: Palgrave Macmillan, 2013), 151. My decision to avoid the term 'structure' is based on my own experience; confusions arose when I described my concept as a 'structural mechanism'. See Berg, 'Structural Mechanism, Law, and the Dalit Question in India'. For this book, I have therefore modified my concept for both didactic and conceptual reasons.
95. James Manor, 'Prologue: Caste and Politics in Recent Times', in *Caste in Indian Politics*, ed. Rajni Kothari and James Manor, 2nd edn (Hyderabad: Orient BlackSwan, 2010).
96. Michel Foucault, 'The Subject and Power', in *Power, Essential Works of Foucault 1954-1984*, ed. James D. Faubion (London: Penguin Books, 2002), 342; Chantal Mouffe, *Agonistics: Thinking the World Politically* (London: Verso, 2013); Friedrich Nietzsche, 'Homer's Contest', in *On the Genealogy of Morality*, ed. Keith Ansell-Pearson, rev. student edn, Cambridge Texts in the History of Political Thought (Cambridge: Cambridge University Press, 2007); Mark Wenman, *Agonistic Democracy: Constituent Power in the Era of Globalisation* (Cambridge: Cambridge University Press, 2013); Dana Richard Villa, *Politics, Philosophy, Terror: Essays on the Thought of Hannah Arendt* (Princeton, NJ: Princeton University Press, 1999).
97. Nikolai Roskamm, 'On the Other Side of "Agonism": "The Enemy," the "Outside," and the Role of Antagonism', *Planning Theory* 14, no. 4 (2015): 384–403, doi:10.1177/1473095214533959.
98. Jacob S. Hacker, Paul Pierson and Kathleen Thelen, 'Drift and Conversion: Hidden Faces of Institutional Change', in *Advances in Comparative-Historical Analysis*, ed. James Mahoney and Kathleen A. Thelen, Strategies for Social Inquiry (New York: Cambridge University Press, 2015).

99. Glynos and Howarth, *Logics of Critical Explanation in Social and Political Theory.*
100. Ibid.
101. Kothari, 'Introduction'.
102. M. S. Srinivas, 'The Dominant Caste in Rampura', *American Anthropologist* 61, no. 1 (1959): 1–16.
103. Rudolph and Rudolph, *The Modernity of Tradition*; Kothari, 'Introduction'.
104. Rajni Kothari, 'Rise of the Dalits and the Renewed Debate on Caste', *Economic and Political Weekly* 29, no. 26 (1994): 1589–94; Sudha Pai, *Dalit Assertion and the Unfinished Democratic Revolution: The Bahujan Samaj Party in Uttar Pradesh* (New Delhi: Sage Publications, 2002); Jaffrelot, *India's Silent Revolution.*
105. *NDTV,* 'Caste Fine, Not Casteism, Says BJP's Yogi Adityanath', 5 March 2017, accessed 21 May 2017, https://www.youtube.com/watch?v=gE4RONcQIUA&feature=youtu.be; *Times of India,* 'My Cabinet Colleagues Are Vegetarians, Yet Not Weak: Adityanath Yogi', 1 May 2017, accessed 23 June 2017, http://timesofindia.indiatimes.com/city/lucknow/my-cabinet-colleagues-are-vegetarian-yet-not-weak-adityanath-yogi/articleshow/58463422.cms.
106. Dirks, *Castes of Mind.*
107. For a critique of the exaggerated usage of Foucault in critical theory, see Colin Gordon, 'Expelled Questions: Foucault, the Left and the Law', in *Re-reading Foucault: On Law, Power and Rights*, ed. Ben Golder (London: Routledge, 2013), 13.
108. Michel Foucault, *The Archaeology of Knowledge* (London: Routledge, 1989).
109. Chatterjee, *The Politics of the Governed.*
110. Kapur et al., 'Rethinking Inequality'.
111. Stuart Corbridge and John Harriss, *Reinventing India: Liberalization, Hindu Nationalism and Popular Democracy* (Malden, MA: Polity Press, 2000).
112. Smriti Sharma, 'Caste-Based Crimes and Economic Status: Evidence from India', *Journal of Comparative Economics* 43, no. 1 (2015): 204–26, doi:10.1016/j.jce.2014.10.005. Similarly, lynching of blacks in the USA occurred more often as a response to labour market competition and the fact that blacks were free rather than slaves, see Gregory N. Price, William A. Darity and Alvin E. Headen, 'Does the Stigma of Slavery Explain the Maltreatment of Blacks by Whites? The Case of Lynchings', *The Journal of Socio-Economics* 37, no. 1 (2008): 167–93, doi:10.1016/j.socec.2007.06.001.
113. My analysis thus differs from a recent discussion of the Green Revolution, see Aditya Dasgupta, 'Technological Change and Political Turnover: The Democratizing Effects of the Green Revolution in India', *American Political Science Review* 112, no. 4 (2018): 918–38, doi:10.1017/S000305541800031X.
114. Thelen, 'How Institutions Evolve'.
115. Wenman, *Agonistic Democracy*; Mouffe, *Agonistics.*

1

Foundations of Caste and Constitutional Democracy

Ambedkar, Equality and Law

The idea of a casteless society has been important to anti-caste leaders since premodern times. Anti-caste movements gained momentum in the middle of the nineteenth century, and the so-called non-Brahmin movements in the Madras and Bombay Presidencies were vibrant by the time Ambedkar was born in 1891. Ambedkar's father, for example, was inspired by the low-caste leader Mahatma Jyotirao Phule, who also came from Maharashtra. In the twenty-first century, one could find posters of Ambedkar in many Dalit homes, for example, in rural south India and elsewhere in the country. Statues of Ambedkar have been erected in cities such as Mumbai, Hyderabad and Kanpur. Occasionally, statues are vandalized by members of other castes, and in some cases, they have had to be protected,[1] but the proliferation of statues is nonetheless significant. Ambedkar's role as a symbol of assertion is a result of his contribution to the crafting of constitutional entitlements for the Scheduled Castes (SCs) and his relentless critique of caste. He marks a new chapter in the anti-caste project, representing constitutional entitlements and claims to universal values. In addition to his advanced scholarly thought, he created a legacy as a statesman who was instrumental in designing India's constitution with entitlements and principles such as equality.[2]

In this chapter, I focus on two topics of Ambedkar's legacy, namely his theory of caste annihilation and his contribution to the Constitution of India, 1950. The two topics must be unpacked separately if one is to understand each of them and how they relate to one another. The idea of abolishing caste is a revolutionary intellectual project of emancipation, whereas the second topic is a story about a liberal democrat who struggled but followed his vision for social reform by taking part in the negotiations and participating in the development of India's constitution. Ambedkar made a number of different contributions and was engaged in theoretical and practical battles. In a seminal essay, Professor Upendra Baxi discussed his roles and enumerated seven dimensions of Ambedkar's career.[3] Political theory and constitutional politics, which I focus on, are two dimensions noted in Baxi's discussion, and they cannot be mixed up if one is to understand Ambedkar's different types of contributions. First, I focus on Ambedkar as a 'militant' writer who made contributions relevant to political theory and, second, as a 'liberal democrat' in the constitutional process who negotiated with other politicians and lawmakers. Ambedkar is characterized as a modern Manu,[4] corresponding to the ancient lawgiver, for his contribution to the constitution of the postcolonial Indian state. In practice, he became both a statesman and an innovative thinker.

Ambedkar's scholarly critique of caste should be viewed as a contribution to political theory; he critically examines social and religious practices while simultaneously advocating democratic principles and reforms. His work is relevant to different strands of current political thought, such as post-foundationalism and republican theory of freedom.[5] Yet caution needs to be exercised when using these labels because each includes different bedfellows. For example, freedom from domination and republicanism comprises several approaches. A prominent one includes the methodological individualism of Quentin Skinner and the Cambridge School, which also informs Aishwary Kumar's discussion of Ambedkar and Gandhi, although Kumar argues that Ambedkar draws on Rousseauist revolutionary thought and early modern republicanism.[6] Republicanism is also relevant when, for example, Arendt points to how Machiavelli's theory of action and his concept of *virtù* illustrate that freedom is inherent in political action.[7] In my view, Ambedkar's conceptual contribution requires recognition of how he distinguishes between the social, political and religious domains when developing his project for freedom against domination. He characterizes each domain, explains the persistence of caste and has an acute interest in identifying how democratic change could occur. Caste-based domination was his key object of study, and conceptually, Ambedkar viewed caste as a matter of ontology because of how the belief in caste constitutes social relations.

Ambedkar offers a theory about how caste-based domination is constituted and how religious ideas provide a foundation for social order. Caste has a grip on those who practise it. But by focusing on how caste is constitutive of social relations, his approach dovetails with central concerns in post-foundational theory in which hegemony and political ontology are considered historically contingent.[8] Comparing Ambedkar's social and political thought with post-foundational theory, such as the works of Ernesto Laclau, offers considerable potential. The late Laclau offers a theory of hegemony in which he distinguishes between social and political practices, as well as provides a concept of political ontology.[9] He distinguishes between political ontology and studies of action. Ambedkar, though, provides an explanation of how caste is ontologically grounded while contributing to democratic solutions based on Enlightenment ideals. However, Ambedkar combines a radical perspective on political theory with a pragmatic approach to democratic struggles.

The process of drafting India's constitution represents a framework somewhat different from the one Ambedkar focuses on in his radical text 'Annihilation of Caste'.[10] He was a liberal democrat who had discussed, negotiated and compromised with his opponents. He made a significant contribution to the drafting of India's constitution even though the constituent assembly (1946–9) consisted of many upper-caste men and *zamindar*s (landlords) who had other ideas about India's future.[11] However, Ambedkar emerged as a statesman in this context while coping with humiliations and conflicts. One of the conflicts that has gained a great deal of attention is his struggle with Mahatma Gandhi in the early 1930s. The dispute with Gandhi is important in India's constitutional history, especially in explaining the position of the untouchables in the religious order and Gandhi's idea of a holistic nation. It shows how Ambedkar struggled with the hegemonic articulation of Indian nationalism at the time. But, conceptually, the conflict with Gandhi could be a red herring if it distracts attention from Ambedkar's account of how caste is ontologically grounded.[12]

In this chapter, I first outline a short history of anti-caste struggles across several regions before I provide an account of Ambedkar's career, his emerging movement and the human rights articulations of the late 1920s. This provides the background for my introduction of the basic perspectives of his social and political thought. Next, I explain a psychological element of his theory of caste, which I classify as the ontological drive and grip of caste. Finally, I examine the discussion of caste during the drafting of India's constitution. I go on to examine Ambedkar's historical battles with Gandhi in the 1930s and his later contributions to the constituent assembly from 1946 to 1949. The chapter thus introduces Ambedkar's theory of caste and his contribution to India's constitution in order to provide a basis for an examination of law and caste-based dominance.

Histories of Anti-Caste Struggles

The current Dalit movement involves young and old activists, who draw on a long history of struggles, various incidents and writings as they engage with contemporary issues. They are part of a long history of critiques of hierarchy and inequality that exist in the Hindu social order. The general trend during the postcolonial period has been that the emerging middle class of Dalit activists have read Ambedkar's work and established Ambedkarite movements. This is what happened in Uttar Pradesh in the 1960s and 1970s, providing a basis for the Ambedkarization that anticipated the larger political transformation in the state in the 1980s and 1990s.[13] Similarly, Ambedkar was a significant source of inspiration for activists across the country. In the 1970s, however, there were many possibilities for the Dalit mobilization to emerge as a sustained and countrywide mobilization. The Dalit Panthers was a militant organization established in Maharashtra in 1971, which speeded up the momentum for a cultural and literary movement in India. This was in practice the starting point for using the term 'Dalit' as a self-chosen designation for a political movement that identified with Ambedkar.

There are many starting points for anti-caste movements, and some of them include the views of people from the colonial period and even from pre-British India. In fact, there were outspoken anti-caste intellectuals in premodern India, such as articulate subaltern figures in the fifteenth century. Kabir (1440–1518) and Ravidas (1450–1520) were two subaltern intellectuals from north India who left critical legacies in the form of their poetry and the practices associated with part of a *bhakti* (devotional) tradition. Both were born in untouchable castes. Ravidas was a Chamar (leatherworker) by caste, and Kabir was from a weaver community.[14] The two poet saints questioned hierarchical religion. Their teachings have been revived several times, including in transnational revivals such as the one in Britain in 2009.[15] Ravidas envisioned an egalitarian city – Begumpura – that was unified and did not involve any sadness, while Kabir questioned the doctrine of rebirth and wrote many radical poems. Part of one of Kabir's poems reads: 'Pandit, look at your heart to know. Tell me how untouchability was born – untouchability is what you made so'.[16] Kabir was a critical poet who felt that caste obstructed human freedom. While the medieval *bhakti* movements undermined Brahmins' monopoly and questioned their birth-given status, it has not been clear that they managed to break away from caste.[17] This applied to *bhakti* movements of Mahars in Maharashtra, where there were instances of melancholy and concealed obedience to ideas of rebirth.[18] As Jaffrelot underlines, Ambedkar did not only grow up with these egalitarian traditions and the questioning of hierarchy, but he also developed the critique of them by using a new emancipatory approach.[19] In fact, Ambedkar's anti-caste approach was characterized by a commitment to universalizing democratic principles.

Ambedkar took part in a transformation towards more universal perspectives in the anti-caste movement, thus following the trend initiated by Phule and the non-Brahmin movement. Indeed, he championed the values of the French Enlightenment, namely liberty, equality and fraternity, which he took to be the basis of democracy. At the end of his life, he converted to Buddhism, but the Buddha that he embraced was outward-looking, universal and engaged rather than inward-looking and meditative.[20] Ambedkar's Buddhist conversion was based on his understanding of Indian history – he saw Buddhism and Brahminism as being historically opposite. He identified a sharp difference between Buddha's idea that 'all are equal' and Brahminism which had introduced inequality. Ambedkar wanted to revive the historical battle for equality between Brahminism and Buddhism.[21] This is one part of the repertoire that the current Dalit movement has inherited.

Ambedkar's career and his ideas about emancipation were an extension of an anti-caste tradition. While he became a symbol at an all-India level, there were nonetheless important regional differences among the activists. Each region had its specific trajectory and movements, which included the non-Brahmin movements in Maharashtra, the Madras Presidency, Travancore (today Kerala) and Punjab. There were noteworthy differences and commonalities across these movements. At the end of the nineteenth century, there were noteworthy anti-caste movements which included those with transnational visions of freedom from oppression and slavery.

Phule was the leader of the non-Brahmin movement in the Marathi-speaking areas in western India – today Maharashtra. Phule was born in 1827. His family was from the Mali (Shudra) caste that traditionally engaged in gardening. In the nineteenth century, colonial powers gained opportunities to develop their institutions due to a decline in the power of the Peshwas, the traditional ruling elite.[22] The colonial government did not pay much attention to the untouchable castes. The administration mostly recruited members of the higher castes, especially Brahmins. But Scottish missionaries were interested in developing institutions, such as schools, and to convert the lower castes. Phule was among the students attending a school in Pune run by missionaries of the Free Church of Scotland.[23] There were several sources of inspiration for this generation of social reformers beyond the missionary schools, including a vernacular press. As a young man, Phule and his friends were inspired by ideas about being liberated from colonial rule and social reforms. He later became increasingly interested in the work of Thomas Paine. Phule developed an understanding of Paine that differed from that of Brahmin activists, who used Paine to support their anti-colonial rhetoric.[24] In 1873, Phule published his book on slavery. It was dedicated to 'the good people of the United States' for freeing black people from slavery and expressed a desire that Indians would emancipate 'their Shudra Brethren from the trammels of Brahmin thraldom'.[25] But this book represents a relentless critique of Brahmin power. Even in the first sentence, he declares 'that the Brahmins were not the aborigines of India'.[26] This remark is part of Phule's anti-caste critique and represents a step outside the Vedic paradigm that dominated the Hindu revival at the time.[27] Phule reinterpreted the well-known theory of Aryan invasion. The idea of the Aryans was projected by mid-nineteenth-century Hindu reformers as a theory about a mythic Aryan period, representing a golden age of Vedic texts and practices.[28] Yet Phule claimed that Brahmins were descendants of Aryans who invaded the subcontinent that was once populated by lower castes.[29] Phule was deeply engaged in a broad non-Brahmin movement at that time, and he combined this critique with demands for primary education for the lower castes and a keen interest in women's rights. The non-Brahmin movement was well established in Maharashtra via meetings and activities in rural and urban centres in the 1880s. As the historian Rosalind O'Hanlon writes, 'The non-brahman ideology developed out of real caste antagonism within Indian society'.[30] There was a considerable difference in the level of education between the Brahmins and the lower castes. The social and educational inequalities and the prevalence of Brahmins in the colonial administration were the key concerns for a social reformer such as Phule.

There was a similarly vibrant non-Brahmin movement in the Madras Presidency in south India at that time. The development of this movement is considered to have been a reaction to the institutionalization of Hindu law and Brahmin power in the colonial state during the course of the nineteenth century.[31] One of the main leaders of the anti-caste movement in Madras was Pandit C. Iyothee Thass (1845–1914). Although Thass had collaborated with the members of the nationalist movement early on, he ended up disagreeing with the Indian Congress on positions of Hindu identity and caste in the early 1890s. On the basis of his archival research and his study of Thass's writings in the anti-caste publication *The Tamilian*, Ayyathurai underlines how Thass challenged assumptions about common identity and the interest in social reform.[32] Thass felt that the Brahmin and upper-caste participants had no interest in discussing the problems of the Parayars as this was handled by British officials. To recognize the Parayars, Thass demanded that the oppressed classes should be allowed to enter Vishnu and Siva temples. But this claim was rejected wholeheartedly by the assembly members; Thass then responded by rejecting the Hindu gods and claiming that the Parayars did not have any caste identity – indeed, they were casteless people.[33] Thass later developed his critique of the caste system by pointing out that Parayars were originally Buddhists. He thus revived a Buddhist tradition in his relentless anti-caste struggle several decades before Ambedkar decided to convert to Buddhism in Nagpur in 1956.

There were therefore several regional movements fighting against caste-based oppression in addition to the non-Brahmin movements in Madras and Maharashtra. The movements in Punjab in the north and in the Travancore and Malabar regions (today's Kerala) of south-west India were also significant. The history of social reforms in Punjab was characterized by internal critiques of the Sikh religion. The movement in Kerala was, comparatively, based more on class discourses and was deeply engaged in abolishing slavery and creating land reforms. The land reforms in Kerala were implemented prior to India's independence and were not hampered by opposition from landowners in the courts like Nehru's attempts at land reforms in the First Constitutional Amendment.[34] This early amendment, which followed deliberations in the constituent assembly, was struck down by the high court in Bihar in the 1950s. The land reforms in Kerala, which had been carried out prior to India's independence, did not benefit the untouchable castes in equal measure. In Malabar, there had been notorious hierarchical traditions; the traditions included practices such as 'unseeability' which meant that excluded groups had to hide when they encountered a person from a higher caste.[35]

What the anti-caste struggles across different regions had in common was that they represented collective political projects. Thass's Buddhist movement in Madras and Phule's non-Brahmin movement in Maharashtra are prime examples of this. Ideas of social reform were not reducible to individuals, and the movements were based on a collective political commitment to the struggle for freedom from oppression and caste. This struggle represented a struggle for a new mode of existence in which the members of these movements would be recognized as equals. As such, lower-caste intellectuals like Phule and Thass spearheaded movements that were free from the mentalities of the caste hierarchy. Ambedkar's contribution represents a new and significant extension of this emancipatory project.

Ambedkar's Career and Democratic Ideals

The non-Brahmin movement had a significant impact on the lower castes in Maharashtra at the time that Bhimrao Ambedkar was born, in 1891. He was the youngest of fourteen children, and only five of them survived.[36] Ambedkar's father, Ramji Sakpal, was inspired by Jyotirao Phule. The family belonged to a section of society whose social and economic positions were better than that of other untouchable castes. Ambedkar's family seemed to have had a regular income as part of a middle class. His father served in the military. Because of his family background, Ambedkar could enjoy more opportunities than many members of his own caste – the Mahars. The British army had recruited many Mahar men, particularly from the Ratnagiri district where Ambedkar's family lived.[37]

The Mahars are one of the leading castes among the untouchables in Maharashtra. The three largest untouchable *jati*s (castes) in the state are the Mahars, the Mangs and the Chambhars, although the Mahars are the most populous of these three leading castes.[38] While the Mangs used to be ropemakers and basketmakers, the Mahars were not closely identified with one occupation in the traditional division of labour. They were general village servants. According to Gokhale, their social history includes having 'rights' to ask for and be given food by villagers, but they were also called on to perform tasks such as being messengers, watchmen and disposers of dead animals, often cows. Their handling of dead cattle was decisive in them being regarded as an untouchable caste, although the Mahars were not engaged in sanitation and sweeping villages like other untouchable castes.[39] The Mahars were entitled to own land, but their landholdings were inadequate for the whole population and were often of poor quality.[40] Colonialism also appears to have undermined their ability to keep their landholdings, given the colonial inclination to support larger landowners. Overall, the Mahars were available as village servants throughout the state and were thoroughly exploited. Religion was the only area in which they had a choice. Gokhale reports that the critique of Hinduism launched by Christian missionaries emboldened the production of anti-caste critique among the Mahars, although not many of them converted to Christianity.[41] The Mahars were generally associated with the *bhakti* tradition which had more egalitarian practices than Hinduism. And yet the *bhakti* tradition did not represent a systemic denial of Hinduism. The Mahars would occasionally be able to participate in some village festivals, but they were excluded from entering the temples.

Ambedkar's family and the Mahars were inspired by the non-Brahmin movements and were emboldened by several appeals to equality and education from social reformers and the *bhakti* tradition as well as Christian missionaries.[42] These various demands for social reforms coexisted with enduring reminders of social injustices and discrimination. Ambedkar's upbringing differed from that of many Mahars. Life in the military cantonment seems somehow to have protected him from untouchability practices as a child.[43] But he soon learnt about how caste involved humiliating experience. His sister had to cut his hair as no barber wanted to cut it. During his upbringing, therefore, Ambedkar experienced both upward mobility and discrimination. Given his later significance, his biography has become a legendary example of the mechanism of oppression that characterizes the Dalit situation in modern India. Stories about his struggles have been used by Dalit leaders during the postcolonial period to educate members of the Dalit movement about what his approach represented.[44]

One of the pivotal stories from Ambedkar's life is his experience as a nine-year-old boy. He had been stranded in a railway station along with his brother, and they had problems with further transportation since no one wanted to deal with them. One carter had eventually agreed to take them to their destination on the condition that he should be paid double and that the brothers should drive the cart themselves while the cartman walked along on foot to avoid sitting beside them. Ambedkar and his brother were denied drinking water for one and a half days while travelling by the bullock cart to reach their father.

In high school, Bhimrao and his brother found that no teachers wanted to touch their notebook nor ask them questions.[45] It was a government school, infused with casteism. There were restrictive rules for accessing drinking water. He and his brother were not allowed to study Sanskrit, the language essential for studying the Vedas – the sacred texts that should neither be read nor heard by Shudras or the untouchables.[46] One day, the teacher asked Ambedkar to go to the blackboard to solve a geometrical theorem.[47] As Bhimrao walked forward in the room, the entire class rushed to fetch their lunch boxes from behind the blackboard in order to avoid their food being polluted by Bhimrao's presence.[48] The schoolchildren's parents opposed Bhimrao's presence in the class, and one teacher was prompted to discourage him from continuing his education. The caste prejudice had a severe impact on his situation at school.

It was a rare achievement for the untouchables to complete high school. A gathering was therefore organized in Bombay, which included a social reformer, to celebrate Ambedkar's successful graduation.[49] He also completed an undergraduate degree at Elphinstone College in Bombay and started working for the Baroda state (today's Gujarat) state administration in January 1913 to repay his sponsor, the maharaja of Baroda. It was the maharaja of Baroda who also granted Ambedkar a scholarship to study overseas. The maharaja had visited America and was willing to delay Ambedkar's administrative service and support his graduate studies in Columbia University and subsequently in London.[50]

Ambedkar studied at Columbia University in New York from 1913 to 1916, during a vibrant intellectual period at the university. He studied with professors such as John Dewey and learnt from the wider intellectual trends in America at that time. He was absorbed in his studies and was able to continue his overseas studies when he received financial support to study at the London School of Economics for one additional year. Upon returning to India in 1917, Ambedkar was determined to serve the maharaja of Baroda for a prescribed ten-year period. But he faced discrimination in the office where he worked as a military secretary even though he tried to hide his caste. When he stayed in a Parsi hotel, the local community of Parsis was angry with him, and a group of men threatened him, demanding that he should leave the hotel.[51] He returned to Bombay, where he worked as a professor in a commercial college for two years. Ambedkar was acutely aware of the problems of untouchability and how this mattered for relations among staff in government offices in general.[52] Overall, his personal experience consisted of educational successes and a host of humiliating experiences. These opposing experiences represent a narrative that matter for the contemporary Dalit movement.

It was in 1919 that Ambedkar made his first public appearance as a representative of the untouchable castes. Unlike other spokespersons for the untouchables, he did not represent an organization at that time. Ambedkar was invited because he was the only college graduate among the untouchables in the Bombay Presidency. His testimony was lengthy and articulate, but it seems as if Ambedkar and other activists who raised the problems of the Depressed Classes were generally ignored by the Southborough Committee.[53] It was not until 1923 that Ambedkar started to work as a social reformer alongside representing the Depressed Classes in the government.[54] According to Zelliot, Ambedkar's activism largely followed a general pattern established by previous reformers, which involved attending conferences, establishing newspapers and organizations until the mid-1930s, that is, until he declared that he would convert to another religion in 1935 and established a political party in 1936.[55]

A conference in Mahad city in 1927 is widely considered as the starting point for a more united political awakening among the untouchables during this period. It was decided on this occasion that the whole assembly should march towards the drinking-water pool which the Mahad municipality had opened for untouchables in 1926.[56] Ambedkar, movement leaders and others drank from the water pool.[57] At the same time, it was rumoured that the untouchables would also enter a temple, which resulted in riots and prompted caste Hindus to attack the untouchables. A court case was later filed to prevent the untouchables from using water from this pool. The objection from caste Hindus was that this was private property. Ambedkar won the case after three years of arguing in court. But the caste Hindus appealed to Bombay High Court, and it was not until 1937 that the untouchables were finally entitled to use the water from the pool.[58]

In addition to the non-violent march to access the pool, the conference in Mahad in 1927 was marked by the symbolic burning of the *Manusmrti* (Laws of Manu).[59] A resolution was passed at the conference to reject the religious authority of this Hindu law book which taught social inequality and caste-related cruelty. This resolution appeared more than twenty years before the Universal Declaration of Human Rights. The clear affirmation of dignity and the critique of a dominating Hindu religion at the Mahad conference are a reminder of how rights struggles have a rich history across time and space. The resolution could be viewed as comparable to the affirmation of universal rights during the French Revolution and clearly contradicts current arguments in global intellectual history (advanced by the American lawyer Samuel Moyn) that modern human rights only came into existence in the 1970s.[60] The statement of the untouchables' conference in 1927 was acutely informed by a notion of universal rights and is comparable with the ideals of the French Enlightenment. It says,

> Taking into consideration the fact that the laws which are proclaimed in the name of Manu, the Hindu law-giver, and which are contained in the Manu Smriti and which are recognized as the Code for the Hindus are insulting to persons of low caste, are calculated to deprive them of the rights of a human being and crush their personality. Comparing them in the light of the rights of men recognized all over the civilized world, this conference is of the opinion that this Manu Smriti is not entitled to any respect and is undeserving of being called a sacred book to show its deep and profound contempt for it, the Conference resolves to burn a copy thereof, at the end of the proceedings, as a protest against the system of social inequality it embodies in the guise of religion.[61]

The declaration combines an appeal to universal equality with a dramatic symbolic conclusion – to burn a book representing a 'system of inequality' disguised as a Brahminical religion. This action also attracted attention as a public attack on Brahminism.[62] According to Zelliot, the idea of burning *Manusmrti* was suggested by a Chitpavan Brahmin associated with Ambedkar. It caused dramatic reactions.[63] Such radical moves did not suit Ambedkar's character. He preferred more peaceful modes of action, such as arguing in court rather than urging his followers to fight for their rights in the streets. His involvement in movements for temple access was also unclear; in fact, readers in the early 1930s expressed frustration about Ambedkar's declining interest in temple entry.[64] He nonetheless provided leadership to the Mahar movement. Above all, he broke away from earlier approaches when he claimed in the mid-1930s that he would convert to another religion rather than remain in the fold of Hinduism.

Ambedkar's participation in the constitutional deliberations at the time of the Simon Commission in 1929 represented an important step towards national politics. He took part in several Round Table Conferences that the imperial power conducted in London. The battle with Gandhi at the time of the Second Round Table Conference in 1931 has gained considerable attention in the secondary literature as a key episode in the history of how the constitution was framed. This is no coincidence as it represents an event that Ambedkar recounted with bitterness when he wrote his book *What Congress and Gandhi Have Done to the Untouchables* in 1945.[65] At the Second Round Table Conference in London in 1931, Ambedkar had demanded a separate electorate for the untouchables, thus drawing on the policy that had been introduced for the Muslims in 1909. Gandhi, who represented the Congress party, sought to avoid any division of the Hindu community and was insistent that the untouchables were part of the Hindu order. Gandhi opposed Ambedkar's idea that the Depressed Classes should be entitled to vote in separate elections.

The distinction between touchables and untouchables is central to Ambedkar's understanding of caste and the Hindu social order. The distinction pervaded the social order and created a systematic exclusion of the untouchables. While they had ontological significance, the concerns that Ambedkar voiced in the constitutional debates were very practical. The basic facts were that the untouchables lived outside villages and were not allowed to enter the main parts of the villages unless under specific conditions. Ambedkar felt that separate elections would not only enable the untouchables to vote but also that their interests would be articulated in official forums if they could elect their own representatives. But Gandhi opposed the idea and even protested against the colonial recognition of this policy of a separate electorate in the ensuing Communal Award by saying that he would fast until he died. As Baxi has put it, Gandhi gambled with his life.[66] The act gained national attention and put considerable pressure on Ambedkar to change his position. Ambedkar gave up his demand and made a compromise with Gandhi, agreeing that seats should be reserved for the untouchables. He was bitter about Gandhi and his decision to fast, and he explained, 'All eyes naturally turned to me as the man of the moment or rather as the villain of the piece',[67] that is, of the Communal Award. This episode has become pivotal to defining the space, foes and struggles for Dalits in the contemporary Indian state. At the same time, the tussle with Gandhi was also decisive in Ambedkar's emergence as a political actor of national importance.

There is no doubt that Gandhi was a crucial interlocutor and political opponent for Ambedkar, but it is unfortunate if this constitutional battle becomes an all-pervading frame of reference for discussing Ambedkar's intellectual battle with caste.[68] The most significant problem is that it reduces Ambedkar's theory of caste to a specific history in constitutional politics. One of Ambedkar's key concerns seemed to be what an excessive focus on individual action tends to neglect, namely how the social and political order is produced.

Ambedkar's key concern in the essay 'Annihilation of Caste' appears to be how to overcome the persistence of caste. For him, caste was an embedded form of dominance that was produced by endogamy and religious beliefs. This concern with the caste order represents a distinct theme that is not merely reducible to constitutional politics, rather, it is a relevant motivation for his participation in constitutional politics.

Ambedkar on Caste, Religious Foundation and Change

There is a noteworthy thematic continuity in Ambedkar's struggle with untouchability and caste. The French sociologist Oliver Herrenschmidt has argued that Ambedkar deployed several systematic observations and novel concepts in analysing the Hindu social order. These were that India is a cultural unity, that there is a system of castes with a religious foundation, that the caste system is characterized by graded inequality and, finally, that caste is a matter of social psychology and a state of mind.[69] I agree with Herrenschmidt that Ambedkar's sociology is remarkably coherent and that these interrelated presuppositions offer different analytical possibilities.

The wide range of Ambedkar's writings and speeches includes several themes and discussions, but there are three important references that are useful to explain his social and political thought. The first is his early text 'Castes of India: Their Mechanisms, Genesis and Development',[70] written in 1916 while he was studying at Columbia University, the second text is his radical anti-caste critique from 1936, 'Annihilation of Caste',[71] and the third is his unpublished comparison of slavery and untouchability.[72] By comparing the first two texts, one may suggest that religion became an increasing interest in Ambedkar's thoughts on the anti-caste struggle. The third text shows how he also used an international comparison of slavery and untouchability to address a conceptual problem, namely to explain his assumption that untouchability was more enduring than slavery.[73]

The sociological question concerning caste as a self-enclosed group runs through Ambedkar's thinking. He engages with this theme in a sociological paper 'Castes in India', mentioned earlier. This early essay includes a definition of caste as a self-enclosed group in a manner that resembles Weber's definition of status group formation. Ambedkar strongly emphasizes how endogamy – marrying within the caste – is decisive for the origin of caste.[74] The observation reflects an enduring interest in his work. His relentless battle in the constituent assembly and subsequent legislative debates to create reforms for women can be viewed in the context of his interest in what gender inequality and marriage practices implied for the Hindu social order. Moreover, the question of marriage figures prominently in Ambedkar's perhaps most sustained theoretical discussion of caste and the Hindu social order, namely the essay 'Annihilation of Caste'. But this text is more militant than his early sociological essay because it moves beyond the question of inter-caste marriage to developing a resolved critique on the divine basis of caste.

The questions of endogamous practices and religion offer promises for conceptual discussions of how caste embeds different dimensions. These possibilities are not necessarily developed in the secondary literature. In fact, there are prominent accounts that tend to divert attention away from discussions of Ambedkar's texts to his historical dispute with Gandhi. One of these digressions is evident in Roy's discussion of the 'The Doctor and the Saint'.[75] While introducing 'Annihilation of Caste', she ends up discussing the relation between Gandhi's work and ideas of reform and that of Ambedkar. This is partly a result of Ambedkar's choice because he attached Gandhi's response in a republication of 'Annihilation of Caste' alongside his own critique of the Mahatma. In any case, this critical episode has gained a life of its own. A second deviation in the literature appears in Kumar's sophisticated discussion of Ambedkar as a republican in Rousseau's sense.[76] Unfortunately, Kumar's discussion reflects loyalties to conceptual schools such as Quentin Skinner's contextualism and the neo-Roman approach to civil liberties, which do not correspond well with Ambedkar's core concerns with overcoming religion, oppression and the many dimensions of caste. Therefore, while I agree with Kumar's statement that Ambedkar's discussion of freedom from caste in 'Annihilation of Caste' is a revolutionary engagement with justice, he does not spell out the key questions of Ambedkar's 'interpretative *coup de force*'.[77] My own way of making sense of Ambedkar's approach is to consider it as a problem-driven analysis of caste into which he incorporates different dimensions of caste in a sustained engagement with democratic ideals. What is crucial in this context is that his central object of study is the persistence of caste-based oppression which corresponds to an interest in explaining how caste is produced and how it could be abolished. Here, the focus on the production of caste and casteism represents an ontological dimension in Ambedkar's approach.

The context in which Ambedkar wrote 'Annihilation of Caste' sheds light on the critical responses to it that emerged. Ambedkar wrote this text after he was invited to speak to an association that had been created to break away from caste. This organization was called Jat-Pat-Todak Mandal, meaning 'Society for the Abolition of Caste'. The Jat-Pat-Todak Mandal was created in 1924 in Lahore city, the capital of the Punjab province, which is in today's Pakistan.[78] In 1935, the organization invited Ambedkar to be the president of its conference because its members identified with his idea that caste should be eradicated. Yet although it was determined to work for the eradication of the caste system, the Jat-Pat-Todak Mandal decided to withdraw its invitation when it realized how thoroughly Ambedkar criticized caste and its supporting religion.[79] It later explained that it withdrew its invitation because Ambedkar claimed he would leave the Hindu fold. The chairman explained that such a step would destroy the basis for the organization's conference, and yet he considered Ambedkar's text to be 'the most learned thesis on the subject' of caste and worth reading across the country.[80] In his analysis of religious rebels in Punjab, Mark Juergensmeyer explains that the Jat-Pat-Todak Mandal was mainly focused on inter-caste marriage as a strategy for breaking away from caste.[81] In his essay 'Castes of India' from 1916, Ambedkar had also highlighted that endogamous marriages generated caste society. But the organization had close historical ties with Arya Samaj, a Hindu reform movement, and its members were not prepared to leave the Hindu religion in the manner that Ambedkar advocated.

In 'Annihilation of Caste', Ambedkar endorses the ideas of the Jat-Pak-Todak Mandal while moving a step further than this group. He combines observations on both the production and the reproduction of caste as a social system. He first endorses the organization's idea that inter-caste marriage is an effective strategy for abolishing caste; indeed, he highlights that inter-caste marriage is the 'real remedy for breaking Caste'.[82] But Ambedkar's next claim is that intra-caste marriages have become an embedded feature of Indian society because of its religious foundation. He underlines that no Hindu would like to marry into a different caste because it would violate sacred dogmas. Quite provocatively, he states that the 'real remedy is to destroy the belief in the sanctity of the *Shastras*'. In other words, while intra-caste marriage reproduces castes as a social system, this second theme is about how caste is produced by religious beliefs. Ambedkar concedes that it requires extra courage to ask Hindus to confront their religion, but he underlines that it is precisely 'the religion which has produced in them this notion of the sacredness of Caste'.[83]

The definition of caste as a sacred 'notion' is significant because of how it identifies caste as a question of mentality. And Ambedkar often defines caste as a matter of social psychology.[84] In 'Annihilation of Caste', Ambedkar defines caste as a 'notion' and 'a state of mind' and even claims that the 'destruction' of caste 'means a *notional* change'.[85] Elsewhere, Ambedkar defines caste as 'an aspect of social psychology' which he then characterizes as an element in an antagonism between groups.[86] But there is an emphasis on mentality and consciousness in Ambedkar's discussion of caste as a 'notion' and 'state of mind'. It implies a passion – or 'beliefs' – and a commitment to practising caste.

This emphasis on the individual's mind and embedded belief in caste that Ambedkar uses in his account of caste differs from the classic sociologies of caste in the works of Louis Dumont and M. N. Srinivas or André Béteille. Dumont, for example, uses a structuralist approach to explain that caste is constituted as a holistic system by way of the exclusion of two complementary elements, the Brahmins and the untouchables. Dumont avoids relying on psychological approaches as doing this would resemble individualism which he rejects for methodological reasons. Srinivas, on the other hand, is more empirical and focuses on the composition of villages. For Ambedkar, caste is also a question of a mentality. The link between the 'notion' of caste and its practices is 'the belief in the sanctity of the *Shastras*'.[87] This is a systematic attempt to pinpoint the origins of caste. According to Ambedkar, caste is produced by a 'notion of sacredness'.

But the constitution of a society composed of castes goes beyond the religious domain by involving social relations overall. Ambedkar's idea of the constitution of society is therefore very different from that of the sociologist Anthony Giddens, whose well-known discussion of the constitution of society focuses on individual action and the possibility of amending rules in the process of applying them.[88] Ambedkar was not an individualist. Instead, he focused on how social inequality is embedded in religion. And overturning a religion involves a collective project that goes beyond questions of how individual action is constituted. His critique of religion and idea of abandoning Hinduism were undoubtedly revolutionary. In practice, however, Ambedkar seems to have been a diplomat. According to Zelliot, it was not Ambedkar who suggested that *Manusmrti* should be burnt at the time of the conference in Mahad. But his intellectual remedy is thoroughly revolutionary. He argues that breaking up caste would require removing the religious authority of the Hindu texts. Ambedkar reiterates this claim using several rhetorical strategies. He states, for instance, that 'a new life cannot enter a body that is dead' and that the 'old body must die before a new body can come into existence and a new life can enter into it'.[89]

This metaphorical language suggests that freedom requires a new point of departure outside the religion of caste. The aim is to create a new religious order corresponding to Enlightenment ideals. Ambedkar's commitment to rationalism does not mean that he denies religion. On the contrary, religion is part and parcel of his perspective on the constitution of a political order, which he envisions as an order that has relevance for social and cultural practices. In fact, although he is militant in his writings on religion, he agrees with the conservative British philosopher Edmund Burke who stated, 'True religion is the foundation of society, the basis on which all true Civil Government rests.'[90] This statement involves several assumptions that are worth spelling out. 'True religion' is an expression that serves several purposes for Ambedkar's idea of what resembles a utopian ideal. The concept of truth corresponds to a set of principles and an ethical space; Ambedkar's idea is precisely that it is only through religious conversion that such a just order could be accomplished. He had not decided the religion he would choose at the time of writing 'Annihilation of Caste'. In this essay, his remarks about religion are tied up in a question about democracy and Enlightenment. He argues that a new religion would require 'a new doctrinal basis … that will be in consonance with Liberty, Equality and Fraternity; in short, with Democracy'.[91]

This definition of religion is open to several questions and the application of several approaches because Ambedkar does not offer much conceptual support for these principles. In practice, he identifies principles with ideas about freedom and truth.[92] He champions the level of principles and draws a sharp distinction between a religion of rules and a religion of principles. He considers Hinduism to be a bundle of rules, 'all mixed up'. Textually, Ambedkar seems to draw on John Dewey's discussion of ethics in which the American professor discusses reflective morality.[93] But Ambedkar's statement should be viewed in a broad sense if one should avoid misunderstandings. For example, it is closer to the views of Enlightenment philosophers such as Kant and Montesquieu than to Wittgenstein's beliefs expressed in his late philosophy of language. In fact, some of Ambedkar's discussions appear strange to modern readers interested in the social sciences who are familiar with how Wittgenstein's concept of rules has inspired prominent contributions such as those of Bourdieu and Giddens. Wittgenstein, an analytical philosopher from Austria, argues that rules, rather than being abstract entities, are concrete forms of knowledge involving how to apply words in context in a meaningful manner. This is also partly how Ambedkar portrays Hinduism, but he rejects it as a source of moral deprivation, narrowmindedness and lack of freedom. For Ambedkar, rules are practical guidelines that correspond to habits and prescribe courses of action in ways that do not allow for much independent thought – 'like cooking recipes'.[94] Here, rules create a mechanical mode of life, whereas principles require a meaningful intellectual life. For him, principles will require an ethical approach characterized by conscious and responsible action. True religious acts require principles, not rules. Hinduism constitutes a religion that is in sharp contrast to a religion of principles that Ambedkar champions. He makes use of this distinction between principles and rules to claim that Hinduism constitutes such an idiosyncratic assortment of rules that it does not qualify to be called a religion. He states that 'what the Hindus call Religion is really Law or at best legalized class-ethics',[95] and argues that once people accept that Hinduism is a law and not a religion, they will be willing to change. But the change will not come if Hinduism is looked upon as a religion. At any rate, Ambedkar is not against religion, but he underlines the need for religious reform, the end of hereditary priesthood and a religion based on principles.[96] In other words, his idea is that a 'true' religion provides a 'foundation' for a just social order which can be made more consistent if democratic principles are applied. Indeed, his main claim in the famous text 'Annihilation of Caste' is that insofar as religion produces a social and political order, it requires democratic reforms and commitments to truth.

The idea that religion is a societal 'foundation' deserves further scrutiny because it refers to practised religion and not simply religion as a static structure, like the foundations of a building. By following Burke's idea that true religion provides a basis for civil government, a foundation is not the same as a superstructure in a Marxist sense, nor is a foundation the same as Carl Schmitt's idea of sovereign power as the condition for social order. Schmitt's approach is decisionist, when he suggested that the concept of 'the political was a precondition for a state; this referred to the ruler's ability to distinguish between friend and 'foe', that is, a public enemy.[97] Although the distinction between friend and foe resonates with Ambedkar's ontologically qualified distinction between touchables and untouchables, there are clear differences. The relation between touchables and untouchables represents an ontological difference which creates hegemony and antagonism among members of a population. This is where the late Laclau offers a lucid way to make sense of Ambedkar's distinction between the untouchables and touchables. Laclau played with the concept of the political, arguing it was of primary importance to social relations.[98] He was determined to deconstruct the so-called concept of the political and to explain how it represents a hegemonic logic residing in a social formation which incorporates social relations and therefore goes further than a decisionistic approach to the political.[99] Antagonism is the key term in Laclau's approach, and it explains how one pole negates the other pole. Antagonism provides a ground for the existence of a society. Such a ground for social order also involves an abyss which represents a possibility that the ground may change.[100] This is the idea in post-foundationalism, emphasized by Laclau and Marchart – an ontology (ground) is not entirely stable.

Ambedkar's concept of graded inequality is premised on an antagonism between touchables and untouchables, which represents the ontological difference in the caste system. His essay 'Annihilation of Caste' does not provide by itself a complete understanding of the foundation of the society of castes. In the essay, Ambedkar suggests that the foundation of the Hindu social order is the belief in the sanctity of the *shastras*. He also uses this religious perspective to explain everyday material conditions and enduring exploitations. Furthermore, the ontological distinction between touchable and untouchable castes is particularly prominent in one of Ambedkar's unpublished papers.[101] Villages would often be divided between touchables who lived in the main village, whereas the untouchables would be assigned to settlements outside the main village. According to Ambedkar, the exclusion of the untouchables reproduces the Hindu social order as a system of graded inequalities where touchables will affirm their status by never aligning with the the untouchables. The foundation of the social order is therefore reflected in this distinction. The difference between touchables and untouchables is embedded in the social order and village organization.[102]

While one may view the distinction between touchables and untouchables as the basis for the system of caste-based exclusion that Ambedkar describes, his ideas about religion is a key premise in this overall approach. His conversion to Buddhism at the end of his life also reflects a genuine interest in this theme. However, his statement about '*notional* change' does not have much conceptual support except for the emphasis on religious authority. The main claim is that destroying the Hindu texts is required to abolish caste. There are several questions and loose ends beyond this claim, which he does not resolve in 'Annihilation of Caste'. His claim about principles seems very general, and he does not offer any concrete alternative to the religious foundation of caste beyond the general Enlightenment principles. Yet Ambedkar is consistent and perceptive about the psychological passions that make caste an active dimension in social relations because it is 'a state of mind'.

The relevance of social psychology is a noteworthy aspect of his explanation of caste. By stating that caste is a 'state of mind', Ambedkar pinpoints that there is a passion associated with the sanctity of the *shastras*. From Ambedkar's perspective, struggles for temple access do not make sense. Temple access figured prominently in the nationalist movement, but it became more pivotal for Gandhi than Ambedkar. Instead, Ambedkar's anti-caste struggle reflects a deeper concern with what I will refer to as the ontological grip of caste.

Ontological Drive and Grip of Caste

The discussion of true religion and religion being a foundation for society represents Ambedkar's conceptual reflections on political ontology and his view that the foundation is not simply a monolithic structure. On the contrary, Ambedkar describes an ontology of caste that he wants to replace with an Enlightened democratic order. He also has a consistent interest in describing how the ontological dimension plays out in everyday psychology as a concrete caste mentality. This comprises two levels – the political ontology and everyday interactions – and he offers a striking account of the ways in which the ontology of caste plays out in everyday relations.

Hegemonic analysis is concerned with how practices are integral to a given ontology. This was highlighted by Marchart in his analysis of Laclau whose theory he characterized as 'political ontology'.[103] Laclau's approach thus captures some of the concerns that are otherwise understood by the political that institutes politics and ontology. His earlier collaborator, Mouffe, distinguished between the ontological and the ontic level to make sense of the difference between the political and politics. This distinction has been at the centre of analysing hegemony and transformations in a political order.[104] The political refers to the institutionalization of a dominating order which appears powerful, and yet incomplete and open to change. However, an excessive focus on the concept of the political may create misunderstandings. This book therefore discusses the concept of the political in terms of Laclau's concept of antagonism to make sense of Ambedkar's thought. The question of meaning is crucial in Laclau's approach. Names and meanings not only have force but their meanings are produced through the hegemonic articulation.[105] Ambedkar's contribution to the theory of caste is to specifically explain an ontological difference between touchables and untouchables and how it gains force and meanings through multiple forms of humiliation, exclusion or violence.

Furthermore, Ambedkar's focus on how caste is produced shows an interest in how an ontological desire is generated through religious beliefs. Recall Ambedkar's claim that intra-caste marriages will continue if people believe that the scriptures of Hinduism are holy. It is the sanctity of the scriptures that makes caste persist. In explaining how caste is practised and given 'a perpetual lease of life', Ambedkar explains what grips the subjects and makes them fully committed to maintaining caste.[106] Here, his observations can be further explained using psychoanalytical terms. Where Laclau is criticized for not explaining what it is that forces subjects to carry out their social and political action, psychoanalytical theory offers concepts to explain how ideological visions are produced and sustained through practices.[107] One term used by Jason Glynos and David Howarth to supplement social and political logics is 'fantasmatic logics'. I find this term unhelpful and leave it aside, and I will instead refer to the unconscious drive and 'life instinct' in psychoanalysis as an ontological desire.[108] This corresponds well with Ambedkar's explanation of how there is an embedded desire in people's minds to observe caste. This corresponds also with what Glynos, in his discussion of psychoanalysis in political theory, refers to as the 'grip of ideology'.[109] In fact, Ambedkar's portrayal of an ontological desire can be called the everyday grip of caste.

Mainstream sociology of caste has used a terminology that does not account for the significance of religious texts in everyday social relations. In fact, in making a claim that scriptures matter, Ambedkar tends to use what has been dismissed as a 'book view' approach to caste. The concept of the 'book view' as a term was invented in early postcolonial sociology in India. The concepts of the book view and the field view were used by the founding father of the sociology of caste in India, Srinivas, and subsequently by André Béteille and his followers. Srinivas's concept of the book view represented a critical corrective to Brahminical emphasis on logic and ancient texts. Srinivas felt that reading old texts gave a misleading impression of the social reality, and he heralded a professional commitment adopting the field view in order to acquire more accurate data. This approach makes sense in the context of anthropology to justify ethnographic research and reject repetition of scriptures such as the Vedas as the source of all truths. The distinction between the book view and the field view was useful to emphasize that there was a need for empirical ethnography. But the distinction has become a dichotomy that undermines reflexivity about the role of ideology in ethnographic practice. It does not clarify how caste continues to maintain its grip and encourages people to practise caste. Even though ethnography is essential, the rejection of the book view comes with an inadequate understanding of what grips people who practise caste. It is therefore significant that Srinivas, who championed the distinction between the book view and the field view, did not properly explain the significance of caste as a mentality in his own fieldwork. Being a Brahmin himself, his fieldwork experiences reflect the fact that he was treated as a man from the highest caste. In his seminal ethnographic account, Srinivas explains how villagers had several expectations of how he as a Brahmin should behave in relation to them.[110] Where did these expectations of caste come from if Srinivas rejected the book view? The promise of Ambedkar's account of caste is that it offers tools to explain how caste grips subjects in everyday practices.

It is in 'Annihilation of Caste' that Ambedkar is at his most articulate on the mentality of caste. He had not always been equally convinced that religious scriptures were decisive for the existence of caste. In fact, there is a noteworthy difference between 'Annihilation of Caste' (1937) and the text 'Castes in India' (1916) written twenty years earlier while he was a student at Columbia University. In the early sociological text, Ambedkar advances class, gender and endogamy as the key factors of the creation of caste. He describes caste as a self-enclosed class, reinforced by endogamy – marrying within the caste – and involving a strict interest in avoiding any marriage outside a particular caste.[111] This text has a stronger emphasis on stratification and gender, so much so that he marginalizes the religious perspective. In fact, Ambedkar's statements in 'Castes in India' are meant to sideline the centrality of religious texts and Brahmins. He states, for instance, 'Caste existed long before Manu' and that it would be too much to expect the Brahmins to have created the caste system on their own.[112] Rather than focusing on religious sanctity, Ambedkar argues that castes have been imitating Brahmins. While this is an implicit reference to Brahmin texts, there is a remarkable shift from his 1916 essay to his work of the mid-1930s in which Ambedkar is far more articulate about how religious authority is decisive for the continuity of caste. The statement quoted above agreed with that of Jat-Pat-Todak Mandal in the mid-1930s because he underlined that caste was a class that had been self-enclosed through the practice of endogamy. But in 'Annihilation of Caste', Ambedkar moves beyond that position and brings the anti-caste struggle to a new level; he introduces another 'real remedy' which is 'to destroy the belief in the sanctity of the *Shastras*'.[113] This is the intellectual version of burning *The Laws of Manu*.

Religion thus gains significance in Ambedkar's anti-caste struggle, representing an interest in the question of the ontological drive of caste and the need for a new religious foundation. His plea for notational change involves a type of social psychology.[114] The development of Ambedkar's political thought reflects an enduring concern with the grip of caste. Viewed alongside the ontological distinction between touchables and untouchables, the ontological drive and life instinct have relevance for everyday hegemony and caste-based violence.

Constitutional Politics and Emerging Policies

The history of policymaking represents a domain with its own trajectory, concepts and options, but there are significant continuities between Ambedkar's conceptual account of caste and his policy recommendations. His request for a separate electorate for the untouchables corresponds to the ontological difference between touchables and untouchables noted in his conceptual discussions. However, his struggles during the drafting of the constitution involve constant encounters with the powerful elite leading the nationalist movement. He faced opposition, particularly from the dominating Congress party. Ambedkar's experience with conflicts and debates reflects the ruling hegemony at the time, and the history of constitutional debates involved a process that included several battles that proved crucial for the constitutional trajectory. It was during this constant interface with hegemonic articulation and elite power that he made his momentous contribution to the development of India's legal framework. The single fact that most students in India learn about him today is that he wrote the Indian constitution, and it is right that they are taught this fact. Although there were many participants in the constituent assembly of 1946–49 and many lengthy discussions took place,

Ambedkar had a crucial role in the drafting process. As Jaffrelot emphasizes, many participants in the drafting committee were often absent and Ambedkar had to write much of the draft on his own.[115] While emerging as a leading constitutional expert, Ambedkar developed an innovative approach to a democratic constitution while using, among other things, an international perspective on law. The process of developing India's constitution began at the start of the century as a response to problems of governance that had arisen for the colonial government as well as to the demand for representation among an articulate educated class in India. Ambedkar's participation in this process created a new and distinct chapter in the history of anti-caste struggles. He became an increasingly central actor during this process, emerging as a leader of India's untouchables – known as the Depressed Classes at that time. This condescending expression was used in official parlance not only during the 1920s, when Ambedkar started his career, but also throughout the independence struggle, when it recurred as an informal expression.

It was during this constitutional process that Ambedkar fought and negotiated for policies that he believed could ameliorate the situation for the untouchables. The most well-known episode was the conflict with Mahatma Gandhi in the early 1930s over the question of having a separate electorate for the untouchables. Gandhi had become a central figure in the nationalist movement. He was able to bring together a larger section of the population and develop a more popular movement than the educated elite was able to organize.[116] Gandhi's decision to follow up his threat of fasting until he died over the question of a separate electorate was therefore a very powerful act. Ambedkar later recounted this conflict with great bitterness. He felt that Gandhi and the Congress party repressed the interests of the untouchables while projecting themselves as their representatives.[117] Nonetheless, both Gandhi and Ambedkar participated in a historical process that comprised activists and leaders in India who negotiated with the colonial government regarding designing new policies. The Indian National Congress (the Congress party) had been established in 1885 and comprised members of an educated elite until the First World War. The Congress party had therefore not been into a broad popular movement before Gandhi joined their movement from 1917 to 1918, but they now emerged with confidence and resolution about his tactic of non-cooperation with the colonial government.[118]

Following the social transformations in India and the country's experiences of the First World War, the colonial government organized a commission led by Montagu and Chelmsford to review India's system of governance. One of the problems they identified in the reforms of 1909 was the way in which the system of governance blended autocracy with constitutional government.[119] Their other concerns were that the reforms of 1909 did not provide adequate answers to Indian political problems of representation and that the administrative processes had slowed down.

The Montagu–Chelmsford Committee thus addressed several organizational aspects while suggesting that it was necessary to give the people of India more responsibilities.[120] Nonetheless, a central question initiated in the Morley–Minto Reforms of 1909 was that of group-based entitlement. The historian Jalal argues that granting a separate category for Muslims represented the momentous step of creating group-based ('communal') policy.[121] She emphasizes that the effect of the Montagu–Chelmsford Reforms of 1919 and the Government of India Act, 1935, intensified the intra-Muslim factionalism. In addition, the relationship between a Hindu-dominated Congress party and Muslim leaders was estranged when the independence movement was active. The idea of having a separate electorate did recur as an option during the constitutional debates. It was this policy proposal that Ambedkar later adopted in relation to the untouchables.

It was during the second period of constitutional reforms associated with the *Montagu and Chelmsford Report* that Ambedkar emerged as a representative of the untouchables. He was recruited to the Southborough Committee in 1919 because he was the only person from the untouchable castes in Bombay who had a university degree.[122] While discussing popular representation of India's diverse groups and problems of equality, he rejected territorial representation as was unable to secure voices for minorities. The distinction between touchables and untouchables gained relevance at this point. To address these 'real divisions' in society which were embedded in the agrarian structure, and the fact that people's sympathies were determined before elections occurred, Ambedkar suggested a 'form of low pitched franchise' to secure greater balance between non-Brahmins and Brahmins.[123] It should be kept in mind that Brahmins gained considerable institutional power in the colonial state during the nineteenth century.[124] Ambedkar, then, condemned Brahmins for having misused their control within the government, and he argued that it would be inadequate to simply allocate one or two seats for the untouchables in a large assembly of upper castes (whom he compared to Tories).

Ambedkar argued in favour of proportional representation. While doing so, he supported the policy of having a separate electorate for Muslims to include groups in dialogue in elected assemblies.[125] But it was only a decade later that he adopted this policy as a possibility for the untouchables as well.

India's independence movement had gained momentum during the 1920s, and the Indian National Congress decided to boycott the Simon Commission. While objecting to the fact that the commission had no Indian representative, the Congress party decided to organize its own committee to spell out an alternative set of principles for an independent constitution for India. The committee was chaired by the Congress leader Motilal Nehru, and it created the Congress party's most important constitutional documents. Nehru's committee offered no special provisions for the Depressed Classes, nor a separate electorate for Muslims. Instead, it was argued that discrimination would disappear with adult suffrage and education, and the *Nehru Report* therefore projected abstract principles rather than any group-based minority rights. Meanwhile, the Congress party was challenged by the right-wing Hindu Mahasabha. This had an impact on the report, and nationalism was promoted at the expense of any concession to minorities, which were dismissed as 'communalist'.[126] The *Nehru Report* thus estranged minorities while projecting the nation as a collection of individuals.[127]

Unlike the Congress party, Ambedkar participated in discussions organized by the Simon Commission, and it was during these deliberations that he gained a keen interest in the idea of having a separate electorate for the untouchable castes. In fact, contrary to the views of the Congress party and Hindu nationalists, the Simon Commission recommended that the separate electorate should continue for minorities such as the Muslims while granting reserved seats to the untouchables. It was against this background that Ambedkar also proposed having a separate electorate at the Round Table Conferences that were held in London between 1930 and 1932 so that political representation had sufficient legitimacy among all major parties, the Congress party included.[128]

It was during the Second Round Table Conference that Gandhi was sent as the representative of Congress, where he objected to Ambedkar's demand for a separate electorate for the untouchables. Although the notion of having a separate electorate was a new policy for Ambedkar, he viewed it as a reflection of the 'fundamental issue'; he asked, '*Are the Untouchables a separate element in the national life of India or are they not?*'[129] This was an existential question for both Ambedkar and Gandhi. According to Ambedkar, the untouchables were a separate element in Indian society. The Congress party, on the other hand, did not see any other alternative than defining the untouchables as a part of Hindu society. Indeed, Gandhi's position on caste is a clear case of reforming Hinduism from within the system. He wanted to reject untouchability and caste, but the type of caste he rejected was *jati* and not *varna*. In fact, Gandhi upheld the *varna* system as essential for creating an organic whole and as a good normative order that reflected 'the law of Nature'.[130] For Ambedkar, Gandhi's position was problematic in a fundamental sense because the *varna* system involved the basic premises of graded inequality that created untouchability and caste-based oppression in the first place.

Contrary to Gandhi, Ambedkar sought to overcome caste and considered *varna* to be a purely ideological imposition on the untouchables. He argued that 'Hindu society insists on segregation of the Untouchables.'[131] The separate electorate should work as a non-territorial system that meant the untouchables would be eligible to vote in separate elections. Gandhi claimed it would perpetuate a split in the social and political system and would be unhelpful for the untouchables. Thus, while Gandhi sought to accommodate differences at the conference, he claimed that 'the claims advanced on behalf of the Untouchables' is 'the unkindest cut of all'.[132] Indeed, Gandhi concluded by dismissing Ambedkar's demand and declared,

> I cannot possibly tolerate what is in store for Hinduism if there are two divisions set forth in the villages. Those who speak of the political rights of Untouchables do not know their India, do not know how the Indian society is today constructed, and therefore I want to say with all the emphasis that I can command that if I was the only person to resist this thing I would resist it with my life.[133]

Gandhi thus introduced a political gamble – putting his own life at stake – in this relentless emphasis on India as a holistic society. He was willing to see the separate electorate as an issue of life and death. Tensions also loomed among the supporters of Gandhi and Ambedkar as they returned to Bombay in late December 1931: up to forty people were hospitalized when supporters of Gandhi and Ambedkar gathered to welcome their leaders with decorations, slogans and greetings.[134] And Gandhi did follow up with his most powerful method in his non-violent struggle, fasting, suggesting that he would 'resist it with my life' after the colonial government announced its Communal Award in August 1932. At that time, the British prime minister confirmed that the government had decided to allow the untouchables to become a separate electorate. Gandhi responded immediately; he started to fast, shocking Congress leaders and the entire country by his determination to fast until he died.[135]

Gandhi's fast not only represented a direct challenge for Ambedkar but also increased the pressure on him and the possibilities of threats against the untouchables because of the considerable public attention given to the fast. To avoid negative consequences and public resentment against the untouchables, Ambedkar chose to compromise. He gave up his demand for a separate electorate for the untouchables. As Baxi puts it, Gandhi gambled on Ambedkar's character and won.[136] Gandhi had identified him as a liberal democrat rather than a man of revolutionary action. Ambedkar later recalled this episode with great bitterness. The result of Gandhi's action was that rather than being allowed to form a separate electorate, the untouchables were granted reserved rights. This policy was also adopted in the Government of India Act, 1935, the main constitutional document that was passed as law before India's independent constitution. This Act adopted the term 'Scheduled Castes' which thereby officially replaced the old designation, Depressed Classes, to refer to the untouchable castes.[137] The Scheduled Castes Order was created in 1936, and its main purpose was to enumerate castes that were entitled to use reservation policies. The Scheduled Castes Order was an equal opportunities policy which became a model for India's constitution of 1950. It was then reconfirmed that the SC status could only be granted on a religious basis. The constitution stated that 'no person who states a religion different from the Hindu religion shall be deemed to be a member of a Scheduled Caste'.[138] This religious criterion for granting the protection of constitutional provisions has been subject to debates since independence. It represents one of the path-dependent questions concerning India's constitutional state, having been determined by how important the Hindu religion was for constitutional politics at the time of the independence movement.

The constitutional debate during the colonial period culminated in the constituent assembly debates which lasted from 1946 to 1949. The assembly was fully aware of the unique opportunity it had to create a constitution for the country and how India differed from Britain. When it met for the first time on 9 December 1946, it received supportive messages from the USA, China and Australian governments, and the last-mentioned government declared that the constituent assembly was a 'sign of a new era for India'.[139] The assembly endorsed a constitution that brought fundamental principles such as equality and equality of opportunity into focus. Ambedkar rose to the task of serving as the leader of the drafting committee in the assembly and emerged as a statesman with constitutional expertise. Gandhi did not participate in the assembly, but his ideas were supported by several members of it. Although the members of the assembly emphasized that it was well-balanced with representatives from every religion, there was also a social bias. It is an exaggeration to claim that it was 'a highly representative body'.[140] There was a level of diversity, but such an assessment would be blind to the elite bias of the assembly. As Corbridge and Harriss argue, the Congress party was a centralized organization for an educated elite. The constituent assembly consisted of a higher proportion of upper-caste people, Brahmins and other higher-castes, than appeared in the general population.[141] Despite the elite bias, it is true that the assembly was characterized by its modernist visions, such as those of Jawaharlal Nehru. He championed modernization and industrialization and believed that socialism would replace differences. Nehru emphasized class, whereas Ambedkar addressed the problem of the untouchables and caste, but both believed in modern economic development.

The result of the debates that took place from 1946 to 1949 was that India adopted a comprehensive constitution. While affirming sovereignty and democracy, the constitution adopted the Irish constitutional distinction between the fundamental rights and directive principles. This approach was important for welfare policies. Directive principles created leeway for regional states, while the section on fundamental rights became a prominent and defining feature of India's constitution. Fundamental rights were discussed early on and comprised a policy of non-discrimination (Article 15) and policies concerning equal opportunity for all citizens in public employment (Article 16). The term 'reservation' is mentioned in the fourth subclause of Article 16 where it is stated that there could be provisions for adequate representation of any 'backward class of citizens' in public employment. The SCs and Scheduled Tribes (STs) were the only classes of citizens that these policies applied to at the time of independence. The Other Backward Classes (OBCs) became subject to investigations later.

It was historically significant that the Constitution of India adopted an equal opportunity policy to advance reservation for the SCs, but this policy had important limitations because of the lack of any other substantial social reforms that could enable impoverished classes of people to succeed in formal education. Entitlement to reserved posts in education and public employment did not sufficiently address the multidimensional problem of class, property, inheritance and gender inequalities. First, the constitution did not lead to land reforms and such policies were struck down by north Indian landowners in the courts.[142] The lack of redistribution of land and property created a limited basis for a social transformation among majority of the people who were part of the exploitative agricultural mode of production. Land reforms had proven crucial for social development in Kerala, south-west India, prior to India's independence, but this precedent did not translate into an all-India policy in the Constitution of India.

Second, caste intersects with gender and family. After independence, therefore, Ambedkar made a relentless effort to craft a new bill to ensure greater scope for women's rights. The so-called Hindu Code Bill dealt with the question of the role of religion in governing marriage and inheritance. Several reform movements were active during the colonial period, starting with that of the Hindu reformer Ram Mohan Roy (1772–1833) and the Act against self-immolation of widows in 1829.[143] In 1937, Hindu women were granted more rights to property, although the relevant Act did not imply full rights to ownership for widows.[144] These laws addressed Brahmin orthodoxy.

It was to complete social reforms through the constitution that Ambedkar used his position to propose a new Hindu Code Bill when Prime Minister Nehru granted him the possibility of reconsidering the existing drafts. Ambedkar's proposition was to accept only monogamous marriages, to extend gender equality, to grant women rights to inherit property and to eliminate caste barriers in civil marriage.[145] The bill was introduced in the constituent assembly, that is, to the same assembly members who had endorsed the clear principles of equality in the Constitution of India. But the Hindu Code Bill created strong reactions among traditionalists in the assembly, and the sections regarding marriage and divorce were amended beyond recognition. After this legislative defeat, Ambedkar resigned from Nehru's government because he felt Nehru had abandoned him due to the power of the conservative members of the Congress party. Nehru gave up supporting women's rights because he realized that the bill was not only resented by central leaders in the assembly but that it also represented an effective possibility for Hindu hardliners such as the Hindu Mahasabha to mobilize popular protests.[146] So, despite Ambedkar's contribution to crafting the Indian constitution, he failed to reform issues involving religion, family and gender. He was acutely aware of how significant questions of gender and women's social position were for a more egalitarian order. Indeed, it was precisely questions about gender and marriage, especially endogamous marriages, that he had highlighted in his anthropological essay about caste-based closures as a student in 1916.[147] During the debates on the Hindu code bill in 1951, he declared, 'Whatever else Hindu society may adopt, it will never give up its social structure for the enslavement of the *Sudra* and the enslavement of women. It is for this reason that law must now come to their rescue in order that society may move on.'[148] On 27 September 1951, shortly after making this statement, Ambedkar resigned from Nehru's cabinet. By avoiding intervening in the domains of marriage, inheritance and gender equality, the lawmakers established a non-interventionist approach to a dimension of the society that contributes to the overall reproduction of graded inequality in a society made up of castes.

Summary

Ambedkar's struggle for justice is an extension of a long history of anti-caste critiques and struggles for freedom from caste-based oppression. He championed Enlightenment ideals and called for the universalization of rights that anti-caste intellectuals had pursued before him. Through his several roles, especially as a constitutional expert, he has become a symbol of emancipation, dignity and constitutional entitlements for Dalits in the postcolonial state. As Zelliot underlines, Ambedkar transcended the sub-caste and regional level that had been the framework for earlier anti-caste struggles and gained recognition both as a national leader for the untouchables and as a statesman.[149] The goal of this chapter has not been to simply reiterate Ambedkar's career. I have tried to highlight his ongoing significance for explaining a central dimension in Indian society today.

In this chapter, I have delineated Ambedkar's theory of caste and his contribution to constitutional politics to fully understand his scholarly insights and political achievements. He was theoretically 'militant', while being a liberal democrat in constitutional politics. Conventional discussions have focused on his trajectory and career, but an undue focus on this story may end up romanticizing how he became a statesman despite being from a caste considered untouchable, excluded and 'Depressed'. Zelliot's classic account illustrates this inclination.[150] At the same time, Ambedkar's career offers crucial insights into many experiences that Dalits face in contemporary India. His biography comprises episodes illustrating how his success as an educated man and lawgiver was fraught with setbacks.

These lessons, moreover, explain why contemporary Dalits can identify with the experiences of discrimination that he faced during his lifetime while celebrating his contribution to India's constitution. Overall, Ambedkar represents a process that I call the mechanism of oppression in the Dalit situation, that is, how upward mobility coexists with humiliation.

In terms of social and political thought, I have outlined three essential approaches he uses in his scholarship on caste. The first approach is a sociological explanation of the reproduction of caste through intra-caste marriage. Ambedkar argued in 1916 that castes are created by members of certain classes and status groups that seek to close the door to their class or group to members of other classes or groups by practising endogamous marriage. The second approach reflects religion and ontology. In 'Annihilation of Caste', Ambedkar argues that the abolition of caste requires an end to the mentality of caste by destroying the religious sanctity that creates this grip of caste. The final approach concerns how his ontological distinction between touchables and untouchables reveals an embedded social inequality. The ontological distinction is a source of exclusion and constitutes a system he refers to as a system of graded inequality. This concept integrates questions of ontology, religion and social stratification. The concept of graded inequality shows how caste represents a complex system that cannot be reduced to a question of either religion or inequality. The concept of graded inequality explains why upward mobility can provoke a backlash.

I have underlined that a key question in Ambedkar's scholarship is his interest in explaining how caste is produced. In this chapter, I have pointed out how Ambedkar describes what I refer to as an ontological desire to practise caste. Ambedkar characterizes caste as a mentality which will not vanish without a '*notional* change' involving the destruction of the religious sanctity that produces a belief in caste.[151] Ambedkar's scholarly account of caste is radical, and the controversies emerging after 'Annihilation of Caste' was published were understandable given how caste was institutionalized in the Hindu social order. His legacy as a lawmaker is part of the same struggle, although he used a pragmatic strategy of aiming to ameliorate the situation for the untouchables. Whether he was being militant as an intellectual or diplomatic as a politician, he championed Enlightenment ideals.

The commitment to Enlightenment ideals runs through Ambedkar's writings about freedom from caste-based domination and bolsters his idea of a democratic order and democratic reforms. The Constitution of India also emphasized Enlightenment ideals, like constitutions of other countries. It is noteworthy that in 1927, the Dalit movement made demands that read like an early version of the Universal Declaration of Human Rights, which was created twenty years later.[152] By claiming that everyone is born with equal worth, the human rights resolution of the untouchable movement rejected the idea of grading that shapes the caste mentality. However, the legal response to caste in the Constitution of India did not result in noteworthy reforms in domains such as gender and marriage, which means that it did not aim at changing the ways in which caste is being reproduced.

While the affirmation of key liberal principles by the constituent assembly was noteworthy, it is important to specify the type of liberalism that the assembly endorsed. The lawmakers had conservative motivations when they avoided substantial reforms to legislation regulating marriage and gender equality. Theoretically, their decisions also corresponded to their belief in non-intervention as a liberal principle which involves the state not regulating matters that belong to the (private) domain – such as marriage and women's inheritance. This represented a negative conception of freedom. Ambedkar had a different conception of freedom when he wanted to enable women to inherit property in the same manner as men. In the context of the Hindu Code Bill, he aimed at creating greater freedom among men and women so that they could make choices irrespective of dominating actors and norms.

Reservation was the main problem-solving strategy that the constituent assembly endorsed to ameliorate the historically oppressed SCs and STs. This was an identification of inequality rather than caste ontology, and it was not supported by substantial redistribution of property and landholdings by way of land reforms. In addition, the theological principle became decisive when it was declared that beneficiaries of the reservation policy had to profess Hinduism as their religion. The effect of the reservation policy – the policy of equal opportunity – has been a degree of upward mobility and the emergence of a new middle class among Dalits. Political mobilization emerged most spectacularly in Uttar Pradesh, where political entrepreneurs, such as Kanshi Ram, benefitted from the growing middle class among Dalits and other lower castes. One may argue that the constituent assembly adopted the policy of equal opportunity for 'backward classes of citizens' for performative reasons. The next chapter will examine one of the inadequacies of the equality legislation in the context of caste, especially the fact that the declared abolition of untouchability addressed the symptom rather than the cause of caste-based domination. It is nonetheless significant that untouchability was criminalized by the Constitution of India. It is also significant that equal opportunity policies were developed even though the legislators did not properly address how inequality was embedded in the agrarian structure, such as through land reforms or through gender and marriage practices.

Notes

1. D. Karthikeyan and Hugo Gorringe, 'Rescuing Ambedkar', *Frontline*, 2012, accessed 5 July 2019, https://www.frontline.in/static/html/fl2919/stories/20121005291913600.htm.

2. Christophe Jaffrelot, *Dr. Ambedkar and Untouchability: Analysing and Fighting Caste* (London: Hurst, 2005); Eleanor Zelliot, *From Untouchable to Dalit: Essays on the Ambedkar Movement* (New Delhi: Manohar, 2001).
3. Upendra Baxi, 'Emancipation as Justice: Legacy and Vision of Dr Ambedkar', in *From Periphery to Centre Stage*, ed. Kripal Chandra Yadav (New Delhi: Manohar, 2000).
4. Dhananjay Keer, *Dr. Ambedkar: Life and Mission*, 3rd edn (Bombay: Popular Prakashan, 2003).
5. Oliver Marchart, *Post-Foundational Political Thought: Political Difference in Nancy, Lefort, Badiou and Laclau* (Edinburgh: Edinburgh University Press, 2007); Philip Pettit, *Just Freedom: A Moral Compass for a Complex World* (New York: W. W. Norton & Company, 2014).
6. Aishwary Kumar, *Radical Equality: Ambedkar, Gandhi, and the Risk of Democracy*, Cultural Memory in the Present (Stanford, CA: Stanford University Press, 2015), pp. 9, 226.
7. Hannah Arendt, *Between Past and Future: Eight Exercises in Political Thought* (New York: Penguin Books, 2006), 151; Mark Wenman, *Agonistic Democracy: Constituent Power in the Era of Globalisation* (Cambridge: Cambridge University Press, 2013), chap. 1.
8. Ernesto Laclau and Chantal Mouffe, *Hegemony and Socialist Strategy: Towards a Radical Democratic Politics* (London: Verso, 2001), chap. 4; Wenman, *Agonistic Democracy*, 5.
9. Ernesto Laclau, *The Rhetorical Foundations of Society* (London: Verso, 2014); Marchart, *Post-Foundational Political Thought.*
10. This text has become one of Ambedkar's well-known books, but he originally characterized it as an essay; see Ambedkar, B. R. 'Annihilation of Caste', in *Dr. Babasaheb Ambedkar Writings and Speeches*, ed. Vasant Moon, vol. 1. (Bombay: Education Department, Government of Maharashtra, 1989), 23–96.
11. Partha Chatterjee, 'A Possible India: Essays in Political Criticism', in *The Partha Chatterjee Omnibus* (New Delhi: Oxford University Press, 1999), 42; Stuart Corbridge and John Harriss, *Reinventing India: Liberalization, Hindu Nationalism and Popular* Democracy (Malden: Polity Press, 2000), 24; Rochana Bajpai, *Debating Difference: Group Rights and Liberal Democracy in India* (New Delhi: Oxford University Press, 2011), 46.
12. This is what has happened to Arundhati Roy's well-known discussion of Ambedkar. While the new and annotated edition of *Annihilation of Caste* is a valuable source for any student of Ambedkar, Roy's introductory essay provides a comparison of Ambedkar and Gandhi which distracts attention from the main claims in the book. See Arundhati Roy, 'The Doctor and the Saint', in *The Annihilation of Caste: The Annotated Critical Edition, B. R. Ambedkar*, ed. S. Anand (London: Verso), 15–179.
13. Jagpal Singh, 'Ambedkarisation and Assertion of Dalit Identity: Socio-Cultural Protest in Meerut District of Western Uttar Pradesh', *Economic and Political Weekly* 33, no. 40 (1998): 2611–18, doi:10.2307/4407245.

14. Gail Omvedt, *Seeking Begumpura: The Social Vision of Anticaste Intellectuals* (New Delhi: Navayana, 2008), 91.
15. Gurharpal Singh, 'Religious Transnationalism and Development Initiatives: The Dera Sachkhand Ballan', *Economic and Political Weekly* 47, no. 1 (2012): 53–60, accessed 3 October 2018, https://www.epw.in/journal/2012/01/religion-and-citizenship-special-issues/religious-transnationalism-and-development.
16. Omvedt, *Seeking Begumpura*, 99.
17. M. S. A. Rao, 'Some Conceptual Issues in the Study of Caste, Class, Ethnicity and Dominance', in *Dominance and State Power in Modern India: Decline of a Social Order*, ed. Francine R. Frankel and M. S.A. Rao, vol. 1 (Delhi: Oxford University Press, 1989), pp. 1, 29.
18. Jayashree Gokhale, *From Concessions to Confrontation: The Politics of an Indian Untouchable Community* (Bombay: Popular Prakashan, 1993), 41–2; Jaffrelot, *Dr. Ambedkar and Untouchability*, 20.
19. Jaffrelot, *Dr. Ambedkar and Untouchability*, 20.
20. Gary M. Tartakov, 'The Navayāna Creation of the Buddha Image', in *Reconstructing the World: B. R. Ambedkar and Buddhism in India*, ed. Surendra Jondhale and Johannes Beltz (New Delhi: Oxford University Press, 2004), 174.
21. Bhimrao Ramji Ambedkar, *The Buddha and His Dhamma* (Nagpur: Buddha Bhoomi Publication, 1997), 301–4; Gail Omvedt, *Buddhism in India: Challenging Brahmanism and Caste* (New Delhi: Sage Publications, 2003).
22. Rosalind O'Hanlon, *Caste Conflict and Ideology: Mahatma Jotirao Phule and Low Caste Protest in Nineteenth-Century Western India* (Cambridge: Cambridge University Press, 1985), 4.
23. Ibid., 105.
24. Ibid., 111.
25. Govind P. Deśapāṇḍe, ed., *Selected Writings of Jotirao Phule*, with annotations and introduction by Govind P. Deśapāṇḍe (New Delhi: Leftword, 2002), 25.
26. Ibid., 27.
27. Dorothy Matilda Figueira, *Aryans, Jews, Brahmins: Theorizing Authority through Myths of Identity*, SUNY Series, the Margins of Literature (Albany, Great Britain: State University of New York Press, 2002).
28. Ibid.
29. Ibid., 147–50.
30. O'Hanlon, *Caste Conflict and Ideology*, 8.
31. David Anthony Washbrook, 'Law, State and Agrarian Society in Colonial India', *Modern Asian Studies* 15, no. 3 (1981), 653; Mathias Samuel Soundra Pandian, *Brahmin & Non-Brahmin: Genealogies of the Tamil Political Present* (Delhi: Permanent Black, 2007).
32. Gajendran Ayyathurai, 'Foundations of Anti-Caste Consciousness: Pandit Iyothee Thass, Tamil Buddhism, and the Marginalized in South India', unpublished PhD thesis, Columbia University, New York, 2011, p. 23–4.
33. Ibid.

34. Granville Austin, *Working a Democratic Constitution: A History of the Indian Experience*, Second impression. First published 1999 (New Delhi: Oxford University Press, 2004).
35. Robert Deliège, *The Untouchables of India* (Oxford: Berg, 1999), 96.
36. Keer, *Dr. Ambedkar*, 10.
37. Gokhale, *From Concessions to Confrontation*, 50.
38. Ibid., 27.
39. Zelliot, *Dr. Babasaheb Ambedkar and the Untouchable Movement* (New Delhi: Blumoon Books, 2004), 17.
40. Gokhale, *From Concessions to Confrontation*, 29–31.
41. Ibid., 41.
42. Zelliot, *Dr. Babasaheb Ambedkar and the Untouchable Movement*, 11; O'Hanlon, *Caste Conflict and Ideology*.
43. Oliver Mendelsohn and Marika Vicziany, *The Untouchables: Subordination, Poverty and the State in Modern India* (Cambridge: Cambridge University Press, 1998), 88.
44. See Chapter 3 for one of its significant example.
45. Keer, *Dr. Ambedkar*, 14.
46. Ambedkar studied Sanskrit later in his life during a three-month stay in Bonn while he was attending university in Europe.
47. Vasant Moon, *Dr. Babasaheb Ambedkar*, trans. Asha Damle (New Delhi: National Book Trust, 2002), 4.
48. Keer, *Dr. Ambedkar*, 18.
49. Ibid., 19.
50. Zelliot, *Dr. Babasaheb Ambedkar and The Untouchable Movement*, 64.
51. Kripal Chandra Yadav, ed., *From Periphery to Centre Stage* (New Delhi: Manohar, 2000), 25–30; Zelliot, *Dr. Babasaheb Ambedkar and The Untouchable Movement*, 67.
52. Ambedkar refers to the story of a young man who had moved to Gujarat to serve in the state administration in the mid-1930s. The man, who was from the Bhangi caste, struggled to find a room to rent and to use the water in the office as the water-carrying man did not want to share his water with an untouchable. He was also asked to stand at a distance from his colleagues and had faced hostilities when he sat on an office chair; see Yadav, ed., *From Periphery to Centre Stage*, 35–7.
53. Eleanor Zelliot, 'Learning the Use of Political Means: The Mahars of Maharashtra', in *Caste in Indian Politics*, ed. Rajni Kothari (New Delhi: Orient Longman, 1970), 39.
54. Zelliot, *Dr. Babasaheb Ambedkar and The Untouchable Movement*, 68.
55. Ibid., chaps. 2, 4 and 5.
56. Keer, *Dr. Ambedkar*, 70.
57. Zelliot, *Dr. Babasaheb Ambedkar and The Untouchable Movement*, 76.
58. *Times of India*, 'Untouchables Win', 17 October 1931, accessed 20 September 2018, https://search.proquest.com/docview/325523999?accountid=11144; *Times of India*, 'Right of Using Tank', 1 January 1937, https://search.proquest.com/docview/325343193?accountid=11144.

59. Zelliot, *Dr. Babasaheb Ambedkar and The Untouchable Movement*, 77.
60. Lynn Hunt, *Inventing Human Rights: A History* (New York: Norton, 2008); Samuel Moyn, *The Last Utopia: Human Rights in History* (Cambridge, MA: Belknap Press of Harvard University Press, 2012), 1.
61. Bhimrao Ramji Ambedkar, 'Political', in *Dr. Babasaheb Ambedkar Writings and Speeches: Unpublished Writings*, ed. Vasant Moon, vol. 5 (Bombay: Education Department, Government of Maharashtra, 1989), 254.
62. *Times of India*, 'The Burning of Manu', 30 January 1928, accessed 15 March 2016, https://search.proquest.com/docview/346271176?accountid=11144.
63. Zelliot, *Dr. Babasaheb Ambedkar and The Untouchable Movement*, 77.
64. *Times of India*, 'Untouchability and Temple Entry: Important Movement', 18 November 1932, accessed 20 September 2018, https://search.proquest.com/docview/324543375?accountid=9735.
65. Bhimrao Ramji Ambedkar, 'What Congress and Gandhi Have Done to the Untouchables: Mr. Gandhi and the Emancipation of the Untouchables', in *Dr. Babasaheb Ambedkar Writings and Speeches*, ed. Vasant Moon, vol. 9 (Bombay: Education Department, Government of Maharashtra, 1991), 9.
66. Baxi, 'Emancipation as Justice', 61.
67. Ambedkar, 'What Congress and Gandhi Have Done to the Untouchables', 88.
68. Roy, 'The Doctor and the Saint'.
69. Olivier Herrenschmidt, 'Ambedkar and the Hindu Social Order', in *Reconstructing the World: B. R. Ambedkar and Buddhism in India*, ed. Surendra Jondhale and Johannes Beltz (New Delhi: Oxford University Press, 2004), 37–48.
70. Bhimrao Ramji Ambedkar, 'Castes in India: Their Mechanism, Genesis and Development', paper read before the Anthropology Seminar of Dr A. A. Goldenwizer at the Columbia University, New York, on 9 May 1916, in *Dr. Babasaheb Ambedkar Writings and Speeches*, ed. Vasant Moon, vol. 1 (Bombay: Education Department, Government of Maharashtra, 1989).
71. Bhimrao Ramji Ambedkar, 'Annihilation of Caste', in *Dr. Babasaheb Ambedkar Writings and Speeches*, ed. Vasant Moon, vol. 1 (Bombay: Education Department, Government of Maharashtra, 1989).
72. Bhimrao Ramji Ambedkar, 'Untouchables or the Children of India's Ghetto', in *Dr. Babasaheb Ambedkar Writings and Speeches: Unpublished Writings*, vol. 5, ed. Vasant Moon (Bombay: Education Department, Government of Maharashtra, 1989).
73. Dag-Erik Berg, 'Foregrounding Contingency in Caste-Based Dominance: Ambedkar, Hegemony, and the Pariah Concept', *Philosophy & Social Criticism* 44, no. 8 (2018): 843–64, doi:10.1177/0191453717744007.
74. Ambedkar, 'Castes in India', 14. Endogamy is the custom of marrying within the caste, clan or local community.
75. Roy, 'The Doctor and the Saint'.
76. Kumar, *Radical Equality*, 9, 230.
77. Ibid., 220.

78. Bhagwan Das, *In Pursuit of Ambedkar* (New Delhi: Navayana Pub, 2009), 21.
79. *Times of India*, 'Surprise for Dr. Ambedkar: Attack on Caste and Its Sequel', 1 January 1936.
80. Ambedkar, 'Annihilation of Caste', 84.
81. Mark Juergensmeyer, *Religious Rebels in the Punjab: The Ad Dharm Challenge to Caste* (New Delhi: Navayana, 2009), 39.
82. Ambedkar, 'Annihilation of Caste', 67.
83. Ibid., 69.
84. Herrenschmidt, 'Ambedkar and the Hindu Social Order', 46. It should be added that social psychology is another theme that John Dewey, Ambedkar's teacher at the Columbia University, aimed at developing to make more sense of habits and social life than could be gained by simply focusing on inner private life. See John Dewey, 'The Place of Habit in Conduct', in *The Essential Dewey: Vol. 2, Ethics, Logics, Psychology*, ed. Larry A. Hickman and Thomas M. Alexander (Bloomington, IN: Indiana University Press, 1998), 48.
85. Ambedkar, 'Annihilation of Caste', 68; author's italics.
86. Bhimrao Ramji Ambedkar, 'The Untouchables: Who Were They and Why They Became Untouchables?', in *Dr. Babasaheb Ambedkar Writings and Speeches*, ed. Vasant Moon, vol. 7 (Bombay: Education Department, Government of Maharashtra, 1990), 370.
87. Ibid., 68.
88. Anthony Giddens, *The Constitution of Society: Outline of the Theory of Structuration* (Cambridge: Polity, 1984).
89. Ambedkar, 'Annihilation of Caste', 78.
90. Ibid., 76.
91. Ibid., 77.
92. For a comparable instance, see Arendt, *Between Past and Future*, 150–1.
93. John Dewey, 'Moral Judgement and Knowledge: From Ethics (1932)', in *Ethics, Logics, Psychology*, vol. 2 , ed. Larry A. Hickman and Thomas M. Alexander, The Essential Dewey (Bloomington, IN: Indiana University Press, 1998).
94. Ambedkar, 'Annihilation of Caste', 75; cf. Dewey, 'Moral Judgement and Knowledge', 338.
95. Ambedkar, 'Annihilation of Caste', 75.
96. Ibid., 76–7.
97. Carl Schmitt, *The Concept of the Political* (Chicago and London: University of Chicago Press, 1996), 26.
98. Ernesto Laclau, *New Reflections on the Revolution of Our Time* (London: Verso, 1990), 33.
99. Laclau, *The Rhetorical Foundations of Society*, 7. This is a point where Laclau's approach differs from that of his earlier co-writer, Chantal Mouffe.
100. Marchart, *Post-Foundational Political Thought*; Laclau, *The Rhetorical Foundations of Society*.
101. Ambedkar, 'Untouchables or the Children of India's Ghetto'.

102. Berg, 'Foregrounding Contingency in Caste-Based Dominance'.
103. Laclau's discourse theory therefore differs from how Foucault understood the term 'discourse' which has a stronger emphasis on history than ontology.
104. Marchart, *Post-Foundational Political Thought*, 1–2.
105. Laclau, *The Rhetorical Foundations of Society*; Jason Glynos and David R. Howarth, *Logics of Critical Explanation in Social and Political Theory* (New York: Routledge, 2007), 145.
106. Ambedkar, 'Annihilation of Caste', 74.
107. Glynos and Howarth, *Logics of Critical Explanation in Social and Political Theory*.
108. Jacques Lacan, *The Four Fundamental Concepts of Psychoanalysis*, the seminar of Jacques Lacan trans. with notes by Bruce Fink; book 11 (New York: Norton, 1998), 198.
109. Jason Glynos, 'The Grip of Ideology: A Lacanian Approach to the Theory of Ideology', *Journal of Political Ideologies* 6, no. 2 (2001): 191–214.
110. Mysore Narasimhachar Srinivas, *The Remembered Village*, 2nd edn, Oxford India Perennials (New Delhi: Oxford University Press, 2012).
111. This, he suggests, explained why a practice such as *sati* was invented, because a widow or 'surplus woman' had to be 'disposed of' to avoid her marrying outside the caste. See Ambedkar, 'Castes in India', 11. See also note 74 for 'endogamy'.
112. Ibid., 16.
113. Ambedkar, 'Annihilation of Caste', 68.
114. Herrenschmidt, 'Ambedkar and the Hindu Social Order'.
115. Jaffrelot, *Dr. Ambedkar and Untouchability*, 108.
116. Sudipta Kaviraj, 'On State, Society and Discourse in India', in *Rethinking Third World Politics*, ed. James Manor (London: Longman, 1991).
117. Ambedkar, 'What Congress and Gandhi Have Done to the Untouchables'.
118. Sugata Bose and Ayesha Jalal, *Modern South Asia: History, Culture, Political Economy*, 3rd edn (London: Routledge, 2011), 112.
119. Edwin Samuel Montagu and Frederic John Napier Thesiger Chelmsford. *Report on Indian Constitutional Reforms,* East India (Constitutional Reforms), presented to both Houses of Parliament by command of His Majesty (London: H. M. S. O., 1918), 63.
120. Ibid., 147.
121. Ayesha Jalal, *Democracy and Authoritarianism in South Asia: A Comparative and Historical Perspective* (Cambridge: Cambridge University Press, 1995), 13.
122. Jaffrelot, *Dr. Ambedkar and Untouchability*, 53.
123. Bhimrao Ramji Ambedkar, 'Evidence before the Southborough Committee on Franchise: Examined on 27th 1919', in *Dr. Babasaheb Ambedkar Writings and Speeches*, ed. Vasant Moon, vol. 1 (Bombay: Education Department, Government of Maharashtra, 1989), 255.
124. Washbrook, 'Law, State and Agrarian Society in Colonial India', 653.
125. Ambedkar, 'Evidence before the Southborough Committee on Franchise', 255–68.
126. Bose and Jalal, *Modern South Asia*, 119.

127. Jaffrelot, *Dr. Ambedkar and Untouchability*, 56.
128. Bajpai, *Debating Difference*, 33–34; Bose and Jalal, *Modern South Asia*, 119; Judith M. Brown, *Modern India: The Origins of an Asian Democracy* (Oxford: Oxford University Press, 1994), 282.
129. Ambedkar, 'What Congress and Gandhi Have Done to the Untouchables', 181; originally italics.
130. Mahatma K. Gandhi, 'Caste Must Go', in *Caste and Democratic Politics in India*, ed. Ghanshayam Shah (New Delhi: Permanent Black, 2002), 82.
131. Ambedkar, 'The Untouchables: Who Were They and Why They Became Untouchables?', 266.
132. Bhimrao Ramji Ambedkar, 'Dr. Ambedkar at the Round Table Conferences', in *Dr. Babasaheb Ambedkar Writings and Speeches*, ed. Vasant Moon and Hari Narke, vol. 2, 2nd edn (Bombay: Government of Maharashtra, 2005), 662.
133. Ibid., 663.
134. *Times of India*, 'Huge Crowds Welcome Mr. Gandhi: Depressed Classes' Counter-Demonstration, Impressions of Second Round Table Conference', 29 December 1931, accessed 20 September 2018, https://search.proquest.com/docview/325423172?accountid=9735.
135. Jawaharlal Nehru, *An Autobiography* (New Delhi: Jawaharlal Nehru Memorial Fund, 1980), 370.
136. Baxi, 'Emancipation as Justice', 61.
137. Christophe Jaffrelot, 'The Impact of Affirmative Action in India: More Political than Socioeconomic', *India Review* 5, no. 2 (2006): 174.
138. Government of India, *The Constitution (Scheduled Castes) Order*, 1950, http://lawmin.nic.in/legislative/election/volume%201/rules%20&%20order%20under%20Constitution/THE%20CONSTITUTION%20(SCHEDULED%20CASTES)%20ORDER,%201950.pdf.
139. Constituent Assembly of India, 'Monday, the 9th December 1946', Constituent Assembly of India Debates (Proceedings), vol. I (New Delhi: Lok Sabha Secretariat, Government of India), accessed 11 July 2019, http://164.100.47.194/Loksabha/Debates/cadebatefiles/C09121946.html.
140. Granville Austin, *The Indian Constitution: Cornerstone of a Nation* (New Delhi: Oxford University Press, 1999), 14.
141. Corbridge and Harriss, *Reinventing India*, 23; see also Chatterjee, 'A Possible India', 42.
142. Austin, *Working a Democratic Constitution*, chap. 3.
143. Olivier Herrenschmidt, 'The Indians' Impossible Civil Code', *European Journal of Sociology/Archives Européennes de Sociologie* 50, no. 2 (2009): 316, doi: 10.1017/S0003975609990154.
144. Reba Som, 'Jawaharlal Nehru and the Hindu Code: A Victory of Symbol over Substance?' *Modern Asian Studies* 28, no. 1 (1994): 170, doi: 10.1017/S0026749X00011732.

145. Som, 'Jawaharlal Nehru and the Hindu Code', 171; Jaffrelot, *Dr. Ambedkar and Untouchability*, 115; Bhimrao Ramji Ambedkar, *Dr. Babasaheb Ambedkar Writings and Speeches*, ed. Vasant Moon, vol. 14, no. 1 (New Delhi: Dr. Ambedkar Foundation, 2014).
146. Jaffrelot, *Dr. Ambedkar and Untouchability*, 116; Som, 'Jawaharlal Nehru and the Hindu Code'.
147. Ambedkar, 'Castes in India'.
148. B. R. Ambedkar, 'Hindu Code Bill (Clause by Clause Discussion)', in *Dr. Babasaheb Ambedkar Writings and Speeches*, ed. Vasant Moon, vol. 14, no. 1 (New Delhi: Dr. Ambedkar Foundation, 2014), pp. 2, 14, 1146, accessed 8 November 2018, https://www.mea.gov.in/Images/attach/amb/Volume_14_02.pdf.
149. Zelliot, *From Untouchable to Dalit*, 53.
150. Ibid.
151. Ambedkar, 'Annihilation of Caste', 68.
152. Berg, 'Foregrounding Contingency in Caste-Based Dominance'.

2

Law beyond Untouchability

From Temple Entry to Atrocity and Legal Change

During the independence movement, the key concerns that emerged regarding ameliorating the situation for untouchable castes were temple entry and access to public places. Access to public spaces and facilities, such as the water tank in Mahad, was important to Ambedkar's movement in the 1920s. Ambedkar led temple entry movements such as the one in Pune in 1929, but he seemed to have lost interest in this strategy by the early 1930s.[1] In fact, it was Gandhi who gained prominence in the movement that wanted to establish temple entry for untouchable castes during the independence movement. The constituent assembly later adopted an article that abolished untouchability and prohibited and criminalized its practices (Article 17). The article represents a strategy for addressing the problem of untouchability in the independent Indian state. In Gandhi's perspective, temple access represented an idea of holism and a vision of accommodating everyone, including every caste within the Hindu fold. He wanted to harmonize society and integrate untouchables into the Hindu social order in ways that corresponded with the adaptation of the rites and customs of the superior castes.[2] Gandhi was one of the several social reformers within the Hindu fold, and the focus on temple access for untouchables represented an element of social reform in the nationalist movement. But the idea of temple entry introduced the idea of religious inclusion into the public sphere. It represented a discourse that did not entirely correspond with the basic problems of exclusion that the Dalits encountered. This early approach was unhelpful in relation to curbing the caste-based violence that frequently happened to Dalits. Caste-based violence was a legal anomaly, and it resulted in several changes in law and terminology during the postcolonial period.

In this chapter, I argue that the focus on temple access in this early approach to caste was inadequate to address caste-based oppression. The hegemonic narrative at the time of the independence focused on untouchability and access to temples, but this approach underwent changes because gaining entry to temples would not solve the persistent trend of caste-based violence. New discourses created legal changes. These changes could be viewed as learning processes that concerned how the Dalit problem of enduring oppression could be conceptualized. It became clear that a concept such as civil rights and the idea of temple entry misrepresented the basic problems of Dalits, especially caste-based violence. This early approach reflects the failure of Gandhi and other reformers to acknowledge the extent to which caste-based dominance was premised on an ontological difference between touchables and untouchables.

In what follows, I first explain the characteristics of the early-postcolonial approach in eliminating untouchability. Second, I point out how untouchability and temple entry are two references that must be critically re-examined while clarifying legal distinctions and the everyday expression of civil rights. Third, I examine how the abolition of untouchability, expressed in Article 17 of the Constitution of India, creates significant paradoxes. Article 17 involves several potential legal discourses as it includes criminal and civil elements in the constitutional law. The concept of untouchability corresponded to civil wrongs while generating a religious understanding. Collective attacks on Dalits as organized caste-based violence represented an anomaly; it could not be properly handled by the existing framework and paved the way for the Scheduled Castes and Scheduled Tribes (Prevention of Atrocities) Act (PoA Act), 1989. Fourth, I explain how the persistence of caste-based violence during the postcolonial period was discussed in the 1980s, and I put into focus how a conceptual and discoursive change occurred when a government committee decided to replace the focus from untouchability to atrocity and a criminal law approach. Fifth, I emphasize the significance of the brutal trend of caste-related atrocities. These extreme events created a recognition that caste-based violence constitutes an enduring phenomenon in India. The atrocities throw up new insights, which can be used to contextualize laws and related discourses and to rethink ways of making sense of the Dalit situation in India. I conclude by discussing how the legal changes related to Article 17 make sense in terms of Foucault's concept of discourse. Foucauldian analytics (which was once used by Nicholas Dirks in his discussion of caste[3]) is helpful to account for what the legal changes imply, but it does not explain the persistent trend of collectively organized attacks. Indeed, a different starting point is required to explain casteism and caste-based violence. Here, the ontological difference between touchables and untouchables provides a basis for explaining why the aim of atrocities is to 'teach Dalits a lesson'.

Untouchability and Temple Entry Movements

One of the remarkable elements of the Constitution of India is the way in which it includes statements that negate hierarchical notions. The constituent assembly decided to abolish untouchability untouchability (Article 17). Caste was not abolished; however, it is worth underlining that this paradox was pointed out during the discussions.

> I do not understand how you can abolish untouchability without abolishing the very caste system. Untouchability is nothing but the symptom of the disease, namely, the caste system.[4]

This statement did not gain much attention in the constituent assembly, but it brings the paradox into focus: the assembly abolished the effect rather than the cause. It was also argued in the assembly that one should try to specify untouchability, but this was not followed up. On 29 April 1947, however, the conservative leader Sardar V. Patel introduced the clause that later became part of the article in the constitution that abolished untouchability. The clause read, 'Untouchability in any form is abolished and the imposition on that account shall be an offence.'[5] This is a striking sentence because the latter part of it does not follow from the first. In any case, this suggestion later became part of Article 17 in the Constitution of India and in the section on fundamental rights. The constituent assembly decided to abolish, prohibit and make untouchability a punishable offence. There was no significant disagreement about this proposition. But it became clear during the postcolonial period that this formulation was an inadequate legal approach in view of the persistent trend of caste-based violence.

The abolition of untouchability in India's constitution of 1950 appeared to be firmly decided, but this would be a superficial understanding. The abolition of untouchability comprises noteworthy sociological and conceptual paradoxes, among other things, because it is premised on there being a gap between untouchability and caste. In one of Ambedkar's unpublished manuscripts, he argues that those 'who propose to deal with untouchability without damaging the caste system, rest their case on verse 4 of Chapter X of the Manu Smriti. In the verse, Manu says that there are only four varnas and that there is no fifth varna'. Ambedkar concedes that the untouchables may be understood to be part of the fourth *varna*, but he underlines that this may also mean that there are people outside the *varna* system who are not meant to be incorporated into Hindu society. He states that Manu kept referring to people outside the four *varna*s as *bayha*s or *varna bahya*s, 'which means those outside the varna system'.[6] Ambedkar did not make any such objections when the abolition of untouchability was discussed by the constituent assembly in 1947. But the remarks just quoted represent a critique of the abolition of untouchability: it does not damage the caste system which creates untouchability.

The debates in the constituent assembly were characterized by visions of equality, and the Constitution of India is very articulate on equality, with several articles that concern in the Fundamental Rights section. Recall Marc Galanter's seminal characterization of the spirit in the constituent assembly: he argues that there was a determination to compensate for historical injustices committed against outcastes and marginalized groups, specifically theScheduled Castes (SCs), Scheduled Tribes (STs) and Other Backward Classes (OBCs). Galanter addresses the policy of equal opportunity and feels that the concept of 'compensatory discrimination' fitted well with the Indian situation.[7] But this concept has its limits. It does not explain how some of the declarations in the constitution appear more performative than substantial. Article 17 is a case in point. It reads,

> 'Untouchability' is abolished and its practise in any form is forbidden. The enforcement of any disability arising out of 'Untouchability' shall be an offence punishable in accordance with law.

The article became the basis for the later Untouchability (Offences) Act, 1955, which was amended and renamed the Protection of Civil Rights Act in 1976. Article 17 was thus central to legislation related to untouchability. It is a law that deals with non-discrimination rather than a policy of equal opportunity. But the first sentence in Article 17 reflects a paradox, as the last part of the sentence does not follow from the first part, as noted above. It is relevant to ask how a practice can be prohibited if it has already been abolished. It could be suggested that the sentence is a performative act or an overly general declaration to demonstrate an egalitarian vision for a modern India. Yet it has legal implications because it prohibits untouchability.

Ambedkar's remarks suggest that abolishing untouchability did not affect the belief in caste. On the contrary, it could have been seen as consistent with viewing the Hindu caste order as a consistent whole with caste differences. But the dominating narrative at the time of independence focused on access to public space as a civil right. This was represented most notably by Gandhi, the leading social reformer in the nationalist movement and an active participant in the temple entry movement. As Dalton emphasizes, Gandhi followed up the social reforms initiated by others, but his desire for social harmony was comparatively noteworthy.[8] Temple entry appears to be one of his attempts to create social harmony while integrating the untouchables into Hindu society.

Gandhi became dedicated to the temple access movement after the struggle with Ambedkar in 1932 over the question of whether the untouchables should be granted a separate electorate. He had addressed the problem of untouchability earlier. In 1921, he argued that untouchability was a 'blot on Hinduism' and that it should be removed.[9] He endorsed a struggle for temple entry in Kerala in 1921, though low-caste leaders had convinced him they were not actually untouchables.[10] But it was after the battle with Ambedkar in 1932 that he became more articulate on the need to allow temple access for the untouchables. He then emphasized how the movement against untouchability had gained force and how there was an interest in creating a legal ban on preventing temple entry, which could replace colonial laws that had supported Hindu orthodoxy.[11]

Gandhi's reform movement was situated between orthodox Hindus (the *sanatanis*[12]) and other Hindu reformers. At the end of 1932, Gandhi had addressed the question of temple access to the Guruvayaur temple in Cochin, Kerala. His request appeared to be a mixture of demands on behalf of the untouchables and concessions made to the practitioners of untouchability. Gandhi did not want to offend these practitioners of untouchability. In fact, despite arguing that untouchability was a blot on Hinduism, he allowed the temple to be ritually purified. While he allowed untouchability to be practised by those who believed in the values of caste, Gandhi toured the country to raise the issue of untouchability. The best organized and most peaceful temple entry movement occurred in Kerala. It was a milestone for this movement when the Maharajah of Travancore issued a temple-entry proclamation in 1936, declaring that all temples in Travancore should be open to the untouchables.[13] Reforms were modest, but the focus on temple access became a visible strategy that aimed to ameliorate the plight of untouchables within the framework of Hindu and national unity. As with processes of 'Sanskritization', which characterizes the process whereby lower castes adopt Brahmin rites and customs, the goal of these reforms was not to overturn the caste system but to adopt relatively more inclusive practices.[14]

There were basic differences in Ambedkar's and Gandhi's struggles for temple access in terms of policy, strategy and ontology. Ambedkar considered this struggle to be a question of civil rights and access to public space in general, whereas Gandhi considered temple access to be a question of religious reform and national cohesion, and his ideas evolved over time. Ambedkar argued, for instance, that the untouchables had already struggled for access to temples and public wells in 1929 to demand their 'civic rights'.[15] They had approached the Mahatma who at that time had criticized their plan of using *satyagraha* (non-violent resistance) against Hindus to ameliorate their situation. But Gandhi had argued that *satyagraha* was meant to be used only in the struggle against the colonial powers.[16] The fact that Gandhi changed his position on temple entry may reflect the ways in which temple access gained more importance in the nationalist movement. As Galanter underlines, temple entry was the area that perhaps troubled reformers and politicians concerned with Hindu unity the most.[17] Gandhi became central to this publicly visible topic. He used temple entry in his strategy for creating national unity, although his ideas were not new among Hindu reformers.[18]

While manoeuvring between various positions, the Mahatma made strong, albeit complex, claims about caste and the scope for social reform in Hinduism.

He argued that Lord Krishna had taught doctrines of equality in the *Bhagavad Gita* while adding that it is impossible to attain *swaraj* (independence) if 'the Hindus wilfully regard untouchability as their religion'.[19] Gandhi's critique of untouchability is fraught with contradictions. On the one hand, he conceded that untouchability existed in a limited sense, and he advised the untouchables to follow self-purification rules and observe internal and external 'laws of sanitations'.[20] On the other hand, he argued, 'Temple-entry is the one spiritual act that would constitute the message of freedom to the "untouchables" and assure them that they are not outcastes before God.'[21]

Gandhi's intricate discussion of untouchability and caste shows that he approached social reforms for the untouchables from a very different viewpoint to that of Ambedkar. His position on untouchability reflects a pragmatic denial of any ontological difference between touchables and untouchables as well as recognition of this dimension in the Hindu caste order. Ambedkar criticized him for endorsing practices that recognized the antagonism between touchables and untouchables, arguing it was inconsistent with the Mahatma's claim that a separate electorate for the untouchables would divide them from the caste Hindus.[22]

The basic motivation for wanting to incorporate the untouchables in the Hindu fold corresponds to Gandhi's overall strategy of harmonizing the Hindu social order while affirming its religious identity at the expense of other religions.[23] Gaining entry to temples became one method of being included in the nationalist movement. The different positions of Gandhi and Ambedkar on the untouchables is further evident in how Gandhi's rhetoric and ideas about social reforms are based on approaching the issues concerning the untouchables from a religious point of view. This was evident in the name he chose for the untouchables, Harijans, according to him 'means "a man of God"'.[24] In 1933, he started a journal with this name. Gandhi also claimed that untouchability is not a product of 'the caste system but of the distinction of high and low that has crept into Hinduism'.[25] Although he criticizes the hierarchical grading in Hinduism as a source of corruption, he states that the fourfold division of *varna* is a natural order. In fact, Gandhi views society as an organic whole, explaining that each class complements the others and contributes to 'the whole body of Hinduism'.[26] He does not think that the *varna* system is the source of the hierarchical grading. His idea of an egalitarian promise amid this fourfold division of society must be understood, he says, by considering his ideas about the two terms *jati* and *varna*. This position is relevant when Gandhi explains *varna* and *jati* in his reaction to Ambedkar's radical text 'Annihilation of Caste'. In his journal *Harijan*, in an article dated 18 July 1936, Gandhi claims, 'Varna and Ashrama are institutions which have nothing to do with castes'. Ambedkar rejected this view. Even representatives of the Jat-Pat Todak Mandal, who had withdrawn their invitation to Ambedkar to be the president at their conference after they had read a draft of his speech, claimed that Gandhi's distinction 'between caste and Varna is too subtle to be grasped by people in general'.[27]

When Gandhi dismissed caste, he was referring to *jati* rather than *varna*. The word *jati* has similar roots to the word *jana*, meaning 'to be born'.[28] *Jati* is used to describe the everyday understanding of caste and designates the heritage or occupation a person is born into. Ambedkar agreed with Gandhi that caste and *varna* differed, but he claimed that Gandhi was unable to explain the difference between the two concepts as well as how they overlap and refer to 'the pursuit of ancestral calling'.[29] Ambedkar further claimed that Gandhi tended to 'spiritualise politics', confuse his roles as Mahatma and a politician and was more motivated by politics than truth.[30] Recall from the discussion of 'Annihilation of Caste': Ambedkar argues that the beliefs in Hindu scriptures must be abolished because they create caste mentalities. Gandhi's focus, on the other hand, was on harmonizing the social order through religious reform and incorporating the untouchables into Hindu society. He also claimed (unlike the constitution-makers) that untouchability could only be removed through religious reform and not by the force of law alone.[31]

While Galanter rightly says that members of the constituent assembly were determined to pursue equality, the previous discussion shows that there was no determination to abolish caste. Gandhi is an example of someone who felt deep ambivalence about caste-based reforms. According to Ambedkar, the idea of removing untouchability could be consistent with Manu's teaching while Manu thought that where there was no fifth *varna*, he could still refer to people outside the *varna* system. In a system of graded inequality, which Ambedkar argued was a trademark of a Hindu social order, every member of touchable castes would aspire to be somebody and, as such, would need others to look down on as 'nobodies'.[32]

The idea of seeing the untouchables as members of the Hindu religion was undoubtedly motivated by a desire to increase the numerical strength of Hinduism as compared to Islam and by a wish for social harmonization. The temple entry was nonetheless part of an early civil rights agenda among egalitarian movements. The League for Equal Civic Rights was one of these numerous movements and was established in 1918 by a group of Syrian Christians in Travancore who fought for equal opportunities for all groups in public service and even for the end of untouchability.[33] While civil rights activists focused on access to roads and public buildings, there was limited success in creating temple entry for the untouchables. Overall, the idea of temple entry for the untouchables remained problematic and insubstantial and was often transformed into a question of religious inclusion.

An examination of the temple entry movement suggests that it is worthwhile, considering whether the concept of untouchability undermines an accurate understanding of caste-based exclusion. In other words, is the concept of untouchability part of the problem? The term reproduces a religious discourse and makes temple entry a central focus, and this discoursive configuration creates a legal impasse. Therefore, it is helpful to take a step back to explain how the temple entry movement compares with different domains of law and to delineate different concepts such as civil rights and civil law.

Civil Rights versus Branches of Law

One needs to distinguish between civil rights and civil law. The concept of civil rights has served as a rhetorical strategy in a struggle for democratic recognition of excluded groups. There are also historical links between Gandhi's non-violent movement in India and the black civil rights movement in the USA, but there are also clear differences. To avoid confusion, it is useful to explain the relation between civil rights in the USA and of Gandhi, before explaining why civil rights is a general concept that does not make sense at the level of law.

The concept of civil rights is well known from the struggles in the USA such as Martin Luther King's movement for black people in America. The concept of 'civil rights' or 'civil rights struggles' appears to characterize a policy or movement that is aiming for recognition and equal treatment of particular social groups, such as black people and white people in the USA. It is based, like the temple entry movements in India, on the idea that all people deserve access to public space on an equal basis. However, the concept of civil rights itself is open to many interpretations.[34] In the USA, the development of civil rights moved in fits and starts until the 1960s, when it became the main label used to characterize the black struggle for dignity and equal rights.[35] Internationally, the civil rights concept is largely informed by the black movement in the USA that was struggling to gain equal treatment and to oppose the spatial segregation that was imposed by the Jim Crow laws. The movement led by people like Martin Luther King culminated in the creation of the Civil Rights Act, 1964, in the USA, and this Act made equal opportunity a public policy in the country.

Martin Luther King's call for full recognition and integration of black people into American society resonates with Gandhi's approach. In fact, King and his associates were inspired by Gandhi's political thought, his ideas of civil disobedience and his resistance with non-violent methods. Workshops on non-violence were organized, inspiring individuals such as Rosa Parks not to give up her seat for a white man in 1955. She had been trained in Gandhian techniques in the movement of Martin Luther King and other activists who were struggling to gain equal access to public space.[36]

But it would be misleading to consider civil rights to be the same as civil law. Indeed, while designating struggles for equal treatment and legal protection, the concept of civil rights has limited value for understanding law. Therefore, one needs to step outside the rhetoric of civil rights when explaining the relation between Dalits and law. It was partly the ambiguities that could be introduced by the rhetoric of civil rights that made it necessary for lawmakers in India to rethink the legal approach to preventing caste-based violence. To explain the legal changes that occurred, it is useful to introduce some basic legal distinctions.

The term 'civil law' is concerned with law. The concept of civil law can be understood in several ways, most generally as a branch of law that is distinct from common law or Roman law. In common law traditions, such as those that operate in the UK, the USA and India, civil law is a concept that is distinguished from criminal law. The latter is important for this discussion, and I wish to further unpack this distinction in order to discuss how caste-based oppression was conceptualized.

According to Glanville Williams' text book on law, there are two main branches of law, criminal and civil.[37] The difference is between civil wrongs (sometimes referred to as civil offences) and criminal law. This is a key legal distinction, and each domain of law has its own characteristics, procedures and implications. It is therefore important to determine whether a piece of legislation is located under one of these domains. Each domain of law resonates with certain political discourses and ideas more than others. When the constituent assembly abolished, prohibited and punished untouchability, it was not clear how this related to the different domains of law. Article 17 represents a starting point. And yet the history of approaching untouchability as a problem concerning temple entry had an impact on the popular understandings in the early-postcolonial period.

There was a growing concern with caste-based atrocities during the postcolonial period. And the problem of caste-based atrocities represents a legal anomaly in a situation in which Gandhi's rhetoric of accommodating differences and the movements for temple access had shaped the public approach to untouchability. An adequate legal approach to the atrocities inflicted on Dalits required a break with the idea of temple access as well as with the concept of untouchability itself. In other words, although one may criticize the constituent assembly for not having elaborated the meanings of untouchability, the postcolonial history shows that the concept of untouchability was itself an obstacle to the conceptualization of atrocities.

Article 17: Meanings and Discourses

It is by interrogating the concept of untouchability, its affinity with religion and the history of the temple access movement, one can break down and understand the expressions used in civil rights and legislation for a more equal social order during the postcolonial period. It appears that the concept of untouchability corresponds better with the domain of law known as civil wrongs rather than criminal law.

Caste-based violence is a different theme, and so it corresponds to a different domain of law.

Ambedkar asked, '[W]hy are the untouchables always beaten?'[38] He offers an ontological explanation, arguing that the untouchables are nobodies in a system of graded inequality. But he did not translate this observation – about caste-based atrocities – into a discussion of law in the constituent assembly. My suggestion is that Ambedkar did not have the opportunity to fully answer this question in light of the inadequate legal basis at the time he made his leading contribution to developing the Constitution of India. During the early-postcolonial period, moreover, the main attempt was to develop the legislation that applied to the SCs with direct reference to Article 17. According to Anupama Rao, the legislative developments between 1947 and 1955 can be characterized as 'legal equalization' where the 'practice of untouchability was criminalized'.[39] While these statements appear to confirm the general idea that criminalization of untouchability was constitutionalized, they reflect different discourses. In fact, Article 17 does not constitute one coherent unit because there are several discourses at stake in the two sentences concerning the prohibition of untouchability in the Constitution of India.

Recall Glanville Williams' explanation that there are two great branches of law, criminal and civil. The main difference between these two domains of law is found in the legal consequences that follow a violation of law.[40] In my view, the legislation that aimed to address the problems experienced by the untouchables in the early-postcolonial period was largely shaped by the notion of the practice of untouchability being a civil wrong. While creating ambiguities, Article 17 invokes three different legal approaches and related discourses. It jumbles together constitutional law, civil wrongs and criminal law, and each of these legal domains have their own discursive characteristics and implications. First, Article 17 is included among fundamental rights in the constitution and reflects the overall egalitarian principles that were used in the crafting of the Constitution of India. Equality is considered such a central principle that it was later declared to be part of the constitution's 'basic structure'.[41] Second, by considering the idea of avoiding defamation of character and assault and with its aim of not offending the untouchables by denying them access to temples, the article resonates with general tort and civil wrongs. The general understanding of the situation of the untouchables at that time was that they were denied access to temples. Yet the final sentence in Article 17 indicates that untouchability is 'punishable', which suggests that untouchability has been criminalized. But this was not straightforward in practice. No criminal proceedings or punishments took place after Article 17 was created as part of the Constitution of India. Therefore, the criminalization of untouchability was a theoretical possibility rather than an effective law; the law lacked consequences and did not stipulate crimes. This lacuna was addressed in the subsequent Untouchability (Offences) Act, 1955, in which punishments were prescribed.[42] There were debates in parliament on ways to address caste-based oppression. But the debates reflect an unresolved tension between the two domains of law, civil wrongs and criminal law, and this tension appeared unresolved for several reasons. The overall problem was the discoursive hegemony of the temple entry movement, which was amplified by the nationalist movement and ideas about social inclusion. In addition, the term 'untouchability' reinforced the articulation of caste-based exclusion as a matter of religion and the focus on access to public spaces such as temples.

Several legal changes took place in the early-twentieth century. Various pieces of legislation emerged across regional states to address untouchability before India gained independence in 1950. In 1917, the untouchable activists who had touched holy water in Madras had been prosecuted by the government. Three decades later, the government of Madras had created three Acts in 1947 and in 1948 to address temple entry and to remove 'civil disabilities'. A similar legislation was passed in several other states, such as Andhra Pradesh, Kerala, Bihar and Uttar Pradesh.[43] Most of it appeared in the late 1940s. After independence, the central government attempted to develop its legislation to prevent untouchability. To collect information, in January 1950, the government of India sent out requests for information to state governments about the practice of untouchability in the state, civil disabilities and possible punishments prescribed by the state laws.[44] The responses arrived in 1953. In addition to statements from associations representing the Harijans and Depressed Classes, these responses formed the basis for drafting the bill of 1954. The bill was discussed in parliament and the Untouchability (Offences) Act was approved in May 1955.

The troubling issue in these and subsequent debates was that untouchability had not been fully defined. The concern with the concept of untouchability gained significance after a judge declared in a court judgment in 1957 in Karnataka that neither the Untouchability (Offences) Act nor the constitution defined the term 'untouchability'. In fact, the judge emphasized that the constitution put untouchability in inverted commas. He suggested that this was done to try to avoid the fact that untouchability was made explicit and reproduced through legal practice. The judge also underlined that the constituent assembly had addressed the plight of castes that had been discriminated against historically. Their plight was not to be understood in a 'literal' sense, by which he meant that Article 17 does not apply to those who experience untouchability 'temporarily or otherwise by various reasons'.[45] The petitioners complained that members of the Jain community practised untouchability when worshippers approached Jain temples in Bangalore. In other words, the law was elusive. Article 17 and the subsequent Untouchability (Offences) Act, 1955, provided a weak basis on which to intervene in untouchability practices. The judge in Karnataka ended up arguing that it would even be contrary to the law to specify what untouchability was about.

The legal challenge appeared to be how to define untouchability more clearly, as if the legislation could be improved by answering the following question: what is untouchability? This question was raised, for example, in a committee report to the Ministry of Law and Social Welfare in 1969. The question 'What is untouchability?' encouraged specification of the meanings of terms such as 'disabilities' and of actions such as access to public spaces.[46] On the one hand, answering this question appears to involve a formalistic elaboration of the relation between a concept and its domain of relevance. On the other hand, it also seems to introduce a religious horizon as well as the forms and characteristics of untouchability.

In practice, the recurring issues seemed to involve (a) access to public space, (b) offences against untouchability and (c) the essence and meaning of untouchability. This is summarized in the Untouchability (Offences) Act, 1955, where the term in parentheses relates to the word 'untouchability'. If the term 'offences' means the same as civil offences, this Act is not primarily conceptualized as a criminal piece of legislation as offence is often used as a less accurate expression for civil wrong.[47] By conceptualizing offences in terms of untouchability, this Act tends to reproduce the image created by the temple entry movements as a problem of access to public spaces, particularly temples. Moreover, religion seems to provide the conscious or unconscious reference point for conceptualizing the problem of the social exclusion of untouchable castes. In other words, the Untouchability (Offences) Act not only involves a conflict between two different legal domains and discourses but it also has a greater affinity with civil wrongs than criminal law. Moreover, the concept of untouchability provided support for viewing untouchability as a matter of civil 'offence'. This understanding was further consolidated by asking about the essence of untouchability. In short, the concept of untouchability became part of the problem of developing an adequate legal response.

Legislators were concerned with the caste-based violence throughout the postcolonial period, and members of parliament were determined to criminalize it. The next major change occurred in 1976, when the Untouchability (Offences) Act, 1955, was revised, developed and renamed as the Protection of Civil Rights Act in 1976.[48] The 1955 Act provided the framework for new and more detailed provisions, and this worked within the paradigm of Article 17 of the constitution. The revised Act of 1976 introduced further punishments for violence and discrimination against members of the SCs and STs.

The name of the Act seems to be an extension of the overall idea of civil rights. Giving the 1976 Act a new name emphasized the concept of civil rights, and the Act defines them as follows: '"civil rights" means any right accruing to a person by reason of the abolition of "untouchability" by Article 17 of the Constitution'. This statement affirms how historically untouchable castes were granted equal dignity. But the content of the Act and the concept of civil rights reconfirm the idea that the goal was to grant members of the SCs access to public spaces. This legal tradition thus carried forward this ambiguity with the concept of untouchability and the conceptualizing of violence against the background of temple entry or civil rights as a problem of access to public space. The 1976, Act did not overcome the tension between two legal domains, civil wrongs (or civil offences) and criminal law, despite consistent efforts to addressing the practice and 'preaching' of untouchability.

During the postcolonial period, the legal framework coexisted with an enduring trend of caste-based violence against members of the untouchable castes, and the Protection of Civil Rights Act, 1976, was not primarily designed to address this trend. As Baxi writes, the police did not have an adequate legal approach to handling large-scale violence based on caste. In 1979, the Bureau of Police Research suggested that charges brought for violations against the SCs should explicitly mention how cruelty, brutality or wickedness had been part of collective actions carried out to 'teach Harijans a lesson'.[49] In other words, the legal framework was still inadequate for effective police action even after the Civil Rights Act of 1976. Like members of the public, researchers in the Indian police were concerned with how to prevent – or if that failed, how to follow up – cases of caste-based violence. Overall, 'atrocity' emerged as a common-sense term to account for caste-based violence. In the 1980s, the term atrocity gained official recognition and enabled a discoursive break with the concept of untouchability. Violence was no longer an anomaly. Instead, the concept of untouchability and the individualizing civil rights approach were replaced with a clearer approach under the criminal law – the PoA Act, 1989.

Discoursive Change and the PoA Act, 1989

A series of atrocities across the country, virtually 'starting' with the attack in Kilvenmani in 1968, generated a growing demand for an improvement in the anti-atrocity legislation. The creation of the Protection of Civil Rights Act, 1976, reflects the overall demand for improved legislation. As Rao explains, there were discussions about the nature of untouchability and law enforcement in parliament at the time of the creation of the Untouchability (Offences) Act, 1955. However, the enduring trend of large-scale massacres throughout the postcolonial period provoked many reactions at the centre of Indian politics, and massacres continued even after stricter procedures and measures had been adopted to protect civil rights in 1976. There were, for instance, several large-scale massacres in the late 1970s and during the 1980s in Bihar. Atrocity was therefore a topical term. Dalit delegations, such as the one made up of leaders and representatives from the Dalit Mahasabha in Andhra Pradesh, approached Delhi to demand official actions to prevent atrocities. During this period, the group called the Parliamentary Forum for Scheduled Castes and Scheduled Tribes, consisting of members of parliament, has been central in the ongoing lobbying in parliament. Massacres and atrocities are often discussed in the national parliament,[50] and there are formal reasons for doing so. The Indian state combines federalism with a strong central government, and it is particularly centralized with respect to law and order. As Subramanian explains, '[T]he law and order situation in the states, especially regarding subjects such as atrocities against Scheduled Castes and Tribes is a matter more often debated in Parliament than in state assemblies.'[51]

It was in the context of continued atrocities, demands from Dalit movements and recurring debates in parliament that the creation of new laws to prevent caste-based violence became a critical task. The atrocities were decisive for Rajiv Gandhi who in 1987 declared that there must be a special Act to deal with the problem of atrocities against untouchables and tribal people.[52] Rajiv Gandhi made this promise in an annual speech outside the Red Fort in Old Delhi on 15 August 1987. In principle, a home minister should develop this idea and prepare an Act. But it was a minister of law at that time, a Dalit from Karnataka, who wanted to accomplish the prime minister's promise. He organized a committee to develop the Act. P. S. Krishnan was invited to be a member of this committee because he was a state official with extensive fieldwork experience and insight into the type of problems Dalits faced. The discussions that this committee conducted are worth emphasizing. When I interviewed Krishnan, he explained that the discussions started with a stated interest in defining untouchability. Such a point of departure was consistent with the persistent discussion about how to address untouchability as a practice that should be prohibited. The common understanding was that untouchability had not been properly defined and that the weak definition was the reason for the inadequate approach to date. However, the discussions of this drafting committee gained a new point of departure when it was suggested that one should address caste-based violence as a problem of atrocity rather than of untouchability. Krishnan suggested that rather than defining untouchability, one should ask, 'What is an atrocity?' The adoption of this concept was not trivial. By using the common-sense term atrocity as an official term, one could more clearly break away from the framework of civil rights and develop a new and more determined piece of legislation under criminal law. In other words, the adoption of the concept of atrocity enabled a discoursive change to occur, and this supported the crafting of a new piece of criminal law.

The new approach prompted the committee to use the Indian Penal Code as the legal starting point when they sought to specify and define atrocity. In an interview, Krishnan emphasized how he could make use of his many visits to

Dalit villages, including many where Dalits had been victims of atrocities. Most bureaucrats would not conduct a survey in the countryside. Before participating in the drafting committee, Krishnan had come across a case in which Dalits were forced to eat obnoxious material, and he proposed that this should be punishable.[53] Broadly, there were many different experiences that were brought forward from various actors in this process. One of the demands, for example, was that there should be a special court to deal with the perpetrators of atrocities. This demand was inspired by a similar provision in the Indian Penal Code. The demand for a special court had been made by people such as the Dalit Mahasabha leaders in Andhra Pradesh after the Karamchedu massacre in 1985.[54]

The PoA Act was established on 11 September 1989. It includes a range of specific definitions, prescribes punishments and gives the concept of atrocity a firm legal status. As well as referring to instances covered by the Indian Penal Code, such as rape and murder, the Act defines atrocities in several ways that are specific to the SCs and STs. These definitions include forcing members of these categories to work as bonded labourers, forcing them to 'drink or eat any inedible or obnoxious substances', exploiting women sexually, 'corrupt[ing]' their water, occupying the SC/ST-owned land or property, preventing them from gaining access to public places, humiliating them by parading them naked in public or using derogatory caste-related names to address them.[55] By focusing on atrocities, the PoA Act represented a clear move away from civil law to criminal law. The new Act replaced previous Acts such as the Protection of Civil Rights Act, 1955. That Act had been developed with reference to the constitution's Article 17, which declares untouchability to be 'abolished and its practise in any form forbidden'. The 1955 Act was modelled on civil liberties. In 1976, Lok Sabha changed and renamed the same Act as Untouchability (Offences) Act. This new Act did not contain sufficient steps to curb caste-related atrocities, and legal practice was still shaped by the idea of using a definition of untouchability as a starting point. This had been the initial idea during the preparation of the PoA Act before the committee agreed on a new point of departure, namely to focus on atrocity as a more appropriate concept.[56]

The new legal approach to atrocities could more effectively integrate the different kinds of violence and forms of oppression used against Dalits. The history of the PoA Act, 1989, represents a discursive change in the legal approach to Dalits. It was generated by ongoing debates and demands for legislation that was more appropriate for preventing caste-related atrocities. Moreover, the legal approach to caste-based violence was enhanced by locating the Act under the India Penal Code. The different kinds of atrocities carried out against Dalits and Adivasis could therefore amount to more specific punishments. Overall, the PoA Act, 1989, and the rules that followed in 1995 represent a firm legal affirmation that crimes against the untouchables will be punished. It is a strict law with wide powers. Unlike the

Indian Penal Code, the Act does not allow the death penalty.[57] However, one of its considerable and well-known powers is that offenders can be imprisoned without any provisions for being released on bail. This is precisely the provision that the two-judge bench at the Supreme Court argued would result in an 'abuse of law of arrest' in their judgment of 20 March 2018.[58] A principal and director of technical education in the state of Maharashtra had been accused in January 2006 of abusing his power to write confidential reports that deliberately damaged the career and reputation of an employee, a person from an SC. The highest court of the country struck down this accusation as a 'clear abuse of process of court' and even modified the provision for anticipatory bail.[59] The judgment created considerable protests among Dalits across the country, from Chennai and Hyderabad in south India to New Delhi in north India, and nine people were killed in north Indian states on 2 April, shortly after the judgment was given.[60] The BJP (Bharatiya Janata Party) government introduced a bill to restore the provision, and the amendment bill was endorsed by the Indian parliament on 6 August of the same year.[61] While the provision in the PoA Act is hugely unpopular, especially among BJP supporters, it is an aspect of the law that is based on experience gained from atrocity cases.

The Persistence of Caste-Related Atrocities

The organized atrocities and acts of large-scale violence against Dalits represent a more extreme dimension of caste-based oppression which differs from everyday discrimination and abuse. Everyday forms of discriminations are different in villages and towns.[62] Discrimination is more explicit in the countryside since it is easier to identify a person's background in villages where everyone knows the relatives of the person in question. In urban contexts, caste is often more hidden but can be discerned by recognizing diet, place of origin and family occupations.[63] During the postcolonial period, however, massacres of Dalits emerged as a major problem and concern. They occurred in different parts of the country and have mainly been individual cases emerging out of local conflicts. The organized attacks are normally rural phenomena.[64] The media covers some events. Social media has made large numbers of atrocities visible today, even for a global audience, but many events have historically been unnoticed. The list of massacres is, in any case, such that it represents a consistent dimension of violence during India's modernity.

The killing of forty-four Dalits in Kilvenmani village (also known by its Tamil name Keezhvenmani) in Tamil Nadu on 25 December 1968 represents an early event of caste brutality and ongoing attacks against Dalits in the postcolonial state.[65] On this occasion, landlords locked the Dalits into a hut and burnt them alive. This was a reaction to their demand for higher wages, which had been supported by the communist movement. Forty-four people died, and many were women, children and elderly people.[66] On 27 May 1977, eleven Dalits and two lower-caste peop were killed in Belchi in Bihar. Several massacres followed in Bihar, such as the one in Pipra in 1980 and in Nonki-Nagawa in 1988.[67]

The trend of caste-related violence did not stop. There were several brutal cases of violence during the modern period, often as a direct result of Dalits trying to participate more fully in society or making particular demands. In 1997, fifty-eight Dalits were killed in Lakshmanpur-Bathe in Bihar.[68] In 1997, six Dalits were murdered in Melavalavu in Tamil Nadu after a Dalit had been elected to the presidency of the panchayat, the village council. In October 2002, five Dalits were lynched in Haryana after a rumour, that they had slaughtered a cow, had circulated.[69] In Andhra Pradesh, the two major massacres, Karamchedu in 1985 and Tsundur in 1991, were reactions to Dalit assertion. In Karnataka, six Dalits were burnt alive in Kambalapalli in 2000 after years of tension.[70] The massacre in Khairlanji in Maharashtra on 29 September 2006 was one of the last major events that occurred in the new millennium. In Khairlanji, four members of a family were killed. The mother, her daughter and two sons were tortured to death; the mother and daughter had been gang raped and their bodies were mutilated. The father escaped. The atrocity occurred after a long struggle for better wages and protests about wrongful acts carried out against Dalit property – the destruction of a rice field and a shop. The attack happened after one of the Dalit women had accused an OBC man in a neighbouring village of committing an atrocity.

It is difficult to compare the postcolonial trend of caste-based violence with the situation prior to India's independence. Violence against the untouchables occurred during the colonial period as well. Hierarchical practices were prevalent. In Travancore, some members of higher castes were entitled to kill the untouchables who did not get out of their way.[71] But the large-scale massacres of the postcolonial period have created an assumption among Dalit activists and observers that these brutal cases represent a trend that is distinctive of the postcolonial period. Many of these massacres occur during disputes between landlords and landless labourers. It is significant to note that many landowners, who are often the culprits, are not necessarily members of the Brahmin castes, that is, not from the priestly castes who are deemed to be ritually superior. Although Brahmins gained considerable power over policymaking in the colonial state, they do not figure prominently in the history of collectively organized massacres. Instead, several massacres were committed by landowning castes, traditionally Shudra castes, such as those in coastal Andhra. They moved up in the hierarchy of castes by acquiring economic and political power; they rearticulated their origins and claimed they were Kshatriyas. Their mobility reflects a certain flexibility in the caste system, once theorized by Srinivas, in which lower castes can move up in the hierarchy and claim Kshatriya status.[72] This occurred among Telugu castes such as Reddys, Kammas and Velamas.[73] While the Reddys and Kammas rose in the non-Brahmin movement, their egalitarian agenda changed into a pursuit of superior status for their own castes.[74] Reddys projected a glorious past, and Velamas engaged a Brahmin historian to explain that they were 'pure Kshatriyas'.[75]

While challenging Brahmin power, Reddys and Kammas cultivated the *varna* scheme and acquired a taste for Vedic culture. Articulations of status became important as competition among them increased. By starting to read the Vedas and wearing sacred threads, Kammas became attached to Brahmin orthodoxy.[76] These processes reflect Sanskritization, where social mobility is based on the reproduction of tradition rather than on revolutionary change of the caste system.[77] While the caste system is viewed as one of graded inequality, however, the untouchables will be kept at bay while touchable castes compete and rearticulate superiority.[78] This appears to be the case with the non-Brahmin movement in Andhra, where, according to Ramaswamy, members of superior castes 'never thought of equating themselves with the untouchables'.[79]

The rearticulation of caste not only increased with competition over power and dominance, but it also corresponded with significant changes in the political economy in coastal Andhra. Here, agricultural reforms during the colonial and postcolonial periods had been very profitable for the landowning peasant castes. As Srinivasulu underlines, caste became central to the articulations of social conflicts in Andhra.[80] The re-embedding of caste mentalities in the agrarian economy provides an important background to the massacres. The massacres of Dalits, in Tsundur and Karamchedu, were both systematically coordinated attacks that were carried out to 'teach Dalits a lesson' (see Chapters 3 and 4). This expression has even been used during attacks, such as the one in Karamchedu. The logic of teaching a lesson is also used among Dalit activists to explain how the massacres are organized spectacles to affirm that members of their caste should remain inferior and should not assert any demands or correct the behaviour of members of the dominant castes. The attack in Khairlanji also began in a similar manner, that is, first in talks about 'showing the *dheds* (a derogatory term for Dalits in Maharashtra) their place' and later in slogans about beating 'the bastards' or killing the Mahars.[81]

It is not clear whether the trend of collective attacks against Dalits is an entirely new phenomenon. Teltumbde has been among those who has highlighted that the massacres of Dalits represent a new and more brutal phenomenon in the context of caste. He argues that while caste-based violence was historically committed by individuals, there is a postcolonial trend in which this type of violence is 'carried out collectively, in a loosely planned manner, as a spectacle of demonstrative justice'.[82] Although his claim is not accompanied by a historical comparison or evidence, it reflects an impression among experienced observers. But there are very few, if any, systematic studies that substantiate the argument that caste-based violence is intensifying during the postcolonial period and the attacks are carried out in a more collective manner than before. Keeping the comparisons across historical periods aside, the mechanism of oppression is nonetheless a consistent logic in the massacres.

Atrocities often reflect an embedded antagonism in which claims of equality by untouchable castes may result in backlashes. This corresponds to the ontological difference in the system of graded inequality, which, Ambedkar argues, means that the untouchables are treated as 'no-bodies'.[83] There are many accounts of intensification of caste-based violence, but Krishnan, a civil servant, pundit and former secretary to the central government, makes a statement that summarizes many of them. He argues, 'As the resistance of the Dalits has grown, so the frequency and brutal ferocity of atrocities have grown apace'.[84] Overall, caste-based violence occurs as acts that aim to 'teach Dalits a lesson' about behaving submissively towards locally dominant castes. This assumption was also held by researchers in the Indian police force, who in the 1980s felt that the legal framework had to be improved to try to prevent these massacres.[85]

To sum up, the atrocities constitute a more important dimension of the social realities for Dalits than the early postcolonial legislation had been designed to address. The framework of Article 17 and the subsequent Acts of 1955 and 1976 were insufficient to address the collective attacks that were often carried out to 'teach Dalits a lesson'. Three decades since its creation, the PoA Act has become significant in the public discourse; it is a tool that can be used by the Dalit movement, but it is deeply resented by representatives of caste Hindus. But the large-scale massacres leave a lasting trauma and may remain subject to ongoing mobilization. For instance, the Communist Party of India (Marxist) (CPI[M]) organizes an annual anniversary to remember the victims of the Kilvenmani massacre of 1968. Karamchedu was crucial in the formation of the modern Dalit movement in Andhra Pradesh. No doubt other issues, such as sub-categorization, preoccupy contemporary Dalit movements in Andhra Pradesh. But Karamchedu was among the critical events that speeded up the momentum among Dalit activists to demand a more adequate legal framework to prevent atrocities against Dalits and Adivasis. Despite their different agendas, several leaders of Dalit activists in states such as Telangana and Andhra Pradesh took a clear stance in objecting to the modifications of the PoA Act that were carried out in the Supreme Court judgment of 20 March 2018 where the PoA Act was modified. In Telangana, the cultural leader and revolutionary activist Gaddar argued that the PoA Act should be placed outside the reach of judicial review, while Manda Krishna Madiga criticized the right-wing government for weakening the Act and led a delegation of Madiga activists to protest in Delhi in August of the same year.[86]

Beyond Untouchability

The above discussion shows that the constituent assembly did not exactly address the problem of caste-based violence against the members of so-called untouchable castes when they drafted the Constitution of India. They did condemn untouchability and endorsed its abolition, and this statement matters for several questions that have been raised. Untouchability practices have been traditionally applied to menstruating women as well. According to *The Laws of Manu*, an untouchable person, 'a menstruating woman and impotent man' should not be 'watching the priests dine'.[87] Although this is an ancient text, some temples prohibit menstruating women from entering. A landmark judgment was delivered by the Supreme Court on 28 September 2018 when it ruled that the 'social exclusion of women, based on menstrual status' at the Lord Ayyappa temple in Kerala is an untouchability practice that violates the constitution.[88]

In terms of addressing caste-based oppression, however, it has been previously shown that Article 17 was open to ideological and juridical disputes. The decision to abolish untouchability appears to be an affirmation of the spirit of the constituent assembly. Equality was a principle that had a significant impact on the discussions in the assembly, and it is central to the section titled Fundamental Rights in the Constitution of India. The abolition of untouchability follows this overall approach. In addition, the main leaders, such as Nehru, influenced the constituent assembly with a vision about modernizing India.[89] Yet Article 17 still reads as a performative and ambiguous statement. The ambiguity is partly expressed by putting untouchability in inverted commas, which was emphasized in a subsequent judgment from Karnataka High Court in 1957.

The constitution's Article 17 should be understood primarily as a performative act which left many questions open for later interpretations. In fact, when viewed as a statement, it represents what philosophers refer to as a 'speech act'. In John Searle's philosophy of language, a speech act can be a performative declaration with some sociological relevance. The creation of an institution could be a direct result of a performative action, and speech acts are essential for the reality that humans create.[90] From this perspective, Article 17 could be viewed as a performative act, but its meaning is ambiguous, especially because it did not remove the cause of untouchability. Finally, although Article 17 declares that caste should be punishable, it is not enough to view this article as a criminalization of untouchability.

Article 17 is not a coherent whole; it involves different legal discourses. But it does represent a starting point for a significant learning process that occurred during the postcolonial period. The most important lesson was the discoursive break from untouchability and civil offence to the concepts of atrocity and criminal law. This conceptual change can be traced to the drafting committees. Conceptually, this process can be further unpacked by using Foucault's concept of discourse. This notorious term is considered 'frustratingly unclear', but the advantage of Foucault's concept of discourse is that it can be used to delineate possible forms of understanding which are analytically distinct from social practices.[91] Similarly, the different domains at play in Article 17, such as constitutional principles and civil and criminal laws, represent domains of understanding regulated by concepts, their interconnections and legal meanings. In his *The Archaeology of Knowledge*, Foucault also highlights how certain understandings of the world are produced because a powerful concept or the constellation of certain concepts brings one object rather than another object into mind. The ruling 'discursive formation' determines the objects that become visible.[92] Likewise, the concept of untouchability served a particular discourse.

At the time of independence, the concept of untouchability gained meaning in relation to temple entry, which therefore became the main way of addressing caste-based exclusion. While a temple is a religious site, the idea of temple entry appeared to gain meaning as part of a civil rights struggle, and this was sustained by the nationalist movement. But the old concept of civil rights served to sustain the given discourse, which is often inclusionary holism and the inclination to focus on a religious site. Additionally, the concept of untouchability misrepresents the understanding of law. Civil rights is a summarizing concept that stands for equal recognition and access to public space. As such, it could support the idea that temple entry is a civil rights struggle. Article 17 was followed up with attempts to make untouchability practices punishable under the Untouchability (Offences) Act, 1955, and the Protection of Civil Rights Act, 1976, but this development seemed to combine two different branches of law. It was only by moving away from the concept of untouchability to atrocity that one could more clearly break away from civil wrongs or civil offences and move to criminal law. The discoursive formation centred around untouchability tended to individualize exclusion and undermine the development of criminal law to address atrocities. On the one hand, the ongoing deliberations after independence enabled an unpacking of the several possible relevant discourses and the creation of a more comprehensive legislation under criminal law. On the other hand, the lesson learnt from law was that the framework of untouchability and civil wrongs was inadequate to address caste-based exclusion in a comprehensive legal manner that would include protection for victims and punishments of perpetrators. Many Dalits do not plan to enter temples because they follow other traditions. Some have demanded temple access, and some still feel humiliated for being barred from participation in religious festivals. But violence is a topic that requires a different legal approach.

The main lesson learnt about the relation between Dalits and the law is that the Dalit question is concerned with casteism as an ideology and with recurring violence, which constitute a persistent social and political practice outside the domain of law. Here, one needs to step outside the Foucauldian analytics and to focus on oppression and how caste is constituted. Ambedkar's claim that the idea of removing untouchability was consistent with the belief in caste is noteworthy. He argues that 'religious minded Hindus' would be opposed to carrying out social reforms and removing untouchability, whereas a 'politically-minded Hindu' would consider the idea useful as it created a democratic image but did not alienate caste Hindus.[93]

Recall that Ambedkar considered the belief in caste to be decisive for the constitution of a society made up of different castes. While underlining the idea that social reforms appear impossible if Hindus consider Hindu legal texts to be holy scriptures, Ambedkar offers several sociological observations to explain how untouchability is embedded in the Hindu social order. A key sociological concept, which combines sociological and ontological meanings, is graded inequality. Ambedkar states that 'untouchability cannot disappear' because the principle of graded inequality is embedded in the Hindu social order.[94] This concept refers to a system characterized by the grading of its members, and no one is in a completely underprivileged class except the untouchables. The privileges are enjoyed by those who are graded. This is a system of rank in which recognition is secured by always being able to look down on the untouchables as 'no-bodies' and, in doing so, being 'somebody'.[95] From this perspective, there is no scope for equal recognition of the untouchables because caste is sacred, eternal and integral to the Hindu social order.[96]

Ambedkar was engaged in temple entry movements in the 1920s, for example, at the Kala Ram temple at Nasik from 1930 to 1935.[97] His campaign could no doubt be characterized as a civil rights struggle for non-discrimination, but he also ended up rejecting the Hindu religion by converting to Buddhism. Gandhi approached social reform through the Hindu religion. He was ambivalent about eliminating untouchability and tried, among other things, to appease orthodox Hindus by allowing them to ritually purify temples. Ambedkar felt that Gandhi's idea of harmonizing differences was impossible in a religious system that reproduced a belief in caste.

During the postcolonial period, the trend of caste-based violence and organized atrocities gained more prominence. There were still significant and ongoing cases in which Dalits had been prevented from visiting temples. These include the long-term dispute about whether Dalits could pull the temple car during the Kandadevi temple festival in southern Tamil Nadu, which has been discussed many times – by Gandhi in 1934 and by members of the Madurai Bench of the Madras High Court in 2014.[98] Disputes about temple entry are real struggles with exclusion from public space. But this chapter has pointed out how the all-India approach to atrocities required stepping outside the concept of untouchability and associated legal provisions if it was to provide adequate legal protections from caste-based violence.

Ambedkar's account of an ontological difference and a desire to keep the untouchables at bay offers an explanation of the persistence of social exclusion. But the numerous massacres that have occurred, from the massacre at Kilvenmani to the one that took place at Tsundur, provide separate insights into the situation of Dalits in postcolonial development. The main lesson that has been learnt from the numerous brutal massacres is that they often occur because of a desire to 'teach Dalits a lesson'. This observation is a common-sense one. Among the many activists and observers that I have interviewed during my fieldwork, this widespread insight appears to be such a basic assumption that one may refer to it as an immediate and first step to explaining the Dalit situation in India today. This common-sense explanation of the Dalit situation can be characterized as a mechanism of oppression in which demands, resistance or upward mobility may result in backlashes.[99] This mechanism of oppression is relevant in virtually all massacres. The belief in caste, then, becomes a central logic when caste-based violence occurs. It is to such logic that the next two chapters are devoted.

Notes

1. *Times of India*, 'Right of Entry to Poona Parvati Temple', 17 October 1929, accessed 20 September 2018, https://search.proquest.com/docview/613812370?accountid=9735; *Times of India*, 'Untouchability and Temple Entry: Important Movement', 18 November 1932, accessed 20 September 2018, https://search.proquest.com/docview/324543375?accountid=9735.
2. Dennis Dalton, 'The Gandhian View of Caste, and Caste after Gandhi', in *India and Ceylon: Unity and Diversity*, ed. Philip Mason (London: Oxford University Press, 1967), 161; Judith M. Brown, ed., *Mahatma Gandhi: The Essential Writings* (Oxford: Oxford University Press, 2008), 226; see also M. N. Srinivas, 'A Note on Sanskritization and Westernization', *The Far Eastern Quarterly* 15, no. 4 (1956): 481, doi:10.2307/2941919.
3. Nicholas B. Dirks, *Castes of Mind: Colonialism and the Making of Modern India* (Princeton, NJ: Princeton University Press, 2001).
4. Constituent Assembly of India, 'Constituent Assembly Debates: Volume III, 28th April to 2nd May 1947', in *Constituent Assembly Debates: Official Report*, vol 3, 6 vols. (New Delhi: Lok Sabha Secretariat, 1946–1950), 403.
5. Ibid., 434.
6. Bhimrao Ramji Ambedkar, 'Untouchables or the Children of India's Ghetto', in *Dr. Babasaheb Ambedkar Writings and Speeches: Unpublished Writings*, ed. Vasant Moon, vol. 5 (Bombay: Education Department, Government of Maharashtra, 1989), 100.

7. Marc Galanter, *Competing Equalities: Law and the Backward Classes in India* (Berkeley, CA: University of California Press, 1984), 3.
8. Dalton, 'The Gandhian View of Caste, and Caste after Gandhi', 167.
9. Brown, *Mahatma Gandhi*, 218.
10. Robin Jeffrey, 'Temple-Entry Movement in Travancore, 1860–1940', *Social Scientist* 4, no. 8 (1976): 14, doi:10.2307/3516377.
11. Brown, *Mahatma Gandhi*, 226.
12. The *sanatanis* adhered to ideas of eternal religion or law (*sanatana dharma*). They represented an orthodox Hindu reform movement with a strict interest in maintaining the caste order and were reluctant to incorporating lower castes among the twice-born. See Christophe Jaffrelot, *Religion, Caste and Politics in India* (London: Hurst, 2011), 95; C. J. Fuller, *The Camphor Flame: Popular Hinduism and Society in India* (Princeton, NJ: Princeton University Press, 1992), 10.
13. Department of Social Welfare, *Report of the Committee on Untouchability, Economic and Educational Development of the Scheduled Castes and Connected Documents*, L2 Dept of SW 69-2) (New Delhi: Department of Social Welfare, Government of India, 1969), 3; Oliver Mendelsohn and Marika Vicziany, *The Untouchables: Subordination, Poverty and the State in Modern India* (Cambridge: Cambridge University Press, 1998) 106–7.
14. Mysore Narasimhachar Srinivas, 'Caste in Modern India', *The Journal of Asian Studies* 16, no. 4 (1957): 531; Srinivas, 'A Note on Sanskritization and Westernization'.
15. Bhimrao Ramji Ambedkar, 'What Congress and Gandhi Have Done to the Untouchables: Mr. Gandhi and the Emancipation of the Untouchables', in *Dr. Babasaheb Ambedkar Writings and Speeches*, ed. Vasant Moon, vol. 9 (Bombay: Education Department, Government of Maharashtra, 1991), 264.
16. Ibid.
17. Marc Galanter, 'Temple-Entry and the Untouchability (Offences) Act, 1955', *Journal of the Indian Law Institute* 6 (1964): 185, accessed 6 February 2016,http://marcgalanter.net/Documents/templeentryandtheuntouchabilityact.pdf.
18. Dalton, 'The Gandhian View of Caste, and Caste after Gandhi', 168.
19. Brown, *Mahatma Gandhi*, 216.
20. Ibid., 226.
21. Ibid.
22. Ambedkar, 'Untouchables or the Children of India's Ghetto', 347.
23. Nathaniel Roberts, *To be Cared for: The Power of Conversion and Foreignness of Belonging in an Indian Slum*. The Anthropology of Christianity, vol. 20 (Oakland, CA: University of California Press, 2016), 134.
24. Brown, *Mahatma Gandhi*, 227. Ambedkar translates this designation as 'Children of God', which he felt was condescending. Bhimrao Ramji Ambedkar, 'Political', in *Dr. Babasaheb Ambedkar Writings and Speeches: Unpublished Writings*, ed. Vasant Moon, vol. 5 (Bombay: Education Department, Government of Maharashtra, 1989), 364.

25. Brown, *Mahatma Gandhi*, 215.
26. Ibid., 216.
27. Bhimrao Ramji Ambedkar, 'Annihilation of Caste', in *Dr. Babasaheb Ambedkar Writings and Speeches*, ed. Vasant Moon, vol. 1 (Bombay: Education Department, Government of Maharashtra, 1989), 83–4.
28. Christophe Jaffrelot, 'The Impact of Affirmative Action in India: More Political than Socioeconomic', *India Review* 5, no. 2 (2006): 188.
29. Ambedkar, 'Annihilation of Caste', 92.
30. Ibid., 93.
31. Brown, *Mahatma Gandhi*, 218.
32. Ambedkar, 'Untouchables or the Children of India's Ghetto', 100–2.
33. Jeffrey, 'Temple-Entry Movement in Travancore, 1860–1940', 13.
34. It could be understood as a term that can be used to back up civil liberties and legislation against a government's violations of people's freedoms and individual lives, such as in liberal constitutions in the USA or Europe, or as expressed in the 'Universal Declaration of Human Rights', as opposed to social and political rights. This is not the meaning that I consider relevant for discussing civil rights in this context.
35. Charles R. Epp, *The Rights Revolution: Lawyers, Activists, and Supreme Courts in Comparative Perspective* (Chicago: University of Chicago Press, 1998), 27.
36. Lloyd I. Rudolph and Susanne Hoeber Rudolph, *Postmodern Gandhi and Other Essays: Gandhi in the World and at Home*, rev. edn (Chicago and London: University of Chicago Press, 2006), 33.
37. A. T. H. Smith, ed., *Glanville Williams: Learning the Law*, 15th ed. (London: Sweet & Maxwell, 2013).
38. Ambedkar, 'Political', 265.
39. Anupama Rao, *The Caste Question: Dalits and the Politics of Modern India* (Berkeley, LA: University of California Press, 2009), 167.
40. Smith, *Glanville Williams*.
41. For a discussion on this doctrine, see Sudhir Krishnaswamy, *Democracy and Constitutionalism in India: A Study of the Basic Structure Doctrine* (New Delhi: Oxford University Press, 2009).
42. Ministry of Law and Justice, Protection of Civil Rights Act, 1955, Act No. 22 of 1955 (Government of India, 8 May 1955), accessed 1 December 2016, http://lawmin.nic.in/ld/P-ACT/1955/A1955-22.pdf.
43. Department of Social Welfare, *Report of the Committee on Untouchability*, 3–5.
44. Ibid., 6.
45. *Devarajiah vs B. Padmanna* (Karnataka High Court, 10 September 1957), accessed 26 Feburary 2016, http://indiankanoon.org/doc/337685/.
46. Department of Social Welfare, *Report of the Committee on Untouchability*, 7.
47. Smith, *Glanville Williams*.
48. Ministry of Law and Justice, Rights Act Protection of Civil, 1955.
49. Upendra Baxi, 'Historic New Law: Protecting SC/ST Rights', *Times of India*, 15 September 1989.

50. Emphasized by P. S. Krishnan, in an interview with the author, Hyderabad, 5 March 2008.
51. K. S. Subramanian, *Political Violence and the Police in India* (New Delhi: Sage Publications, 2007), 19.
52. P. S. Krishnan, in an interview with the author, 5 March 2008; ibid., New Delhi, May 2009. See also P. S. Krishnan, 'Walls in Minds', *Frontline* 26, no. 24 (2009), accessed 1 February 2018, http://www.frontline.in/static/html/fl2624/stories/20091204262402500.htm.
53. Such instances have continued after the PoA Act. A case of this kind occurred on 22 May 2002 in Thinniyam village in Tiruchi district, Tamil Nadu, where two Dalit men were forced to feed each other human excreta. According to the journalist Viswanathan, the incident happened after the men had supported another member of the Dalit community who demanded money back after the local panchayat leader and her husband failed to deliver the favour he had paid them to do; see S. Viswanathan, *Dalits in Dravidian Land: Frontline Reports on Anti-Dalit Violence in Tamil Nadu (1995–2004)* (Pondicherry: Navayana, 2005), 241–2.
54. Bojja Tharakam, in an interview with the author, Hyderabad, March 2008.
55. P. S. Narayana, *Commentary on the Scheduled Castes and the Scheduled Tribes (Prevention of Atrocities) Act, 1989 & Rules, 1995 and Protection of Civil Rights Act, 1955 & Rules, 1977*, 5th edn (Hyderabad: Gogia Law Agency, 2006), 19.
56. P. S. Krishnan, in an interview with the author, 5 March 2008.
57. For this reason, the special public prosecutor of the Tsundur court argued in court that while the accused should be convicted in accordance with the PoA Act, 1989, the sentence should be prescribed in accordance with the Indian Penal Code. The prosecutor wanted to argue for the death penalty in making this distinction between conviction and sentence. B. Chandrasekar, a lawyer from Guntur, in an interview with the author, Warangal, January 2009.
58. *Dr. Subhash Kashinath Mahajan versus the State of Maharashtra and Anr.* (New Delhi: Supreme Court of India, 20 March 2018), 88, accessed 4 April 2018, http://supremecourtofindia.nic.in/supremecourt/2017/22086/22086_2017_Judgement_20-Mar-2018.pdf.
59. Ibid., 87.
60. *Scroll.in*, 'Bharat Bandh: Nine Killed, Hundreds Detained as Protests Turn Violent in Several States', 2 April 2018, accessed 2 November 2018, https://scroll.in/latest/874124/bharat-bandh-dalit-protestors-block-trains-in-bihar-odisha-against-scs-order-on-sc-st-act.
61. The Scheduled Castes and the Scheduled Tribes (Prevention of Atrocities) Amendment Bill, 2018, Government of India (August 2), accessed 10 July 2019, http://www.prsindia.org/uploads/media/Prevention%20of%20Atrocities/Scheduled%20Castes%20and%20the%20Scheduled%20Tribes%20(Prevention%20of%20Atrocities)%20Amendment%20Bill,%202018.pdf; *Times of India*, 'Parliament Passes Bill to Restore Original SC_ST Atrocity Law', 9 August 2018, accessed 29 October 2018, https://timesofindia.indiatimes.com/india/parliament-okays-bill-to-restore-original-sc/st-atrocity-law/articleshow/65340768.cms.

62. For a comprehensive mapping of different forms of untouchability conducted by an NGO, see Navsarjan Trust and Robert F. Kennedy Center for Justice & Human Rights, *Understanding Untouchability: A Comprehensive Study of Practices and Conditions in 1589 Villages* (2010).
63. For an ethnographic account of caste in the city, see Roberts, *To Be Cared for*, 54ff.
64. Debashis Chakraborty, D. Shyam Babu and Manashi Chakravorty, 'Atrocities on Dalits: What the District Level Data Say on State-Society Complicity', *Economic and Political Weekly* 41, no. 24 (2006): 2478–81.
65. This history of atrocities has become part of common knowledge in the Dalit movement, such as among my informants in Andhra Pradesh and Tamil Nadu; they reflected on how an atrocity could be a part of a larger trend. For background, see for example, Paul R. Brass, *The Politics of India since Independence*, 2nd edn (Cambridge: Cambridge University Press, 1994), 326; P. S. Krishnan, 'Untouchability and Atrocities', in *The Emerging Dalit Identity: The Re-assertion of the Subalterns*, ed. Walter Fernandes (New Delhi: Indian Social Institute, 1996); Anand Teltumbde, *The Persistence of Caste: The Khairlanji Murders and India's Hidden Apartheid* (New Delhi: Navayana Publishing, 2010).
66. Viswanathan, *Dalits in Dravidian Land*, 29; Teltumbde, *The Persistence of Caste*, 60.
67. Krishnan, 'Untouchability and Atrocities', 133.
68. Teltumbde, *The Persistence of Caste*, 60.
69. Surinder S. Jodhka and Murli Dhar, 'Cow, Caste and Communal Politics: Dalit Killings in Jhajjar', *Economic and Political Weekly* 38, no. 3 (2003).
70. P. M. Jayshree et al., eds., *Case Papers: Summary & Jury's Interim Observations and Recommendations,* Dalit Human Rights Violations: Atrocities against Dalits in India, vol. 1 (Ahmedabad and Madurai: National Campaign on Dalit Human Rights, 2000).
71. Jeffrey, 'Temple-Entry Movement in Travancore, 1860–1940', 5.
72. Mysore Narasimhachar Srinivas, *Social Change in Modern India* (New Delhi: Orient Longman, 1995).
73. Yamada Keiko, 'Politics and Representation of Caste Identity in Regional Historiography', *Indian Economic & Social History Review* 45, no. 3 (2008), doi:10.1177/001946460804500302.
74. Uma Ramaswamy, 'The Belief System of the Non-brahmin Movement in India: The Andhra Case', *Asian Survey* 18, no. 3 (1978): 299, doi:10.2307/2643221.
75. Ibid.; Keiko, 'Politics and Representation of Caste Identity in Regional Historiography', 363.
76. Keiko, 'Politics and Representation of Caste Identity in Regional Historiography', 358–59. Sacred threads (often red threads) are worn by men over the left shoulder and across the upper body as a sign to indicate that the person belongs to the twice-born castes. Superior status can be demonstrated by men when the sacred thread is displayed and visible on their upper body.
77. Srinivas, 'Caste in Modern India', 531.

78. Ambedkar, 'Untouchables or the Children of India's Ghetto', 102.
79. Ramaswamy, 'The Belief System of the Non-brahmin Movement in India', 297. The Dalit leader and former member of the non-Brahmin movement in Andhra Pradesh, Katti Padma Rao, made the same point in an interview with the author, Hyderabad, February 2008.
80. K. Srinivasulu, 'Caste, Class and Social Articulation in Andhra Pradesh: Mapping Differential Regional Trajectories', Working Paper 179, Overseas Development Institute, London, 2002, accessed 10 July 2019, https://www.odi.org/sites/odi.org.uk/files/odi-assets/publications-opinion-files/2692.pdf; see also Brass, *The Politics of India Since Independence*, 325–8; Teltumbde, *The Persistence of Caste*, 56.
81. Teltumbde, *The Persistence of Caste*, 100.
82. Ibid., 31.
83. Ambedkar, 'Untouchables or the Children of India's Ghetto', 102.
84. P. S. Krishnan, 'Atrocities against Dalits: Retrospect and Prospect', *Combat Law: The Human Rights & Law Bimonthly* 8, nos. 5–6 (2009): 10, accessed 10 July 2019,https://www.yumpu.com/en/document/view/38026162/pdf-437mb-combat-law/2.
85. Baxi, 'Historic New Law'.
86. *Hindu*, 'Gaddar for SC/ST Act in 9th Schedule', 15 May 2018, accessed 16 May 2018, http://www.thehindu.com/todays-paper/tp-national/tp-andhrapradesh/gaddar-for-scst-act-in-9th-schedule/article23888169.ece; *Hans India*, 'MRPS Leaders to Participate in Meet on SC/ST Act in New Delhi', 6 August 2018, accessed 31 October 2018, http://www.thehansindia.com/posts/index/Telangana/2018-08-06/MRPS-leaders-to-participate-in-meet-on-SCST-Act-in-New-Delhi/403770; *Hans India*, 'MRPS Slams BJP for Trying Dilute SC, ST Act', 1 June 2018, accessed 14 September 2018, http://www.thehansindia.com/posts/index/Khammam-Tab/2018-06-01/MRPS-slams-BJP-for-trying-dilute-SC-ST-Act/385744.
87. Manu, *The Laws of Manu: With an Introduction and Notes*, trans. Wendy Doniger and Brian K. Smith (New Delhi: Penguin Books India, 1991), 68.
88. *Indian Young Lawyers Association & Ors. vs The State of Kerala & Ors* (New Delhi: Supreme Court of India, 28 September 2018), accessed 30 October 2018,x` https://www.sci.gov.in/supremecourt/2006/18956/18956_2006_Judgement_28-Sep-2018.pdf.
89. Sunil Khilnani, *The Idea of India* (London: Penguin Books, 1998).
90. John R. Searle, 'Social Ontology: Some Basic Principles', *Anthropological Theory* 6, no. 1 (2006), doi:10.1177/1463499606061731.
91. David R. Howarth, *Discourse* (Buckingham: Open University Press, 2000), 48–9.
92. Michel Foucault, *The Archaeology of Knowledge* (London: Routledge, 1989), 49.
93. Ambedkar, 'Untouchables or the Children of India's Ghetto', 100.
94. Ibid., 101.
95. Ibid., 101–2.
96. Ibid., 102.

97. Department of Social Welfare, *Report of the Committee on Untouchability*, 4.
98. *Hindu*, 'Kandadevi Temple Car Festival Mired in Controversy', 2 July 2014, accessed 24 October 2018, https://www.thehindu.com/news/cities/Madurai/kandadevi-temple-car-festival-mired-in-controversy/article6169348.ece.
99. Dag-Erik Berg, 'Structural Mechanism, Law, and the Dalit Question in India', *Asian Journal of Law and Society* 2, no. 1 (2015): 21–33, doi:10.1017/als.2014.14.

3

The Karamchedu Killings and the Struggle to Uncover Untouchability

Three cases of caste-based violence, occurring in coastal Andhra, are central to the postcolonial history of Andhra Dalits. The first case occurred in the village of Kanchikacherla (Krishna district) on 24 February 1968; a boy was tied to a post in the middle of the village, beaten and then burnt alive.[1] Another extremely grave instance took place in Karamchedu village (Prakasam district) on 22 July 1985, resulting in the deaths of six Dalits, while the third, with eight fatalities, was in Tsundur village (Guntur district) on 6 August 1991. These brutal events were all carried out by local dominant castes as comprehensive attacks on Dalits in the most prosperous part of the Telugu-speaking regions, which was Andhra Pradesh state until 2014. While the event in Kanchikacherla was central for the first generation of activists during the postcolonial period in this state, the cases in Karamchedu and Tsundur have shaped the second generation. These events occurred a generation or two earlier to Rohith Vemula's suicide at the University of Hyderabad. The history of the Dalit movement in Andhra Pradesh and Telangana has included many important episodes and many different forms of protests.[2] The history of anti-caste mobilizations in Madras, Bombay and other regions at the beginning of the twentieth century is well known. At that time, there were active Dalit leaders in coastal Andhra as well as in Hyderabad city.[3] There had been a radical reform movement concerned with issues such as gender, dowry and untouchability in coastal Andhra run by members of the regional elite in the nineteenth century. But the identity- and caste-based mobilization among Andhra Dalits gained momentum in the early 1920s. The Dalits' social reform movements emerged at the same time as a strong regional movement in Andhra, which mobilized separation of the Telugu-speaking areas of Madras Presidency.[4] The Dalit movements had a different trajectory and source of inspiration, naming themselves 'Adi-Andhra' in 1917 in Vijayawada city (coastal Andhra) and 'Adi-Hindu' in 1922 in Hyderabad.[5] They named their organizations with the prefix

'Adi' to indicate that they were original inhabitants – indigenous sons of the soil. The Adi-Andhra Mahasabha (great assembly of the natives of Andhra) had counterparts in other regions in colonial India, and these early Dalit movements identified themselves with a wider subaltern critique of the Aryan invasion. Recall that reformers such as Mahatma Phule turned the Hindu narrative about the Aryans being the people of Vedas who arrived on the subcontinent on its head.[6] Phule distinguished between the Aryans, who traced their origins to a Vedic Golden Age with notions of caste, and the non-Aryans, whom he referred to as an indigenous population. This counter-hegemonic discourse was important for the Dravidian movement in south India. The adoption of the term 'Adi' was used to define oppressed groups as the original inhabitants, in opposition to dominant castes who they argued were invaders on the subcontinent.[7] The Adi-Dravida activists of 1917 dismissed any reference to caste, including the idea that they were a fifth category – Panchamas – as such a reference did not make the step outside of caste and signify their identity as sons of the soil.[8] The movement was articulate and yet complex. In fact, there are subsequent examples of how members of the Adi-Andhra movement in 1932 endorsed a Gandhian assimilation programme rather than Ambedkar's idea of a separate electorate.[9] At any rate, the adoption of terms such as Adi-Andhra and Adi-Hindu represented different regional identities among Dalits. The Adi-Andhra was a vibrant movement in the 1920s, but the term today designates just one group in the census.

The term 'Andhra' is not synonymous with the Telugu language, and the regional differences in Telugu-speaking areas made Andhra an unstable designation for the movement's state. The three regions, Telangana, Rayalaseema and coastal Andhra, were united in one Telugu-speaking state in 1956.[10] But the term 'Andhra' mainly referred to coastal Andhra. This region also acquired a competitive advantage after the state of Andhra Pradesh was established in 1956, as powerful groups in this region gained cultural and economic power in the state.[11] While there were several starting points for the movement demanding a separate Telangana state, it gathered momentum after 2008, and the Telugu-speaking state Andhra Pradesh was divided into two new states, Telangana and Andhra Pradesh, in 2014. The goal in this chapter is to explain how this region offers significant insights into the sociology of caste, modernity and Dalit studies than has been traditionally reflected in the scholarship. Andhra now referred to the current state of Andhra Pradesh, formerly known as coastal Andhra and Rayalaseema. But the insights concerning caste and class dynamics in this chapter should be viewed as lessons from the Telugu-speaking areas as a whole.

In this chapter, I reintroduce the Karamchedu massacre as a central event that in crucial ways formed the basis for the modern Dalit movement in the old state of Andhra Pradesh. As the political scientist Gudavarthy says this event became decisive for an 'independent dalit movement' in modern Andhra Pradesh.[12] In fact, as one of the leaders at that time, Bojja Tharakam, explained, 'Karamchedu became more than just a village' – 'Karamchedu became a phrase', which 'also non-Dalits know'.[13] The event displayed the brutality of caste and foregrounded a social dimension that movements in the state were forced to address. The movement called the 'Dalit Mahasabha' was formed after the attack in a situation in which the activists broke away from the dominating class discourse, dominant among the existing movements in the state to address untouchability and caste.

I argue that the Karamchedu massacre shows how the Dalit project could be understood as an emancipatory one that broke away from an all-encompassing class-based approach to oppression. The killings in Karamchedu do not just show the mechanism of oppression in the Dalit situation, where upward mobility and egalitarian behaviour provoked a backlash. In fact, one of the key lessons learnt from Karamchedu was the way in which political power had emboldened the landowning peasant caste to carry out the attack.

The dominant caste in Karamchedu village was the Kamma caste which comprised 6,000 people in a population of 13,600 villagers. This included 2,000 Scheduled Castes (Dalits), among whom 1,100 were Madigas and 900 were Malas.[14] Politically, the Kammas were powerful and closely connected to the ruling Telugu Desam Party (TDP).[15] Overall, the Karamchedu killings could be understood as an example of how a group of power-holders used their dominance to exercise force and re-embed caste in the corporate agrarian development. This social and political order formed the background to the new Dalit movement.

This chapter outlines the history of the Dalit Mahasabha from its beginnings as a coherent front after Karamchedu in 1985 until its fragmentation at the time of the Tsundur event in 1991. A central goal of this chapter is to highlight what can be referred to as the ontological and historical significance that this event has had for the Dalit movement in the state. The two categories of caste and class are at the very centre of this history.

The history of the Dalit movement in Andhra Pradesh includes important lessons concerning the relation between caste and class. These lessons are relevant for Dalit studies in general. According to Kancha Ilaiah (whose name is now Kancha Ilaiah Shepard), Andhra Pradesh is 'considered a blind spot for Dalit struggles and a bright spot for class struggles, as this has been the place where the historic Telangana armed struggle and subsequently Naxalite revolt took place'.[16] The literature on Dalits has traditionally been dominated by the examination of states such as Maharashtra, Tamil Nadu and Uttar Pradesh. The effect of studying these paradigmatic cases is that caste is foregrounded largely at the expense of class. In my view, the history of the Dalit movement in Andhra Pradesh could be usefully compared to the discoursive situation in Tamil Nadu and Kerala. To put it in broad terms, while Tamil Nadu is a state where caste is consistently articulated in public discourse at the expense of class, the situation in Kerala is characterized by a strong egalitarian discourse that excludes references to caste identities.[17]

The Karamchedu massacre provides insights into the relation between the analysis of caste and the analysis of class; the event generated discussions and insights that resulted in a discoursive conflict in which Dalit activists criticized how the all-encompassing class discourse of the Maoist movement had made casteism invisible. As Ratnam notes, the Naxalites' dominant position in the 1970s had made it difficult for a Dalit assertion, such as the vibrant Dalit Panther movement in Maharashtra, to gain ground in Andhra Pradesh.[18] The Maoist movement accommodated many individuals from Dalit castes, yet Karamchedu represents 'a turning point in the growth of the Dalit movement'.[19] The Bangalore-based magazine *Dalit Voice* reported that Karamchedu produced 'young militants' who had 'no patience to wait' nor were they 'prepared to look up to the upper castes for solutions'.[20] The Dalit movement in Andhra Pradesh gained support from Dalit activists outside the state as well.

In what follows, I first introduce Karamchedu, the massacre and its historical significance. Next, I explain the broader context in which this event occurred and how caste dominance was integral to the oppression of Dalits in the agrarian structure. This provides a background for discussing how the Dalit movement distinguished itself from the communists, the Maoists and the radical left movement in its approach to oppression. In this context, Ambedkar became the emancipatory symbol for the Dalit movement.[21] Finally, I emphasize how the difference between the Dalit and Maoist movements could clearly be seen in their different approaches to law.

The Karamchedu Incident: An Eye-Opener

The massacre in Karamchedu village happened on 17 July 1985, the day after a Madiga boy had rebuked a Kamma boy for washing his buffalo in a tank where Dalits drew water from.[22] The Madiga boy was disabled, but his rebuke so angered the Kamma boy that he beat the Madiga boy with his cattle whip. A Madiga woman who was also present at the water tank intervened. When the Kamma boy hit her as well, she struck back using her water bucket. An elderly Dalit tried to calm the situation down, and the Kamma boy left but not before issuing a warning. He later brought friends and relatives to interrogate the Madiga woman back at the Madiga *wada* (settlement).

The Dalits might have anticipated upper-caste retaliation after this episode, but it was hardly expected that hundreds of Kammas would mobilize and launch a major attack early next morning. The residents of the Madiga *wada*, who did not have a reputation for being assertive, were attacked. Even pregnant women and mothers with small children were beaten. The entire colony was damaged. People were tortured and chased, houses were set on fire and Dalits fled the village in large numbers. They arrived in the neighbouring town of Chirala, some 8 kilometres away, where many of them were hospitalized. Six Madigas died in the attack.

The news of the Karamchedu massacre mobilized people throughout the state. Activists in Chirala, such as Katti Padma Rao, were present and ensured that the victims reached the town, and activists across the entire state followed up and mobilized to protest against the attack. Indeed, the brutal incident was the starting point for a greater consciousness of the relevance of caste among Dalits, non-Dalits and even a strong revolutionary movement like the Naxalites. Karamchedu pushed the momentum for a whole generation of activists and largely shaped the course of movements on Dalit issues in the state. As mentioned earlier, the Dalit Mahasabha was formed as an immediate response to the Karamchedu massacre.

There were significant reactions far beyond the fold of Dalits as well. The massacre destroyed the myth among committed social activists that caste was 'a thing of the past'.[23] In an interview before his untimely death, K. Balagopal emphasized the historical significance of Karamchedu for his generation of activists by characterizing it as the event that 'opened our eyes' to the caste question. In other words, Karamchedu was the brutal massacre that changed the established idea among movements that oppression was a function of feudalism and class. It put caste at the centre of a new and strong direction for activism and debates. The event made caste-based oppression visible, creating shock and reactions among the general population.

The killings in Karamchedu gained political significance among the leading parties in the state. The TDP was in power at the time. The Congress party criticized them for the incident, while representatives of the TDP struck back by criticizing the shortcomings that had occurred under Congress rule.[24] Political power constitutes a decisive dimension in the history of the massacre because of the ways in which the event relates to the TDP. The landlords in Karamchedu had connections to the political party at the time. The TDP had been created in March 1982 by the famous movie actor N. T. Rama Rao (known as NTR), who came to power in January 1983. The TDP replaced a long period of Congress rule at a time when the latter was in crisis, weakened by factionalism and allegations of corruption and therefore lacking in legitimacy.[25] Kamma farmers turned to the TDP as the new political alternative.[26] Many 'backward castes' had been politically alienated at that time given Indira Gandhi's strategy of creating alliances between upper castes and Dalits.[27] Fundamentally, the TDP seized power at a critical moment through populist appeals, by championing Telugu identity and by reaching out to new groups.[28]

The situation in Karamchedu village should be viewed in the context of this political development. It was reported that the Kamma castes in the village were emboldened by connections to powerful people.[29] The daughter of the new chief minister of Andhra Pradesh had married a man from Karamchedu, the son of a wealthy landowner.[30] It was a central allegation after the massacre that some of N. T. Rama Rao's in-laws in Karamchedu were actively involved in the attack against the Madigas on 17 July 1985.[31]

In short, the rise of the TDP and the direct connections that the Kamma landlords had with political honchos emboldened them to act, abusing their tenants and intensifying the caste-based violence. While the Kamma landlords were economically and politically powerful, their dominance did not primarily derive from their ritual status. But the ritual dimension mattered in relation to the Dalits. In this part of Andhra, Malas and Madigas are comparatively more well-educated and assertive than other oppressed Dalit and tribal groups in the coastal region.[32] The dominant castes questioned the new habits and confidence of Dalits – and attacked them. The Karamchedu and Tsundur massacres are thus two incidents that reveal the ways in which the local dominant castes violently resented the social development and modern lifestyle of Dalits. During the attack on 17 July, the Kamma landlords had abused the victims by shouting, 'Madiga dogs! Have you learnt your lesson well for having opposed the Kammas?'[33]

Agriculture, Caste and Development in Coastal Andhra

The regional context is significant for understanding the events in Karamchedu. As a state created along linguistic lines in 1956, Andhra Pradesh consisted of three main regions: Rayalaseema in the south, coastal Andhra in the east and Telangana in the west. Hyderabad city, the capital of the state, is part of Telangana. There was a relentless fight for a separate Telugu state even before India's independence. It was because of this linguistic identification that Andhra Pradesh, in 1956, became the first state in postcolonial India to be established based on language.[34] The large south Indian state was nonetheless inherently unstable as the regions differ substantially, and their differences explain later political developments. Rayalaseema in the south is, overall, a dry area with a predominantly agrarian economy where the Reddys form a landowning caste. Telangana, the least-developed region of the state, was part of the Nizam's dominion that was ruled from Hyderabad city. While the other parts of Andhra belonged to the Madras Presidency, the Nizam maintained relative autonomy during the British colonial period. Coastal Andhra is the most prosperous region. It is argued that there was already suspicion in areas such as Telangana by 1956 that 'Andhra folks' would overrun the region because of their entrepreneurial classes and educational advantage.[35]

In addition to the development of modern educational institutions during colonial times, the coastal belt emerged as a strong modern economy because of its fertile land and irrigation, which contributed to the region's very productive agricultural businesses. The result of the agricultural developments since the late nineteenth and early twentieth centuries was a type of farmer-capitalism in the region. Agricultural production has continued to be the main economic basis of its development, although later there were investments in new industries such as cement and steel.[36]

The feudal legacy has been challenged across the Telugu-speaking areas in the form of several struggles against oppression in the agrarian mode of production. The peasant rebellions against feudal oppression in Telangana and the princely state of Hyderabad that took place since before India's independence are well known, but there were also notable Maoist movements in coastal Andhra. For example, a movement was started in the tribal area of Srikakulam in the late 1960s. Here, the new legislation that had been created after independence to protect Adivasis and their land had been undermined by more powerful economic interests in the area. While representing a beginning for the Naxalite movement in Andhra Pradesh, the rebellion that occurred in Srikakulam district was in fact more violent and lasted longer than the initial revolt in Naxalbari, West Bengal.[37] But the coastal region was also a stronghold for the non-Brahmin movement and has had a special role in the emergence of the modern Dalit movement. What is decisive here is that the Karamchedu and Tsundur massacres both occurred in prosperous coastal Andhra.

Geographically, Karamchedu and Tsundur are situated in two neighbouring districts in Andhra. The situation in Karamchedu reflects the general phenomenon in coastal Andhra, where Kammas, who were Shudras, are often the dominant caste. But the Kammas have moved from relying mostly on agriculture to becoming a specific business class through the development of a strong corporate culture and associational loyalties.[38] In Tsundur, the Reddys constitute the dominant caste. Like the Kammas, the Reddys are also Shudras historically who have gained a dominating position in terms of economic, social and political power in the state. During the colonial period, the Reddys participated in non-Brahmin movements and demanded Kshatriya status,[39] and they represent 'upper' or 'forward' castes today.

What characterized Karamchedu village was its high degree of capital-intensive production. It was a very prosperous village, primarily because of its tobacco cultivation and export. It was precisely this capitalist development that became evident after the Karamchedu massacre.[40] It could be said that the massacre indicates that caste may not only be an intense experience but may also be intensified in situations in which social norms are changing. Here, I follow up on what Katti Padma Rao, one of the main leaders of the Dalits at the time of the events in

Karamchedu, explained to me.[41] In his view, the struggle against Brahmin power in Andhra Pradesh has reinforced the significance of caste.[42]

My own way of making sense of the violent casteism is to identify how the mechanism of oppression was at play when political power emboldened members of the dominant castes to use violence against Dalits. The relevance of caste is not simply a case of how caste has become politicized[43] or has been given 'a new lease of life'.[44] It is also relevant to the atrocity that occurred in Laxmipetha in 2012, where the dominant caste Kapu had been emboldened by controlling political power.[45]

During colonialism, Brahmins had occupied a significant role in politics and were a privileged elite. A significant shift in landownership started in the late 1940s when, according to Satyanarayana,[46] Brahmins sold land to non-Brahmin castes such as the Kamma and Kapu. The effect was that a new dominant peasantry, made up of agricultural castes with a strong determination to cultivate their land, emerged in coastal Andhra and Rayalaseema. Moreover, the developments among Kammas were characterized by their strong attachment and commitment to agricultural production.[47] This ethos of production and business was decisive because the rich Kamma peasantry was able to develop a strong position in commercial agriculture, including the growth and export of tobacco (such as in Karamchedu). Their surplus wealth was reinvested in other businesses and used for lending. Indeed, although territorial control has remained crucial to consolidating their power, the Kammas had started a range of businesses from agricultural products to transport and cinemas.[48] From the end of the colonial period, therefore, Kammas, Reddys and Kapus grew to become the nouveau riche peasantry and the dominant caste in Srinivas's sense of the term. Yet Kammas were, overall, underrepresented politically as the Congress was dominated by Reddys.

By the early 1980s, the Kamma caste had gained a significant position in Andhra Pradesh. Ceilings on land possessions introduced in the early 1970s and job reservations for residents from Telangana in Hyderabad had encouraged Kammas to go into business. The Kammas gained significant political power in the early 1980s. The social mobility of these powerful caste is noteworthy. None of the Kammas, Reddys and Kapus were historically similar to Brahmins who could claim ritual superiority in the caste system, and yet their dominance makes them upper castes. The events in Karamchedu and Tsundur also affirm that their claims to ritual superiority were decisive in relation to the Dalits. No doubt they used force to make Dalits comply as loyal labourers.[49] It was reported that Karamchedu landlords would personally turn up in houses to beat labourers who had been absent from work and that labourers in the village would be at risk of being excluded from work for up to nine months if they were absent from work for some reason.

More broadly, the emergence of this powerful social class could be viewed as an example of the possibilities for social mobility in the traditional caste system.

According to Srinivas, it was the 'political fluidity' in the traditional system that allowed entire castes to move up in the social hierarchy. He argued, 'Any caste that achieved political power at the local level could advance a claim to be Kshatriyas''.[50] In the present case, the Kammas already constituted an affluent and politically powerful group at the beginning of the twentieth century. Their political movement included an articulation of a distinct identity as Kshatriyas. As Yamada shows, local Kamma historians were active in providing evidence for Kammas' status as Kshatriya.[51] He argues that these claims were developed in conjunction with the colonial census that counted and categorized people. This movement overlapped with the Andhra movement that started in 1913.[52] Yamada also underlines that it was a central impetus in the Kamma movement to claim that Kammas were Kshatriyas. Although the claim reflects the relevance of the traditional caste system, their position as a dominant social class was mainly based on their economic and political power.

But there is more at stake in the massacre than simply a system of stratification. It also shows that ritual status and ideology of caste add force to the perpetrators' determination to act as if these elements confirm that there is an ontological difference between touchables and untouchables that justifies violence being inflicted on the latter. As such, the violent attack connects with ritual status and is not reducible to stratification alone. The reconfiguration of the social order creates new contingencies. Srinivas argues that education and constitutional rights are likely to 'increase rather than decrease' the level of 'local clashes'.[53] Events such as those in Karamchedu, meanwhile, indicate that the caste-based violence happens during a re-embedding of caste where a sense of graded inequality comprises religion, stratification and a sense of ontological difference in which the 'Untouchables are nobodies'.[54] The Karamchedu massacre occurred because the Madigas 'corrected' the behaviour of the Kammas. Their honour as landowners was challenged, and notions of ritual superiority added force to the desire to 'teach Dalits a lesson'.

Social and political power among dominant Kamma landlords increased at the same time as there was upward mobility among Dalits in the village. Just as the Tsundur Dalits had gained confidence at this time, so had the Dalits in Karamchedu, and they behaved in accordance with a more egalitarian self-conception than was prescribed by their traditionally attributed status as untouchables. This seems to have applied to both Madigas and Malas in the village. However, most Dalits in Karamchedu were Madigas who are traditionally ranked lower than the Malas. D. N. Reddy reported that the Kamma landlords in Karamchedu preferred 'the Madigas, because they are supposed to be more submissive and the Malas more aggressive'.[55] Although there were both assertive and non-assertive Dalits in the village, the Dalits of Karamchedu had by and large started to adopt a more egalitarian mode of behaviour. They did not vacate the front seats on buses or in the cinema when Kammas approached or asked them for the seat. It was explained to me that Kammas in Karamchedu became determined 'to teach the Dalits a lesson', since Dalits did not comply with their sense of superiority.[56]

In short, social transformation involves upward mobility among Dalits, on the one hand, and increased political power among the Kammas landlords, given the rise of the TDP party that was in power in 1985, on the other. The mechanism of oppression was part of caste relations in the village, but it was political power that enabled the dominant castes to violently re-embed caste relations in the village to the point of carrying out an organized attack.

The Formation of the Dalit Mahasabha

The brutality of casteism in the massacre in Karamchedu became visible to a larger audience because the media reported the incident. This added to the information that was disseminated throughout the movement. There had been many atrocities against Dalits just prior to Karamchedu, including killings and the burning of houses in Chittoor district.[57] But the wide reporting in the media after Karamchedu affected the popular response to caste-based oppression.[58]

The attack in Karamchedu become decisive for the emergence of Dalit assertion in Andhra Pradesh. At this crucial moment, Dalit leaders were able to mobilize a movement and define the incident as a moment that was exclusively relevant to the Dalit question. The leaders organized meetings and action and created a strong intellectual backbone for an independent movement. A collective political subjectivity emerged in a situation that was initially characterized by feelings of devastation, anger and bitterness.

The centre of this anti-caste struggle was the camp (*shibiram*), organized in the neighbouring town of Chirala, some 8 to 10 kilometres away from Karamchedu. This camp was organized in Chirala because the Karamchedu Dalits had fled there en masse to seek refuge in a church after they ran away from the attack carried out in their village. The victims had not been protected by the police. Constables in Karamchedu did not intervene in the clashes, and the police in Chirala were beating and arresting panicked Dalit youths who had escaped to the town rather than safeguarding and helping them.[59] The victims were, instead, accompanied by activists, Dalit leaders and a local movement of poor people who supported the victims.

The two central Dalit leaders during this crisis were Tharakam, from Hyderabad, and Katti Padma Rao, from coastal Andhra, and both were experienced and well-educated social activists.[60] As Balagopal explains, 'Karamchedu brought' these two well-known and respected leaders 'into the streets'.[61] They were determined to address the Dalit question; their presence and leadership ensured confidence in this difficult situation. Katti Padma Rao lived in Chirala at the time of the Karamchedu massacre and witnessed the Dalits who had fled the village as they arrived in Chirala. He visited the local hospital where victims received medical help; some victims later died of their injuries.[62] He was thus in the middle of the situation from the very beginning. Local people supported the victims by providing food, but many victims were too shocked to eat. A local movement made up of youngsters living in the Scheduled Caste (SC) hostels, rickshaw pullers, workers from factories and mills and others continued to provide support. Poor people brought money, food and other necessities while encouraging the victims by saying, 'Keep up the fight.'[63]

About 500 victims from Karamchedu stayed in the camp. The significance of the camp and the shelter in Chirala was such that the victims refused the help offered by the government because it was based on a condition that they must return to Karamchedu. The victims did not accept the offer of the district collector, which consisted of 150 meal coupons for the 500 people in the camp. They responded, 'We don't want to move. We feel safe here.'[64] Katti Padma Rao underlines that the victims refused the offer because it was insignificant and that their 'opposition' to this offer was 'one type of fighting'.[65] The victims never returned to Karamchedu, preferring to settle in Chirala.[66]

The camp was thus the centre of Dalit protests and embodied the immediate impact of oppression, untouchability and the struggle for justice.[67] There was a sense of anguish in the camp, but the atmosphere was also characterized by the firm determination not to compromise with any representatives of the state or the established political parties or civic society organizations.[68] Indeed, there was a strict demand that only Dalits should represent and speak on behalf of the Dalits.

Representation became a crucial principle that was used to demarcate and develop a Dalit identity movement. There was a determination to prevent groups other than the Dalits from using the camp as their arena. Only Dalits could mount the dais and speak to the audience during meetings. A Maoist leader, who had come to help, was denied entry because he was a Brahmin.[69] Moreover, this attitude reflected the overall political assertion that traditional terms for lower castes, such as Harijan, Madiga and Mala, were humiliating and should be explicitly disowned. The group insisted on using the term 'Dalit' and identifying itself with Ambedkar.[70] Dalit subjectivity and a sense of collective power gained momentum. The movement became a significant and visible one in Andhra Pradesh. Meetings in Chirala attracted huge crowds. People travelled by train in large numbers from all over Andhra Pradesh to attend the gatherings of activists because they were so determined to participate in the new movement. Activists in neighbouring states mobilized their support as well. In interviews, Tharakam explained how he was in contact with leaders in several Indian states and cities, calling leaders in Punjab,

Delhi, Calcutta, Bihar and Orissa on the phone, while visiting the neighbouring states of Maharashtra, Karnataka and Tamil Nadu to explain about the atrocity and the challenges that confronted the new movement. Moreover, because a leader like Tharakam had collaborated with Ezhilmalai (now Dalit Ezhilmalai) in Tamil Nadu earlier, it was easy to gain immediate support from that state. Activists from Tamil Nadu thus travelled to Andhra to participate in the broad Dalit movement; this included young and emerging activists who were then exposed to the events that had occurred in Karamchedu.[71]

The name of the new movement was Andhra Pradesh Dalit Mahasabha. Tharakam became the founding president and Katti Padma Rao the general secretary.[72] Mahasabha means grand assembly. Several significant aspects of the meeting at which the Dalit Mahasabha was established should be noted. The most significant of these was that the new movement signalled the Dalits as a new collective political subject. This new anti-caste movement, which comprised Dalits and non-Dalits, shifted from having an exclusive focus on class to one that emphasized untouchability and caste as an essential part of oppression which had to be addressed if emancipation and well-being were to be attained. And the All-India Dalits Coordination Committee in Karamchedu, which was an ad hoc organization, spearheaded a state-wide march to the state legislative assembly of Andhra Pradesh in Hyderabad in which about 500,000 people participated.[73]

The Dalit Subject, Emancipation and Caste

The formation of a Dalit movement that developed a new and distinctive project of emancipation deserves to be understood as a phenomenon that extends beyond the collection of individuals. The articulation of a new political subject represented a change, and it is useful to distinguish between ontological and historical data to conceptualize the new visions of emancipation from oppression. The distinction between ontological and historical occurrences is central to the French philosopher Alain Badiou's theory, as when he distinguishes between a historical situation and an event. For him, the term 'situation' signifies the historical facts, whereas an 'event' is a concept that indicates a new possibility and a mode of existence that is repressed and made invisible by the ruling ontology.[74] This is how caste-based domination was made invisible by the ruling understating of the conditions that existed in the agrarian mode of production, and yet caste remained a possible topic in the situation.

Badiou's concept of subject is integral to this theory of emancipation. Viewed as a subject engaged in following up a new goal and possibility, Badiou's concept of political subject should be distinguished from discussions of subjectivity that have been streamlined by Foucault's post-structuralist analytics. For Badiou, the subject involves a commitment to truth and a procedure that evolves from the new possibility (the event). He defines the subject as one who shows 'fidelity' as 'a process of truth' and a right procedure.[75] Here, the connection between an event and a subject is decisive and designates a new possibility; he claims that a subject emerges with the event where a new procedure is used in a firm commitment to truth.[76] An event, therefore, represents a break with the ruling ontology and a possible new mode of existence. Badiou states, 'To belong to the situation is everyone's natural destiny, but to belong to the composition of a subject of truth concerns a particular route, a sustained break.'[77]

Karamchedu could be understood by utilizing Badiou's philosophy, although it should be underscored how the longer trajectory of Dalit activism in the region provided a basis for the new movement to gain momentum. The incident brought a new political subject into view, characterized by a renewed commitment to target the truths of casteism. This was a Dalit subject which had a coherent political configuration rather than a multitude of individuals. What is decisive here is the creation of Dalit subjectivity as a distinctive political movement and a distinct discoursive approach. Historically, there had been vibrant mobilization of Adi-Andhras in the 1920s as well as activism in the initial decades after independence.[78] But the social and political activism in the 1970s and early 1980s was dominated by class discourses, and the new Dalit subject represented a distinct formation which rejected any assimilation with other approaches.

The Dalit movement gained its shape and momentum during the period when the camp was a centre of activism, and it was demanded that the government should provide adequate support and compensation to the victims. Organizationally, the most decisive step occurred at the meeting that took place on 1 September 1985 in Chirala, when it was decided to establish an independent Dalit movement.[79] This was a significant gathering of people. It is estimated that around 300,000 people participated in marches and rallies on that day. The revolutionary poet Gaddar, a Dalit from Telangana associated with the revolutionary movement, inaugurated the meeting by reading out a poem that the writer Kalekuri Prasad had composed for the 'Dalit Tigers' who had 'fought with the Karamchedu landlords'.[80]

Oppression of landless labourers in the agrarian structure had conditioned an enduring movement to address forms of material exploitation in Andhra Pradesh. But since the Maoist movement was in the foreground of the struggle, the new Dalit movement had to confront and break away from the approach of the radical left. Although many Dalits participated in the Maoist movement, their more specific problems of caste and the stigma of untouchability were not represented ideologically by the Maoists nor did Dalits figure prominently among the leaders.

The term 'radical left' basically refers to the Naxalites that emerged in the 1970s. They replaced the traditional left of the Dalits, since the latter had largely ceased to address issues of land redistribution after the abolishment of the *zamindari* system.[81] The Maoists created new aspirations in the struggle against oppression; they organized campaigns, such as 'go to the village', and attracted many Dalits living in villages.[82] They addressed land-related problems and deprivation, issues that were fundamental to Dalits. The traditional left was associated with the old communist party, which had become the 'parliamentary left' because of its participation in the parliamentary system that the Naxalites rejected.

While many Dalits sympathized with the Maoists because of their mobilization among landless labourers, the general problem was how they focused on generic categories of oppression such as class and landownership to the point of relegating caste and untouchability to the margins. Sympathizers included Dalit leaders such as Tharakam and Katti Padma Rao. Tharakam had been central in the Ambedkarite movement in Telangana and practised law at the Andhra Pradesh High Court for the government. But his support for the Maoists was not as clear as Gaddar's, the revolutionary poet, whose cultural performances have become legendary in Andhra Pradesh.[83] Gaddar has been a central figure in the Maoist movement since the 1970s. In short, the Maoist movement included many Dalits and Adivasis and made a wide impact on the ways in which oppression was conceptualized. But the overall trend in the terms they used to refer to caste was to view it as reflections of bourgeoisie ideology, which was harmful for the struggle. This was also how the Maoists approached the events in Karamchedu – they viewed the massacre as a conflict between landless labourers and proprietary classes.

This ideological approach translated into a slow adjustment to the new terminology. Maoists were slow to pick up the term 'Dalit' as a generic label; in fact, their use of the name Harijan on one of their pamphlets was resented by Dalit activists in the new movement.[84] In spite of their sympathy and determination to fight for the Karamchedu Dalits, the Maoist movement did not identify with the Dalit subjectivity that emerged because of their resistance to engaging in an analysis of caste. This does not mean that the Maoists were hesitant to condemn the killings. On the contrary, they condemned the attack and wanted to retaliate by using their own strategy – violence – against the Kamma landowners. Thus, while the Dalit movement filed a legal case, the Maoists rejected the ineffective state apparatus and killed the main person accused of carrying out the atrocities.

The Maoist movement, nonetheless, constitutes an important part of the ideological learning process that took place among activists in the state after the attack in Karamchedu. The massacre provoked internal discussions among the Maoists about how to identify with the caste question.[85] U. Samba Siva Rao, who was a Naxalite at that time, explained to me in an interview (January 2008) that the Karamchedu massacre was taken seriously among the Maoists and that caste was a matter of ongoing debate from 1985 to 1987. There were also discussions about caste among Maoists after this period. But the question was sensitive in the movement, and the result of these internal ideological debates was that members in favour of addressing caste were expelled and labelled as 'anti-revolutionaries'. One of them is Kancha Ilaiah who has since that time emerged as a major intellectual on questions concerning social dominance, caste and religion. Ilaiah found the upper-caste leaders' response to Karamchedu to be 'caste blind'.[86] Activists such as Kancha Ilaiah and Samba Siva Rao are from Shudra castes and today identify with the larger movement known as Dalit-Bahujan. In any case, the debates and flow of people from the Maoist movement to the Dalit movement have contributed to the approach in this region where caste and class analyses have been combined in nuanced and sophisticated ways.

The new Dalit movement comprised a generation of activists who had either a direct or an indirect relation to the class perspective of the revolutionary movement. However, Tharakam and Katti Padma Rao made Ambedkar's strategy of annihilation of caste the fundamental strategy for the new Dalit movement. It was essentially the Ambedkarite perspective that previous members and sympathizers of the Maoist movement embraced in the new anti-caste movement post Karamchedu. For example, after he was expelled from the Naxalite movement in 1987, Samba Siva Rao participated in the group that founded the journal called *Edureeta* (which means 'swimming against the tide') around 1989–90. The group comprised previous Naxalites who had started reading Ambedkar seriously. One of the most prominent members of the group was K. G. Satyamurthy, a Dalit, who had been among the main leaders of the underground revolutionary movement in the 1970s.[87] These intellectuals addressed caste-based issues while drawing on their insights into Marxist class analysis, thereby contributing to 'a new caste-class theory'.[88] The journal has contributed to making caste and class a permanent focus for activists in the state who analyse oppression.

Following the Karamchedu massacre, the new anti-caste movement comprised Dalits and non-Dalits. The Dalit Mahasabha produced a generation of very dynamic activists with practical skills and intellectual seriousness; magazines were published and theoretical debates took place. Tharakam and Katti Padma Rao were at the forefront of the movement, sustaining its momentum through many meetings, rallies and speeches.

Ambedkar: Symbol of Emancipation

It was the introduction of Ambedkar to the Dalit movement, in the form of his life story and writings, that provided the basis for the new ideological development among Dalits in the state. The Dalit leaders were already very familiar with the details of his life and his writings. Tharakam vividly recalled having seen

Ambedkar in Delhi in 1956.[89] In the middle of several approaches and experiences, Ambedkar became the central reference through which the entire Dalit problem could be addressed as the movement broke away from the dominating ideological framework of the left-wing movement.

In an interview, Tharakam explained that he and his colleagues used to quote Ambedkar regularly. They referred to episodes from Ambedkar's life in their analysis of untouchability. In this way, they educated members of the movement and developed its anti-caste approach. Tharakam described how, after almost every incident of caste discrimination, they could refer to a similar situation that had occurred in Ambedkar's life. This includes an episode such as Ambedkar's fight to take water from the Chawdar tank in the Maharashtrian municipality Mahad in the late 1920s.[90] Invoking Ambedkar thus became a way to address issues that the movement faced. He was a symbol that members of the movement could identify with in their struggle, and he summarized the problem of caste-based exclusion and provided a rational vison of emancipation. Ambedkar's life and the terminology he used represented the most vital part of the new and distinct Dalit approach that used a combination of caste and class analyses in the development of their movement and its approach.

In establishing the publication *Nalupu* in 1989, Tharakam continued the work to build the movement among Dalits and oppressed people. *Nalupu* spread practical information regarding legal rights, atrocities against women and Dalits in general. This publication had a distinguished editorial team and became a central ideological medium for Dalit intellectuals in the period it lasted, from 1989 to 1993. It initiated a notable theoretical debate on Ambedkar's theory of annihilation of caste.[91]

Ambedkarite movements existed in Andhra Pradesh prior to Karamchedu, but the massacre contributed to the emergence of Ambedkar as a powerful symbol who provided a rationality, representing a new possibility outside the existing social and political movements.[92] Some of Ambedkar's writings had been translated into Telugu before Karamchedu, such as 'Annihilation of Caste',[93] perhaps the most important of his writings in terms of its influence and conceptualization of caste, which had been translated during the 1970s. The Republican Party of India, started by Ambedkar, made attempts to address the conditions of landless Dalits in the 1960s. In the mid-1970s, Tharakam followed up this struggle through the Ambedkar Youth Association, which he had started in Nizamabad in 1971.[94] This movement aimed to tackle the problems experienced by landless Dalits. The movement did not have a breakthrough at that time, but it erected statues of Ambedkar and celebrated his birthday. A statue of Ambedkar erected in Hyderabad in 1968 was central to these birthday celebrations on 14 April of that year. Although it was present in the region, the Ambedkar movement was not represented in the public discourse as a distinctive subject at this time to the same extent as after Karamchedu.

Law and Delegations to Delhi

It is at the level of strategy and action that the Dalit movement gained some of its distinction and identity. There was also a crucial difference between the Maoist movement and the Dalit Mahasabha at this level. This was most clearly seen when a member of the Naxalite movement killed the man accused of organizing the Karamchedu carnage. According to Balagopal, the killing was a surprise because the Naxalites had not been significantly active in the area. The Dalit Mahasabha – which had been at the centre of the struggle after the Karamchedu massacre – opposed violent means of protest. The Dalit Mahasabha had filed a private complaint in the court so as to include individuals who had been left out of the police investigations.[95] But it was not until 2008 that the final verdict arrived. On 19 December 2008, the Supreme Court of India accepted an appeal made ten years earlier. The highest court in the country sentenced the main accused person to life imprisonment and thirty others to three-years imprisonment.[96]

The main lesson that can be learnt from Karamchedu is not simply that justice was delayed by the Supreme Court judgment that was made more than twenty years after the occurrence. Rather, the incident should be viewed in the context of the overall development of all-India legislation that aimed to curb the problem of atrocities against Dalits. First, Karamchedu created its own 'feedback mechanism' and protests in the political system. The Dalit Mahasabha organized delegations to New Delhi to demand justice and to voice their concerns about the lack of legal protection for Dalits. Second, the legal situation at the time of Karamchedu was more amorphous than when the massacre in Tsundur occurred six years later. Karamchedu occurred before the passing of the Scheduled Castes and Scheduled Tribes (Prevention of Atrocities) Act (PoA Act), 1989, which was designed to target discrimination against Dalits and Adivasis. As explained in Chapter 2, the Act is a special piece of legislation that comes under Indian criminal law, but its content and punishments differ from the general criminal code. Karamchedu, notably, was dealt with under general criminal law, whereas the later Tsundur trial was conducted under the PoA Act, 1989.

After the Karamchedu massacre, there were consistent demands from Andhra Pradesh for a special Act to deal with major atrocities based on caste. The PoA Act was consented to by the president of India on 11 September 1989. Although the chronology could suggest that there is a direct, causal connection between the demands from Andhra Pradesh and the Act, this is not entirely accurate. In fact, the Act was a result of many atrocities in different parts of the country, starting from the late 1960s. The problem of atrocities had been a recurring concern, and the Parliamentary Forum for Scheduled Castes and Scheduled Tribes had made various suggestions about providing legal protection earlier.[97] Although Karamchedu was not the single cause behind the Act, the Andhra Pradesh Dalit Mahasabha has been more articulate on law and legal action than many Dalit movements in the country. The Karamchedu massacre reinforced the mobilization for adequate legal protection and the demand for all-India legislation to address atrocities.

Summary

The massacre in Karamchedu is a significant case that has a range of historical and theoretical implications. It had a major impact on activists in the state as it brought into view how casteism was integral to the agrarian economy. Despite earlier activism and several atrocities, this brutal attack represented a new point of departure for an independent Dalit movement. As a particularly violent re-embedding of casteism, it had revealed both social and political logics integral to the agrarian economy. Sociologically, the attack on Dalits in Karamchedu confirmed what I refer to as the mechanism of oppression in the Dalit situation, where upward mobility and assertiveness may create a backlash. But it was the relevance of political power that appeared decisive for members of the landowning castes; they appeared able to exercise their dominance in new and powerful ways by carrying out the organized attack while the local police obeyed the state power. Political power among dominant castes created leeway and extra impetus for acting violently in this re-embedding of status and social relations. The violent casteism was a result of state power and electoral success.

What made Karamchedu such a significant event was the extent to which it destroyed the myth that caste was a thing of the past. In this situation, though, Dalit leaders were able to organize the movement in both practical and ideological ways. Indeed, educated Dalits and members of the middle class gave the Dalit movement a clear direction after Karamchedu.[98] The Dalit movement now appeared to be a coherent configuration of activists who were determined to move in a new direction while remaining committed to the idea of emancipation from casteism. It constituted an organized and common commitment to attaining dignity and a new mode of existence. In addition to providing members of the movement with a sense of identification with Ambedkar's struggles with untouchability and exclusion, he represented ideas about emancipation and a struggle for dignity and legal protection in the state.

The Dalit Mahasabha was committed to following non-violent procedures in the framework of the constitutional state, and one of its central demands was that more adequate legislation should be created to punish perpetrators of caste-based massacres. This approach was part of a discoursive rupture in two ways. First, the movement's demand for better legal protection and for prosecution of accused persons reinforced the national concerns about the lack of adequate legal approaches to atrocities. Second, the commitment to a Dalit agenda involved a significant conceptual development that meant a sustained intellectual break with the class discourse of the left. Events at the camp and the politics of representation that was developed there led to the movement being able to distinguish itself from the radical left and to come across as a distinctively Dalit movement. Many of its activists were inspired by the left-wing movement. This makes the story of Dalit Mahasabha comparatively noteworthy, as the movement had a more consistent focus on how caste and class relate than one finds in other south Indian states such as Tamil Nadu and Kerala. The emergence of a Dalit movement required a break with revolutionary ideology and its class discourse. This is somewhat different from the creation of the Adi-Andhra Mahasabha in 1917, a distinct movement that negotiated with the Congress-led nationalist movement during the 1920s.[99] The Adi-Andhra movement became a regional chapter of a broader movement when it defined its members as natives of Andhra. Similarly, the story of Karamchedu became part of a national movement in several ways: the Dalit Mahasabha was able to develop its cooperation with movements outside Andhra Pradesh in terms of direct involvement in the aftermath and at conferences and during activities later on.

Today, the situation among Dalits in Telangana and Andhra Pradesh is characterized by multiplicity rather than unity. A new sub-caste movement has emerged and has caused controversy among Dalit subgroups (primarily Malas and Madigas) over sub-classification of the SC category.[100] The history of Karamchedu nonetheless remains paramount. The Dalit mobilization in Andhra Pradesh during the 1980s is noteworthy for the study of Dalit mobilization and identity formation and the failure of a one-dimensional class analysis to address how caste was an embedded feature of oppression.

Notes

1. *Times of India*, 'Eyewitness Account Given: Burning of Harijan Boy', 3 May 1968, accessed April 25, 2016, http://search.proquest.com/docview/614027427/fulltextPDF/97566C7EEE244A2PQ/2?accountid=11144.
2. Gail Omvedt, *Dalits and the Democratic Revolution: Dr. Ambedkar and the Dalit Movement in Colonial India* (New Delhi: Sage Publications, 1994); Yagati Chinna Rao, *Dalits Struggle for Identity: Andhra and Hyderabad 1900–1950* (New Delhi: Kanishka, 2003); Adapa Satyanarayana, 'Dalit Protest Literature in Telugu: A Historical Perspective', *Economic and Political Weekly* 30, no. 3 (1995); K. Laxminarayana et al., 'Laxmipet Dalit Killings', *Economic and Political Weekly* 47, nos. 47–8 (2012): 26–28.
3. Rao, *Dalits Struggle for Identity*.

4. David Anthony Washbrook, *The Emergence of Provincial Politics: The Madras Presidency, 1870–1920* (Cambridge: Cambridge University Press, 1976), 250; Lise Mitchel, *Language, Emotion, and Politics in South India: The Making of a Mother Tongue* (Bloomington: Indiana University Press, 2009).
5. Chinnaiah Jangam, 'Dilemmas of Dalit Agenda: Political Subjugation and Self-Emancipation in Telugu Country, 1919–1950', in *Dalit Studies*, ed. Ramnarayan S. Rawat and Kusuma Satyanarayana (Durham: Duke University Press, 2016), 108; Nagam Kumaraswamy, 'Dalits and Autonomy: Towards Construction of Dalit Movement in Andhra Pradesh', PhD thesis, Department of Political Science, Osmania University, 2011, p. 83; N. Chandra Bhanu Murthy, 'Identity, Autonomy and Emancipation: The Agendas of the Adi-Andhra Movement in South India, 1917–30', *The Indian Economic & Social History Review* 53, no. 2 (2016): 226, doi:10.1177/0019464616634841.
6. Figueira, Dorothy Matilda. *Aryans, Jews, Brahmins: Theorizing Authority Through Myths of Identity*, SUNY Series, the Margins of Literature (Albany: State University of New York Press, 2002), 144–50.
7. Omvedt, *Dalits and the Democratic Revolution*, 117.
8. Kumaraswamy, *Dalits and Autonomy*, 84; Murthy, 'Identity, Autonomy and Emancipation'.
9. Jangam, 'Dilemmas of Dalit Agenda', 126.
10. Mitchel, *Language, Emotion, and Politics in South India*, 39–43.
11. Carol Upadhya, 'Amaravati and the New Andhra: Reterritorialization of a Region', *Journal of South Asian Development* 12, no. 2 (2017): 7, doi:10.1177/0973174117712324.
12. Ajay Gudavarthy, 'Dalit and Naxalite Movements in AP: Solidarity or Hegemony?', *Economic and Political Weekly* 40, no. 51 (2005); K. Y. Ratnam, 'The Dalit Movement in Andhra Pradesh: A Study of Political Consciousness and Identity', PhD thesis, Centre for Political Studies, School of Social Sciences, University, Jawaharlal Nehru, New Delhi, 2014; K. Y. Ratnam, 'The Dalit Movement and Democratization in Andhra Pradesh', Working Paper No. 13, East-West Center in Washington, Washington, DC, 2008, accessed 10 July 2019, https://www.eastwestcenter.org/fileadmin/stored/pdfs/ewcwwp013.pdf.
13. Bojja Tharakam, in an interview with the author, Hyderabad, January 2008.
14. Salaha, *Karamchedu: Report by Fact Finding Team* (Hyderabad: Hyderabad Book Trust, 1985), 1.
15. K. Balagopal, 'Karamchedu: Second Anniversary', *Economic and Political Weekly* 22, no. 33 (1987); K. Balagopal, 'The Karamchedu Killings: The Essence of the NTR Phenomenon', *Economic and Political Weekly* 20, no. 31 (1985): 1298.
16. Kancha Ilaiah, 'Caste or Class or Caste-Class: A Study in Dalitbahujan Consciousness and Struggles in Andhra Pradesh in 1980s', in *Caste, Class, Gender*, ed. Manoranjan Mohanty (New Delhi: Sage Publications, 2004): 229.
17. There are new publications emerging on Andhra Dalits which make this important history more accessible beyond the state. This includes books such as Chinnaiah

Jangam, *Dalits and the Making of Modern India*, (New Delhi: Oxford University Press, 2017) and Sambaiah Gundimeda, *Dalit Politics in Contemporary India* (Abingdon: Routledge, 2016), although their discussions differ somewhat from mine.

18. Ratnam, 'The Dalit Movement in Andhra Pradesh'.
19. Satyanarayana, 'Dalit Protest Literature in Telugu', 171.
20. "Karamchedu Massacre Helps Dalit Militancy', *Dalit Voice* 5, no. 2 (1985): 15.
21. Dag-Erik Berg, 'Dalits and the Constitutional State: Untouchability, Dalit Movements and Legal Approaches to Equality and Social Justice for India's Scheduled Castes', PhD thesis, Department of Administration and Organization Theory, University of Bergen, 2011; Ilaiah, 'Caste or Class or Caste-Class', 240.
22. For detailed reports on the massacres, see Salaha, *Karamchedu: Report by Fact Finding Team*; Andhra Pradesh Civil Liberties Committee, *The Karamchedu Massacre: A Report* (Guntur: Andhra Pradesh Civil Liberties Committee, 1985), on file with the author.
23. K. Balagopal, activist in the People's Union for Civil Liberties at the time of Karamchedu, in an interview with the author, Hyderabad, January 2008.
24. Ratnam, 'The Dalit Movement in Andhra Pradesh', 107.
25. Atul Kohli, 'The NTR Phenomenon in Andhra Pradesh: Political Change in a South Indian State', *Asian Survey* 28, no. 10 (1988); G. Ram Reddy, 'The Politics of Accommodation: Caste, Class and Dominance in Andhra Pradesh', in *Dominance and State Power in Modern India*, ed. Francine R. Frankel and M. S. A. Rao, 2 vols. (Delhi: Oxford University Press, 1989); K. C. Suri, 'Telugu Desam Party: Rise and Prospects for Future', *Economic and Political Weekly* 39, nos. 14–15 (2004).
26. Balagopal, 'Karamchedu', 1380.
27. Suri, 'Telugu Desam Party', 1482.
28. Kohli, 'The NTR Phenomenon in Andhra Pradesh', 1016; Reddy, 'The Politics of Accommodation', 287.
29. Salaha, *Karamchedu: Report by Fact Finding Team*, 8.
30. Balagopal, 'Karamchedu'; Balagopal, 'The Karamchedu Killings', 1298.
31. Balagopal, 'Karamchedu', 1378.
32. K. Balagopal, 'Post-Chundur and Other Chundurs', *Economic and Political Weekly* 26, no. 42 (1991): 2399, accessed 15 October 2015, http://www.epw.in/system/files/pdf/1991_26/42/post_chundur_and_other_chundurs.pdf.
33. Salaha, *Karamchedu: Report by Fact Finding Team*, 27.
34. Mitchel, *Language, Emotion, and Politics in South India.*
35. Kingshuk Nag, *Battleground Telangana: Chronicle of an Agitation* (New Delhi: HarperCollins Publishers India, 2011), 11.
36. Sanjaya Baru, 'Economic Policy and the Development of Capitalism in India: The Role of Regional Capitalists and Political Parties', in *Transforming India*, ed. Francine R. Frankel et al. (New Delhi: Oxford University Press, 2000), 216; Harish Damodaran, *India's New Capitalists: Caste, Business, and Industry in a Modern Nation* (Ranikhet: Permanent Black, 2008); Carol B. Upadhya, 'The Farmer-Capitalists of Coastal Andhra Pradesh', *Economic and Political Weekly* 23, no. 28 (1988).

37. Reddy, 'The Politics of Accommodation', 314–15; Brass, *The Politics of India Since Independence*, 324.
38. Upadhya, 'The Farmer-Capitalists of Coastal Andhra Pradesh', 1438.
39. Yamada Keiko, 'Politics and Representation of Caste Identity in Regional Historiography', *Indian Economic & Social History Review* 45, no. 3 (2008): 363.
40. D. Narasimha Reddy, 'Karamchedu: A Dialectic without Development', *Economic and Political Weekly* 20 (1985): 1547.
41. Katti Padma Rao, interview with the author, Hyderabad, 15 February 2008.
42. See Katti Padma Rao, *Caste and Alternative Culture* (Chennai: The Gurukul Lutheran Theological College & Research Institute, 1998), 10.
43. Rajni Kothari, 'Introduction', in *Caste in Indian Politics*, ed. Rajni Kothari (New Delhi: Orient Longman, 1970), 20.
44. M. N. Srinivas, 'Caste in Modern India', *The Journal of Asian Studies* 16, no. 4 (1957): 529.
45. Bojja Tharakam, 'Laxmipeta: Deadly Combination of Caste and Political Power', *Economic and Political Weekly* 47, no. 28 (2012), accessed 11 July 2019, http://www.epw.in/journal/2012/28/web-exclusives/laxmipeta-deadly-combination-caste-and-political-power.html.
46. Adapa Satyanarayana, 'Caste and Class in Rural Andhra', in *Caste and Class in India*, ed. Kanhaiya Lal Sharma (Jaipur: Rawat Publishers, 1994).
47. Ibid., 378.
48. Damodaran, *India's New Capitalists*, 103; Upadhya, 'The Farmer-Capitalists of Coastal Andhra Pradesh'; Dalel Benbabaali, 'Caste Dominance and Territory in South India: Understanding Kammas' Socio-Spatial Mobility', *Modern Asian Studies* 52, no. 6 (2018), doi:10.1017/S0026749X16000755.
49. Andhra Pradesh Civil Liberties Committee, 'The Karamchedu Massacre', 3.
50. Srinivas, *Social Change in Modern India (1966)* (New Delhi: Orient Longman, 1995), 99.
51. Yamada Keiko, 'Origin and Historical Evolution of the Identity of Modern Telugus', *Economic and Political Weekly* 45, no. 34 (2010).
52. Keiko, 'Politics and Representation of Caste Identity in Regional Historiography', 363.
53. Srinivas, *Social Change in Modern India*, 98.
54. Bhimrao Ramji Ambedkar, 'Untouchables or the Children of India's Ghetto', in *Dr. Babasaheb Ambedkar Writings and Speeches: Unpublished Writings*, ed. Vasant Moon, vol. 5 (Bombay: Education Department, Government of Maharashtra, 1989), 102.
55. Reddy, 'Karamchedu', 1547.
56. Bojja Tharakam in an interview with the author, Hyderabad, February 2008.
57. Balagopal, 'The Karamchedu Killings', 1299.
58. Ratnam, 'The Dalit Movement and Democratization in Andhra Pradesh', 19.
59. Reddy, 'Karamchedu', 1548.
60. Ratnam, 'The Dalit Movement and Democratization in Andhra Pradesh', 20.

61. Balagopal, 'Karamchedu', 1378.
62. Katti Padma Rao in an interview with the author, 15 February 2008.
63. Reddy, 'Karamchedu', 1548.
64. Cited in ibid., 1548.
65. Katti Padma Rao in an interview with the author, 15 February 2008.
66. This information is based on interviews conducted during fieldwork in Hyderabad in 2008.
67. Ratnam, 'The Dalit Movement and Democratization in Andhra Pradesh', 19.
68. Ratnam, 'The Dalit Movement in Andhra Pradesh'.
69. Ilaiah, 'Caste or Class or Caste-Class', 242.
70. Bojja Tharakam in an interview with the author, Hyderabad, 2008.
71. Bojja Tharakam in an interview with the author, Hyderabad, 2008; ibid., 2014; Paul Panneer Selvam in an interview with the author, Chennai, 2014.
72. The movement was led by Katti Padma Rao, from coastal Andhra, and Bojja Tharakam, from Hyderabad. Although they had different personalities, both were well educated and powerful speakers. Bojja Tharakam was a lawyer who practised in Andhra Pradesh High Court on behalf of his government, whereas Katti Padma Rao was a teacher of Sanskrit. Tharakam had left his job in Hyderabad to join the movement. Both were committed social activists. Katti Padma Rao had until that time been a leader of the rationalist movement in Andhra Pradesh, and he had also participated in the anti-Brahmin movement before joining the rationalist movement.
73. Ratnam, 'The Dalit Movement and Democratization in Andhra Pradesh', 21.
74. Alain Badiou, *Being and Event* (London: Continuum, 2005), 184; Alain Badiou and Fabien Tarby, *Philosophy and the Event* (Cambridge: Polity, 2013), 9.
75. Alain Badiou, *Ethics: An Essay on the Understanding of Evil* (London: Verso, 2002), 43.
76. Ibid.
77. Ibid., 46.
78. Sambaiah Gundimeda, 'Dalit Activism in Telugu Country, 1917–30', *South Asia Research* 36, no. 3 (2016), doi:10.1177/0262728016663270; Jangam, 'Dilemmas of Dalit Agenda'; Kumaraswamy, *Dalits and Autonomy*; Murthy, 'Identity, Autonomy and Emancipation'; Omvedt, *Dalits and the Democratic Revolution*; Satyanarayana, 'Dalit Protest Literature in Telugu'; Rao, *Dalits Struggle for Identity*; Jangam, *Dalits and the Making of Modern India*.
79. Ratnam, 'The Dalit Movement in Andhra Pradesh', 111.
80. Ibid.
81. The *zamindari* system was one of the agricultural systems. For discussion, see Satyanarayana, 'Caste and Class in Rural Andhra'.
82. Ratnam, 'The Dalit Movement and Democratization in Andhra Pradesh', 16; Karli Srinivasulu, 'The Caste Question in the Naxalite Movement', *Economic and Political Weekly* 52, no. 21 (2017): 49–50, http://www.epw.in/journal/2017/21/naxalbari-and-after/naxalbari-chhattisgarh.html. This method is still being used. As Gaddar emphasized to me in an interview (23 March 2008), one could only understand the

nature of the Dalit problem after having lived among landless Dalits for a couple of months. This experience is what the Maoist movement expected from anyone who joined them, and this is still the case today.

83. P. Kesava Kumar, 'Popular Culture and Ideology: The Phenomenon of Gaddar', *Economic and Political Weekly* 45, no. 7 (2010).
84. Ratnam, 'The Dalit Movement in Andhra Pradesh', 107–8.
85. Ratnam, 'The Dalit Movement and Democratization in Andhra Pradesh', 16.
86. Ilaiah, 'Caste or Class or Caste-Class', 240.
87. For a new biographical account published by his relative, see Sujatha Gidla, *Ants among Elephants: An Untouchable Family and the Making of Modern India* (New York: Farrar, Straus and Giroux, 2018).
88. Ilaiah, 'Caste or Class or Caste-Class', 249.
89. Tharakam explained in an interview to the author, December 2014.
90. Tharakam in an interview with the author, February 2008.
91. Ajay Gudavarthy, *The Politics of Post-Civil Society: Contemporary History of Political Movements in India* (New Delhi: Sage Publications, 2013), 82–3; Ilaiah, 'Caste or Class or Caste-Class', 248; Ratnam, 'The Dalit Movement in Andhra Pradesh', 120; Ratnam, email message to author, 8 December 2018.
92. Karamchedu led to different forms of expressions. The Dalit literary movement, for instance, includes notable poetry written by Dalit women. See, for instance, Rani, Challapalli Swaroopa. 'Dalit Women's Writing in Telugu'. *Economic and Political Weekly* 33, no. 17 (1998): 21–4, doi:10.2307/4406697.
93. Bhimrao Ramji Ambedkar, 'Annihilation of Caste', in *Dr. Babasaheb Ambedkar Writings and Speeches*, ed. Vasant Moon, vol. 1 (Bombay: Education Department, Government of Maharashtra, 1989).
94. Ratnam, 'The Dalit Movement and Democratization in Andhra Pradesh', 16–17.
95. K. Balagopal, '"Law and Order" on Lease', *Economic and Political Weekly* 24, no. 24 (1989): 1323, doi:10.2307/4394952.
96. *Times of India*, 'SC Convicts 31 in Karamchedu Dalit Massacre', 20 December 2008, accessed 10 July 2019, https://timesofindia.indiatimes.com/city/hyderabad/SC-convicts-31-in-Karamchedu-Dalit-massacre/articleshow/3864622.cms?referral=PM.
97. *Times of India*, 'Use MISA to end Atrocities on Harijans', 1 December 1974, accessed 20 September 2018, https://search.proquest.com/docview/750801793?accountid=9735.
98. Mallepalli Laxmaiah, a Dalit activist and journalist, in an interview with the author, Hyderabad, January 2008.
99. Murthy, 'Identity, Autonomy and Emancipation'.
100. See Chapter 6.

4

Casteism and the Tsundur Atrocity

The postcolonial history of India involves many of these brutal cases of organized caste-based violence in the rural landscape. The attacks in Andhra Pradesh, in Karamchedu in Prakasam district (1985) and in Tsundur village in the neighbouring Guntur district (1991), represent two brutal instances, although several other atrocities took place before, between and after Karamchedu and Tsundur.[1] At a national level, the early and well-known incidents that occurred during this grim postcolonial trend happened in Kilvenmani village in the Thanjavur district in southern Tamil Nadu, where forty-four Dalits were burnt to death in December 1968. But the cases in Thanjavur and coastal Andhra suggest that modern agricultural technology provided the material basis for the social changes in these villages that led to extreme brutality. As Paul Brass indicates, it is useful to be cautious when explaining violence in the agrarian context simply by referring to a 'Green revolution' rather than to more historical explanations.[2] In fact, it is also important to underline caste as a factor in this context. Some of the cases that happened at the same time as the brutal assault in Kilvenmani are not simply cases of violence in a feudal agrarian structure. Caste relations are embedded in the agrarian mode of production, and the term 'feudalism' appears inadequate to explain casteism and violence. It is useful to revisit the ontological difference that Ambedkar emphasized exists between touchables and untouchables, between 'some bodies' and 'nobodies',[3] to understand how the desire to 'teach Dalits a lesson' could play out.

Cases of amorous encounters and upward mobility represent possibilities that transgress basic ideas about differences in an ontology of caste. The incident that took place in Kanchikacherla village on 24 February 1968 in Krishna district could be viewed in this context. On that day, Kotesu, a 'Harijan boy', was burnt alive.[4] Kotesu had been charged with stealing two pots and a tumbler, and a group of seven people had tied him to a post in the village, beaten him and later burnt him. While the accusation of theft resonates with a stereotype about Dalits being less trustworthy people, Kotesu's parents had another explanation; they thought that Kotesu was having a love affair with the landlord's daughter. This brutal punishment in Kanchikacherla had an impact on this first generation of Dalit activists after independence; the Dalit leader Eshwari Bai raised the issue in the state assembly.[5] The case was also reported in national newspapers, and a Congress politician provoked reactions when he referred to the incident in Kanchikacherla as an example of how the peasantry could exercise justice and prevent thefts.[6] The accounts of Kotesu's crime therefore differ from being theft to a friendly, if not an amorous, relationship with the landlord's daughter. In any case, the incident in Kanchikacherla had an impact on Dalit activists at that time. The cases that have been central for the contemporary generation of Dalit activists, however, have been those at Karamchedu and Tsundur and, more recently, the suicide of Rohith Vemula. These instances have affected the understanding of how caste-based violence may occur in India today, and the brutal attack in Tsundur, and its scale and details, is one of the key narratives shaping the movements' sense of injustice.

The atrocity in Tsundur village happened on 6 August 1991; eight Dalits were killed in a carefully planned attack. There were tensions in the village at the time of the incident that had arisen after a period of disputes among the youths in the village. If the burning of Kotesu in Kanchikacherla was carried out to prevent the possibility of a love affair between a Dalit boy and a caste Hindu girl, the massacre in Tsundur involves a greater deal. The attacks on the Dalits of Tsundur were carried out to 'teach them a lesson', primarily to try to make them submissive and to comply with their position as the untouchables and to aim to ensure that they do not resist the authority of the caste Hindus. For caste Hindus in the village, the attack was also a matter of maintaining their reputation in relation to neighbouring villages. The massacre is an extreme instance of this logic, as it shows how collective the violence was organized in order to maintain their status and re-embed social relations in the village in line with the norms of dominating caste.

This brutal attack occurred in a context of social and political transformation in the village. There was upward mobility and assertiveness among the Tsundur Dalits, and this provoked a backlash. I had encountered several versions of the mechanism of oppression characterizing the Dalit situation earlier (via interlocutors who were either Dalit activists or people who were close observers), and the same explanation was presented here. This time, however, I learnt about the scale and details of this organized violence that I had never encountered before. Caste Hindus used other explanations for the event that occurred, such as that Dalit boys flirted with upper-caste girls. Although I was also told by one of the Dalit men who had been attacked that this was not true, each of these explanations suggests that caste is central to making sense of why this violence occurred.

In this chapter, I start in the first section by explaining the process of social change in the village and how there were tensions between the two groups that involved strikes, violence and negotiations. The tensions arose in a context in which the facts did not correspond to the ontology of caste and in which there were often ongoing incentives among Dalits to deinstitutionalize caste that corresponded to the attempts to reinstitutionalize caste of some members of the landowning and dominant caste. In the second section, I explain what happened in the main incident in the attack on 6 August 1991. While my main source is the comprehensive Tsundur judgment of 2007 along with the statements of the then special public prosecutor, the facts are, naturally, contested because the perpetrators may be punished. In the third section, I explain what happened after the attack and how the police appeared to be complicit in the attack because of their actions and their poor recording of the initial evidence. Finally, I explain the wider reactions to the massacre in Tsundur. This case provides a background for understanding why many activists in this state participated in the World Conference against Racism in South Africa in 2001, ten years after the attack in this village. As an example of a case of violent casteism, the event of Tsundur illustrates what authors such as Teltumbde[7] have argued, which is that atrocities are conducted as collectively organized attacks by the dominating castes to kill Dalits.

Social Change, Assertion and Conflict in Tsundur

On 7 July 1991, a group of Dalit boys went to see a film at the cinema in Tsundur.[8] The cinema had been built one year earlier. Before that time, the inhabitants of Tsundur had to visit the neighbouring village, Modukuru, to watch films. Among the group of Dalit boys was a postgraduate student, Govathoti Ravi, who had come to spend his holiday in his home village. During the film, his friend's foot touched the leg of the chair in front of him, where an upper-caste boy sat. The upper-caste boy rose and criticized the Dalit boy for touching his seat. From his seat, next to his friend, Ravi reacted to these remarks, which he felt were unreasonable and offensive. He told the Reddy boy, 'Don't use those kinds of words', and excused his friend, saying that his action was neither intended nor did the touch create any harm. Ravi explained that it had all happened by mistake.[9] But the Reddy boy tried to gather support against the two Dalit boys. The episode created tensions, but nothing serious happened that evening. Ravi went to see the *mandal* president, a Dalit and a relative, and accepted his advice not to worry about this incident and to take no further action. He left for Ongole (a town in the neighbouring district, Prakasam) to meet his friend from college.

When Ravi returned from Ongole on the six o'clock train the next evening, however, he was met by a group of sixty to seventy upper-caste men, who started to chase him. They had been waiting for him to return. Seeing the crowd starting to chase him with iron rods, sticks and knives, Ravi ran away. He ran nearly 2 kilometres into the fields before he was found and beaten. The whole upper-caste group gathered around him, and it felt, Ravi explained, as if the whole group of sixty to seventy upper-caste men kicked him at once.[10] This was, he recollected, when he fell unconscious. He was beaten for half an hour; then there was some respite before they returned to continue the beating. The group of men forced Ravi to drink liquor mixed with urine, handed him over to the police and told them that he had caused problems after drinking alcohol.

His friend, whose foot had touched the Reddy boy's chair in the cinema, was not beaten. Instead, the reaction was directed against Ravi, who, during the beating, was told, 'You, the man who opposed us' – 'How dare you?' He had corrected the behaviour of a member of the caste Hindus and had now been 'taught a lesson' about how he should be subordinate. But the upper-caste anger about Dalit assertion was not limited to him. In fact, the crowd that had come to ask Ravi's father about his son's whereabouts earlier that day had tied up and beaten him to such an extent that he was unable to walk. The father was not aware of the incident at the cinema the previous night. He was a teacher in the village, but his poor health after the beating forced him to resign from his job and move his family to Tenali, the neighbouring town, so that he could access regular medical treatment.

After the incident in the cinema in July 1991, the upper-caste villagers imposed a social boycott on the Dalits of Tsundur. Social boycotts are often used in India to discourage Dalits from acting independently and from demanding higher wages, better work conditions or access to village festivals. Although there had been tensions in Tsundur village for nearly a year, no one could have anticipated the scale of violence that was about to take place, even after Ravi and his father were badly beaten. The village atmosphere was tense – so much that both upper-caste villagers and Dalits arranged internal meetings about these increasing tensions that had arisen after a long period of social changes.

Broadly speaking, the ongoing social and political changes in Tsundur had been evident from the fact that Dalits aspired to access higher education and modern jobs. Dalits had also acquired the habit of having tea and snacks in 'hotels'[11] in the village's main street, where upper-caste villagers used to sit without the company of Dalits. The Tsundur Dalits had started to wear better clothes than the upper-caste citizens. In the agricultural fields, the upper-caste parents commented on how neat and tidy the Dalit children looked.[12]

The tensions were mostly felt among the village youths and had been apparent in Tsundur at least since a quarrel between some of the young people had occurred during a drama one year earlier. This minor incident happened when a Dalit boy sat on a brick while watching the theatrical performance in the open space near the temple. But upper-caste citizens would not tolerate the fact that he sat on the brick. They got angry and started a quarrel, which resulted in injuries on both sides. The episode may be considered as a starting point for the violent process that followed because a series of events took place later that related to the drama.[13]

It was at this time that the Ambedkar Youth Association was organized and became the basis for activism among Dalit youths in Tsundur. Dalit youths had, in fact, become more politically assertive generally. The Ambedkar Youth Association was funded by six to eight members in 1990, and Ravi was among the founders. He had been inspired to start the Ambedkar Youth Association during his undergraduate studies in Krishna district. And when he returned home, he joined his friends and acted as the secretary of the association.[14] The association was active between 1989 and 1991. It was an important symbolic event when the Ambedkar Youth Association organized the erection of a statue of Dr Ambedkar in April 1990 during the celebrations to mark the centenary since Ambedkar's birth, an event celebrated all over India. Statues of Ambedkar can be found all over India today, be that a road junction in a village in Tamil Nadu or at the centre of a city such as Mumbai or Lucknow. This process of identifying with Ambedkar's life and erecting statues of him has, as mentioned previously, been labelled Ambedkarization, and this has largely characterized Dalit mobilization.[15] In Tsundur, the Ambedkar Youth Association erected the statue in the middle of the village along the main road. The statue faced the church located on the opposite side of the road. The upper-caste citizens kept quiet during the period that the statue was being erected.[16]

Ambedkar, the symbol of Dalit assertion and modern identity, became very visible in the Tsundur village centre. I happened to see the statue before it was pointed out to me when I first visited the village in February 2008. Standing by the village's main road, I saw the towering statue nearly 100 metres away. I recognized the posture and could clearly see that what looked like a statue of Ambedkar had been placed at the centre of the village. My observation was confirmed – it was Ambedkar, but I only came to learn about the history of that statue later. In essence, the statues of Ambedkar have become the most visible signs of Dalit assertion in India,[17] and the Ambedkar Youth Association in Tsundur had boldly brought its ideas to the fore. The group's assertion of Dalit identity by erecting the statue of Ambedkar thus fitted with the wider trend of Dalit mobilization in India, labelled Ambedkarization.[18]

There seems to have been a greater degree of Ambedkarization in Tsundur than in neighbouring villages, such as Modukuru, insofar as Ambedkarization means making Dalit identity visible and being assertive by erecting statues of Ambedkar. Both villages are in Tsundur Mandal, the larger administrative unit that has its centre in Tsundur village. In Modukuru village, however, the statue of Ambedkar is located inside the Dalitwada and not in the village centre, like in

Tsundur. The comparison between Tsundur and Modukuru provides an important insight into the context and potential dynamics of both villages. On the one hand, the caste composition is almost the same. In both villages, the Reddys and Telagas are dominant castes, although Reddys are by far the most numerous. The Reddy community represents what the sociologist Srinivas would have referred to as the dominant caste: they are numerically predominant and enjoy economic and political leverage but are not too low in the ritual hierarchy.[19] In Tsundur, the upper-caste villagers constitute a coherent and dominant section of the society in terms of numbers and their landholdings and economic power. There are close connections in terms of caste and kinship between the villages. For example, the Brahmin priest in Tsundur's Siva temple was residing with his family in Modukuru when I met him briefly in 2008. The upper-caste dominance appears so similar in these villages that one of my Dalit informants in Tsundur asserted that the upper-caste people in both villages are equally dominant in terms of land and economic power. The upper castes are dominant in all fields, including politics, their relationships with the police and their numerical size.

But Modukuru and Tsundur differ in two important ways. First, there are more Dalits in Tsundur than in Modukuru. And second, the Modukuru Reddys appear to be richer and have greater economic assets than those in Tsundur.[20] The overall impression is that the Modukuru Reddys appear to use their leverage to pressurize their counterparts in Tsundur to curb the Dalits in that village.

The upper castes in this region have a common reputation for being particularly traditional. This characteristic can mean several things, ranging from observing rituals and having hierarchical beliefs to wearing traditional clothes rather than shirts and trousers. Even today, more upper-caste people than Dalits wear traditional clothes in Tsundur, which is a basic hint that the former are more traditional. Although there have been social and economic changes in Tsundur Mandal since the early 1990s, I was informed that many caste Hindus appeared in court wearing traditional clothing.[21] In his study of the Tsundur massacre, K. Muruli asserts that the Reddy-dominated villages in Guntur were 'extremely traditional and conservative … compared to the surrounding areas that are dominated by the Kammas'.[22] Muruli adds that there were elements of caste-based exclusion, such as Dalits were not invited into upper-caste villagers' homes.

Untouchability was not apparent in Tsundur, at least during the 1980s, when a young and educated generation acquired a taste for egalitarianism. On the one hand, people like Ravi claimed that there was no untouchability; rather, it was the class that was a problem in the village. He explained there were some instances in Valiveru, a neighbouring village, where Dalits were not allowed to enter hotels. But in the Tsundur cinema, for instance, seats were taken according to the order in which people appeared and purchased their tickets, which could result in Dalits sitting side by side with upper-caste people. Untouchability was not evident, and the so-called two-tumbler system was a thing of the past.

Hierarchy and status-grading appeared more evident whenever Dalits and upper-castes were assembled for meetings. During discussions, Dalits were expected to sit on the floor, while the upper-caste people sat at a higher level than them. But it is at this point that the generational difference seems to play a role. Dalits used to be represented by elderly people, who were more submissive to the established rules than the younger generation. But this does not mean that untouchability practices, such as the two-tumbler system and prohibitions on Dalits wearing sandals when walking in upper-caste localities, were practised.

In brief, the situation in Tsundur did not appear very clear-cut as far as untouchability was concerned. Yet an elderly widow in the Dalitwada, Mrs Jakraiah, offered me some examples of subtle forms of discrimination that seem to have been the pattern in the village.[23] Mrs Jakraiah said that Dalits were respected while working in the agricultural fields. When I asked about the situation for women, she denied that Dalit women were abused by upper-caste men. She said that the problem used to be that Dalits were abused 'by name' in public places, which indicates how caste-related names for Dalits are derogatory and that their use is a source of humiliation and stigma. But she insisted that there were, in fact, friendly relationships in the fields and seemed to describe a situation of almost mutual dependency: the upper-caste villagers needed a labour force, whereas Dalits needed an income to live on. She explained that religion separated the castes in that the upper castes have temples and Dalits go to church.

No doubt the castes were separated in terms of religion and where they lived. The upper-caste people lived in one part of the village, Dalits in the other. But, nonetheless, there were social and political changes. The growing assertion by Dalit youths of their rights was crucial. But there were several reasons behind the social and economic changes. During my field trip in March of 2008, U. Bullikotaiah, a Tsundur Dalit, enumerated three factors when he explained the social change in Tsundur. As some of his earlier relatives, he had been politically active. Bullikotaiah had contested as an independent candidate in the 1981 elections. At that time, he gained such a powerful position that the upper-caste people wanted to make a compromise so that he should not undermine their campaign.

There were social changes in the village during the 1980s. Reflecting on these changes, Bullikotaiah argued that education, the construction of the railway station and political assertion were the three main factors which altered the situation for Dalits and changed their relationships with members of the dominant castes. The political mobilization made the social changes more visible. The most important effect of the social changes was that Dalits started questioning the situation, and education seems to have been decisive in their increasing assertiveness.

The creation of a railway station in the 1980s made it possible for the Tsundur Dalits to travel outside the village for their daily work. But, more importantly, the railway required manpower and provided employment for 200 illiterate Dalits. Of these 200 Dalits, 180 were given permanent jobs. George Fernandes was the railway minister while the Janata Party was in power at the central level. According to Bullikotaiah, George Fernandes decided that those who had been employed for six months by the railway authority would be granted permanent employment. There was already a double railway track passing by Tsundur village, connecting Tsundur with Chennai and Kolkata. But the railway needed labourers to clean the tracks and to deal with goods. In other words, the need for manual labour created job opportunities for Dalits.

The railway station was instrumental in creating new social habits, such as Dalits using the village hotels for refreshments. This new practice even resulted in Dalits sitting next to upper-caste villagers in the local teahouses (cafés or 'hotels'). Bullikotaiah explained further that the new practices created a sense of equality among Dalits because they started feeling more equal with their upper-caste counterparts. Thus, employment on the railways and a reliable income created a greater sense of freedom, at least among the section of the Tsundur Dalits who were employed on the railways. The upper-caste villagers, however, used to leave the hotels when Dalits arrived to drink tea.

The social and economic changes were perhaps most visible among the many Dalit students. It had become possible to prioritize education as the basic way for social and economic advancement precisely because of the remarkable sense of social security that emerged with employment in the government sector. In addition to being employed in the railway, Tsundur Dalits were also employed in banks and telephone departments.[24] Moreover, upper-caste children were not interested in education at that time, since their families owned land and they could be confident about having a secure income in the future. But Dalit families were much keener to educate their children so that they become independent. So, while upper-caste children had no incentive to ensure their future through formal education, Dalit children aspired to earn a decent living through their studies. Today, everyone wants an education.[25] Formal education has become imperative across Indian society. In 1991, however, the upper-caste people in Tsundur were not educationally forward and there was, according to Srinivasulu, a 'much higher' degree of literacy among Dalits than among Reddys.[26]

In 1991, there were an estimated 200 matriculated Dalit children studying outside the village,[27] in places such as the town of Tenali and the city of Guntur. Some studied till tenth standard, that is, until they were about sixteen years old, others were undergraduates and there were even fifteen postgraduate students. These figures contrast with the estimated fifty Reddy and Naidu students studying outside the village at this time.[28] The students commuted and therefore used the same means of transportation, such as buses and auto-rickshaws, including 'share autos'. But education was also a more tangible factor in the village's everyday life. Most children went to school. There was a primary school in the village and another in the Dalit hamlet. But the comprehensive school was in Modukuru, and the children Dalit therefore interacted daily with children from caste Hindu families when walking to school. During the 1980s, there were an estimated 200 Dalit children walking to Modukuru every day. Ravi remembered how Dalit children 'spoke freely with upper-caste students' at that time.[29] Other Dalits in Tsundur did not recall major incidents between the girls and boys, except some friendly teasing. The upper-caste villagers, on the other hand, did not appreciate seeing their daughters walking in crowds in which lower-caste students were so prominent in terms of numbers, style of clothing and educational merit. Although it seems as if there were more upper-caste boys than girls studying, the difference in numbers between the sexes was not particularly wide. It was in any case with reference to the girls that upper-caste villagers voiced their serious apprehension. They accused the Dalit boys of teasing and even abusing the girls. Although Dalit boys found that the allegations were 'fabricated',[30] they were indeed serious charges. And the situation for the girls and the alleged abuse later became the basic explanations for upper-caste villagers' understanding of the problems that arose in the village.[31]

The upper-caste allegations gained momentum because the charge against the Dalit boys of abusing the upper-caste girls relates to the wider theme of the moral status of girls and women. It also serves to project immorality onto Dalits. In a theoretical perspective, an inter-caste marriage is a violation of the ontological difference that shapes the caste system, its grading and identities. Caste is reproduced by organizing marriages within the same caste, and girls widely represent the family's virtue and moral reputation. It is argued elsewhere that it creates a sense of insecurity among caste Hindu men if Dalit boys start – or are capable of starting – a relationship with a girl from the dominant caste community.[32] Other sociologists argue, moreover, that gender and caste interrelate in such a way that the grading of caste is expressed through men's ability to exercise manhood, either by controlling the women in their family or by humiliating members of lower castes by humiliating the women in their family. The widespread understanding is that a woman's character represents the family's moral status. At any rate, Tsundur Dalits argued that the main reason for the increased tensions between upper-caste people and Dalits in the village was envy. The upper-caste villagers were envious of the increasing education, sophistication, cultural capital and modern outlook of Dalits.

The social changes in Tsundur, in any case, involved new types of situations and possibilities that did not correspond to the ontology of caste in which members of the dominant castes could expect that touchables and untouchables would be separated and that the latter would be insignificant and submissive. Instead, the visible sign of the upwardly mobile Dalit youth seemed to have created a sense of ontological insecurity among members of the dominant castes as well as a desire to reinstitutionalize caste relations. Ontological insecurity refers to a psychological sense of anxiety.[33] But the idea of 'teaching Dalits a lesson' reflects an ontological drive to reinstitutionalize a dominant caste order.

Given the social changes and the series of 'provocative' events, members of the landowning and caste Hindu community wanted to strike back in a more organized manner. The incident in the cinema seems to have represented a starting point for the upper-caste villagers' interest in striking back. The dominant castes appeared to have united through a common idea of acting against Dalits in the village.[34]

The tense atmosphere was also reflected by the fact that several individual incidents had been registered with the police. They included cases against some Malas from Tsundur village concerning attacks on some upper-caste Telagas that were alleged to have taken place on 13 and 14 October 1990. On 7 August 1991, some Dalits were also registered for a criminal offence after a reported attack on Chidipudi Punna Reddy. And just a few days after the cinema incident, the police had registered criminal cases against several upper-caste Reddys as well as a group of Malas.[35] Indeed, according to the Tsundur judgment, the animosities had, by the end of July 1991, reached a dramatic climax, with clashes between the two communities in Tsundur village. It is stated that

> the Harijans were thrown out of employment and they were subjected to social boycott by not being called for coolie work and taking back the leased lands given to them and forcing them to go out of the village. The Harijans were also frequently insulted by the upper-caste leaders by instigating their caste people, to throw them out of the village.[36]

In this hostile atmosphere between the communities, the police had mobilized a large number of officials to prevent further violence. The social boycott of Dalits further affirmed the split; it implied, for instance, that Dalits were unable to use shops owned by upper-caste people to buy groceries and medicines. Also, travelling outside the village for work meant that Dalits returned home late, often after sunset. Some people believed that the electricity was cut off as Dalits returned home, making cooking difficult and leaving them in complete darkness for the rest of the night. When such tactics occur, they may reflect a wider phenomenon of collusion between upper-caste people and public officials. Upper-caste people generally exercise control over public services. Yet Muruli reports that there was one police constable, who happened to be from a 'backward caste', who interfered to avoid the power to the Dalitwada from being cut.[37]

The increasing animosities in the village made both upper-castes and Dalits arrange internal consultations about how to deal with the situation. On 9 July, for instance, the upper-caste people decided to impose social boycott on the Dalits in the home of the village *sarpanch* (village head), Modugala Sambi Reddy.[38] The boycott was also coordinated with neighbouring villages to prevent Dalits from obtaining work as labourers nearby. The boycott merely reflected a divided village in which each part defined the other as a foe. The almost war-like situation included several criminal cases on either side and was therefore well known by the Tenali police. The upper-caste determination was in any case to strike back against the 'provocation of Harijans'.[39] They wanted to 'teach the Dalits a lesson'.[40]

A meeting was organized on 4 August 1991. On this day, some 200 Reddys and Telagas met at the house of the *sarpanch* in Tsundur village to discuss how to teach the Tsundur Dalits a lesson. The participants included Reddys and Telagas from nearby villages such as Modukuru, Munnangivaripalem and Valiveru. They concluded that they were 'not to tolerate any other incidents or insult or molestations to their women folk and decided to drive them out of the village for ever'.[41] They reconvened two days later and exercised their anger to an extreme end.

The Attack on 6 August 1991

Large numbers of upper-caste people reunited on 6 August 1991.[42] Some 100 upper-caste people met a police officer, and one complaint reported to the police that day was about an alleged assault by a Dalit on two upper-caste persons.[43] But the upper-caste group had a common intention: a plan 'to kill the Harijans'.[44] Thus, a group of more than 200 upper-caste people, Reddy and Telaga, started marching from the upper-caste settlement in the village towards the Dalit colony. The group passed the police station, armed with iron rods, axes, spears, sticks and iron pipes.[45] When the upper-caste people approached the centre of the village and had the upper-caste settlement behind them, they split into two groups. One group headed towards Church Road, the main road in the village dividing the upper-caste settlement from the Dalit settlement ('Dalitwada' or 'Malapalle'[46]). The other group went straight ahead along the railway track into the fields and onto the other side of the Dalitwada. The move was well planned. The group had arranged tractors and other vehicles for transportation. For instance, G. Sambi Reddy, from Munnangivaripalem, a neighbouring village, had come with his tractor and trailer, which accommodated as many as fifty or even sixty people, and they were prepared to attack. Reddys and Telagas from Modukuru mobilized and were waiting in the fields.

Earlier that day, the police had raided the Dalitwada several times, and there were rumours that they were planning to arrest individual Dalits. The actions of the police had made most Dalit men flee into the agricultural fields and hide in the fields rather than staying at home. And Tsundur Dalits had good reasons to flee. Many police cases had recently been registered against Dalits resulting from the tensions in the village, and more cases were anticipated because of the police action. The police mobilized in large numbers to arrest Dalits and 'entered into their palle' at about 11 a.m.[47] In addition, the police 'started beating male persons of the palle'.[48] The Dalit men had left their homes unarmed and were unable to defend themselves against the deadly attack about to come.

The police action thus enabled the attackers to target individual Dalits who were hiding unarmed in the fields. While the armed upper-caste people chased Dalits who had taken refuge in the fields nearly an hour earlier, the police watched the whole situation at a distance and did not interfere or defend the Dalits. Some Dalits left along the Tsundur–Modukuru Road. When the upper-caste people came, however, Dalits fled into the fields. Three of them hid in a jasmine garden. Among them was Jaladi Mattaiah who was forty years old and had not participated in any public demonstrations and had not committed any offence against the upper-caste villagers. Mattaiah had usually spent much of his time with upper-caste people and knew them very well. He was, or so his son remembers, a gentle person. He had no criminal record. Mattaiah was still hiding in the jasmine garden when the group of angry upper-caste people approached one hour later. The group, which arrived from Church Road on tractors and turned towards Modukuru, was led by Modugula Sambi Reddy. The group got out of the tractors and started running into the fields, shouting loudly that they were 'going to finish off the Harijans'.[49] Some chased those Dalits who were then running towards the channel that ran by the village, others ran towards the irrigation canal. Then there were cries from the jasmine garden. Mattaiah was attacked; his ear was speared, and his head was hit with an axe a couple of times. Jaladi Immaniel, a thirty-five-year-old Mala who had also sought shelter in the garden, was also struck by an axe. Modugula Sambi Reddy, attacked his head with an axe, another man did the same to the middle of his forehead, and then he was stabbed in the face and cut with a knife near his lower lip. Mallela Subba Rao (also a thirty-five-year-old Mala) was not wounded with an axe, but instead he was hit with iron rods on his head, right leg and chest. The other attackers joined in, and their participation resulted in his violent death.[50] The three men who had been attacked in the jasmine garden died from their injuries.

At the same time, some women from the Dalitwada went to the southern railway gate, which is on the other side of the Dalitwada. They wanted to see what was going on and saw a large crowd of Reddys and Telagas armed with sticks, rods, axes and spears moving and shouting that they should kill any Dalits they could spot.[51] This was the group of upper-caste people who had gone along the railway track earlier and had 'chased the Harijans towards Modukuru side and on the eastern bund of the new channel'.[52]

At least ten Dalit men were running away towards Modukuru. But having reached the Modukuru railway gate, where there is a small bridge across the canal, they were stopped by a group of upper-caste villagers from Modukuru, who were waiting for them in the field. Thus, squeezed in between the two groups of chasers, the fleeing Dalits were caught and attacked. Mandru Ramesh was struck by an axe on his right hand and wrist, and a knife was plunged into his neck.[53] At the Modukuru railway gate, Jaladi Issac, Sankuru Samson and Devarapalli Jayaraju were all killed in front of the cattle shed that stood next to the road that the railway station was on.[54] Issac was hit in the head with an axe and beaten with iron rods on his head and legs.[55] Samson was hit and was injured in the face by an axe; his eyeballs were removed and his right ear was cut off, and inevitably, he died.[56] Jayaraju was not struck by an axe, but he received so many other injuries that he also died.[57] The killings that occurred in front of the cattle shed must have been a very violent sight indeed.

Meanwhile, the group that had killed the Dalits in the jasmine garden had now travelled in a tractor down to the panchayat office in Modukuru. It is reported that the killers in the jasmine garden had praised their achievements loudly when they returned to the tractor.[58] The tractor belonged to G. Sambi Reddy from Munnangivaripalem, who also drove it. But the group had not finished its mission: it was on target once again when it reached Modukuru, that is, when it came across some Dalits[59] who had happened to separate from the group while running towards the Modukuru railway gate and had reached the centre of the village (Modukuru) instead.[60] Thus, the group, led by the Tsundur *sarpanch*, started chasing these Dalits towards Modukuru gate. One murder attempt failed. In fact, although Tanamchintala Adam[61] was hit with an axe on his right leg and elbow, he managed to escape and ran towards the Modukuru railway gate. Here, he was beaten and then witnessed Issac, Samson and Jayaraju being attacked before he eventually managed to escape.[62]

Angalakuduru Raja Mohan was also with the Dalits who had ended up at the panchayat office in Modukuru, and he – once he was chased – ran along with the group of Dalits towards the Modukuru railway gate. Raja Mohan was killed; the post-mortem examination concluded that he had died because of a head injury.[63] Meanwhile, a group of Dalits managed to get away from the Modukuru railway gate and hurried towards Moparru, east of Modukuru. After some time, a public bus appeared, which had come from Modukuru, and several of the upper-caste perpetrators got off it. They were armed and started chasing the Tsundur Dalits who escaped into the fields.[64] Dayiri Dhana Raj[65] was chased nearly all the way back to Tsundur, where he was attacked and beaten, and blood was removed from his body with a syringe. He was also forced to drink drain water and urine. But Dhana Raj was lucky. He was left alive in the fields, though under guard;

Dhana Raj managed to escape from the guard and swam across the canal. He was eventually rescued by some Dalit women, who dressed him up as a woman; wearing a sari like any other woman, he was put on a train from Tsundur station to Tenali the same night.[66]

Altogether, eight Dalits were killed in this major assault and five other persons were seriously injured on this day, 6 August 1991.[67] The dead bodies were not left behind in the fields, however. Instead, they were put into sacks and thrown in the nearby canals. The first three bodies were thrown in the Tungabadra irrigation canal, on the western side of the Tsundur–Modukuru Road.[68] The other bodies were left elsewhere: one to the west of Modukur village, and the remaining bodies were found in 'the new channel' and in a 'branch canal' on the eastern side of Modukuru.[69] Eyewitnesses claimed to have seen bodies being packed into sacks, which the culprits kicked 'with their legs' before they threw them into the nearby canals.[70] In short, this was a well-planned attack, resulting in a massacre of Tsundur Dalits in which the upper-caste people became extremely cruel in their determination to 'teach the Dalits a lesson'. Later, the incident became a major reason for social mobilization and complex processes in legal institutions evolving over many years.

Dead Bodies and Questions about the Police

One of the remaining key questions relating to the events of 6 August concerns the actions – or the inaction – of the police. There were several dead bodies in the village, and there had been a very violent attack in the agricultural fields. It was two years since the Prevention of Atrocities Act (PoA) had been created as an all-India piece of legislation. However, no effective action was taken by public officials to prevent the massacre or to retrieve information about it after it had happened. For instance, there were no reports at the police station on 6 August about the organized attack, which has later been referred to as the main incident in the context of tensions in Tsundur. The police did 'not know what happened in the fields and surrounding villages'.[71] A head constable from Tsundur police station reported in the later trial that a group of policemen had been looking for Reddys and Telagas, that is, the 300 upper-caste men who had passed 'in front of the police station armed with deadly weapons'[72] and who had chased the Dalits on the eastern bund of the canal on the day of the massacre. The police did not catch anyone, however, and they had been instructed to return to the station in Tsundur.[73] Later that day, G. Sambi Reddy from Munnangivaripalem had appeared at the police station. He had arrived on his tractor which some hours earlier had been used to drive the perpetrators. G. Sambi Reddy asked the police to escort his children from a nearby school back to his village, which they did so as to protect them.[74]

The police in Tsundur did not inquire into the killings of the Dalits before 11.30 p.m. on 6 August, after receiving information from the police in Tenali about dead bodies in the tank in Kondareddy.[75] The Tenali police heard about the incident in Tsundur when they were recording the statements of the injured Dalits who had been hospitalized in the government hospital in Tenali that night. Yet the Tsundur police did not find any dead bodies when they first went out to search early in the morning on 7 August. Later that morning, police personnel arrived from Tenali and organized search for dead bodies in several directions. They did not find any, however. Instead, it was the local Dalits who found them. Two bodies had been put into sacks, and eight bodies were recovered from canals within a radius of 7 kilometres from the centre of Tsundur.[76]

The crime was not registered as a coordinated or major criminal case by the police, and this raised a serious question about law enforcement during the trial. The special public prosecutor was very critical of the police in Tsundur during the trial; he claimed that the police had undermined the evidence needed for further criminal investigation and the later prosecution. He argued that the '[p]olice have not chosen to book a grand crime' but rather twelve individual 'crimes'. And he added 'that there are contentions by the SCs that their narratives of the events were not properly recorded by the Police'.[77] In an interview, the prosecutor explained that the quality of the 'first information reports' (FIRs) became 'a very serious matter in the trial'.[78] Thus, there was ample space for the defence lawyers to argue that the prosecution's twelve FIRs were insufficient to prove that anyone was guilty of committing the violent crimes. The reports were inconsistent. And the poor quality of the evidence made it hard to show that the upper-caste people conspired to kill the Dalits, that is, that they were acting as a group in a so-called unlawful assembly with a common intent to commit a crime. The police appeared more prepared to protect the landowners' children than the victims of the attack that day.

The defence lawyers claimed during the trial, however, that the case was only brought because of 'the so-called Human Rights activists' hue and cry … for publicity and for various other reasons of their selfish goals, but there is no truth in it'.[79] The truth was therefore disputed, and the discussion concerning the evidence concerned the police's management of events as they had registered the reports of the incidents from the day of the attack. It was also disputed whether the police sought to curb any subsequent Dalit mobilization and undermine the protests from gaining momentum.

Public Responses and Dalit Activism

The magnitude of 6 August greatly shocked Tsundur Dalits. The news about the major violence committed in the fields of Tsundur and Modukuru not only reached neighbouring towns and villages but the incident was also reported by national media. The massacre in Tsundur was reported in the newspaper *Times of India* to be 'the most gruesome ever witnessed in the state' in 'terms of toll, diabolic planning and ruthless execution'.[80] Regional political leaders, furthermore, condemned the attack. The chief minister, N. T. Rama Rao – who ruled at the time of the Karamchedu massacre in 1985 – argued that the Congress government was unable to ensure law and order in the state and that the central government should impose presidential rule in the state.[81] There were therefore many interests at stake in the case. Meanwhile, regional activists mobilized and so did activists in neighbouring states to gather facts about the event.[82] Katti Padma Rao became a prominent Dalit leader in this context, organizing 'dharnas', a special camp to support the victims, and calling for state-wide action. Katti Padma Rao lives in nearby Tsundur, in Ponnur town, and had led the movement Dalit Mahasabha that had been established in 1985 after Karamchedu along with Bojja Tharakam. Both attended the camp in Tsundur along with other prominent activists.[83]

The burial was led by the social movements, and Maoists were among those who were determined to ensure that the victims were given a Christian burial. In fact, the leaders of the more militant activists, the Naxalites, made their point by burying the deceased Dalit victims in the centre of the village.[84] The usual burial ground for Dalits is located on the outskirts of the village. Unlike Christians, Hindus do not bury their dead, and the burial in the centre of the village was therefore also contested for religious reasons.[85] Today, the graves have become powerful manifestations in the village centre. They remain visible on a slope while there are shops on each side and on the opposite side of Church Road. The politically significant burial caused a large crowd to assemble and included many activists and social movements from the whole of Andhra Pradesh.

While there were prominent Dalit leaders in Tsundur after the attack, the local Dalits had been led by Kommerla Anil Kumar up to that time. He was a young man and had been an active youth leader and a prime witness to the Tsundur massacre.[86] Anil Kumar was, in short, a key person in the Dalitwada; he could act and encourage the Tsundur Dalits. He was a crucial witness to the carnage and was able to confirm how the plot was carried out and how the local police may have been complicit in covering it up. It was therefore a blow for the Tsundur Dalits when he was shot by police on 17 September 1991 in the Malapalle.[87]

This young, articulate Dalit leader was murdered about one week after the Tsundur massacre had been discussed in the Indian parliament. At that time, the Dalit, Bihar politician Ram Vilas Paswan asked the government to clarify its measures to prevent these atrocities. Indeed, the Tsundur massacre was heavily condemned during this parliamentary debate on 9 September 1991. The representative from Tenali, Professor V. Umareddy, stated to the assembly and its speaker, 'Sir, a shameful incident has been inflicted on Harijans in my own Constituency of Tenali in Andhra Pradesh ... a naked attack on the very social order of the country.'[88] It was certainly a serious assembly that addressed the brutal killings of the Scheduled Castes (SCs). A representative from Karnataka state, V. Sreenivasa Prasad, went as far as to compare untouchability with apartheid in his clearly self-critical reflection:

> Sir, we have always been talking of antiapartheid in this country. What moral right has this country got to talk about anti-apartheid? We can see apartheid in every nook and corner of this country in the form of untouchability.[89]

In spite of this flow of self-critical statements uttered in the national parliament in New Delhi on 9 September, the Tsundur police killed Anil Kumar eight days later. However, although that murder certainly made an impact, the story did not end with Anil Kumar. The Tsundur victims faced a multifaceted struggle for justice involving many movements and activists. It is nonetheless significant that activists who were active in the Tsundur camp would also participate in the World Conference against Racism in Durban 2001 ten years later. However, the government of India objected to any comparison to South Africa regarding caste and race at this conference and in the ensuing 'Durban process' at the United Nations to avoid drawing international attention to caste-based oppression.[90]

Summary

The chapter has offered a detailed description of the tensions, plot and attack in Tsundur village to identify how the organized caste-based attack occurred and how the events played out socially, politically and institutionally. I will follow up the institutional processes in Chapter 5. But the facts that have emerged from this case study suggest that the police force had been more keen to act in accordance with the interest of the dominant order than to ensure protection for Dalits or to implement law effectively. For instance, while eight Dalits were killed by a large crowd of armed caste Hindus from the landowning community, the police had dispersed the Tsundur Dalits. On the day of the attack, the police provided more protection for children of landowners than for those who were attacked in the agricultural fields. The poor registration of evidence in the FIRs after the attack adds another reason to allege that either the police do not effectively implement the rule of law or they may even have been complicit in covering up the attack.

The social and political contexts are nonetheless decisive in explaining why the massacre was planned and carried out at all. The massacre was a violent backlash after a period of upward mobility and assertion among Tsundur Dalits. This is a familiar mechanism which I have referred to as the mechanism of oppression in the Dalit situation. The social changes in the village resulted in a dis-embedding of traditional caste relations, identity and behaviour there. In addition, there were deliberate, political attempts to deinstitutionalize values of caste through growing youth assertion and Ambedkarization in the village. On top of this, an older Dalit student corrected the verbal abuse that a boy from the landowning community used against the Dalit's friend at the cinema. However, there was a big difference between 'teaching the Dalit student a lesson' and 'You, the man who opposed us' – 'How dare you?'[91] and carrying out a large-scale attack.

The idea of 'teaching Dalits a lesson' to the point of eliminating them from the village – either literally or by discouraging Dalits from asserting their rights in the future – adds further credibility to two types of conceptual discussions. First, the attack reflects an ontological drive in a psychological sense. The drive gains force when touchables and untouchables are not properly separated and graded and is aimed at restoring the ontology of caste. When Ambedkar invented his concept of graded inequality, he pointed out how this system of caste involved an ontological difference between touchables and untouchables. The former could feel important by treating the latter as nobodies. With the social changes in Tsundur, however, this ontology of caste could not be taken for granted, and hence, the idea of 'teaching them a lesson' took hold. But the large-scale attack in Tsundur introduces in the second dimension the notion of a dominant caste. The French anthropologist Louis Dumont criticized the sociologist Srinivas for adopting a vague definition of a dominant caste.[92] Yet where Dumont aimed at conceptual clarity in terms of using an advanced structuralist philosophy, Srinivas' multifarious notion of the dominant caste captures several aspects of the power dynamics in Tsundur. As in Srinivas' understanding, the dominant landowning caste – which in Tsundur is primarily the Reddy community – had numerical, economic and political advantages. Their position in the ritual hierarchy was not insignificant. Although this community has historically been associated with Shudras, the Reddy caste demanded Kshatriya status in the non-Brahmin movement, and their higher status in relation to Dalits was crucial. Since the Reddy community in Tsundur supported the Congress government that ruled the state at the time, it had a significant political advantage in relation to the state. In addition, the determination to stop the Tsundur Dalits was encouraged by members of the dominant castes in neighbouring villages. United by anger, the ontological drive to restore their status and subjugate the Dalits, made them exercise their power to an extreme degree. Casteism is an intense experience; derogatory remarks suggest that the identity of the untouchables is radically negated.[93] The attack of 6 August 1991 in Tsundur was nonetheless about exercising extreme power to intensify and violently re-embed the privilege of caste, and yet the narrative elements of this case became integral to the history of the Dalit movement and the evolving caste-related politics in the state.

Notes

1. According to one estimate, twenty-eight incidents of violence against Dalits were registered in the state of Andhra Pradesh, ranging from that in Karamchedu on 17 July 1985 to the one that occurred in Tsundur on 6 August 1991. K. Balagopal, *Ear to the Ground: Selected Writings on Class and Caste* (New Delhi: Navayana, 2011), 472–4.
2. Paul R. Brass, *The Politics of India Since Independence*, 2nd edn (Cambridge: Cambridge University Press, 1994), 326–8.
3. Bhimrao Ramji Ambedkar, 'Untouchables or the Children of India's Ghetto', in *Dr. Babasaheb Ambedkar Writings and Speeches: Unpublished Writings*, ed. Vasant Moon, vol. 5 (Bombay: Education Department, Government of Maharashtra, 1989), 102.
4. *Times of India*, 'Eyewitness Account Given: Burning of Harijan Boy', 3 May 1968, accessed April 25, 2016, http://search.proquest.com/docview/614027427/fulltextPDF/97566C7EEE244A2PQ/2?accountid=11144.
5. Bojja Tharakam, in an interview with the author, Hyderabad, December 2014.
6. K. Seshadri, 'The Telengana Agitation and the Politics of Andhra Pradesh', *The Indian Journal of Political Science* 31, no. 1 (1970): 70–1, doi:10.2307/41854361.
7. Anand Teltumbde, *The Persistence of Caste: The Khairlanji Murders and India's Hidden Apartheid* (New Delhi: Navayana, 2010).
8. There are different spellings of Tsundur in English. The name can be spelled as Tsundur, Tsunduru, Chundur or Chunduru. The signpost at the train station in the village uses 'Tsunduru', while many prefer using the term 'Chundur' when they write about the village as this is closer to the vernacular version. I will use 'Tsundur' for consistency as this spelling is also used in the court judgments and official materials.
9. Govathoti Ravi, in an interview with the author, Tenali, March 2008.
10. Ibid.
11. The word 'hotel' is used synonymously with restaurant and/or café.
12. From interview with Mrs Jakraiah, Panthagani Manikhyamma, Tsundur, 10 March 2008.
13. Nagaswaramrao, advocate and assistant to the special public prosecutor, in an interview with the author, Tenali, February 2008.
14. Ravi, in an interview with the author, March 2008.
15. Sudha Pai, *Dalit Assertion and the Unfinished Democratic Revolution: The Bahujan Samaj Party in Uttar Pradesh* (New Delhi: Sage Publications, 2002), 199; Jagpal Singh, 'Ambedkarisation and Assertion of Dalit Identity: Socio-Cultural Protest in Meerut District of Western Uttar Pradesh', *Economic and Political Weekly* 33, no. 40 (1998): 2611–8, doi:10.2307/4407245.
16. Ravi, in an interview with the author, March 2008.
17. In fact, the Dalit Bahujan Party in Uttar Pradesh has been criticized for being more interested in statues of Ambedkar and ensuring that these are made of the best material than in the social and economic elevation of the poor. However, Ambedkar

is also the framer of the constitution, and he can be respected for his contribution among non-Dalits as well. This was the interpretation the Mandal revenue officer gave me when I visited his office in March 2008. He was new to Tsundur and expressed much respect to Dalits, although he was an upper-caste man himself. I asked him if the statue of Ambedkar was intended as a provocation. He said it was not and that Ambedkar could not be a possession of the Dalits, since non-Dalits also respect him and consider him 'theirs' because he led the work undertaken to create the constitution. I suspect he was being excessively polite, but the point is worth noting. In any case, the Mandal revenue officer of 2008 was talking in a significantly different atmosphere than had been the case sixteen years earlier.

18. Pai, *Dalit Assertion and the Unfinished Democratic Revolution*, 199.
19. M. N. Srinivas, 'The Dominant Caste in Rampura', *American Anthropologist* 61, no. 1 (1959): 141.
20. My main source on the economic difference is the Mandal revenue officer at the time.
21. In an interview in March 2008, B. Chandrasekhar, the special public prosecutor, mentioned that most of the accused upper castes that appeared in court in 2007 wore traditional clothes such as dhotis and lungis rather than jeans.
22. K. Muruli, 'Upper Caste Violence on Dalits: Case Studies of Karamchedu and Chundur Massacres', unpublisehed MPhil dissertation, Department of Political Science, University of Hyderabad, 1995, p. 58.
23. Jakraiah, interview with the author, 10 March 2008.
24. K. Srinivasulu, 'Caste, Class and Social Articulation in Andhra Pradesh: Mapping Differential Regional Trajectories', Working Paper 179, Overseas Development Institute, London, 2002, p. 40, accessed 10 July 2019, https://www.odi.org/sites/odi.org.uk/files/odi-assets/publications-opinion-files/2692.pdf.
25. Moses, in an interview with the author, Tsundur, 10 March 2008.
26. K. Srinivasulu, 'Caste, Class and Social Articulation in Andhra Pradesh'.
27. Andhra Pradesh Civil Liberties Committee, *The Chundur Carnage: AP-Civil Liberties Committee Report*, 6, accessed 26 January 2017, http://balagopal.org/wp-content//uploads/2014/04/Tsunduru/THE%20TSUNDURU%20CARNAGE-APCLC%20REPORT-PUBLISHED%20IN%20AUGUST%201991.pdf.
28. Moses, in an interview with the author, 12 March 2008.
29. Govathoti Ravi, interview with the author, Tenali, 11 March 2008.
30. Ibid.
31. See, for example, Vasanth Kannabiran and Kalpana Kannabiran, 'Caste and Gender: Understanding Dynamics of Power and Violence', *Economic and Political Weekly* 26, no. 37 (1991): 2132, doi:10.2307/41626993.
32. Prem Chowdhry, '"First Our Jobs Then Our Girls": The Dominant Caste Perceptions on the "Rising" Dalits', *Modern Asian Studies* 43, no. 1 (2009), 437–79, doi: 10.1017/S0026749X07003010.
33. For discussion of the concept of ontological security, see Anthony Giddens, *The Constitution of Society: Outline of the Theory of Structuration* (Cambridge: Polity, 1984), 50.

34. Ravi in an interview with the author, 12 March 2008.
35. *Sub-Divisional Police Officer, Tenali* (Crime Nos. 65 to 73 and 89 and 90/91 of Tsundur P.S. and Crime No. 64/91 of Amarthaluru P.S.) *vs Accused 1* (Modugula Sami Reddy - 219) (Tsundur court, 31 August 2007), 23.
36. Ibid.
37. Muruli, *Upper Caste Violence on Dalits*, 65.
38. Ibid., 63.
39. *Sub-Divisional Police Officer, Tenali* (Crime Nos. 65 to 73 and 89 and 90/91 of Tsundur P.S. and Crime No. 64/91 of Amarthaluru P.S.) *vs Accused 1* (Modugula Sami Reddy - 219), 24.
40. G. S. Nageswara Rao, an advocate from Tenali town and assistant to the special public prosecutor in Tsundur court, in an interview with the author, Tenali, February 2008.
41. *Sub-Divisional Police Officer, Tenali* (Crime Nos. 65 to 73 and 89 and 90/91 of Tsundur P.S. and Crime No. 64/91 of Amarthaluru P.S.) *vs Accused 1* (Modugula Sami Reddy - 219), 24.
42. It will be evident in Chapter 5 that what occurred on this day has been disputed because the facts have implications for convictions and sentences. The events that I have mapped are mainly based on a detailed analysis of the comprehensive judgment of 2007, and I have supplemented that with available sources.
43. *Sub-Divisional Police Officer, Tenali* (Crime Nos. 65 to 73 and 89 and 90/91 of Tsundur P.S. and Crime No. 64/91 of Amarthaluru P.S.) *vs Accused 1* (Modugula Sami Reddy - 219), 56.
44. Ibid., 25.
45. Ibid., 41.
46. *Wada* means hamlet in Telugu and is part of a larger village; a Dalitwada would refer to a hamlet where Dalits from castes such as Mala and Madiga live. *Palle* is often a more general term for village, but it is used here also in a more specific sense to designate the Mala hamlet. So, while 'Dalitwada' or 'Harijanwada' are generic designations for Dalit settlements, 'Malapalle' refers specifically to the hamlet of the Mala caste (or a Dalit sub-caste). The majority of Dalits in Tsundur were Malas, which is why the terms 'Dalitwada' and 'Malapalle' are sometimes used interchangeably in this context.
47. *Sub-Divisional Police Officer, Tenali* (Crime Nos. 65 to 73 and 89 and 90/91 of Tsundur P.S. and Crime No. 64/91 of Amarthaluru P.S.) *vs Accused 1* (Modugula Sami Reddy - 219), 41. There was disagreement in the court about when the police entered the *palle* and if they did so at all. It seems clear that the police entered before noon or at least in the middle of the day.
48. Ibid., 42.
49. Ibid., 25.
50. Ibid., 25.
51. Ibid., 26.
52. Ibid., 222.

53. Ibid., 26.
54. Special public prosecutor, 'Written Arguments in SC No. 36/1993. In the Court of the Special Session Judge under the SCs & STs (PoA) Act, 1989 (IV ASJ) Guntur. Camp: Tsundur. SC No. 36/91' unpublished manuscript (1 January 2007), chap. 1, p. 9.
55. *Sub-Divisional Police Officer, Tenali* (Crime Nos. 65 to 73 and 89 and 90/91 of Tsundur P.S. and Crime No. 64/91 of Amarthaluru P.S.) *vs Accused 1* (Modugula Sami Reddy - 219), 151.
56. Ibid., 156.
57. Ibid.,159.
58. Prosecutor, 'Written Arguments in SC no. 36/1993', chap. 1, p. 8.
59. Ibid., chap. 1, p. 9.
60. *Sub-Divisional Police Officer, Tenali* (Crime Nos. 65 to 73 and 89 and 90/91 of Tsundur P.S. and Crime No. 64/91 of Amarthaluru P.S.) *vs Accused 1* (Modugula Sami Reddy - 219), 27.
61. Referred to in the judgment as 'LW.49'.
62. Ibid., 27; Prosecutor, 'Written Arguments in SC no. 36/1993', chap. 1, p. 9.
63. *Sub-Divisional Police Officer, Tenali* (Crime Nos. 65 to 73 and 89 and 90/91 of Tsundur P.S. and Crime No. 64/91 of Amarthaluru P.S.) *vs Accused 1* (Modugula Sami Reddy - 219), 52.
64. Prosecutor, 'Written Arguments in SC no. 36/1993', chap. 1, p. 9.
65. Referred to in the judgment as 'PW.15' (prosecution witness no. 15).
66. Ibid., chap. 1, pp. 9–10.
67. *Sub-Divisional Police Officer, Tenali* (Crime Nos. 65 to 73 and 89 and 90/91 of Tsundur P.S. and Crime No. 64/91 of Amarthaluru P.S.) *vs Accused 1* (Modugula Sami Reddy - 219), 160.
68. Ibid., 197.
69. Ibid., 59–60
70. Ibid., 159–60.
71. Ibid., 57.
72. Ibid., 54.
73. Ibid., 58.
74. Ibid., 55.
75. Ibid., 55.
76. Ibid., 64.
77. Prosecutor, 'Written Arguments in SC no. 36/1993', chap. 1, p. 11.
78. B. Chandrasekhar, Special Public Prosecutor, in an interview with the author, Warangal, 8 February 2008.
79. *Sub-Divisional Police Officer, Tenali* (Crime Nos. 65 to 73 and 89 and 90/91 of Tsundur P.S. and Crime No. 64/91 of Amarthaluru P.S.) *vs Accused 1* (Modugula Sami Reddy - 219), 66.
80. *Times of India*, 'NTR Demands Delhi Rule in AP', 12 August 1991.
81. Ibid.

82. Ajith Kanna, in an interview with the author, August 2016.
83. *Times of India*, 'NTR Demands Delhi Rule in AP'.
84. Gaddar, in an interview with author, March 2008. Gaddar, the revolutionary poet, explained that the Naxalites buried the dead in the middle of the village. This was a Christian burial, rather than a Hindu rite.
85. A Guntur lawyer therefore complained against this burial in the centre of the village, arguing that it was a violation of Hindu law, although this case was never processed. Sanjeeva Reddy, in an interview with the author, Guntur, 12 March 2008.
86. Muruli, *Upper Caste Violence on Dalits*, 70.
87. *Sub-Divisional Police Officer, Tenali* (Crime Nos. 65 to 73 and 89 and 90/91 of Tsundur P.S. and Crime No. 64/91 of Amarthaluru P.S.) *vs Accused 1* (Modugula Sami Reddy - 219), 64.
88. Parliament of India, Lok Sabha Debates, 'Re. Brutal Killing of Harijans in Tsundur Village of Guntur District', 1991, accessed 15 January 2018, http://parliamentofindia.nic.in/ls/lsdeb/ls10/ses1/0409089101.htm.
89. Ibid.
90. Dag-Erik Berg, 'Race as a Political Frontier against Caste: WCAR, Dalits and India's Foreign Policy', *Journal of International Relations and Development* 21, no. 4 (2018): 990–1013, doi: 10.1057/s41268-017-0091-3.
91. Govathoti Ravi in interview with the author, Tenali, 12 March 2008.
92. Louis Dumont, *Homo Hierarchicus: The Caste System and Its Implications* (Chicago: University of Chicago Press, 1980), 161.
93. Dag-Erik Berg, 'Foregrounding Contingency in Caste-Based Dominance: Ambedkar, Hegemony, and the Pariah Concept', *Philosophy & Social Criticism* 44, no. 8 (2018): 843–64, doi:10.1177/0191453717744007.

5

Goals of Law, Goals of Order

Institutional Conversion after Atrocities

The creation of the Scheduled Castes and the Scheduled Tribes (Prevention of Atrocities) Act (PoA Act), 1989, was a milestone in the development of the legal protection of groups that had experienced frequent humiliation and large-scale violence during the postcolonial period. And yet the law does not effectively translate into justice in practice: it is not simply a question of legal design and implementation achieving this. To explain how law can be used, it would be helpful to focus on how law and order are two different things, which may even serve different goals. Foucault argues that the expression of law and order is a 'hybridized monster', and that it is better to speak of 'law or order' because the two phenomena are incompatible and can be compared to the choice of having either milk or lemon in a cup of tea.[1] Separating the two terms, law and order, offers an opportunity to examine how law may not be part of the ways in which an institutional order operates. Once an atrocity occurs, institutions may respond in ways that differ from the route set out in official law. Thus, although the PoA Act is a piece of legislation that should be obeyed, local state institutions may in practice comply with the interests of locally dominant castes instead. This is more than a question of delayed justice. The attack in Tsundur occurred on 6 August 1991, but it was only on August 2007 that the trial court delivered its judgment and sentenced many of the accused. However, processes that take place after a crime has been committed involve crucial questions concerning practical institutional barriers, which aggravate vulnerabilities and the difficulties of securing evidence and the truth about atrocities.

This chapter brings the institutional barriers related to law and order more into focus by examining how caste-related attacks are addressed by institutions of law, that is, the local state and courts. Focusing on the attacks on Dalits in Tsundur village in Andhra Pradesh in 1991 and in Khairlanji in Maharashtra in 2006, I point out how institutions such as police stations and courts are vulnerable to making mistakes and being subjected to direct exploitation. Mohanty has argued that in cases such as those in Kilvenmani, Karamchedu and Khairlanji state officials were complicit in the cover-up of massacres or the prevention of the conviction of members of dominant castes.[2] I will address this assumption in this chapter, but my strategy is to use new concepts to discuss how courts and institutions of law become institutional sites vulnerable to being exploited by powerful groups. I engage with contributions to institutional theory to explain how powerful actors gain significance and may affect the outcome of the process. I adopt a concept created by the political scientist Kathleen Thelen to examine how an organization's official goal can be transformed and 'converted' through the politics that start after a decision is made to implement a policy.[3] The concept of conversion is a novel addition to institutional theory, and I will explain it further as it serves to conceptualize institutional processes in the context of caste-based violence, where members of dominant castes often exercise control over state institutions.

In what follows, I introduce the concept of goal conversion in the first section to explain how law and practice may differ, and then I examine two case studies. In the second section, I explain what happened in the Khairlanji massacre in Maharashtra in 2006. In this brutal atrocity case, there are key lessons to be learnt about institutional processes and local legal decisions. In the third section, I discuss the Tsundur case further. While it was clear in the previous chapter that the police were unable to secure accurate evidence at an early stage, I show how the ambiguities in the data recorded after the incident were exploited at the Andhra Pradesh High Court by judges who became hostile to the fact that Tsundur Dalits had kept up their struggle for justice for a long time. In the final section, I discuss how the two cases require greater attention to how law appears to be vulnerable to manipulation and policy conversion. In fact, power dynamics after the attack, including relations between officials and members of the public, played an important role in converting the official goal of institutions into a new goal, which in practice corresponded with the interests of power holders or members of the dominant caste. Overall, goal conversion is a challenge in a context of inequality, dominance and caste.

Atrocity Law and Goal Conversion in Institutional Theory

Lawmaking is no doubt one important part of how justice can be advanced and how responsive public institutions can make a difference. It was because of the persistent trend of caste-based violence that social activists and members of parliament demanded better legislation and preventive measures. As argued in Chapter 2, the problem has been discussed in the Indian parliament. Several efforts were made over a long period by members of the Parliamentary Forum for Scheduled Castes and Scheduled Tribes to improve the situation.[4] Their interventions have coexisted with continuous demands from Dalit movements across the country. While the Protection of Civil Rights Act developed from 1955 to 1976, the Dalit movements lobbied parliament and speeded up the momentum for a comprehensive piece of legislation. The result was the PoA Act, 1989, which can be viewed as a response to historical atrocities like Belchi in Bihar (1977) and Karamchedu in Andhra Pradesh (1985) as well as many other instances of caste-based violence. The police had been unable to address many such incidents within the framework of the Indian criminal code, and the new law was a significant landmark.[5]

The implementation of this piece of legislation is nevertheless fraught with problems. Although the PoA Act reflects how law can be responsive by integrating social problems into the formal framework, everyday practices in public institutions make the law a part of a state order that represses and exhausts Dalits.[6] The legal system therefore ends up delaying justice, even to the point of extending oppression and divisions. It is worthwhile moving beyond basic observations about whether a piece of legislation is implemented or the political class is responsive to the citizens, however. Institutional processes such as 'drift and conversion often occur beyond the bright glare of legislative politics'.[7] And questions of inequality and dominance have a considerable effect on the outcome of public policy.

Recent contributions to historical institutionalism offer tools that can be used to analyse the organizational processes that occur after a decision has been made or an official goal has been created. These contributions are based on two theoretical points. First, historical institutionalists argue that there is often a considerable emphasis in political studies on high-profile events, which foreground the voter–politician nexus. Such an approach creates discussions about the extent to which decision-makers respond to the demands that are articulated by their citizens. Despite its merits, this conventional emphasis on responsiveness is inadequate to explain many institutional processes and implementation of policies.[8] The application of law in practice could be open to change given the nature of how institutions work in practice. Second, institutional changes go beyond the concept of path dependency. This concept is well established and very prominent in institutional theory, and the word 'path' is frequently used as a metaphor to explain institutional continuity. The problem is that path dependency emphasizes linear developments and stability in ways that do not explain several dynamics and types of institutional change.[9] For example, the implementation of law could be changed by more powerful groups and, thereby, converted in practice. Institutional conversion is a valuable concept in institutional theory; it designates the process whereby institutions designed with one set of goals are redirected to other ends.[10]

It is useful to make a basic premise of institutional theory more explicit to understand what is meant by conversion implying a redirection of goals. Organizational theorists distinguish between organizations and institutions. An institutional theorist Philip Selznick emphasizes that 'organisations are technical instruments, designed as means to define goals'.[11] Institutions, by contrast, involve people whose ideas and interests infuse organizations with values. Selznick's classic definition has the merit of highlighting how organizations are defined by goals. Similarly, legislators may have a goal or intention in mind when they enact a piece of legislation. Legal theorists have reasons to problematize intentions in law.[12] But the legal goal in this context is to grant protection to vulnerable groups; in fact, this is spelled out in its name: the PoA Act, 1989.[13] This piece of legislation therefore does have an official goal, but institutions are subject to social and political processes through which formal goals can be changed. Although institutions transcend individuals, they should be understood in a relational sense. Individuals relate to one another inside an institution, and in this way, technical means become blended with internal interests.[14] Relations with external actors, moreover, may be determined by what Weber defines as social status groups.[15] Indeed, members of institutions may have better relations with members of one social class, external to the organization, than others. It was clear in Chapter 4 that the police in Tsundur village had more friendly relations with the caste Hindus whose children they escorted than with the Dalits who were attacked and killed. Institutions are subject to bias where the internal composition of individuals matters. In the case of Tsundur, geography made a difference as well because the police station is located inside the settlement of the landowning castes. The question in this context is whether institutions of law may serve as tools for preventing atrocities or the goal of the PoA Act was changed in the ensuing processes and to what degree. Here, the distinction between formal goals and institutional outcomes is crucial, where inequality among citizens makes the difference more problematic.

In a classic contribution to explaining outcomes of court cases, Marc Galanter argues that experienced and resourceful litigants succeed more often than inexperienced and less resourceful ones.[16] Entitled 'Why the "Haves" Come Out Ahead', Galanter's article dovetails with the concept of conversion in institutional theory.[17] Institutional conversion implies, as it does in Galanter's account, that power and resources provide the means to redirect official goals. Thelen's concept of conversion involves different dimensions, ranging from ideas to actors.[18] Another political scientist, Robert Leiberman, has explored this phenomenon and argues that political change may occur at the intersection of institutions and ideas.[19] The atrocity cases discussed in this book involve several practical contingencies, such as personnel, the situation concerning the registration of first information reports (FIRs), individual relations, participation in movements and ideas about caste. Each of these factors, or a combination of them, could make a difference and determine the outcome, even making one court judgment different to another in relation to the same case. Thus, although the PoA Act is a comprehensive piece of legislation with strict and non-bailable offences, it could in practice be implemented or redirected in different ways from those for which it was designed.

Atrocity cases such as those in Tsundur and Khairlanji are examples of the state converting the law. The initial goal of ensuring protection for victims was changed to comply with the interests and ideas of actors in the state institutions. Discussions about this aspect rarely figure in debates concerning the PoA Act, which has been either publicly dismissed or subjected to debates about its implementation. On the one hand, the law is seen as controversial by members of dominant castes, who argue that it is often misused by the Scheduled Castes (SCs) and that it will result in unfair treatment and non-bailable imprisonment. Such controversial views reflect a problem of legitimacy surrounding this piece of legislation. On the other hand, there are discussions about how the law is ineffective in practice. After discussions in parliament in August 2010, for instance, the Union Home Minister P. Chidambaram expressed concerns about the state's inability to prevent atrocities against Dalits and Adivasis.[20] He also called for better implementation of the PoA Act and speedier trials to avoid losing evidence justifying the prosecution and to prevent manipulation of the witnesses by the accused. Amendments have been made to the law to improve various aspects of it to ensure more effective justice. For example, the Indian parliament approved amendments in 2015 that granted victims more security. These amendments had been pending for a long period in a standing committee. The Act is far from popular as a political strategy, given that there are powerful castes that strongly oppose this legislation. There is in any case more at stake than simply the implementation of, or the politics surrounding, the legislation, as shown in the case studies of Khairlanji and Tsundur.

The Khairlanji Atrocity and State Institutions

The atrocity in Khairlanji village that occurred on 29 September 2006 is among the main atrocity cases that has gained national attention in India in the new millennium. This incident includes a strong element of sexual violence,[21] which is far more prominent than in cases such as those in Karamchedu and Tsundur. However, the atrocity in Khairlanji includes several of the familiar dynamics of caste-based violence and provides further insights into the critical processes that took place after the attack. Khairlanji is in the eastern part of Maharashtra. The village is near the city of Nagpur, where many Dalits gathered on 14 October, two weeks after the attack, to mark Ambedkar's conversion to Buddhism.

Four family members were brutally attacked on 29 September 2006. Two women were raped, brutally beaten and lynched, along with two sons from the same family. The father was not present when the attack started. In addition to brutal violence, the massacre in Khairlanji is also a story about the negligence of the local police and state repression as protests among Dalits and women activists gained momentum after this attack. The People's Union for Civil Liberties (PUCL) was particularly articulate in its critique of the local police; it argued that there was an 'active complicity of the state administration in the massacre and its cover up'.[22] And when the news about the killings eventually resulted in protests two months after the attack, the police struck down the popular mobilization and demonstrations against the lack of state action to ensure protection and justice for Dalits. The police action was driven by a concern about the order, which thus became an approach that marginalized the relevance of the violent attacks. Facts about the atrocity were suppressed due to a powerful national discourse on Maoists being a security challenge. The local barriers to justice and state reactions thus aggravated a popular sense of alienation and injustice.

The attack on the Bhotmange family can be understood against a familiar backdrop. The Khairlanji atrocity shows – like those in Tsundur and Karamchedu – that assertive Dalits can be attacked to 'teach them a lesson'. While this mechanism of oppression was well understood, the situation was that the Bhotmange family insisted that they could cultivate the 5 acres of land they owned. But their plans would have a specific impact on other villagers because local caste Hindus had always used a path that ran over this piece of land. This path, used daily, would now cease to exist. The Bhotmange couple, Bhaiyyalal and Surekha, had started cultivating their land in 1989, after it had been taken for granted by other villagers that they could use it as a common passage. There were several disputes over this land, starting with a police complaint in 2001.[23] Tensions and fear emerged as the family followed up their demands, but it was in 2006 that these escalated into the cruel attack.

The attack happened during the evening of 29 September, and local Dalits and villagers knew it was happening. It is unclear whether anyone beyond the village was aware of it, though; however, Teltumbde explains that the attack had been planned to 'teach the Bhotmange family a lesson'.[24] They had registered complaints at the police station. The first complaint was against a couple of individuals among the caste Hindus and, later on, they reported a violent attack on a local property owner who had supported the family with his advice. The latter incident became decisive. Tensions rose, especially since the police arrested and then released twelve of the accused persons. Caste Hindus had reportedly threatened to attack the Bhotmange family, and there was fear of violence. The attack on 29 September involved a group of both men and women who were armed with primitive weapons such as cycle chains, knives and iron rods. The mother was preparing dinner when the attack happened. The women were dragged out of the house by the hair and then beaten and stripped while the sons were beaten and their genitals were cut. The daughter was raped and beaten. The dead bodies were thrown into an irrigation canal.[25] Apparently, the attackers planned to keep silent about the attack. Several witnesses felt helpless and terrified by what had happened, and they had been threatened with facing a similar fate if they reported the incident.[26] Bhaiyyalal Bhotmange had witnessed the attack on a distance. He had been too terrified to intervene in the violence inflicted in front of him.

Bhaiyyalal Bhotmange was planning to report the attack at the nearby police station. He was a key witness and victim, but there were several barriers that he could not overcome in this process, and so the incident was not accurately registered. The first barrier for the bereaved father and husband was the lack of goodwill among the police officers. They did not respect him as he approached them for help because he had not paid them a bribe when they had expected him to do so earlier. Thus, when he arrived at the police station, he was asked to sit and wait – his case was not prioritized. He waited until he was asked to accompany the police to identify a dead body – which turned out to be his daughter.[27] The second problem arose at this stage as the local police were unable to secure the data and evidence that could have been crucial to the later processes. The post-mortems were not conducted by a doctor with the relevant forensic expertise.[28] Thus, despite the highly sexualized attacks, the post-mortem reports did not include any evidence of rape.

The court case relating to the Khairlanji atrocity, nevertheless, took place sooner than similar court cases elsewhere (such as in Tsundur). The first trial was heard in a 'fast track' session court in 2008, and the second was heard at the Bombay High Court in 2010.[29] The sentences were severe. The fast-track session court handed down six death penalties, but the high court reduced the sentences to life in prison, fines and one year of rigorous imprisonment. However, it is worth noting how the crime was legally conceptualized. Publicly, it was considered to be a caste-related atrocity case. Yet the PoA Act was not the piece of legislation that was applied. Instead of registering this crime as a caste-based atrocity, it was understood as a 'revenge act' between individuals and therefore classified under regular criminal law. It was this assumption that gained significance in the appeal to the Bombay High Court; the court's judgment had identified this as a revenge act rather than killings carried out due to 'caste hatred'.[30]

It is striking that the PoA Act was sidelined, among other things, because it does not involve capital punishments as in the regular Indian Penal Code. This choice was the result of the discourse used in this context. It is useful to revisit Foucault's complex word 'discourse'[31] in order to underline the understanding that gained relevance in this context. Theoretically, the PoA Act was an available piece of legislation, but it was an option kept at the margins of knowledge and practice. It was not the prime theme in the investigation. Rather, the dispute in Khairlanji was individualized by the investigators. It was highlighted in the judgment that it involved an action taken against Mrs Bhotmange after she had filed complaints with the police. The facts were therefore turned against Mrs Bhotmange, and there was a focus on her personal characteristics. The question of caste mentality was silenced. The local discourse seems to have become embedded in the court's assessment. The judgment was in any case appealed and is now pending in the Supreme Court.[32]

The question of discourse is also relevant to explaining how the police responded to the subsequent popular protests. It was a month until the attack gained public attention. This delay is noteworthy since Khairlanji village is only 125 kilometres away from Nagpur, a centre for the Dalit identity politics. The city is important for the Buddhist movement, which was preparing for the fiftieth anniversary of Ambedkar's conversion to Buddhism on 14 October, which usually attracted visitors from across the country.[33] At the end of October, however, a group led by Dalit women mobilized and were later supported by other female activists, who organized a public protest for 1 November. Young women and men followed their lead and protested against the state.

But the government decided to strike down the mounting mobilization by claiming that the movement was infiltrated by the Maoist group, the Naxalites. The concerns with caste-based and sexual violence were therefore effectively marginalized, and the state's determination to curb the protests was strengthened by viewing it in wider terms with a larger discourse concerning national security. On 13 April that year, the Prime Minister of India Manmohan Singh had highlighted the Naxalite movement as a national problem and declared the Maoist movement to be 'the single biggest internal security challenge ever faced by our country'.[34] The Naxalite movement had been active in western Maharashtra. The national security strategy could therefore gain legitimacy and force as the Dalit women and other female activists organized public protests, objecting to how the state had dealt with the caste-based violence in Khairlanji village.

Once the massacre gained visibility through media coverage, the mobilization gained popular momentum. The protests erupted when people in Maharashtra learnt that a statue of Ambedkar had been beheaded in a different part of the country, Kanpur city in Uttar Pradesh. This act caused anger and represented a typical act of humiliation and hostility towards the rights to equality that Ambedkar had contributed to ensuring for Dalits in the constitution of 1950. The beheading resulted in a considerable number of protests in Kanpur city.[35] This was also the background for the peaceful protestors in Maharashtra becoming hostile and more aggressive. Roads were blocked and six vehicles were damaged. The beheading of the statue of Ambedkar in Kanpur and the resulting Dalit protests triggered anger and Dalit protests in Mumbai and throughout Maharashtra. What started as a peaceful protest against the violence in Khairlanji village, therefore, developed into public anger, burnt train coaches and destruction of public property. Four Dalit protestors died. The chain of events represented a broader movement against constant attacks and humiliations. The political alienation loomed large, especially in a context in which Dalits – such as in Maharashtra – were fragmented. As Teltumbde states, the state repression reinforced the sense of alienation and despair.[36]

To sum up, there were different interpretations at the local, regional and national levels, representing a set of discourses that all contributed to removing the state's recognition of a case of caste-based violence in Khairlanji. The PoA Act, 1989, was not used. Instead, the courts used regular criminal law while the police targeted popular protests as a problem of order. Many of the protestors were women who objected to the fact that the police had not even recorded the sexual assaults. Ashu Saxena, the founder of an action group for the Khairlanji victims, was arrested on 9 November and charged with twenty criminal actions.[37] The demand for justice for the killed and mutilated Bhotmanges was thus criminalized for the sake of order and security.

Tsundur and Changing Interpretations of Law

The atrocity in Tsundur has been less surrounded with questions about the state's claim to be maintaining order than that in Khairlanji. The case in Andhra Pradesh involved significant questions of law, and there was a long delay before the trial started.[38] The first trial was conducted in 2007, sixteen years after the incident. But it was a historic event. A special court had been organized in the village – at the site of the occurrence – which is why the descriptions 'Tsundur court', 'trial Court' or 'camp at Tsundur' are used in relation to the court case.[39] The court, officially referred to as a 'special court' in the PoA Act, was organized in the village school.[40] Victims and locals could therefore easily attend, although the proceedings were carried out in English rather than in their native language, Telugu. There was also great awareness in Andhra Pradesh about caste-based violence as well as about the PoA Act, 1989. The Act was part of the movement's history and demands. The leaders of the Dalit movement had made demands for a provision about atrocity to be included in law after the massacre in Karamchedu in 1985.

Providing evidence about the attack involved many technical challenges. The question concerning the meaning of the evidence gained significance when the case was appealed to Andhra Pradesh High Court. The FIRs were crucial. The FIRs were the first and most authoritative documents that would be used in the trial. Their quality relied on the accurate reporting of the individuals who witnessed the attack as well as how the police officers recorded the information given to them in the immediate aftermath. As explained in Chapter 4, the special public prosecutor of the Tsundur court argued that the quality and meanings of 'the FIR became a very serious matter during the trial' in the Tsundur court.[41] However, the special public prosecutor B. Chandrasekhar passed away due to cancer in January 2013. It was after his death that those convicted for the brutal attack in Tsundur village proceeded with their appeal to the Andhra Pradesh High Court to amend the judgment from 2007. And it was precisely the questions of evidence and the credibility of witnesses that emerged powerfully in this new appeal. The two judges also gave the accused the benefit of doubt, highlighting several problems concerning the evidence and questioning key witnesses. In fact, there is a striking difference between the two judgments – that of the Tsundur court of 2007 and the high court judgment of 2014 – in terms of language, presentation of data, attitude and style. The difference is so prominent that it represents a noteworthy discoursive shift.

There was only one judge in the Tsundur court but two on the high court bench. Their identities differed. The judge in the Tsundur court, Anis, was a Muslim and had little relation to any of the communities involved. She was known as a soft judge in Guntur, whereas the judges in the high court came from the same caste as the accused persons. In fact, one of the high court judges, L. Narasimha Reddy, is well known for heading a non-governmental organisation (NGO) in Hyderabad that identifies with the Hindu reformer Saraswati (1824–83). This ideological background is significant. Saraswati had argued that all *varna*s were part of a moral order and that all of them (not just Brahmins) were entitled to read the sacred Vedic scriptures.[42] Saraswati's movement, Arya Samaj, is a forerunner of contemporary organizations associated with the Hindu nationalism, such as the Keshave Memorial Educational Society in Hyderabad which has been led by Narasimha Reddy since 2004. The judge's involvement in a reform movement provides a noteworthy contrast to the otherwise soft and apolitical Muslim judge. There are apparent differences between the judgments made by each court. The judgment written by Anis in 2007 was sober, extremely detailed and comprehensive, while the two high court judges deployed a crisper and more direct writing style, even to the point of expressing hostilities towards the prosecution.

Convictions following such a brutal massacre can result in serious sentences, and the selection of an appropriate judge was therefore contentious throughout the judicial process. The caste identity of the chosen judge as well as his or her individual characteristics were scrutinized and contested, especially by the people who were accused of this crime.[43] The selection of a judge therefore delayed a special court being set up in Tsundur. In fact, five judges had been involved in the case that led up to the 2007 judgment of the Tsundur camp. They included two Dalit judges; one of them had a reputation for being 'a conviction judge'. There was considerable resistance to this judge because he was a Dalit and because he was known to be swift to convict the accused in cases that he heard. He decided not to deal with the case, apparently due to the mounting resistance that he faced from the accused, who were members of the dominant caste. Other judges also abandoned the case. It was a difficult case to handle. The only judge left after the others had resigned had a reputation for being a soft judge – a so-called non-eviction judge,[44] and she was appointed as the judge in the camp at Tsundur. In the judgment, she convicted fifty-six of the accused, and nineteen of them were sentenced to life imprisonment. She avoided using the death penalty.[45] The decision to avoid the death penalty was both criticized and supported by Dalits, but the accused were nonetheless determined to appeal the judgment in 2007 to the high court in Andhra Pradesh.

The two judges at the Andhra Pradesh High Court delivered a judgment on 22 April 2014 that resulted in the release of all the remaining prisoners. Their judgment includes a clear-cut critique of the evidence, witnesses, prosecution authority and the victims attending the court. They appear unreceptive to the arguments advanced by the prosecution. Unlike in the judgment in 2007, they conduct what is known in rhetoric as a 'radical redescription' in which facts, concepts and norms are reorganized to support a new viewpoint.[46] Their main incentive for doing this seems to have been to express disapproval of any collective organization or political assertion.

The high court judgment adopts the idea that the initial conflict as well as the demand for a legal trial were part of a political campaign carried out by Dalit youths. The judgment starts by referring to how the police felt that 'the youth have fallen into the hands of radical elements, they were brain washed, and were waiting for an opportunity to pollute the otherwise peaceful atmosphere in and around said villages'.[47] The judges conclude by acquitting all the individuals convicted in the trial court in 2007 while adding a statement telling the people of Tsundur that this conflict 'must be buried'.[48] It is noteworthy how the judges describe the demand for justice. They argue that it is part of a political mobilization and therefore not trustworthy. In fact, describing the Dalit youth as 'brain washed' is a strong claim and implies that the younger generation had been used by forces that were external to the village. The expression also implies that the young people were not justified in their actions, nor should they be considered to be rational actors with a deliberative agenda. The high court judges viewed the demand for equality and recognition as an external agenda that aimed 'to pollute' the established social order.[49]

Evidence and truth became important for their critical interrogation. A key step here was to question the trustworthiness of the witnesses. The first witness was considered untrustworthy because he had led the Dalit youth movement. Neither he nor two other witnesses were considered to be telling the truth by the high court bench, first, because they reported timings that were inconsistent and second, because they did not inform anyone about the incident 'for a period of four days'.[50] The judges also questioned whether the witnesses had actually been able to see the killings. They highlighted that while the prosecution's witness 'PW-15' had named 100 accused, he had not been able to mention the names of those who had been running in front of him in a crowd. The witness explained that the facts written in the police report at Tsundur police station the day after the attack were incorrect.[51] The judges did not discuss whether the police officers at Tsundur police station had distorted his narrative the day after the attack. Instead, the high court judgment takes the FIR as the baseline for truth and foregrounds inconsistencies and concluded that 'PW-15 is not truthful'.[52]

The FIRs and the time of reporting the incidents to the police become central to the interrogation of the evidence and the credibility of the witnesses, and the judges criticize the witnesses for their delayed reports to the police. They dismiss the idea that fear and lack of trust in the police were relevant to assessing the time at which the witnesses approached the police. Thus, anxiety among Tsundur Dalits, or what the judges characterized as the 'fear psychosis', is not considered relevant.[53] Instead, the judges contend that fear cannot be a reason for delay. They argue that fear can only explain a delay of a few hours and that any statement collected much later would affect the evidence negatively. Indeed, although the prosecution claimed that the attack amounted to a holocaust, the judges suggest in their judgment that the delay indicates that reports may have been coordinated or that there could have been 'planning to present a version' in a way that suited the accusers.[54] This statement must be viewed in the context of their consistent suspicion of collective organization, however. The judges claim that 'the "Dalit" Organizations started protesting' only when the dead bodies had been found in the canal the day after the attack.[55] It is true that Dalit activists in Guntur and throughout Andhra Pradesh mobilized to support the victims in Tsundur after learning about the massacre. But the two high court judges appear to question the victims' accounts, which were reported before the mobilization started.

The critique of the Dalit youths' moral integrity is another aspect of the judgment which adds to the court's disregard of how 'radical elements' outside the village corrupted the minds of the young people in the village. Here, the two judges state that a Dalit boy had been 'rubbing his shoulders' against three girls from the Reddy community.[56] They thus questioned the moral behaviour of Dalit youths in general. While endorsing some data, namely that a Dalit boy had touched three Reddy girls, they do not clarify whether this account was disputed by Dalits in court. Instead, they adopt data that supports a narrative of moral corruption. In short, while acknowledging the loss of the 'precious lives of 8 persons', the high court judgment has a one-dimensional approach.[57] The judges highlight data that serve to question the moral integrity and truthfulness of Dalits while arguing that they are unable to find any evidence to convict the accused.

Unlike the trial court of 2007, the high court not only trusted the version of events given by the Tsundur police but also seemed to adopt their version. While overruling the 2007 judgment, the high court judges argue, for instance, that the 'theory of the chasing by the police turns out to be false' because some Dalits were reported to have been present with the police.[58] However, it should be kept in mind that the tensions in the village were such that there was considerable suspicion about the police. Several criminal cases were filed against Dalits, including an alleged attempt to murder a Reddy landlord. It should also be kept in mind that the police station was in the village and that Dalits, therefore, would have to cross the main road in the village and walk past the settlement of the attackers to file a complaint. The 2014 judgment did not discuss the extent to which the poor quality of the FIRs could indicate that the Tsundur police force was complicit in the attack. Rather, the judgment approves the defence lawyers' approach, emphasizes inconsistencies, discredits the witnesses and stresses the lack of evidence for any of the killings that had been committed in this case.

Religious identity was the final theme that was used to rule out future prosecutions under the PoA Act. It is concluded in the judgment that since the Dalit victims had converted to Christianity, there is therefore no legal basis for using the PoA Act to prosecute the accused upper castes. It is explained that the defence lawyers had 'cross-examined the witnesses at length to prove that they have been converted into Christianity'.[59] Since the PoA Act is designed for the SCs, the law could not be applied to Christians. This question did not become a problem in 2007, when the Tsundur Dalits were classified as Hindus and the SCs.

There was a striking intensity regarding questions concerning caste in the Andhra Pradesh High Court. In 2007, the special public prosecutor in Tsundur camp, B. Chandrasekhar, was a human rights defender from a Brahmin community who had strong local ties and connections with the human rights movement in the state. B. Chandrasekhar appeared to be respected during the proceedings. In 2014, the prosecution was not respected. Instead, the high court bench criticized the prosecution for insufficient evidence and for failing to prove the exact time of the killings on 6 August 1991. The special public prosecutor appearing in the high court was Tharakam, who – along with V. Raghunath – argued on behalf of the victims.

When the prosecution argued that they had lost confidence in having a fair trial because of the situation in the high court, the judges responded by using a powerful tool. The bench argued that this critique was contempt of court. This allegation is a noteworthy step, as any action viewed as contempt of court can be penalized to protect the authority of courts. But the judges changed their minds and stated that the prosecution might have just voiced the opinion of the victims.[60] Tharakam explains the situation in an interview posted on YouTube by the online media platform known as Dalit Camera.[61] Here, the prosecutor states that the court was 'casteist' and that the bench did not want to take the time to hear the testimony of the witnesses. Unlike at the camp at Tsundur, only a few Dalits from Tsundur participated in the high court proceedings. One of them was a victim and was serving as president of the victim's association – Jaladi Moses. He was the son of one of the people who had been killed in the attack. Moses became frustrated with the proceedings and filed an affidavit to show that he had lost faith in the court's ability to deliver justice. The judges criticized his action, arguing that he merely represented an organization and that he was not an actual witness. They also emphasized that his objection amounted to contempt of court. The caste angle was thus brought into play, as the affidavit suggests that the caste mentality had a grip on the judges in their approach to the case. The judges were offended and yet they left the charge of contempt aside by concluding that this was simply a point of view.[62]

The judgment of 22 April 2014 proved controversial. In the immediate aftermath, more than forty organizations representing Dalits and left-wing movements formed a common front in Hyderabad city called the Struggle Committee for Justice to Tsundur Dalits.[63] They agreed that an appeal should be filed in the Supreme Court, and their demand was followed up by the government of Andhra Pradesh. In the petition, the government of Andhra Pradesh asked for special leave to appeal against the high court judgment of 22 April 2014. It was argued in the petition, among other things, that the high court judgment was inaccurate and that it had misrepresented victims' statements. It was also emphasized in the appeal to the Supreme Court that the high court had been unreasonable when it had accused victims of delaying reporting the incidents at the police station. According to the petition, the victims could not be expected to 'immediately rush to the police station and lodge a complaint when their lives themselves were in jeopardy and their kith and kin were brutally beaten'.[64]

The Supreme Court acted three months later by suspending the high court judgment. The highest court in the country therefore put the high court judgment aside until such time as the case had been fully processed in the Supreme Court. This action may have ensured further delays in settling the dispute. A similar appeal occurred after the Karamchedu massacre, and the Supreme Court finally made its judgment in 2008 – more than two decades after the crime was committed. According to Tharakam, the longevity of the legal process implies that the victims do not 'enjoy the tools of justice'.[65]

Empirical Contingencies, Institutions and Power

It is useful to distinguish between law and order when analysing how the atrocity cases have evolved through being dealt with by different legal institutions. Speaking, like Foucault did, about 'law or order' rather than 'law and order' makes it easier to identify how the formal goals of legal protection and recognition of the enduring problem of caste-based violence are not necessarily sustained through courts and institutional practices. The PoA Act, 1989, is widely understood as a powerful piece of legislation. And yet it is also acknowledged that there are problems implementing the Act. Prime Minister Manmohan Singh, for example, expressed 'shock' in 2009 that the conviction rates in cases were lower than 30 per cent; the overall average for the Indian Penal Code was 42 per cent.[66] The situations and figures remained overall stable, and the total conviction rate under PoA Act, 1989, was 25.8 per cent in 2016.[67] Technical questions do complicate the use of the Act, and some of them were addressed in the 2015 amendments. The discussions of the two massacres in Khairlanji and Tsundur in any case suggest several empirical contingencies, that is, possibilities that may be vulnerable to technical error and may be exploited by powerful actors.

The contingencies comprise the characteristics of the appointed judges, their caste identity, their assumptions about political assertiveness as a problem of order and, of course, the registration of the reports of witnesses at the police station immediately after the event. This last-mentioned factor is crucial. The role of the police in the immediate aftermath of atrocities and subsequent proceedings in court make the application of law very open-ended. The evidence offered by the witnesses was put in doubt by the Andhra Pradesh High Court in 2014 and in the Bombay High Court in 2008. No doubt, atrocity cases represent special cases that involve anxious witnesses and police officers who would have to apply laws that they are not accustomed to. Overall, the police appear to have been complicit in covering up the collective attacks in both Khairlanji and Tsundur, but there are nuances worth noting. The story of Khairlanji involves corruption and favours. The bereaved husband had earlier declined to pay bribes to the local police, and after the massacre, he was asked to wait when he went to the police station to report the attacks. The police did not immediately take action when Surekha Bhotmange called the police station in Andhalgaon before the attack, nor did they act when she called a friend during the attack who also called the police urging them to intervene and stop the ongoing attack in Khairlanji.[68] The police station in Andhalgaon was 6 kilometres away from Khairlanji village, and the police actions clearly suggest that they declined to provide the protection that the law prescribes. In the case of Tsundur, the police appear to have written down testimonies without caring about being precise in doing so. Overall, they seem to have been more efficient in maintaining social order than in applying law effectively. This was particularly clear in the case of Khairlanji, where activists were imprisoned as they protested against the state's inadequate legal response.

While evidence provided soon after an alleged crime takes place is crucial for later court proceedings, it is well known that courts are open-ended institutions that allow for various dynamics to play out. Recall how Galanter argues that powerful actors are often at an advantage compared to people with less expertise. In fact, courts represent key arena for institutional conversion.[69] The mandate of the courts is to interpret law, but their interpretations could have implications for how this policy is implemented. The Supreme Court in India is itself a good example of an institution that changes the meanings of law and creates new meanings too. In the 1970s, India's apex court invented the so-called basic structure doctrine, which meant that new legislation would have to be scrutinized by judges who should determine whether the legislation under review can be consistent with the basic structure of the constitution. In the USA, moreover, the Supreme Court was one of the institutions that played a crucial role in the reinterpretation of the Civil Rights Act. What was designed to be a colour-blind piece of legislation was given a new meaning when the Supreme Court decided that employers could not use race-neutral tests and methods to bar applicants with an ethnic minority background.[70] In the cases discussed in this chapter, however, the question of caste became more significant regarding the appointment of judges. Such a bias based on identity can be compared to discussions about juries in the USA, where there is a history of jury bias against black people.[71] The Tsundur case's encounters with bias and individuals' attitudes in court have become decisive for how the case evolved.

Summary

There is a considerable possibility of redirecting law to new goals and conclusions in a context in which facts about an atrocity are not properly recorded and victims face several barriers when they approach the police. In addition, the characteristics of the judges may assume significance. A key lesson that can be learnt from this chapter is that analysing the implementation of law requires a clear distinction between law and order. It is useful to adopt Foucault's observation about how law differs from order almost in the same way as people would choose to have either lemon or milk in a cup of tea. This distinction is useful to explain how the PoA Act can be relegated to the margins in official practices. In fact, the police involved in the Khairlanji atrocity did not use this Act, nor did they mobilize to protect the attacked family. To put it simply, the law did not exist except as an unheeded formal possibility. On the other hand, the series of court cases reveals very well how law cannot be erased as a theoretical possibility; this did not happen in the Tsundur or the Khairlanji cases. The fact that the Supreme Court stayed the Andhra Pradesh High Court judgment seems to restore the relevance of the PoA Act. These processes cannot be grasped by using expressions such as path dependency or the 'hybridized monster' of law and order.

The scope for converting law is particularly relevant for powerful actors, precisely in the sense that is suggested regarding conversion in institutional theory. Here it is argued that although David wins sometimes, 'Goliath has the upper hand.'[72] But the question of law or order is not that straightforward. There is no doubt that dominant castes are economically and politically powerful and should therefore be better placed to endure a lengthy legal battle. At the same time, victims such as those from Tsundur have been able to cooperate with Dalit movements and human rights activists to strengthen their struggles in courts. But the appeal to the Supreme Court implies that the case is not settled and that considerable delays may estrange victims and leave them without the legal protection that was expected. In the Khairlanji atrocity case involving the Bhotmange family, currently pending in the Supreme Court, the bereaved husband passed away on 20 January 2017.[73] Unfortunately, victims do not always live to see the outcome of court processes.

Notes

1. Michel Foucault, 'Lemon and Milk', in *Power: Essential Works of Foucault, 1954-1984*, ed. James D. Faubion (London: Penguin, 2002), 438.
2. Manoranjan Mohanty, 'Kilvenmani, Karamchedu to Khairlanji: Why Atrocities on Dalits Persist?', unpublished paper, July 2007. See also PUCL, *Suppressing the Voice of the Oppressed: State Terror on Protests against the Khairlanji Massacre, A Report to the Nation by an All Indian Team* (2007), accessed 10 April 2017, http://www.pucl.org/major_reports/Report%20on%20Khairlanji%20Massacre,%202007-2.pdf.
3. Kathleen Thelen, 'How Institutions Evolve: Insights from Comparative Historical Analysis', in *Comparative Historical Analysis in the Social Sciences*, ed. James Mahoney and Dietrich Rueschemeyer, Cambridge Studies in Comparative Politics (Cambridge: Cambridge University Press, 2003).
4. For a discussion and analysis, see G. Narayana, 'Rule Making for Scheduled Castes: Analysis of Lok Sabha Debates, 1962–71', *Economic and Political Weekly* 15, no. 8 (1980): 433–40.
5. Upendra Baxi, 'Historic New Law: Protecting SC/ST Rights', *Times of India*, 15 September 1989.
6. Chakraborty, Debashis, D. Shyam Babu and Manashi Chakravorty, 'Atrocities on Dalits: What the District Level Data Say on State-Society Complicity', *Economic and Political Weekly* 41, no. 24 (2006): 2478–81.
7. Jacob S. Hacker, Paul Pierson and Kathleen Thelen, 'Drift and Conversion: Hidden Faces of Institutional Change', in *Advances in Comparative-Historical Analysis*, ed. James Mahoney and Kathleen A. Thelen, Strategies for Social Inquiry (New York: Cambridge University Press, 2015), 181.

8. Ibid., 198–200.
9. Thelen, 'How Institutions Evolve'.
10. Ibid., 228–30; Hacker, Pierson and Thelen, 'Drift and Conversion', 228.
11. Philip Selznick, *Leadership in Administration: A Sociological Interpretation* (Berkeley, CA, and London: University of California Press, 1984 and 1957), 21.
12. Andrei Marmor, *Interpretation and Legal Theory* (Oxford: Hart, 2005), 127–8.
13. Ministry of Law and Justice, The Scheduled Castes and the Scheduled Tribes (Prevention of Atrocities) Act 1989 (Government of India, 1989), accessed 11 December 2017, http://lawmin.nic.in/ld/P-ACT/1989/The%20Scheduled%20Castes%20And%20the%20Scheduled%20Tribes%20%20(Prevention%20of%20Atrocities)%20Act,%201989.pdf.
14. Selznick, *Leadership in Administration*.
15. Max Weber, *Economy and Society: An Outline of Interpretive Sociology* (Berkeley, CA: University of California Press, 1978), 928.
16. Marc Galanter, 'Why the "Haves" Come Out Ahead: Speculations on the Limits of Legal Change', *Law & Society Review* 9, no. 1 (1974): 95–160.
17. Hacker, Pierson and Thelen, 'Drift and Conversion', 200.
18. Thelen, 'How Institutions Evolve'.
19. Robert C. Lieberman, 'Ideas, Institutions, and Political Order: Explaining Political Change', *American Political Science Review* 96, no. 4 (2002), doi:10.1017/S0003055402000394.
20. *Indian Express*, 'Law for SCs, STs Could Be Strengthened: PC', 31 August 2010, accessed 5 February 2018, http://indianexpress.com/article/news-archive/web/law-for-scs-sts-could-be-strengthened-pc/.
21. Anupama Rao, *The Caste Question: Dalits and the Politics of Modern India* (Berkeley, CA: University of California Press, 2009), 237.
22. PUCL, *Suppressing the Voice of the Oppressed*'.
23. S. M. Dahiwale, 'Khairlanji: Insensitivity of Mahar Officers', *Economic and Political Weekly* 44, no. 31 (2009): 29–30.
24. Anand Teltumbde, *Khairlanji: A Strange and Bitter Crop* (New Delhi: Navayana, 2008), 35–8.
25. Ibid., 40–1.
26. Bombay High Court, Criminal Confirmation Case No. 4/2008, in the High Court of Judicature in Bombay, Nagpur Bench, Nagpur, 11, accessed 10 April 2017, http://online.wsj.com/public/resources/documents/Khairlanji.pdf.
27. Teltumbde, *Khairlanji*, 42–3.
28. Dahiwale, 'Khairlanji', 32.
29. Anand Teltumbde, 'High Court's Verdict on Khairlanji: Justice Diminished', *Economic and Political Weekly* 45, no. 32 (2010): 10–11.
30. *Central Bureau of Investigation* (through D.S.P., C.B.I.S.C.B. Chennai) *Camp at Bhandara versus 1. Sakru Mahagu Binjewar* (Bombay High Court), 123.
31. Michel Foucault, *The Archaeology of Knowledge* (London: Routledge, 1989).

32. Anand Teltumbde, '10 Years of Khairlanji: What Do We See?', *Economic and Political Weekly* 51, no. 36 (2016).
33. Teltumbde, *Khairlanji*, 61–2.
34. Manmohan Singh, *PM's Speech at the Chief Minister's Meet on Naxalism* (New Delhi: Prime Minister's Office, 2006).
35. Rediff, 'Damaged Ambedkar Statue Sparks Protests in Kanpur', 29 November 29 2006, accessed 5 February 2018, http://www.rediff.com/news/2006/nov/29statue.htm; Pamela Philipose, 'Khairlanji to Kanpur', *Indian Express*, 2 December 2006, accessed 10 July 2019, http://archive.indianexpress.com/news/khairlanji-to-kanpur/17707/.
36. Anand Teltumbde, *The Persistence of Caste: The Khairlanji Murders and India's Hidden Apartheid* (New Delhi: Navayana, 2010), 134.
37. *Frontline*, 'Enforcing Silence', 15 December 2006, accessed 10 July 2019, http://www.frontline.in/static/html/fl2324/stories/20061215002809800.htm.
38. Chakraborty, Babu and Chakravorty, 'Atrocities on Dalits', 2481.
39. *Sub-Divisional Police Officer, Tenali* (Crime Nos. 65 to 73 and 89 and 90/91 of Tsundur P.S. and Crime No. 64/91 of Amarthaluru P.S.) *vs Accused 1* (Modugula Sami Reddy - 219) (Tsundur court, 31 August 2007).
40. Ministry of Law and Justice, The Scheduled Castes and the Scheduled Tribes (Prevention of Atrocities) Act, 1989, chap. 4.
41. Special Public Prosecutor B. Chandrasekhar in interviews with the author, Guntur, January and February 2008.
42. Susan Bayly, *Caste, Society and Politics in India from the Eighteenth Century to the Modern Age* (Cambridge: Cambridge University Press, 1999), 169.
43. B. Chandrasekhar, in an interview with the author, Guntur, February 2008.
44. Ibid.
45. *Sub-Divisional Police Officer, Tenali* (Crime Nos. 65 to 73 and 89 and 90/91 of Tsundur P.S. and Crime No. 64/91 of Amarthaluru P.S.) *vs Accused 1* (Modugula Sami Reddy - 219), 228.
46. Quentin Skinner, ed., *Visions of Politics: Regarding Method*, vol. 1 (Cambridge: Cambridge University Press, 2002), 182–85.
47. *Chidipudi Srivasava Reddy and Others vs the State of A.P. Rep by the Public Prosecutor*, High Court of A.P. (Andhra Pradesh High Court, Criminal Appeal, 22-04-2014), on file with author (Hyderabad: Andhra Pradesh High Court), 2.
48. Ibid., 73.
49. I encountered somewhat similar statements when I visited a neighbouring village along with my research colleague in 2008. My colleague from University of Hyderabad, who was also from Guntur district, asked some labourers about their opinion of the attack in Tsundur. While one village elder was annoyed about the question, others responded politely that the conflict was basically a problem among young people in Tsundur.
50. *Chidipudi Srivasava Reddy and Others vs the State of A.P. Rep by the Public Prosecutor*, 33.

51. Ibid., 52.
52. Ibid., 55.
53. Ibid., 66.
54. Ibid., 65.
55. Ibid., 9.
56. Ibid., 3.
57. Ibid., 73.
58. Ibid., 10.
59. Ibid., 72.
60. *Hindu*, 'Tsundur Dalit Massacre Case Takes New Turn', 18 March 2014, accessed 24 March 2017, http://www.thehindu.com/news/cities/Vijayawada/Tsundur-Dalit-massacre-case-takes-new-turn/article11416977.ece; Round Table India, 'Tsunduru Trial: Judge Drops Contempt Charges Against Bojja Tharakam', accessed 24 March 2017, https://roundtableindia.co.in/index.php?option=com_content&view=article&id=7314:tsunduru-trial-judge-drops-contempt-charges-against-bojja-tharakam&catid=129:events-and-activism&Itemid=195.
61. Dalit Camera, 'Advocate Tarakam on Tsundur Judgement of AP High Court', YouTube, 23 April 2014, accessed 23 March 2017, https://www.youtube.com/watch?v=BjaazZOVG9Q.
62. *Chidipudi Srivasava Reddy and Others vs the State of A.P. Rep by the Public Prosecutor*, 15.
63. *Hindu*, '1991 Dalit Massacre: Committee to Challenge HC Verdict', 8 May 2014, accessed 16 January 2018, http://www.thehindu.com/news/national/andhra-pradesh/1991-dalit-massacre-committee-to-challenge-hc-verdict/article5989321.ece.
64. State of Andhra Pradesh, Special Leave Petition (CRL), no. 5353-5361/2014, 30 June 2014.
65. *Dalit Camera*, 'Advocate Tarakam on Tsundur Judgement of AP High Court'.
66. *Financial Express*, 'Low Conviction Rate in SC-ST Atrocity Cases Shocking: PM', 8 September 2009.
67. National Crime Records Bureau, *Crime in India 2016. Statistics* (New Delhi: Ministry of Home Affairs, Government of India, 2017), 303, accessed 7 December 2018, http://ncrb.gov.in/StatPublications/CII/CII2016/pdfs/NEWPDFs/Crime%20in%20India%20-%202016%20Complete%20PDF%20291117.pdf.
68. PUCL, *Suppressing the Voice of the Oppressed*, 8.
69. Hacker, Pierson and Thelen, 'Drift and Conversion', 197.
70. Lieberman, 'Ideas, Institutions, and Political Order'.
71. Samuel R. Sommers and Phoebe C. Ellsworth, 'White Juror Bias: An Investigation of Prejudice against Black Defendants in the American Courtroom', *Psychology, Public Policy, and Law* 7, no. 1 (2001): 201–29, doi:10.1037/1076-8971.7.1.201.
72. Hacker, Pierson and Thelen, 'Drift and Conversion', 198.
73. Manoj Mitta, 'From Bihar to Maharashtra via Telangana: Brutal Reminders of Systemic Bias against Dalits', *Scroll.in*, 26 January 2017, accessed 27 January 2017, https://scroll.in/article/827674/from-bihar-to-maharashtra-via-telangana-brutal-reminders-of-systemic-bias-against-dalits.

6

Modernity of Caste

Higher Education, Inequality and Caste Struggles for Reservation

As an integral part of India's modernity, caste is not simply a phenomenon in rural areas or in extreme cases of caste-related violence. It is part of everyday life in modern institutions, where it represents a contingent element in social relations. Caste is, overall, subject to several types of conflicts, ranging from public debates and democratic interaction to humiliation and outright exclusion. In practice, caste is manifested in different ways; it is often identified in terms of politics of inequality, which involves large clusters of castes as well as caste-based discrimination. On the one hand, inequality and struggles for material resources animate caste-based mobilization that presses for new entitlements to reserved quotas. This mobilization comprises radically different groups, from the powerful landowning Jats in north India to the destitute Madigas in Telugu-speaking regions in south India. On the other hand, there is even caste-based discrimination in higher education institutions, which has become more visible in recent years.

According to modernization theory, religion will lose its relevance and tradition will be replaced with a new set of values which are specifically modern. The American political scientists Lloyd and Susanne Rudolph argued in the 1960s that this opposition between modernity and tradition, which was prominent in the European Enlightenment and in Marx's writings, was inadequate. Although they thought that the opposition was heuristically useful, their idea was that modernity and tradition infiltrated each other and that caste was used as an instrument for political mobilization.[1] Their seminal argument is modest and outdated today, and their approach does not quite explain the force with which caste has played out in modern institutions such as higher education institutions.

The controversies regarding caste in higher education and public employment are important when examining why caste seems to be reproduced and even to gain a new intensity in contemporary India. The mechanism of oppression in the Dalit situation is not confined to rural areas. Context matters. But the ontological drive of caste appears to be an integral part of modernity that plays out in different ways, as case studies on the higher education sector suggest.

The politics of reservation policies involves groups and goes beyond electoral politics, but reservation policies also affect elections. The two most central controversies regarding caste-based reservation in India were related to the implementation of the *Mandal Commission Report*. This report was submitted in 1980 and was named after its chairman, B. P. Mandal. Prime Minister V. P. Singh gained power and implemented it in 1990. The implementation generated the first Mandal controversy. The second Mandal controversy emerged after the Congress-led coalition the United Progressive Alliance (UPA) gained power in 2004; this government decided to implement more of the *Mandal Commission Report*, namely to extend seats reserved for the so-called Other Backward Classes (OBCs) to the centrally aided universities as well. Both cases were noteworthy controversies, but it is too easy to view caste as a tool for mobilization or for gaining new votes. The visibility of caste in the new millennium is not simply due to election tactics or reservation policies. Caste seems to have gained new intensity while the Hindu nationalist government led by the Bharatiya Janata Party (BJP) and Narendra Modi has been in power. During this regime, higher education has been targeted and political power has been used to curb opposition while articulating the characteristics of the nation in terms of the privileged values of Hinduism and upper-caste identity. But the visibility of caste-related politics is also a result of long-term political campaigns by various caste groups to address inequality and a lack of recognition. In spite of all of these political movements, the constitution creates a framework that cannot easily be amended by political campaigns.

This chapter is divided into three parts. First, I discuss how conflicts can be conceptualized in democratic theory. This provides a possibility to make sense of different types of conflicts in a democratic system. I use the terms that Chantal Mouffe offers in her discussion of agonistic democracy in which she distinguishes between two types of conflicts associated with antagonism and agon (strife). And I use her scheme to distinguish between ontological discrimination and dissent in a democratic manner while moving beyond her approach to explain how they interrelate in the context of caste. Second, I examine the caste question in higher education, the suicide of Rohith Vemula and how the Hindu nationalist government of Modi has enabled its associates to reinforce caste dominance while gaining control and power. I examine cases in higher education in which caste-based discrimination has intensified in specific political circumstances. Third, I discuss the politics of inequality and the mobilization of caste groups to demand entitlement to reservation. I focus on sub-castes that mobilize to negotiate and demand quotas for their caste, including both rich and poor castes and subaltern groups as well as 'forward castes'. I outline what their struggles in the multilevel form of governance implies in terms of legal change. In short, this chapter sheds more light on the relevance of caste in different domains of the state. Inequality and power struggles create group-based mobilization, and caste values matter in public institutions.

Two Types of Conflict: Antagonism and Agonism

Since democratic dialogue and atrocities are different phenomena, it is helpful to adopt different concepts to be more precise about how to distinguish between them. Since there is both dialogue and atrocity in the modern Indian state, it would be a failure to be silent on one of these practices if the aim is to understand changing forms of caste in India's constitutional democracy. This is where the concepts used in current discussions of agonistic democracy in political theory are useful.[2] I will examine Mouffe's contribution to agonistic democracy. Her discussion has its limitations, but her schematization provides a clear distinction between repression and dissent which she refers to as 'antagonism' and 'agonism'.

In her discussion of democratic theory, Mouffe focuses on the daily disagreements that characterize democratic negotiations or organized protests in relation to a democratic state or its bureaucracy. The Greek term *agon* means conflict or strife.[3] Mouffe is among several political theorists who have brought this concept into discussions of democracy. In doing so, she crafts an approach to democracy that is not based on artificial public reasoning (such as in Habermas' abstract philosophy). Instead, her idea is to consider how disagreements in society may exist and how social movements try to make a difference in the political system without necessarily reaching a consensus. Here, she seems to demarcate democratic dissent from violence; agonism would require some degree of mutual recognition. In an agonistic democracy, opponents will not seek to eradicate their enemies, nor will they consider their demands as illegitimate per se.[4] Instead, this is what characterizes a political antagonism where a conflict turns into an aggressive distinction between friend and enemy and at the same time it is thought that the enemy has no legitimate existence.

Caste-related atrocities reflect antagonisms; they represent a denial of democracy and recognition. However, the drawback in Mouffe's scheme is that she tends to conflate the concept of antagonism with the concept of 'the political'. Although there are different ways of conceptualizing the concept of the political, Mouffe has used the work of Carl Schmitt as a critical foil to conceptualizing it. Schmitt was the notorious author who elaborated the concept of the political in modern political theory, but he did so by understanding it in a decisionistic manner. He relates the concept of the political to the sovereign decision-maker who could use his or her will to make decisions in exceptional situations. This provides insight into what Mouffe means by a lack of recognition of an opponent, and yet Schmitt's formula tends to place the emphasis on decisionism rather than antagonism. For Schmitt, notably, the primary question for any political order is the ability of a ruler to distinguish between the friend of the state and the foe. He argues that the 'specific political distinction to which political actions and motives can be reduced is that between friend and enemy'.[5] Schmitt's conceptual distinction between friend and foe is designed to bolster the powers of a sovereign leader to maintain an order.

Mouffe demarcates her approach from that of Schmitt's decisionism by supplementing the concept of the political with agonistic democracy. In doing so, she defines what dissent is as compared to hostility and violence. According to Mouffe, 'antagonism is a we/they relation in which the two sides are enemies who do not share any common ground'.[6] Agonism, on the other hand, is a condition in which disputes and conflicts exist at the same time as the disputing opponents recognize each other. Thus, agonism represents a democratic we/they relation characterized by recognition, whereas political antagonism designates a violent we/they relation. However, even though Mouffe's scheme provides the possibility of distinguishing between repression and democratic dissent, her concept of antagonism is inadequate for a discussion of casteism.

Antagonism needs a different understanding, namely in the sense that Laclau develops this term as central to his approach to hegemony. In Laclau's approach, antagonism explains how one pole may dominate and, in fact, negate another pole.[7] Antagonism is therefore understood in a relational sense as a hegemonic relation between two poles. Laclau's concept of antagonism presupposes that the two poles are incompatible. Such a relation makes sense at the level of ontology. This does not belong within the domain of empirical political science; it is what Marchart characterizes as political ontology and it sits within the domain of political theory.[8]

Laclau's concept of antagonism can be used to make sense of Ambedkar's concept of graded inequality and the ontological distinction between touchables and untouchables.[9] Ambedkar's distinction between touchables and untouchables is fundamental to the ontology of caste. The concept of graded inequality is more multifaceted. However, one of the characteristics of the Dalit situation is the ways in which they may experience both spectacular violence and possibilities of negotiating with opponents, power holders and members of the state. On the one hand, atrocities represent grave examples of 'teaching Dalits a lesson' about their need to remain submissive, as if they should know that they are 'nobodies' and not 'somebodies'. In this sense, the lives of Dalits become precarious if they act as equal citizens with independent opinions or gain a status that makes them somebody. There are exceptions to these dynamics, such as Dalit business people who might succeed.[10]

But individuals who defy the odds do not rule out the relevance of an antagonism, which is distinctly oppressive when it appears in the lives of the untouchables as opposed to touchables. The case of Vemula shows precisely how he moved from a situation in which his opinions could be respected (as in agonistic democracy) to a condition in which his action was considered illegitimate and the ground for recognition was removed.

Caste in Higher Education amid National Politics

It was an assumption at the time of India's independence that caste would disappear with modernization. This was a central vision of the representatives of the Indian National Congress, particularly Jawaharlal Nehru. Ambedkar was certainly more systematic in combining a critique of caste as an embedded feature of the Indian establishment with a utopian vision, but the idea of modernization and the goal of equal opportunity were nonetheless prominent among the ruling elite. However, the myth of modernization was important for activists who thought in the early 1980s that caste would be part of the past. K. Balagopal, who later became a champion of the human rights struggle in Andhra Pradesh and elsewhere in India, explained in an interview that the Karamchedu massacre was the event that opened his eyes to the caste question (see Chapter 3). But there have been similar experiences in each generation, and the name Rohith Vemula represents an eye-opener for the current generation.

While the Karamchedu massacre had an impact on a generation of activists across south Indian states, Vemula's suicide became the centre of national attention and was even discussed in the Indian parliament. In fact, his suicide compelled Minister of Education Smriti Zubin Irani to respond because her ministry was accused of sending several letters from Delhi urging the administration at the University of Hyderabad to suspend Vemula and other Dalit students. The student's suicide was therefore not only a case in which discrimination had moved from the countryside to the city, it also became evident that his suffering had been aggravated by political decision-makers at the apex of India's political system. The news about the minister of education's involvement in the case created political controversy. The Congress party demanded an investigation into her ministry's involvement in the case.[11]

The case of Vemula's suicide reflects a broader lesson about the ways in which political power can intensify caste relations. The situation in this higher educational institution can be compared to villages where members of dominant castes are emboldened by support from the state. However, the case also provides a rare insight into the relevance of caste in the Hindu nationalist regime. It is a case involving both free speech and caste relations. First, Vemula was targeted because he was an articulate student who organized meetings and made political statements. In August 2015, he participated in the screening of a documentary film about the communal violence in Muzaffarnagar district in Uttar Pradesh during August and September of 2013. The screening of this film in Hyderabad in August 2015 provoked reactions among students of the Akhil Bharatiya Vidyarthi Parishad (ABVP) on campus. The ABVP is an organization that was created in 1948 as an extension of the Rashtriya Swayamsevak Sangh (RSS) and their idea of reaching out to every part of society; the organization has associations with the Hindu nationalist movement in the university sector and was the first student union to attract more than one million members.[12] The ABVP is committed to 'national reconstruction' and social change and to addressing the challenges facing political order, such as 'Islamic' terrorism, Maoism and infiltration of Bangladesh and Kashmir separatists.[13]

As a student wing of the Hindu nationalist movement, the ABVP students on Hyderabad campus were critical of the Ambedkar Student Association (ASA) led by Vemula. Vemula and other members of the ASA complained that the ABVP had disturbed their film screening. At that time, Vemula had also criticized the Indian state's use of the death penalty on his Facebook wall. The topic was controversial because the man who was hanged, Yakub Memon, was accused of carrying out terrorist attacks and bombings in Bombay city in 1993. His execution at the end of July 2015 created a national debate, with leading newspapers arguing that the death penalty was inhuman.[14] Similarly, Vemula had a general human rights concern about capital punishment. On campus, however, the ABVP objected to the protest that Vemula and his friends made against the execution of a Muslim terrorist by calling them 'goons' on Facebook.[15] Vemula and other members of the ASA approached the ABVP as they felt abused and asked for an apology. But the leader of the ABVP filed a police complaint alleging that Vemula had used physical violence against him. Vemula denied this, but the ABVP used its political contacts, such as a regional politician who happened to be a minister in the central government led by the BJP, to curb the political activities of Dalit students. Overall, therefore, the case demonstrated that there was cooperation between members of the state, including the central government in New Delhi, the student movement on the university campus in Hyderabad and the university's vice chancellor.

In addition to the primary aim of the AVBP being to curb opinions that dissented from those on the Hindu nationalist agenda, the conflict on Hyderabad campus was also a matter of caste relations. Leaders of the ASA were highly critical of Vice Chancellor Appa Rao Podile, and they made several statements about how he demonstrated his caste superiority. The Dalit student leaders argued that he behaved in a casteist manner and that he had refused to meet them because he was a man from the Kamma caste. The Kammas have been a peasant caste in the coastal belt, but they have generally become economically and politically very powerful to the point of representing a dominating or 'forward caste'.[16] Kammas were part of the non-Brahmin movement, and yet the caste now identifies itself as being superior to the untouchables. This caste relation became relevant in the conflict that arose between the vice chancellor and articulate members of the ASA. This conflict had quite a long history on campus. Members of the ASA and associated teachers had been in a dispute with the Vice Chancellor, Appa Rao, in 2002. At that time, a member of staff from the Department of Political Science who supported Dalit students was at risk of being expelled from the university. Although the vice chancellor decided to take leave after Vemula's suicide, he returned to the campus in March 2016. Students protested outside his office, and the situation escalated into a violent confrontation with police, activists from the ABVP and members of the ASA. Muslim and Dalit students as well as two university professors were arrested and sent to prison for one week. Vemula's suicide reflects how local conflicts can become violent if both are not recognized as equals. What is particularly relevant in these caste dynamics is the extent to which political power could be used to exercise extraordinary actions against Dalits.

The wave of mobilization of Hindu nationalists during the Modi regime has pushed the momentum for a political approach in which the antagonism reveals a perceptible articulation of hegemony. The distinction between the friends of state power and 'anti-nationals' has been at the centre of this nationalist mobilization. This rhetorical construction of legitimate actors was used to curb the student protests on Hyderabad campus. The term 'anti-national' has become a flexible label that polarizes the public. It is used to criticize actors who disagree with the nationalist movement. The polarization implies a method of institutionalizing new hegemonic power where there is little legitimate space for other subjectivities and political positions.

The labelling of any deviation from a Hindutva order as anti-national has become a politics of othering and has gained momentum since the BJP and Modi won the general elections in 2014. This does not mean that Modi simply orchestrates aggression directly, however. Instead, the BJP's political power has emboldened social and political movements that identify with the Hindutva agenda to carry out more radical political action. The anti-national tag has been used in an intense process of othering to create suspicion and to violently subjugate Muslims, cow traders and Dalits. Muslims have been quickly associated with acts of terror and cow politics have resulted in Dalits being beaten as a punishment for skinning a dead cow or traders have seen their business deteriorate or even grind to a halt. The mobilization of Hindu nationalism has undoubtedly been characterized by a desire to establish a powerful Hindutva authority. In fact, this struggle has implied a cultivation of political antagonisms, which has removed common ground for negotiations between disputing partners.

Caste has become a more explicit dimension in the current Hindu nationalist regime than it was earlier. The evolving dynamics suggest that it is a source of the reinforcement of the power of the Hindu identity rather than simply being a source of the fragmentation of castes. It is therefore problematical to separate religion and caste as if caste is local and religion is national because caste is central to contemporary Hindu national politics. The chief minister of Uttar Pradesh is a radical instance in this regard. After being appointed leader of India's most populous state, Yogi Adityanath explained in an interview on 5 March 2017 that caste is fine for an orderly society whereas casteism is not fine.[17] Yogi, who chose this name to reflect his religious practice, has an articulate position among the Thakurs, from a dominant caste in Uttar Pradesh. As chief minister, he has promoted Hindu values associated with touchable-caste values; emphasizing that his cabinet ministers are vegetarians, he has acted against 'illegal' slaughterhouses and requested that Dalits clean themselves with soap before they attend his public meetings.[18] After a controversial career as a political agitator who has targeted Muslims and projected Hindu values in the past, his policies as chief minister resonate with values that matter for caste relations.

Religion and caste cannot be clearly separated when politicians use the cultural and religious reference points of upper-caste Hindus to develop their policies or articulate their visions of a political community. Leaders of the main Hindu nationalist organization, the RSS, have expressed an interest in reaching out to every member of the society, building the nation and organizing society in accordance with their programme of cultural nationalism.[19] The chief minister of Uttar Pradesh appointed in 2017 is a controversial case, being an example of a belligerent politician and a Hindu priest with a history of making polarizing speeches and using a rhetoric of hate. Overall, the politics that he advocates can be compared to the militant cultural nationalism with an antagonizing approach to Muslims that Savarkar, the author of the book *Hindutva* propagates.[20] Savarkar was the founder of the aggressive right-wing Hindu nationalist movement, which lost its legitimacy after one of its members murdered Gandhi. However different to Gandhi's nationalism and non-violence strategies, the Mahatma still glorified the origins of Hindu culture and values.[21] Caste may occupy a central role in militant and more accommodative understandings of a legitimate political community associated with Vedic culture. It is therefore an incomplete claim that the BJP has an interest in centralizing power, whereas caste mobilization represents a source of decentralizing. This is the argument that the political scientist Paul Brass has advanced, and this was endorsed by Corbridge and Harriss when they concluded that the Indian elite reinvented its power during the period of economic liberalization.[22] But Brass does also point out commonalities between the secular Congress party and the militant Hindu nationalists; they compare by having an 'ideology of state exhalation', and Hindu nationalists would infuse the state more actively with Hindu symbols than secularist regimes normally do.[23] He thus points to commonalities between the two different strategies used by these parties to maintain state power. Brass's approach does in any case not fully capture how caste relations have gained new relevance in the Hindu nationalist agenda of curbing dissent and augmenting Hindu power. Caste appears to be practised as a central framework for understanding the type of values and identities that the nation should practise.

The agenda of subjugating other groups violently goes beyond simply keeping the state united around Hindu symbols. It is a desire to reorder the state and social relations by articulating hegemony in such a way that it curbs dissent and increases subjugation. It allows for an authorization of political power at the expense of agonistic democracy characterized by democratic dissent. In doing so, it has emboldened Hindu nationalist movements to target institutions, especially universities and their administrations.

The case of Vemula introduces a more specific example of how caste relations can become antagonistic in the context of higher education; that is, the grip of caste can gain momentum and create a determination to act forcefully to institutionalize a specific social order. One can explain this grip of caste in terms of Laclau's concepts of social and political logics. Laclau argues that social logics designate rule-following, while 'political logics are related to the institution of the social'.[24] Similarly, a belief in caste augments the desire to institute the social institutions by curbing Dalit activists and turn them into objects for force by branding them as anti-nationals.

Vemula and his friends in the ASA were branded anti-nationals, which made them 'legitimate' targets. However, the action against them and Vemula's suicide follows a familiar trend, namely that political power can intensify casteism and the desire to 'teach Dalits a lesson' about how they should be submissive.[25] The idea of 'teaching Dalits a lesson' was decisive for the caste-related violence that was played out in Karamchedu in 1985 and Tsundur in 1991. Dominant castes were emboldened by the fact that they enjoyed access to political power. In a context in which the Hindu nationalist agenda cultivates authoritarianism and an antagonistic politics, an ideological drive is able to gain force among members of the dominant sections of society. In the case of Vemula, the Hindu nationalist student movement, the ABVP, used its political connections and managed to mobilize a chain of political connections that stretched from the district authorities to the central government in New Delhi. The ABVP student union reported to the vice president of the BJP in Ranga Reddy district, Nandanam Diwakar, about the situation on campus. Diwakar decided to write a letter to the regional politician,

Bandaru Dattatreya, who served as a BJP minister in the Ministry of Labour and Employment in New Delhi. On 10 August 2015, Diwakar, the BJP politician from Ranga Reddy district, wrote to Dattatreya in New Delhi, saying that the ASA had organized a 'series of anti-national activities' and that the ABVP leader N. Susheel Kumar had been attacked 'for protesting against the prayer meeting conducted for Yakub Memon!'[26] This information, the alleged attack and the idea of 'anti-national activities' became the subject of a chain of letters. Dattatreya reported the case to India's Minister of Human Resource Development, Irani, whose office followed up with several letters about anti-national activities and violent attacks on campus, urging the university to act against the students. Dattatreya had argued in his letter dated 17 August 2015 that the centrally funded university in Hyderabad had 'become a den of casteist, extremist and anti-nationalist politics'.[27] While this statement seeks to dismiss the meetings of the student association on identity and human rights by accusing them of being 'casteist' and involving 'anti-nationalist politics', the basic implication of this administrative process was that political power could be used to suspend the students. This exclusion proceeded in two stages. The first step was monetary action. In July 2015, the university stopped paying Vemula his monthly stipend. This was before the letters by BJP politicians were sent to members of the central government with allegations that the university acted too slowly. Although Vemula and his friends complained that this was an attempt to punish him for his political activities, the university administration argued that it was simply an administrative problem. This lack of money put added pressure on Vemula; his family was poor and he had to borrow money from his friends. The second step to suspend Vemula and four other students happened on 3 January 2016; they were told that they were not allowed to use the facilities at the university or attend classes. Vemula and his friends moved out of their university hostel and slept on the streets on campus.

The university administration therefore exercised financial and political pressure on Vemula and his friends, which increased because the student movement, the ABVP, could use its political contacts to reinforce this administrative pressure. However, Vemula could not deal with the pressure and hanged himself on 17 January 2016 in a room that one of his friends had allowed him to sleep in. He left a handwritten suicide note. The writing style and the content of the note were sophisticated, as if it was an act of philosophical self-reflection. He wrote, 'I feel a growing gap between my soul and my body', as if he was a successful academic whose material support was depleted and who was reduced to just a number and counting as just another vote. The letter had a strong rationalistic tone, rejecting religion and any notion of an afterlife while stating, 'My birth is my fatal accident.'[28] Written in English and published widely on the internet, Vemula's suicide note added force to the evolving political debate.

The controversy erupted after it was clear that the central ministry in Delhi had ordered these students to be suspended. The idea that it was political and administrative pressure aggravated the situation for Vemula caused prolonged controversy. Leading politicians, such as Rahul Gandhi, visited the campus, students mobilized in several cities and Vemula's suicide gained media coverage beyond India where it was addressed, for instance, by the editorial board in the *New York Times*.[29] Even the prime minister and the minister for education addressed the issue directly. Vemula's suicide coincided with a larger mobilization concerning cultural nationalism and the Hindu nationalist movement gaining a firmer grasp on social and educational institutions. And yet antagonisms of caste are not new. In fact, caste-based discrimination has been an ongoing topic in higher education throughout the postcolonial period. There have been cases of intensified casteism during periods when the secularist Congress government has been in power as well.

Caste has not only been important during the Hindu nationalist regime, it had also been greatly contested during the secularist regime of the Indian National Congress at the time of the reservation debates a decade earlier, particularly after the ninety-third constitutional amendment was decided in 2005. This new amendment enabled the government to introduce the Central Educational Institution (Reservation in Admission) Bill of 2006 in Lok Sabha. The popular responses to this new amendment aggravated relations between students, and students belonging to the Scheduled Castes (SCs) in the esteemed All India Institute of Medical Sciences (AIIMS) felt bullied and targeted by other students and staff.

The Congress party led the UPA, which assumed power after the 2004 General Elections. Its electoral success was widely understood to be a response by the poorer sections of the society to inadequate social justice following the implementation of policies of liberalization under the BJP. One of the reforms was to implement more of the recommendations that the Mandal Commission had proposed in 1980. The commission dealt with the extension of reservation policies to the OBCs, which, as noted previously, are castes that were not granted access to reservation by the constitution of 1950 in the same manner as the SCs and Scheduled Tribes (STs).

The first controversy concerning the *Mandal Commission Report* occurred in 1990 when the lower-caste government led by Singh introduced some of the recommendations to extend reservation to the OBCs. This decision led to national demonstrations and the landmark Supreme Court case *Indra Sawhney v. Union of India* in 1992.[30] In this case, nine judges ruled that the reserved posts could not exceed 50 per cent of available posts, and this ceiling has been important for subsequent cases. The controversy at that time involved a large-scale mobilization of opponents of reservation, who claimed that it was morally problematic to allocate seats unless the allocation was based on merit and achievements. Supporters of reservation highlighted the historic injustices of Brahminism and caste and that extending this policy was a step towards compensatory justice.[31]

The issues of reservation and the extension of reservation to the OBCs resurfaced when the Congress-led UPA government assumed power in 2004. The result of implementing more suggestions of the Mandal Commission resulted in the so-called second Mandal controversy. The debate was set in motion with parliament's ninety-third constitutional amendment of 2005. This enabled the government to introduce the Central Educational Institution (Reservation in Admission) Bill, 2006 in Lok Sabha. The bill sought to create a 27 per cent quota for the OBCs in the country's centrally financed and leading educational institutions. This included, specifically, institutions of 'national importance set up by an Act of Parliament'.[32] This OBC quota was an extension of reservation quotas that already existed, that is, the 15 per cent quota for the SCs and the 7.5 per cent quota for the STs.

This contentious national politics played out on various campuses, and the situation at the AIIMS in New Delhi was particularly acute. I conducted an interview with one of the SC students at AIIMS some years after the incident.[33] The SC student explained that the anti-reservationists on campus would walk in groups and castigate the SCs they met. The groups could be as large as fifty people, who could start shouting at and abusing any SC students they came across. They could shout slogans, use caste-related names such as 'Chamar' and say, in tune with the basic message of meritocracy, 'You do not deserve to be here'. The use of caste-related names is significant. It is an effective way of bringing the degrading caste stigma into play. Names make explicit the attributed status of untouchables and contribute to radically negating the dignity and existence of Dalits and people categorized as SCs. Thus, while the name Chamar simply means leatherworker, the name conjures up the ritual status of untouchables historically attributed to the group. The Chamar caste is a major Dalit community that is concentrated in north India.[34] It is the largest sub-caste of Dalits in Uttar Pradesh and the electoral backbone of the Bahujan Samaj Party and the politician Mayawati. The Chamar are better off socially and economically than the Valmikis, another Dalit sub-caste, which is traditionally engaged in cleaning. However, by referring to the SC students by caste-related names such as Chamar, the anti-reservationists revived meanings of caste to back up their claim that the Dalits were unfit to study at the college. There is a resonance with the idea of an ontological opposition between touchables and untouchables in the rhetoric. It is an example of what the sociologist Desphande has argued regarding the Mandal 2 debate, namely that the upper-caste identity was projected as being one of people of merit while those who were in the reserved categories were depicted as having no merit.[35] This rhetoric seems to have had particularly solid foundations in premier institutes such as AIIMS.

The bullying at AIIMS could at times involve scribbling derogatory remarks on walls, on the door of an SC student's room or even locking SC students inside their rooms. The government constituted an inquiry, led by Professor Sukhadeo Thorat, to examine the case. The committee reported, among other things, on a case in which a student 'whose room was locked from the outside on several occasions' had to use his mobile phone to ask a friend to open his door.[36] This instance of bullying illustrates how caste may resurface in modern institutions; here, a Dalit's identity is confirmed and abused and his freedom is confined.

The dominating atmosphere at the college, the open hostility and abuse, resulted in a process of segregation. The tensions caused the SC and ST students to move out of their rooms and move to hostel number four and five, where they could stay together on special floors. There are five hostels on campus. The media correctly reported that the practical impact of the intimidating atmosphere was the creation of separate wings, 'one wing' for 'the SC/ST category' and a different one for 'the general category'.[37] But, in practice, most SC/ST students moved to hostel number four and five, which are linked and form a single unit that is separate from the other hostels.

This segregation emerged in a context of fear. Apart from reports on this creation of student ghettos, there were also reports about fear among SC doctors as a direct consequence of the AIIMS director's support of the anti-reservation campaign.[38] The anti-reservationist campaign had thus brought caste-related tension to its peak. This does not mean that caste-related animosities were unknown to AIIMS prior to the demonstrations in 2006. Rather, several issues reflected caste-related tensions earlier. In terms of sports, for example, SC/ST students play football and volleyball, whereas upper-caste students play basketball and cricket. When Dalits try to join a game of cricket, they are often excluded in practice, since they are unlikely to be involved in the game.[39]

Furthermore, the cultural programme Pulse, which is arranged every year, has not accommodated SC/STs as much as other students. Most SC/STs have observed the event, but very few of them have participated in it.[40] In 2003, a Dalit student was beaten up during the event; the administration dismissed the complaint about this. In 2006, SC/ST students put up posters to voice their grievances about harassment, which was viewed as an annoyance and an obstruction of the event.[41] At the time of Pulse in 2006, a provocative CD was circulated, which showed a video of students burning volumes of Ambedkar writings and speeches. The books shown in the video are the influential volumes with blue covers that have been published in all-India editions by the Maharashtra government since the mid-1980s. They have been read with admiration among Dalit activists and intellectuals across India. In brief, burning the books of Ambedkar is also an attack on the policy he represents, reservation for the SCs.

The two cases of Vemula in Hyderabad in 2016 and the situation in AIIMS during the second Mandal controversy were both examples of how casteism could be intensified by political power and decisions. What should have been a situation of mutual recognition (and agonistic relations) between students became antagonistic and hostile. Both of these cases were politically significant, unlike many everyday forms of caste-based discrimination, which do not become the object of political contestations to the same extent. However, everyday forms of discrimination show that caste may be reproduced in new spaces.

The anthropologist Ajantha Subramanian has demonstrated how caste is central to the social life and identity of the most prestigious institutions of higher education in India. She conducted fieldwork in the Indian Institute of Technology (IIT) Madras. The IITs are institutions that should enjoy more autonomy than other educational institutions and were created by the Institutes of Technology Act, 1961, to be 'institutions of national importance'.[42] Through her fieldwork, Subramanian demonstrates how upper-caste students enter a campus believing it to be a space that will reassure them about caste. The campus provides an ontological security of caste, that is, a psychological reassurance about caste relations where one can be free of anxieties about the social world.[43] Students felt that the IIT Madras provided a space where Brahmin students would not be exposed to members of other castes and that the institution represented the values of their caste. Following up Desphande's analysis of the second Mandal controversy, Subramanian provides empirical insights into how upper-caste students have been able to transform their upper-caste status into modern capital. Desphande emphasizes how the idea of caste among the upper castes could be overwritten with merit.[44] In addition to making caste identity implicit, the replacement of caste with an identification with merit further sharpened the difference between those who were entitled to reservation and those who were simply present by virtue of their caste.

To sum up, several cases suggest that caste-based discrimination is occurring in higher education in the new millennium. While caste embeds social life, it is noteworthy that political power and decisions can aggravate caste relations to the point of treating opponents as illegitimate, unequal and worthy of being excluded. Caste is not simply an identity characterized by what sociologists would refer to as conflict or 'contentious politics'. It is more precise to claim that it involves an ontological dimension in which the distinction between touchables and untouchables is used to grade, degrade and humiliate people. Indeed, this distinction represents an antagonism that can swiftly transform democratic relations into hostility and contempt. The reservation debate reproduces this ontological distinction. It is reinvented when caste dominance is expressed in modern terms through the distinction between merit and reservation and the deserving and the undeserving candidates. This applies in the context of Hindu nationalist and

Congress governments. Overall, reservation policies tend to reproduce and politicize understandings of caste without any substantial reforms beyond education.

Sub-caste Mobilization to Demand Quotas and Legal Change

The relevance of caste cannot be entirely understood without grasping the ways in which reservation debates reflect inequality and competing struggles for entitlement to positions guaranteed by the state. Therefore, although Hindu nationalism is a good example of an ideological regime that seeks to centralize power,[45] reservation often resonates with different types of struggles. Reflecting questions about social stratification, reservation movements need to be understood within their legal and regional contexts. Caste embodies a logic of fragmentation. It can be intensely local, especially because in everyday practices it is associated with *jati*s (a caste or sub-caste) or a sub-division of one *jati*. The internal differences among *jati*s play out in the politics of inequality.

Fragmentation is relevant among all caste groups. For example, the two main castes listed as SCs in Telangana and Andhra Pradesh are Madiga and Mala. These are numerically large and significant castes among the SCs, but the hostility between the two Dalit castes has been prominent since the early 1990s. At that time, a group of Madiga activists established a movement for Madigas, championing the plight of their caste. Their struggle, however, resulted in the establishment of an opposing group among the Malas, the Mala Mahanadu. The Madiga movement has in any case launched a movement with a more specific sub-caste agenda. It articulates a specific Madiga identity, and many leaders have chosen to use their caste-related name – Madiga – as a sign of identification. Madiga leaders also encourage their fellow members to describe themselves as Madiga rather than Dalit.[46] In addition to its struggle for identity, the Madiga movement has focused on ways to change the reservation policy for the SCs in a way that would allow Madigas to benefit from this public policy as much as their Mala counterparts. However, the politics of affluent and powerful castes can become embroiled in clear sub-caste agendas. The Jats of north India are an example of a caste that has cultivated an identity as a Kshatriya caste while expressing its pride about Jats being the natural rulers of north Indian villages.[47] According to Dhatta, the movement among the Jats was originally started in 1905 and was inspired by the Arya Samaj movement to identify its members as Kshatriyas.[48] In fact, there is a long history of caste-based mobilization among Jats; its aim has been to ensure that their children have a modern education and occupations beyond agriculture.

Therefore, there are many different sub-caste movements aiming to secure material benefits by being entitled to reservation in education and government jobs. There have also been caste-based movements demanding the creation of new quotas within the existing quotas – such as those for the SCs – or to be entitled to reservation for the first time. Some of these movements, such as the Dalits' Madiga Dandora in Andhra Pradesh and Telangana as well as those of the powerful castes such as Jats in north India and the Marathas in western India, have launched struggles that have involved constitutional battles. There are significant differences between these movements, though. The Madigas are classified under the SCs category and are an underprivileged group from the former untouchable castes. The Jats, Patels and Marathas, on the other hand, are dominant castes who have demanded to be included in the OBCs so that they can qualify for reserved posts in educational institutions or public employment. There are sections among both Jats and Marathas that struggle with inequality, but the larger motivation is the anxiety of losing their dominance on other castes. The creation of new reservation policies would, however, require political decisions and constitutional change to be made. Each of these sub-caste struggles therefore confront a legal framework that cannot easily be adopted to meet their demands. There are differences in the decision-making processes that relate to the OBCs and SCs; the regional states have a greater leeway to design policies for the OBCs than for the SCs, but the overall constitutional framework creates certain paths that cannot be amended by significant mobilization among sub-castes in various parts of the country. In other words, sub-caste mobilization cannot easily amend the goals of existing constitutional policies even in a situation that involves rising inequality.

The strong constitutional path dependence on reservation creates noteworthy questions because social changes have affected certain castes in ways that may aggravate inequality and put the legal goals in a new light. In general, the lack of adaptivity in public policy could create new challenges if the social context is changing. It is argued by political scientists that gridlocks have emerged in the American political system and polarized its legislators because it is difficult to make public policies up to date.[49] This situation represents what institutional theorists refer to as 'drift' – the goals of the organization remain the same while the context changes. Drift thus refers to processes external to the official policy, which itself is kept in place by law.[50]

The Madiga Dandora is a movement that confronts a problem of drift, as it deals with the rising inequalities created by economic liberalization and a lack of constitutional change. There is a long history of demands made by Madigas.[51] The Madiga Dandora movement was established in 1994 in what was then the state of Andhra Pradesh, today Telangana and Andhra Pradesh. The Madigas represents a large sub-caste among the SCs. Their caste was particularly affected by the liberalization of India's economy in the 1990s because the new economic policies undermined their traditional occupation. Traditionally, the Madigas have worked with leather and made traditional sandals. Economic liberalization opened up the markets and industrially manufactured sandals made from plastic were cheaper and outcompeted the traditional sandals that the Madigas had been making. Globalization therefore hit their livelihood and their social conditions worsened. Historically, moreover, the Madigas have been economically disadvantaged compared to a group such as the Malas. Vemula and most of the Tsundur Dalits were Malas. Although the Malas are an oppressed caste and are exploited as a labour force on agricultural fields, they represent a comparatively more successful caste in terms of education. There are comparatively more Malas who gain the seats reserved for the SCs than Madigas and other underprivileged castes among Dalits in Telugu-speaking areas. This inequality between the castes listed as the SCs had gained significance, and the divisions between the castes matter for the political parties. The Telugu Desam Party (TDP) sought continued support for the Madigas and supported their demand to create subcategories among the SCs. Such a step would represent a new reservation policy. Led by the TDP, the government of Andhra Pradesh introduced this policy in 1997 and created the Rationalisation of Reservations Act in 2000.[52] However, the regional government's Act was challenged in court. In 2004, a constitutional bench of five judges ruled that it could not match the fundamental principles in the Constitution of India. It was declared in this judgment (*E.V. Chinnaiah vs State of Andhra Pradesh and Others, 2004*) that a regional government had no legal authority to change the constitution. According to the judgment, moreover, subcategorizing the SCs violated the principle of equality in the constitution.[53]

Despite this setback, the Madiga movement has been determined to follow up its demand to sub-categorize the SCs, but such a policy requires a constitutional amendment. This demand for subcategorization appeared to be temporarily suspended when Madiga activists joined the movement for the creation of a separate Telangana state. Since the creation of the new Telangana state, they have explored collaborating with the new government on various development schemes. The constitutional struggle will nonetheless continue to be fraught with complications and absorbed in a battle with not much leeway in the constitutional framework. The implementation of subcategorization would involve a new government bill and a constitutional amendment, which could quickly be challenged and struck down by a new constitutional bench. This process and gridlock at the apex of the political system reflects one of the mechanisms that keep the constitutional framework in place. The category of the SCs is considered homogenous from a constitutional point of view and related to fundamental articles in the constitution. This stability contrasts with several drifting circumstances that the Madigas have to deal with as they experience social, economic and political changes as well as the institutionalization of two new regional states, Telangana and Andhra Pradesh.

The problem of drift, which emerges when social and economic conditions change at the same time as policy remains the same, does not apply to the same extent to the powerful castes such as the Jats in Haryana and north India and the Marathas in Maharashtra. Their struggles represent a different approach to the politics of inequality. The Jats and Marathas are examples of dominant castes that seek to consolidate their valuable political, social and economic power. Jats and Marathas are both numerically strong. The Jat community extends across several north Indian states such as Haryana, Rajasthan and western Uttar Pradesh. Jats are predominant in the agricultural mode of production and exercise both electoral and economic power. They can therefore be classified as a 'dominant caste' according to Srivinas' concept of this, that is, a numerically significant caste with economic and political power that is not ritually impure.[54]

Therefore, while the Madiga movement in Telangana and Andhra Pradesh is a case of a social movement of a deprived group emerging from below, the situation for Jats and Marathas is radically different. The mobilization of these dominant castes and their demand for reserved posts in education and public employment are revolts from above. The Jats and the Marathas are two powerful groups within their regions, and they have launched political and constitutional struggles to gain reservation as the so-called OBCs. Although there is no doubt that these castes are dominant within their regions, they are also internally complex.

The Jats are traditionally a landowning community, dominating many villages in north India.[55] As a dominant caste, Jats have also carried out attacks on Dalits. This includes the brutal attack by 300 young Jats on the Balmikis (Dalits) in Mirchpur village in April 2010. Two Balmikis were burnt alive and fifty-three houses were set on fire in the attack, which was triggered by the fact that a dog owned by Balmikis had barked at some members of the Jat community in the village.[56] This violent attack on the Balmikis of Mirchpur was a clear exercise of dominance. Although this attack was referred to later as an incident among youths, there were still simmering conflicts between Valmiki (Dalits) and Jat youths several years later.[57] Several members of the local Jat community have been found guilty for the crime, but the legal dispute is likely to continue even after a verdict in Delhi High Court in August 2018.[58] No doubt the Jats are, overall, a dominant caste that frequently exercises its dominance, but the caste is nonetheless internally divided. Some factions among the Jats have even supported the Dalit party Bahujan Samaj Party in Uttar Pradesh elections.[59] There are also powerful elites among the Jats, and it is estimated that a section, constituting one-fifth of the Jats, earns more than half of the total income registered by the caste as a whole.[60] It was in response to the demand by Jats to gain reservation benefits that a leading sociologist on contemporary caste formations claimed:

> The Jats, without doubt, have been the most important and powerful caste community in the rural landscapes of northwest India. The sources of their dominance have typically been their control over agricultural lands, their demographics and their networks beyond the village.[61]

This statement by Jodhka has been substantiated by two economists, Deshpande and Ramachandran, who find no empirical support for the claim that Jats are lagging behind, 'not even in government jobs'.[62] The Jats are instead confronting a situation in which they aspire to have a power base beyond agriculture to compete with other powerful castes. In terms of living standards, however, the powerful castes Jats, Marathas and Patels have greater access to electricity and administrative services provided by the state than other disadvantaged communities. Access to such public services reflects the extent to which the state often serves the interest of established sections of society. There are also more members of these castes who have access to flushable toilets, whereas the situation for impoverished communities is often that they have to defecate in open, public areas. The economists thus point out how there are clear differences in terms of living standards and health prospects among these powerful castes and other castes, historically viewed as underprivileged.[63] According to Deshpande and Ramachandran, the material conditions of these castes – which are referred to as 'forward castes' – do not suggest that they are economically worse off than earlier. Rather, it is argued that these groups consolidated their power between 2004 and 2012.[64]

How, then, can it be explained that the apparent anxiety among these groups about their overall social position has created aggressive political campaigns in recent years? First of all, as the economists noted the discussed argument, the mobilization among dominant castes such as Jats, Patels and Marathas reflects the fact that positive discrimination does cause lower castes to become upwardly mobile.[65] Social transformations and the levelling of a social order, therefore, create counter-reactions. The mechanism of oppression basically implies that dominant castes attack upward mobility with discrimination and violence, whereas these struggles for entitlements are primarily powerful negotiations with the state. Second, the groups have launched contentious campaigns using several types of action. Some members of the Jat community, for example, have engaged in public protests which have become particularly violent at certain junctures, such as in Haryana in February 2016 when thirty people died, shops were vandalized and national main roads were blocked.[66]

The political mobilization among Jats must be viewed in relation to their significant electoral leverage. Reservation for Jats was first endorsed by the UPA government on 4 March 2014. While the BJP initially claimed this was simply a tactic used by the Congress government prior to the general elections to gain the

Jats' vote; the Modi government has endorsed the inclusion of Jats in the OBC category. The National Commission for Backward Classes, however, has opposed the inclusion of Jats in the OBC list.[67] Jats have run both legal and political campaigns in various states. Although the Rajasthan High Court had decided in 2015 that there was not enough data to claim that Jats in two districts should be entitled to benefit from the reservation policy, the state government decided to grant reservation under the OBC category in 2017.[68] Similar political developments have occurred in neighbouring states, such as Haryana. In 2016, Haryana included the Jats in 'Block C' of its Haryana Backward Classes (Reservation in Services and Admission in Educational Institutions) Act, 2016,[69] just a few months after Jats took part in violent protests. But the Act was challenged in the Punjab and Haryana High Court, and it stayed the order in 2017 until further data had been provided by the state to justify the Act.[70] In short, the reservation policy has become an object of contentious political campaigns in which powerful groups such as the Jats may seek to ensure official entitlements in order to secure status and privilege.

Regional states have the authority to change policies related to the OBC category but do not have a similar authority in relation to those for the SCs. There are therefore regional differences in the approach to the OBCs. Early on, for example, the state of Andhra Pradesh subdivided the OBC category and created four subcategories among this large cluster of castes. This policy was not adopted on a national scale until August 2017, when the central government approved the recommendation from its Ministry of Social Justice and Empowerment to make subcategorization of the OBCs into a national policy.[71] This policy initiative may have contributed to a greater emphasis on material conditions in the approach to group-based entitlements. However, it was precisely the subcategorization of the OBCs in Andhra Pradesh that inspired the underprivileged groups among the SCs in the state, particularly the Madigas, launching a campaign to subclassify reservation among the castes listed as the SCs in the state.

Summary

This chapter has outlined how caste has been at the centre of social and political developments in areas such as higher education and in contentious struggles of various sub-castes over new legislation that could ensure that their group is entitled to reservation. I have not endorsed what the Rudolphs characterize as the 'modernity of tradition'.[72] Instead, I have described how caste goes beyond the distinction between modernity and tradition, constituting an ontology of difference as well as a system of inequality. While there is no doubt that caste has strategic significance for mobilization, there are deeper meanings to the modernity of caste. I have shown that caste represents an enduring force in social and political life and that decisions by the central government can intensify caste differences on a university campus. Values of caste are central to the construction of Hindu nationalism as well as to controversies surrounding reservation.

Viewed as an ontological desire, caste represents a force that can transform political debates into antagonistic campaigns and relations. These hostilities can either become a politics of othering on university campuses or become violent in rural and urban contexts. Therefore, there is a short distance between antagonisms and agonistic relations in the context of caste. Democratic competition and debates among castes can transform into a hostile politics of othering, especially in a context in which inequalities appear to be changing along with the positions of groups in a stratified social order.

There are several ways in which distinctions of caste play out in higher education. First, the SC students may become targets for abuse when their caste-related names, such as Chamar or Mala, are used. Using caste-related names thus introduces an ontological distinction between the students; names make attributed status explicit and have the potential to radically negate their identity. Second, anti-reservationists may claim that the students in reserved categories do not qualify on merit to attend a particular higher education institution and therefore do not deserve the place. In an analysis of this perspective, the sociologist Desphande explains how upper-caste students in the second Mandal controversy redefined their upper-caste identity by projecting themselves as people of merit who presented a sharp contrast to people in reserved categories.[73] By creating an identity in which references to caste were erased and people were described in relation to merit, the anti-reservationist rhetoric reproduced a binary distinction of caste hierarchy in a modern form.

Inequality shapes caste-related (or sub-caste-related) politics relating to reservation and entitlements. In this chapter, I have described different types of struggles in contemporary India. I have compared the struggles of underprivileged groups among the SCs with the struggles for reservation entitlements of powerful castes commonly known as 'forward castes'. These struggles reflect the extent to which the entitlements represent a possibility of securing social status and a material economic foundation for the group as a whole. However, there is a radical difference between the struggles of the Madiga Dandora in south India and those of the Jats in north India, and the problem of 'drift' and changing circumstances appears more acute in the context of the Madigas. The Madiga Dandora represents an underprivileged community of the SCs in the Telugu-speaking areas. The fact that the liberalization of India's market economy undermined their livelihood further stimulated their political leaders to demand better access to the reserved positions. Andhra Pradesh's policy subclassifying the SC category was struck down in 2004, since it divided a category that was considered homogenous from a constitutional point of view. The pressure from Jats and other 'forward castes' for inclusion in the OBCs does not involve the same constitutional problems as it does for the Madigas in relation to the SC category. The OBC category is not similarly integral to the constitutional framework; it is possible for regional governments to change the policy relevant to this category. There is a greater leeway for policy change at the regional level than at the constitutional and central levels. This is what has happened concerning Jats in states, such as Rajasthan and Haryana, where the state governments have decided to grant reservation to members of this dominant caste. While there is little material evidence that these dominant castes have become disadvantaged compared to the underprivileged castes like many of the OBCs, their campaigns for reservation show an exercise of power and apprehension about social changes. The Jats have cultivated a transregional mobilization across states such as Haryana, Rajasthan and western Uttar Pradesh to demonstrate for an official status as 'backward' in order to secure reservation and, as such, to consolidate their power.[74]

Reservation has not only become a domain that has been used to address inequalities in a system of social stratification; the caste mobilization also indicates that official entitlements become tools for securing material power and reproducing social status at large. Equal opportunity is a principle in the Constitution of India which informs policies beyond those for group-based reservation. Regional states can develop many different schemes in addition to those designed by the central government.[75] And the path dependency is stronger regarding reservation policy for the SCs and the STs because the legislation for these groups is more explicit in the constitution.

Notes

1. Lloyd I. Rudolph and Susanne Hoeber Rudolph, *The Modernity of Tradition: Political Development in India* (Bombay: Orient Longmans, 1969).
2. Mark Wenman, *Agonistic Democracy: Constituent Power in the Era of Globalisation* (Cambridge: Cambridge University Press, 2013).
3. Ibid., 4.
4. Chantal Mouffe, *On the Political* (Abingdon: Routledge, 2005), 20.
5. Carl Schmitt, *The Concept of the Political* (Chicago and London: University of Chicago Press, 1996), 26.
6. Mouffe, *On the Political*, 20.
7. Ernesto Laclau, *The Rhetorical Foundations of Society* (London: Verso, 2014), 101.
8. Oliver Marchart, *Post-Foundational Political Thought: Political Difference in Nancy, Lefort, Badiou and Laclau* (Edinburgh: Edinburgh University Press, 2007), 146.

9. Bhimrao Ramji Ambedkar, 'Untouchables or the Children of India's Ghetto', in *Dr. Babasaheb Ambedkar Writings and Speeches: Unpublished Writings*, ed. Vasant Moon, vol. 5 (Bombay: Education Department, Government of Maharashtra, 1989), 102.
10. Devesh Kapur, D. Shyam Babu, and Chandra Bhan Prasad, *Defying the Odds: The Rise of Dalit Entrepreneurs* (Gurgaon: Random House India, 2014).
11. *NDTV*, 'Student Suicide: Congress Demands Probe against Smriti Irani', 20 January 2016, accessed 20 June 2017, http://www.ndtv.com/india-news/student-suicide-congress-demands-probe-against-smriti-irani-1268087.
12. Christophe Jaffrelot, *Religion, Caste and Politics in India* (London: Hurst, 2011), 193.
13. Akhil Bharatiya Vidyarthi Parishad, 'History', accessed 27 June 2016, http://abvp.org/history.
14. *BBC News*, 'Yakub Memon: Mumbai Bomb Plotter's Execution Sparks Death Penalty Debate', 30 July 2015, accessed 28 June 2017, http://www.bbc.com/news/world-asia-india-33713805.
15. *NDTV*, 'They Did Namaz for Yakub Memon: BJP Student Leader about Rohith Vemula', 21 January 2016, accessed 21 June 2016, http://www.ndtv.com/hyderabad-news/hyderabad-suicide-have-proof-of-my-assault-says-abvp-man-1268275.
16. G. Ram Reddy, 'The Politics of Accommodation: Caste, Class and Dominance in Andhra Pradesh', in *Dominance and State Power in Modern India*, 2 vols., ed. Francine R. Frankel and M. S. A. Rao (Delhi: Oxford University Press, 1989), 268–74, 305–7; A. Satyanarayana, 'Caste and Class in Rural Andhra', in *Caste and Class in India*, ed. Kanhaiya Lal Sharma (Jaipur: Rawat Publishers, 1994), 378; Aditya Dasgupta, 'Technological Change and Political Turnover: The Democratizing Effects of the Green Revolution in India', *American Political Science Review* 112, no. 4 (2018): 918–38, doi:10.1017/S000305541800031X.
17. *NDTV*, 'Caste Fine, Not Casteism, Says BJP's Yogi Adityanath', 5 March 2017, accessed 21 May 2017, https://www.youtube.com/watch?v=gE4RONcQIUA&feature=youtu.be.
18. *Hindustan Times*, 'Soaps to Dalits: Congress Demands UPCM Yogi Adityanath Apology, Case against Him', 28 May 2017, accessed 21 June 2017, http://www.hindustantimes.com/india-news/soaps-to-dalits-congress-demands-up-cm-yogi-adityanath-apology-case-against-him/story-moCJtxwvG7CtpSJNzG9P9K.html; *Times of India*, 'My Cabinet Colleagues Are Vegetarians, Yet Not Weak: Adityanath Yogi', 1 May 2017, accessed 23 June 2017, http://timesofindia.indiatimes.com/city/lucknow/my-cabinet-colleagues-are-vegetarian-yet-not-weak-adityanath-yogi/articleshow/58463422.cms.
19. Jaffrelot, *Religion, Caste and Politics in India*, 192.
20. Thomas Blom Hansen, *The Saffron Wave: Democracy and Hindu Nationalism in Modern India* (Princeton, NJ: Princeton University Press, 1999), 79.
21. Ibid., 45.

22. Stuart Corbridge and John Harriss, *Reinventing India: Liberalization, Hindu Nationalism and Popular Democracy* (Malden, MA: Polity Press, 2000), 238.
23. Paul R. Brass, *The Politics of India since Independence*, 2nd edn (Cambridge: Cambridge University Press, 1994), 265.
24. Ernesto Laclau, *On Populist Reason* (London: Verso, 2005), 117; Jason Glynos and David R. Howarth, *Logics of Critical Explanation in Social and Political Theory* (New York: Routledge, 2007), 142.
25. Dag-Erik Berg, 'Hindu Nationalism and Caste Exclusion in Indian Universities' openDemocracy, 9 April 2016, accessed 23 May 2016, https://www.opendemocracy.net/openindia/dag-erik-berg/hindu-nationalism-and-caste-exclusion-in-indian-universities.
26. *Wire*, 'Letter Trail Shows HRD Ministry's Keen Interest in "Anti-National" Activities in Hyderabad University', 20 January 2016, p. 4, accessed 26 June 2017, https://thewire.in/19757/letter-trail-shows-hrd-ministrys-keen-interest-in-anti-national-activities-in-hyderabad-university/.
27. Ibid., 5.
28. Rohith Vemula, 'My Birth Is My Fatal Accident: Full Text of Dalit Student Rohith's Suicide Letter', *Indian Express*, 19 January 2016, accessed 20 June 2016, http://indianexpress.com/article/india/india-news-india/dalit-student-suicide-full-text-of-suicide-letter-hyderabad/?utm_content=buffer0c986&utm_medium=social&utm_source=facebook.com&utm_campaign=buffer.
29. Editorial Board, 'Suicide on an Indian Campus', *New York Times*, 27 January 2016, accessed 1 February 2016, http://www.nytimes.com/2016/01/28/opinion/suicide-on-an-indian-campus.html?_r=0.
30. *Indra Sawhney v. Union of India: AIR 1993* (Supreme Court of India, 1992).
31. Myron Weiner, 'The Struggle for Equality: Caste in Indian Politics', in *The Success of India's Democracy*, ed. Atul Kohli, Contemporary South Asia (Cambridge: Cambridge University Press, 2001), 205.
32. The Central Educational Institutions (Reservation in Admission) Bill, 2006, Bill No. 76 of 2006 (2006).
33. Interview with student at AIIMS campus, New Delhi, 10 May 2009.
34. See, for instance, K. S. Singh, *The Scheduled Castes*, Anthropological Survey of India (Delhi: Oxford University Press, 1995), 301.
35. Satish Deshpande, 'Caste and Castelessness: Towards a Biography of the "General Category"', *Economic and Political Weekly* 48 (2013): 32–9, accessed 24 October 2015, http://www.epw.in/perspectives/caste-and-castelessness.html.
36. Sukhadeo Thorat, K. M. Shyamprasad and R. K. Srivastava. *Report of the Committee to Enquire into the Allegation of Differential Treatment of SC/ST Students in all India Institute of Medical Science, Delhi* (New Delhi: University Grant Commission, 2005), 31.
37. Sidharth Pandey, 'Quota Wrangle: Caste War Divides AIIMS', *NDTV*, 16 September 2007.

38. Charu Sudan Kasturi, 'Ghetto in Medical Hostel: Quota Students in AIIMS Allege Being Driven into a Corner', *Telegraph*, Calcutta, 5 July 2006, accessed 6 February 2018, https://www.telegraphindia.com/india/ghetto-in-medical-hostel-quota-students-in-aiims-allege-being-driven-into-a-corner/cid/785574.
39. Thorat, Shyamprasad and Srivastava, *Report of the Committee to Enquire into the Allegation of Differential Treatment of SC/ST Students*. For an account of caste issues in cricket, see S. Anand, *Brahmans & Cricket: Lagaan's Millennial Purana and Other Myths* (Pondicherry: Navayana, 2003).
40. Thorat, Shyamprasad and Srivastava, *Report of the Committee to Enquire into the Allegation of Differential Treatment of SC/ST Students*, 64.
41. In interview with student at AIIMS, New Delhi, 2 June 2007.
42. Ajantha Subramanian, 'Making Merit: The Indian Institutes of Technology and the Social Life of Caste'. *Comparative Studies in Society and History* 57, no. 2 (2015): 291–322, doi:10.1017/S0010417515000043., 291; Ministry of Law and Justice, *The Institutes of Technology Act, 1961* (Government of India, 19 December 1961, accessed 24 November 2018, http://legislative.gov.in/actsofparliamentfromtheyear/institutes-technology-act-1961.
43. The concept of 'ontological security' was coined by Anthony Giddens, and my usage is largely in line with his definition of this term, see Anthony Giddens, *The Constitution of Society: Outline of the Theory of Structuration* (Cambridge: Polity, 1984), pp. 50, 375.
44. Deshpande, 'Caste and Castelessness'.
45. Paul R. Brass, *Theft of an Idol: Text and Context in the Representation of Collective Violence*, Princeton Studies in Culture/Power/History (Princeton, NJ: Princeton University Press, 1997), 281.
46. Let me illustrate this dynamic with reference to my fieldwork and an episode that occurred in Hyderabad in 2007. At that time, I met with a senior movement leader who was a close ally of Manda Krishna Madiga. As we ordered some food and drinks, we started talking to the waiter who was attending to us. I asked him if he knew the senior Madiga leader and which part of Andhra he was from. He explained that he was from Telangana. When the senior Madiga leader asked him about his caste, the waiter looked down and explained that he was a 'Harijan', using the Gandhian name for the untouchables. The Madiga leader corrected this designation; however, what surprised me was that he did not do so by using the general statement that is common among politically conscious Dalits that the term 'Dalit' is better than 'Harijan'. Rather, he urged the waiter to declare that he was a 'Madiga', thus disregarding the two terms that are more common designations for the SCs. This episode shows how the movement could have an impact on everyday situations. The waiter, who was obviously not a political activist, did not appear to be humiliated. On the contrary, he left as a friend and appeared happy whenever I saw him after this meeting.

47. Gaurang R. Sahay, 'Dominance of Jats Is Unabated: Caste and Dominance in the Villages of Western Uttar Pradesh', *Contributions to Indian Sociology* 49, no. 2 (2015): 216–49, doi:10.1177/0971945815575448.
48. Nonica Datta, 'Jats: Trading Caste Status for Empowerment', *Economic and Political Weekly* 34 (1999): 3172; Craig Jeffrey, Roger Jeffery, and Patricia Jeffery, *Degrees without Freedom? Education, Masculinities, and Unemployment in North India* (Stanford, CA: Stanford University Press, 2008).
49. Jacob S. Hacker, Paul Pierson and Kathleen Thelen, 'Drift and Conversion: Hidden Faces of Institutional Change', in *Advances in Comparative-Historical Analysis*, ed. James Mahoney and Kathleen A. Thelen, Strategies for Social Inquiry (New York: Cambridge University Press, 2015), 193.
50. Ibid.
51. P. Muthaiah, 'Dandora: The Madiga Movement for Equal Identity and Social Justice in AP,' *Social Action* 54 (2004): 181.
52. Yagati C. Rao, 'Introduction', in *Dividing Dalits: Writings on Sub-Categorisation of Scheduled Castes*, ed. Yagati C. Rao (Jaipur: Rawat Publications, 2009), 19.
53. *E.V. Chinnaiah vs State of Andhra Pradesh and Ors*, Civil Appeal No. 6758 of 2000, New Delhi: Supreme Court of India, 5 November 2004, http://www.judis.openarchive.in/.
54. Mysore Narasimhachar Srinivas, 'The Dominant Caste in Rampura'. *American Anthropologist* 61, no. 1 (1959): 1.
55. Sahay, 'Dominance of Jats Is Unabated'.
56. Yadav Bhupendra, 'Mirchpur: Assertion and Retaliation', *Economic and Political Weekly* 46, no. 31 (2011).
57. Ankita Dwivedi Johri, 'In Mirchpur, a Race Leads to Clashes, Many Caste Narratives', *Indian Express*, 3 February 2017, accessed 5 February 2018, http://indianexpress.com/article/india/in-mirchpur-a-race-leads-to-clashes-many-caste-narratives-dalit-4505066/.
58. *Indian Express*, 'After Delhi High Court Verdict: Abandoned Dalit Homes, Tension in Air at Mirchpur', 26 August 2018, accessed 24 November 2018, https://indianexpress.com/article/india/after-delhi-high-court-verdict-abandoned-dalit-homes-tension-in-air-at-mirchpur-5325039/.
59. Sahay, 'Dominance of Jats Is Unabated', 247.
60. Christophe Jaffrelot, 'Jats in Wonderlessland', *Indian Express*, 10 March 2017, accessed 22 October 2017, http://indianexpress.com/article/opinion/columns/jats-in-wonderlessland-quote-stir-jat-agitation-obc-status-haryana-employment-4562573/.
61. Surinder S. Jodhka, 'Going Backward', *Indian Express*, 17 March 2014, accessed 30 June 2017, http://indianexpress.com/article/opinion/columns/going-backward/.
62. Ashwini Deshpande and Rajesh Ramachandran, 'Dominant or Backward? Political Economy of Demand for Quotas by Jats, Patels, and Marathas', *Economic and Political Weekly* 52, no. 19 (2017): 89.
63. Ibid., 84.
64. Ibid., 89.

65. Ibid., 81.
66. *Indian Express*, 'Haryana: Jat Agitation Raises Spectre of Last Year's Violence', 19 February 2017, accessed 28 August 2017, http://indianexpress.com/article/india/haryana-jat-agitation-raises-spectre-of-last-years-violence-4532493/.
67. *Hindu*, 'Modi Govt. Backs Quota for Jats', 5 December 2014, accessed 15 October 2015, http://www.thehindu.com/news/national/other-states/Modi-govt.-backs-quota-for-Jats/article10930280.ece.
68. *Hindustan Times*, 'Rajasthan Gives Reservation to Jats of Bharatpur-Dholpur under OBC Category', 23 August 2017, accessed 7 December 2018, http://www.hindustantimes.com/jaipur/rajasthan-gives-reservation-to-jats-of-bharatpur-dholpur-under-obc-category/story-3EvMasr4OhCqLGiX2NJpsM.html.
69. *Haryana Government Gazette*, The Haryana Backward Classes (Reservation in Services and Admission in Educational Institutions) Act, 2016 (Haryana Act No. 15 of 2016), 2016, accessed 2 September 2017, http://haryanascbc.gov.in/writereaddata/Document/1_44_1_Reservtion.pdf.
70. *Hindustan Times*, 'HC Upholds Haryana's Jat Quota Law, Stays Implementation till March 31, 2018', 1 September 2017, http://www.hindustantimes.com/india-news/hc-upholds-haryana-s-jat-reservation-law-puts-implementation-on-hold-till-quantum-of-quota-is-decided/story-s2IBD2YMNNZbHJ1lIccKtO.html.
71. *Indian Express*, 'Cabinet Approval for Panel to Study Quotas within OBC Quota', 24 August 2017, accessed 28 August 2017, http://indianexpress.com/article/india/cabinet-approval-for-panel-to-study-quotas-within-obc-quota-4810787/.
72. Lloyd Rudolph and Susanne Rudolph, *The Modernity of Tradition*.
73. Deshpande, 'Caste and Castelessness'.
74. Datta, 'Jats'.
75. Dag-Erik Berg, 'Scheduled Castes Policies in Interstate Perspective: Constitutional Power, Argumentative Practices, and Governance in India', *India Review* 13, no. 3 (2014): 235–50, doi:10.1080/14736489.2014.937269.

Conclusions on Caste and Law

Caste was embedded in India's social order before independence, but its current visibility is significant. Although this book has examined occurrences from each historical period that has opened a generation's eyes to the caste question, caste seems to be far more visible at the time of writing than before. The rise of the Internet and the digital revolution have made caste more visible to both Indian and international audiences. Inequalities and caste-based discrimination are not simply confined to brutal attacks in the Indian countryside, such as those in Karamchedu in 1985 and Tsundur in 1991. But these two critical cases in Andhra Pradesh throw light on why many Dalit activists from this part of India travelled to the World Conference against Racism in South Africa in 2001 to explain that casteism was the same as racism.

What I have described in this book is the way in which caste represents a social phenomenon that is part of everyday social relations, informing politics and articulations of hegemony. During these nearly seventy-two years years since India gained independence, caste has become more visible and politically charged than the constitution-makers might have assumed. In this book, I have explained how Ambedkar's theory of caste indicates that there is an ontological desire to practise caste. This desire remains relevant in contemporary politics. But there are several dimensions to caste, such as stratification, hierarchy and religion, and Ambedkar incorporated them into his concept of graded inequality. This multidimensionality is significant for law. Indeed, I have pointed out how the legal approach to redressing inequalities and providing protection become subject to several changes after independence.

My theoretical objective has been to provide a critical explanation of the relation between caste and law with a focus on Dalits in India's constitutional democracy, where Dalits are socially excluded (as the untouchables) and officially included (as the Scheduled Castes). In fact, following the atrocity cases, it is reasonable to suggest that Dalits are excluded because of an ontological difference – the antagonism between touchables and untouchables – that Ambedkar foregrounds in his theory of caste. Having followed the approach of the late Laclau outlined by Glynos and Howarth, I have argued that a critical explanation requires several dimensions to be delineated and compared; these involve hegemonic ideas and social and political practices. I have addressed caste-based oppression in India by combining a historical perspective on the development of law with case studies. These case studies indicate how laws are created by contentious struggles, but I have also shown that there are discoursive conflicts in the legal framework which may produce change and new understandings of caste and laws. Legal changes are made to address caste-based discrimination, which reflects how members of the political system respond to social injustices. But institutional characteristics slow down these changes even though caste is played out in violent ways. Social and institutional changes do not always correspond with one another. Capoccia explains this difference by pointing to how, after social changes have occurred, individuals in institutions may be replaced with new individuals who have a slightly different background.[1] But caste mentalities may create a correspondence between the social and institutional levels. A central lesson of this book is also that dominant castes may be able to make state actors, particularly the police, complicit in a massacre either by engaging in coordinated action before the occurrence or by having inadequate or inappropriate reactions after the crime has occurred.

In what follows, I draw some lessons from the discussions in this book, first by providing a critical explanation of the relation between law and caste in what I argue is a political ontology of caste characterized by the distinction between touchables and untouchables. Second, I explain not only why the mechanism of oppression is an accurate characterization of the Dalit situation but also why it goes further than other approaches to explain the institutionalization of caste. Third, I explain how certain dimensions of caste are institutionalized in the legal framework and how the official policies tend to become objects of political discourse, so much so that they become the only visible aspect of caste in the public domain. Finally, I explain the persistence of caste by arguing that the reproduction and intensity of caste and casteism reflect an ontological desire for caste that may bolster social and political action.

Explaining the Relation between Caste and Law

This book has focused on three tasks – first, characterizing the social situation of Dalits; second, specifying the characteristics of institutions and laws and, finally, explaining the continued relevance of caste in India. This has the merit of avoiding, among other things, wholly positivist reporting of what the law says, when it was made and whether the words on paper were applied to a particular situation. It also avoids this book studying caste as just an empirical study of action disguised as 'contentious politics'. Instead, using a broad history and ethnographic materials, I have sought to examine how caste is a long-lasting ideational dimension and to outline key developments of law and how caste is played out within law. In Chapter 1, I outlined Ambedkar's ideas about caste and the ways in which he argues that caste has a grip on subjects who believe that caste is a matter of religion, that is, a sacred dimension of everyday behaviour. Caste relations are not trivial facts. Rather, Ambedkar's explanation of why caste matters for reasons related to ontology, identity and existence is highly relevant to explaining the persistence of caste today. I have emphasized how Ambedkar's term 'graded inequality' involves an explanation of how believers in caste practise it by treating the untouchables as nobodies. This ideational dimension of caste has been reproduced and given new political relevance during the postcolonial period. I focus on the relation between caste and law in several ways. My initial idea was not simply to reiterate anthropological concerns with reifications of caste, nor have I been following an inclination that exists among political scientists to study the politicization of caste with reference to the prototypical voter–politician nexus. Rather, I have sought to examine the evolving relationship between Dalits and institutions of law by incorporating a common-sense approach to characterizing the Dalit situation. This provides a starting point for identifying social mechanisms that are relevant for processes involving law and legal change.

Mechanism of Oppression

My first task was to characterize the legal responses to the Dalit problem. I argued that the Dalits' situation can broadly be characterized as a situation in which upward mobility coexists with enduring atrocity. Such a mechanism of oppression might be identified in the context of other groups, such as that of women, Muslims or Adivasis. But the advantage of acknowledging the mechanism of oppression is that it represents one perspective that is frequently used to make sense of the overall situation for Dalits in contemporary India. This is far from a reductionist perspective. On the contrary, it brings in a common-sense explanation among an organic group of intellectuals, that is, a group of experienced observers in the field.[2] Their accounts can offer new perspectives, which can be used to develop new and more relevant explanations. What I have referred to as a mechanism of oppression is a perspective that can be used to characterize the overall situation of Dalits. It puts into focus how there could be a connection between different legal developments. A lawyer, for example, would distinguish policies of equal opportunity from legislation on caste-based violence because these pieces of legislation belong to different domains of law, which the lawyer cannot mix up. By contrast, the mechanism of oppression provides a perspective from outside the domain of law which introduces the sociological observation of a frequently occurring pattern. While using mechanisms as part of my explanatory strategy, the approach in this book has differed from that found among the work of philosophers (such as Elster, Hedström and Little) who advocate mechanism as a type of explanation because they often tend to focus on microprocesses centred around individuals rather than phenomena such as embedded forms of exclusion.[3] However, the mechanism of oppression does not provide the full explanation. Instead, it represents an overall characterization of an enduring pattern. While resembling a structural problem giving the impression that the problem is constant and endures over time, the concept of mechanism simply designates a recurring pattern. This is where I have followed Elster's emphasis on how mechanisms are often identified in proverbs and that they often come in opposites (haste makes waste, he who hesitates is lost).[4] Proverbs are not trivial; they could rather be viewed as based on historical experience.

Following up the characterization of the Dalit situation found among many organic intellectuals, I have argued that one may view the legal changes as adjustments to this mechanism of oppression in which upward mobility and enduring atrocity coexist. The brutal massacres studied in this book, such as the killings of eight Dalits in Tsundur village in August 1991, were a direct attack on assertive and educated Dalit youths. On the one hand, the legal changes appear to have been an adjustment to the mechanism of oppression. While the reservation policy and the principle of equal opportunity created upward mobility, the persistent attacks and organized massacres created a need for adequate legislation, resulting in the Scheduled Castes and the Scheduled Tribes (Prevention of Atrocities) Act (PoA Act), 1989, which is part of criminal law. This process of legal changes could be viewed as an adaptation to a persistent theme in the Dalit situation in which legal discourses have been unpacked and adjusted.[5] This theme is the enduring norms of exclusion and the facts of oppression. But does the adaptation to the emerging societal challenges represent an effect or a conclusion, or do the new laws also generate new causes for social and political developments?

It is relevant to ask whether policies are outcomes or causes of new social and political developments. The Foucauldian term 'governmentality' has gained prominence in the scholarship on South Asia concerning how to understand the ways in which a population is governed and transformed.[6] Foucault's term is used to identify how there is a certain type of knowledge and dynamic expertise at play through government policies and the various tactics used to control a target population. From this perspective, subjectivities are produced and new mentalities emerge because of how people internalize new knowledge and the techniques of ruling. However, since the Foucauldian terminology emphasizes factors that are antecedent to individual action, it does not focus on how local people negotiate with the state. This lacuna has been addressed by Chatterjee, who has pointed out how state institutions may change their policies when people like slum dwellers negotiate with local officials about whether they can remain in the settlements they have established without official permission.[7] In a perceptive critique, Baviskar and Sundar add that members of middle-class civil society are in fact more likely to bend laws in their own favour, while less privileged groups and 'members of political society strive to become legal'.[8] No doubt the Foucauldian literature offers tools through which one could explain how deviations and resistance at the margins of the social order could be controlled through a flexible law.[9] But Foucault's conceptual architecture is not adequate to address everything.[10] As far as institutional change and, especially, embedded ideas of caste are concerned, one needs a different starting point, where I argue the mechanism of oppression is relevant.

In institutional theory, official laws could be viewed as effects that may in fact generate new directions in which people can act and politics can evolve. Reservation is one such phenomenon. Legal entitlement to students at higher-educational institutions creates contestations about the relevant policies and may politicize conflicts between castes, ranging from divisions among Dalits to the mobilization of powerful castes such as the Jats in north India or the Marathas in Maharashtra.[11] Policy creates politics, and group-based equal opportunity policy has proven important for transforming caste into a key ground for political mobilization.[12] However, the legal changes pertaining to the Dalit situation could be viewed as an institutionalization of specific categories of caste. The formal recognition of certain dimensions of caste may aggravate its significance and create new pressure on politics and identity formations. Political scientists have emphasized, among other things, that 'ideas are embedded in the design of institutions'[13] and that policies are categories of statecraft that shape their social environments.[14] This book has broadly followed such arguments that are associated with historical institutionalism. I have focused on the evolution of laws, their historical origins, the changes in laws, how they are designed and the conversion of law in institutional practices. More than historical institutionalists, however, I have highlighted the ideational dimension of caste and its persistence and intensity as well as noteworthy discourses of law at stake in legal change.

Policy, Power and Discourse

Dealing with caste in public law makes the Indian state more embedded in its social environment. And specific policies that relate to caste tend to increase the significance of given dimensions in a complex social reality. Caste is a multidimensional social system, but each dimension is not equally visible and significant in the legal order. The constitutional principle of equal opportunity and the ensuing reservation policy have foregrounded stratification and inequality, generating a discourse of stratification and entitlements to positions granted by the state. In the context of Dalits and caste, for example, the legal framework tends to reinforce the significance of entitlement to reservation and prevention of atrocity. No doubt the two themes – reservation and atrocity – resonate with the mechanism of oppression as they correspond to themes like upward mobility and backlashes. But other topics associated with caste inequalities remain crucial for the reproduction of the social system. Marriage, for example, is decisive in the reproduction of caste as a social and religious system of grading. Land reform is another key theme, which connects to property and economic power.

In order to explain the significance of some of the policies and their related discourses, it is useful to introduce Foucault's complex concept of discourse. This does not simply designate an approach, a type of speech and a source that creates practices; Foucault also uses the term to explain why one approach is more prominent than other approaches. In his writings, he discusses how one object surfaces and gains prominence to such an extent that it is implemented as if it is the correct and legitimate one. For instance, why would one carry out punishments in a specific way, or why should one treat madness or study grammar or economics in specific ways?[15] Foucault's point is that such practices emerge as discoursive objects because of a given constellation of knowledge and power. A discourse may be privileged as it has authority and power at the expense of another discoursive possibility that is left invisible.

Similarly, the two policies relating to caste in India, reservation and atrocity, appear to be two visible domains. Each domain involves specific legal provisions and official statements with well-known implications that are crucial for equal opportunities and future positions, jobs or punishments. One may therefore argue that the mechanism of oppression – upward mobility and atrocity – is sustained by the fact that there are two pieces of legislation that are visible, consulted and contested. The lack of social reforms in marriage practices and land distribution aggravates inequalities, caste identity and class differences. Marriage deals with love and reproduction, while land reforms involve property relations and modes of production. Both are relevant for reproducing inequalities and aggravating caste relations.

Marriage is crucial for the reproduction of caste, but the legislation concerning it is not as visible as legislation regarding reservation. There are some obvious reasons for a state not intervening in or regulating marriages. Marriage is considered a matter that belongs to the private domain, which is outside the scope of a state based on liberal democratic values. It would therefore be a violation of the state's basic principles to organize marriages across caste to stop reproducing the system.

Yet it is precisely in the context of marriage that caste identity becomes acutely important. Marriages are arranged by parents, who usually start their search for a suitable bride or groom by looking within their own caste. In most newspapers, often on Sundays, there are advertisements in a separate matrimonial section. These are simply part of life. They are not objected to, nor does there seem to be any leeway for organizing a widespread movement against caste-based marriages. In fact, it is often taken for granted that marrying within castes creates ontological security, that is, confidence that an existential self is preserved and so one can be free from anxieties about one's social identity.[16] Marrying within the same caste creates more assurances that the couple will be able to live in peace rather than being challenged and abused by references to caste differences in the family. Inter-caste marriages could expose the couple to the risk of humiliations and abuse. Occasionally, the sanctions for an inter-caste affair can be very violent, and so-called honour killings occur to protect the caste from moral disgrace.[17] There are theological justifications for the prevention of inter-caste marriages. In the best-known Hindu religious text the *Bhagavad Gita*, for example, it is stated that any 'intermingling of the four estates' is a moral problem that obliterates 'caste laws and the eternal family law'.[18] But violent acts by parents, whether it is against a daughter or a son-in-law, could primarily be viewed as motivated by a desire to protect their family's social status and avoid a moral abyss. Overall, the embedded social norm is that marriages are carefully negotiated and organized within the caste.

Land reforms are at the other end of the spectrum, while also largely being outside the constitutional law. There are different trajectories of land reforms across Indian states. There were land reforms in Kerala before India gained independence, and these reforms have created a more egalitarian political culture in Kerala than in most other Indian states. But land reforms were not carried out at an all-India level at the time of independence. The legislation that the constituent assembly elaborated had an emphasis on equal opportunities and reservation. This piece of legislation made the Scheduled Castes (SCs) and the Scheduled Tribes (STs) entitled to have an education. But the possibilities for upward mobility were not supported by reforms concerning property or by land reforms. So, although the entitlement to equal opportunity was granted to individuals from very poor social backgrounds, many would agree with Jaffrelot's comment that the constituent assembly granted this entitlement to the untouchables 'because they were easily identified, too destitute to threaten the upper castes, and bound to remain unthreatening because the [reserved] quotas would never be filled'.[19] The social reforms were inadequate to create social justice. As Jaffrelot argues, moreover, the implications of creating this policy of equal opportunity had a greater political than social impact on the untouchables. The policy created several new questions around which caste groups could mobilize.

The institutionalization of caste therefore means that neither of the two most visible legal provisions concerning caste – entitlement to reservation and prevention of atrocity – are central to the reproduction of caste differences. Reservation and atrocity law are undoubtedly significant and may regulate behaviour across society. But they are not reforms aiming at the first order, where marriage and property would belong. Rather, even though reservation and atrocity legislation are crucial, their significance is secondary to the social reproduction of caste. They represent two important dimensions of the complex phenomenon of caste while creating some upward mobility and legal protection. The institutionalization of caste therefore has specific impacts on certain aspects of the caste system.

The laws regarding equal opportunity and prevention of atrocity are both practical and significant for the Dalit movement. These laws, which include specific lists of entitlements and penalties, are systematically referred to by the existing movements. Some of these movements, such as the Madiga Dandora in south India, have been created to specifically address one of these policies as part of their struggle for social justice. The laws add force to discussions of how upward mobility coexists with discrimination. Many Dalits experience discrimination in educational institutions. This book has discussed the case of the young postgraduate student in Tsundur village who was beaten in 1991 and that of Rohith Vemula, the PhD student who was suspended from the University of Hyderabad in 2015 after having led a student movement on campus. Moreover, the history of legislating to prevent caste-based exclusion reveals several changes that reflect what has been learnt during the lawmaking process. The initial conceptualization of caste exclusion as a matter of temple access was the result of historical movements and a notion of civil wrongs, which did not correspond to the many facts of oppression that had no relation to temples. The creation of the PoA Act was therefore a result of ongoing deliberations and legal and discoursive changes, which recognized and enabled clearer articulations of caste-based violence.

Using concepts from historical institutionalism, I have pointed out how the official policies may be redirected towards new goals in institutional practices. This is a politics of policy conversion. After Vemula passed away, for example, the government of Andhra Pradesh declared that he did not belong to an SC.[20] His mother was from the major Dalit caste, Mala, but she had been adopted by a woman from a backward caste (Vaddera) when she was a child. The woman married Rohith's mother to a man from her own caste, but the husband divorced Rohith's mother after she had given birth to two children because he realized that she was, in fact, a Dalit.[21] Rohith, therefore, grew up as a Dalit and often declared that he was a Dalit, including on a video uploaded on YouTube, but he knew that his family background was complex because his mother had been adopted by a woman with a different caste identity and social status. However, there are legal consequences at stake regarding the question of whether he was a Dalit or, more precisely, a member of an SC. If he was a Dalit, the administration at the University of Hyderabad might be charged under the PoA Act, 1989. If it was declared that he was not a Dalit, the law would not apply and there would be no investigation into how caste-based discrimination was a reason for his suicide. In short, while legal entitlements matter and represent an important part of why India's constitutional democracy is comparatively significant, the policy conversions represent a noteworthy re-embedding of caste-based dominance in practice.

Ontological Desire and Embedded Caste

So, why does caste not vanish? In fact, why does caste persist and even gain new impetus despite a long postcolonial history with elaborate legislation, ideas about modernization and social and political developments? The answer to this final question about the persistence of caste has just been explained – caste identities are reproduced through marriages, and the radical class disadvantage is sustained by lack of reforms regarding property and land. Moreover, the elaborate legislation and democratic system seem to have politicized caste. The significance of caste could be viewed as a result of statecraft, where group-based entitlement makes caste a visible feature in the state. But this old argument of 'seeing like a state'[22] is still inadequate in terms of taking the idea of caste as a social and religious phenomenon into account. If one removes legislation and politicization, caste could be less visible and more difficult to address while still shaping social practices and life chances.

The persistence of caste could be explained not only by the facts of oppression and social reproduction presented in this book but also by ontological terms and ideas. The ontological perspective is useful because it adds an extra dimension that explains the continued relevance of caste and violence. Ambedkar's concept of graded inequality is particularly relevant in this context. It also explains the mechanism of oppression, which was what organic intellectuals described to me over the course of several fieldwork sessions. Conceptually, ontology connects to existence. This is a description that Alain Badiou develops in his abstract philosophy. For Badiou, ontology creates one type of 'being' and existence. But the same ontology represents a denial of a different type of existence. In Badiou's scheme, therefore, ontology creates both existence and non-existence; it gives existence to one modality and represses another possible mode of existence. Badiou's terminology is useful for bringing the ontological dimension of Ambedkar's concept of graded inequality into view. But there are noteworthy differences. Badiou's speculative philosophy does not relate the two antagonistic poles, which is what the late Laclau made more explicit.[23] Ambedkar's ontological distinction is precisely about how each of the two poles that constitute an antagonism negate and remain contingent on the identity of the other. The Dalit identity is radically negated.

Graded inequality also comprises several dimensions where ontology and stratification are two essential dimensions. The term 'stratification' could create confusion, as it could be understood in general and more specific conceptual ways. The sociologist Rosemary Crompton offers a very broad definition of social stratification when she argues that it designates 'the hierarchical ordering of social relationships, and is a general term which describes these systematic structures of inequality'.[24] This definition has little analytical utility. Max Weber offers a clearer conceptual approach to stratification with his concept of status groups. This was elaborated by Bourdieu, who invented terms such as social and cultural capital. The status group approach of Weber refers to how groups gain power and positions in the state and in society and how these groups will create closures to protect their privileges and assert their status. Weber's term resonates with empirical observations. Indeed, the sociological concepts invented by Weber and Bourdieu have been very important for analysing social inequalities. Yet neither Weber nor Bourdieu had any notion of ontology. This is where Ambedkar's concept of graded inequality is distinguished. While addressing social stratification as a matter of inequality, Ambedkar combines it with an ontological approach. The ontological dimension implies a distinction between existence and non-existence and respect and disrespect. This constitutes the antagonism that is still relevant even if there is scope for agonistic democracy.

The ontological desire of caste represents a dimension that was not properly addressed by early sociologists such as Srinivas. One of Srinivas' classic statements appeared in 1957 and reads as follows:

> The provision of constitutional safeguards to the backward sections of the population, especially the Scheduled Castes and Tribes, has given a new lease of life to caste. It is hardly necessary to add that this contrasts with the aim of bringing about a casteless and classless society which most political parties, including the Indian National Congress, profess.[25]

The statement that reservation has 'given a new lease of life to caste' has been repeated by sociologists who have been ambivalent about the reproduction of caste in the postcolonial state. In 2010, Béteille argued that Srinivas' observation had turned out to be correct: reservation has created a preoccupation with caste and community.[26] And yet it is important to contextualize reservation in a sociological sense as a domain at the level of social stratification. Although reservation has undoubtedly become more integral to the institutionalization of caste in the social and political order, the reproduction of caste is stronger in domains such as marriage, kinship and property. As Mendelsohn and Baxi state, the reservation scheme for untouchables was 'calculated to make at best a marginal rather than a frontal attack on the position of Untouchables within Hindu society'.[27] The question is not only whether caste will cease to exist but also whether it creates humiliation, violence and enduring inequalities. Moreover, the intensity of caste must be viewed in terms of the ontological desire that gives caste its lease of life. Unlike Srinivas's seminal accounts of caste, Ambedkar spells out the ontological dimension that explains how mentalities of caste are put into practice over time.

Ambedkar makes sense of the principle of graded inequality by using a clear-cut distinction between the untouchables who are 'nobodies' and Hindus who are 'somebodies'.[28]

The grading involves everyone, including women who menstruate, being subject to the untouchability practices. In the system of graded inequality, self-esteem is bolstered by maintaining the system of untouchability, and caste cannot be dissolved if it is considered sacred and involves religious sanctions. Ambedkar's theory does not only explain why caste and untouchability persist, but it also explains the mechanism of oppression and why caste-based violence occurs. In other words, any upward mobility by the class of people considered to be untouchables implies that touchables will no longer be able to look down on them and that their status as 'somebodies' may be at risk. The upward mobility of the untouchables is problematical in this system given that they are, ontologically speaking, 'nobodies'. The ontological grip of caste is a reason to adopt the mechanism of oppression as a concept that cuts across rural and urban contexts as well as the unhelpful distinction between tradition and modernity. Moreover, the grip of caste explains different forms of conflicts, that is, caste-related atrocities and negotiations. This matters for democratic theory because the grip of caste represents an opportunity to legitimize violence in the middle of a constitutional democracy. The ontological desire cannot be understood simply as a religious question in isolation from social life. Religion intersects with and becomes part of the numerous layers of grading and inequalities, which become embedded in social structures in its divisions and occupations. Indeed, as shown in this book, one of the early lessons learnt in the postcolonial Indian state was that it was inadequate to simply reduce the problem of caste-based dominance to a matter of temple access, which was one of the ways in which religion was reproduced in law as a result of hegemonic articulation. Caste remains embedded by social, political and religious factors, and law has become part of the re-embedding of caste just as much as law creates new possibilities for recognition and freedom in India's constitutional democracy.

Notes

1. Giovanni Capoccia, 'When Do Institutions "Bite"? Historical Institutionalism and the Politics of Institutional Change', *Comparative Political Studies* 49, no. 8 (2016): 1095–127, doi:10.1177/0010414015626449.

2. Kate A. F. Crehan, *Gramsci's Common Sense: Inequality and Its Narratives* (Durham: Duke University Press Books, 2016), 28–33.
3. Peter Hedström and Petri Ylikoski, 'Causal Mechanisms in the Social Sciences', *Annual Review of Sociology* 36 (2010): 49–67, doi:10.2307/25735068; Jon Elster, *Alchemies of the Mind: Rationality and the Emotions* (Cambridge: Cambridge University Press, 1999); Daniel Little, 'The Heterogeneous Social: New Thinking about the Foundations of the Social Sciences', in *Philosophy of the Social Sciences: Philosophical Theory and Scientific Practice*, ed. C. Mantzavinos (Cambridge: Cambridge University Press, 2009), 154–78.
4. Elster, *Alchemies of the Mind*, 12.
5. Dag-Erik Berg, 'Structural Mechanism, Law, and the Dalit Question in India', *Asian Journal of Law and Society* 2, no. 1 (2015): 21–33, doi:10.1017/als.2014.14.
6. Partha Chatterjee, *The Politics of the Governed: Reflections on Popular Politics in Most of the World* (New York: Columbia University Press, 2004).
7. Ibid.
8. Amita Baviskar and Nandini Sundar, 'Democracy versus Economic Transformation?', *Economic and Political Weekly* 43, no. 46 (2008): 88.
9. Ben Golder and Peter Fitzpatrick, *Foucault's Law* (Oxon: Routledge, 2009).
10. Colin Gordon, 'Expelled Questions: Foucault, the Left and the Law', in *Re-reading Foucault: On Law, Power and Rights*, ed. Ben Golder (London: Routledge, 2013), 13.
11. Sumeet Mhaskar, 'Maratha Unrest and Its Linkages with Mumbai's Political Economy', *Wire*, 5 December 2016, accessed 7 December 2016, http://thewire.in/84198/maratha-unrest-linkages-mumbai-political-economy/.
12. Rajni Kothari, 'Introduction', in *Caste in Indian Politics*, ed. Rajni Kothari (New Delhi: Orient Longman, 1970).
13. Daniel Béland and Robert H. Cox, 'Introduction: Ideas and Politics', in *Ideas and Politics in Social Science Research*, ed. Daniel Béland and Robert H. Cox (Oxford: Oxford University Press, 2011).
14. Capoccia, 'When Do Institutions "Bite"?', 10; James C. Scott, *Seeing like a State: How Certain Schemes to Improve the Human Condition Have Failed* (New Haven: Yale University Press, 1998).
15. Michel Foucault, *The Archaeology of Knowledge* (London: Routledge, 1989).
16. Anthony Giddens, *The Constitution of Society: Outline of the Theory of Structuration* (Cambridge: Polity Press, 1984), 50, 375.
17. *Indian Express*, 'Telangana Honour Killing: Son-in-Law Killed, Set Afire by Upper Caste Man', 28 May 2017, access 16 June 2017, http://www.deccanchronicle.com/nation/crime/280517/telangana-honour-killing-son-in-law-killed-set-afire-by-upper-caste-man.html. *Hindu*, '"Honour" Killing of Dalit Youth Shankar in Tamil Nadu: Death for Six, Including Father-in-Law', December 12, 2017, accessed 12 December 2017, http://www.thehindu.com/news/national/tamil-nadu/shankar-murder-case-father-in-law-gets-death-sentence/article21478790.ece?homepage=true.
18. W. J. Johnson, *The Bhagavad Gita* (Oxford: Oxford University Press, 2008), 6.

19. Christophe Jaffrelot, 'The Impact of Affirmative Action in India: More Political than Socioeconomic', *India Review* 5, no. 2 (2006): 186.
20. *Hindustan Times*, 'Rohith Vemula Not a Dalit, Says Collector; Andhra Govt to Cancel SC Certificate', 14 February 2017, accessed 18 February 2017, http://www.hindustantimes.com/india-news/rohith-vemula-s-mother-asked-to-prove-dalit-status-or-get-declared-as-an-obc/story-kflGppKb0Exg5pEPc9qW3K.html.
21. Sudipto Mondal, 'Rohith Vemula: An Unfinished Portrait', *Hindustan Times*, February 2017, accessed 21 February 2017, http://www.hindustantimes.com/static/rohith-vemula-an-unfinished-portrait/index.html.
22. Scott, *Seeing like a State.*
23. Ernesto Laclau, *The Rhetorical Foundations of Society* (London: Verso, 2014), 101.
24. Rosemary Crompton, *Class and Stratification* (Cambridge: Polity Press, 2008), 8.
25. M. N. Srinivas, 'Caste in Modern India', *The Journal of Asian Studies* 16, no. 4 (1957): 529.
26. André Béteille, 'Democracy in Bihar: If Caste Is Not an Issue Now, It May Be so only for a Time', *Telegraph*, Kolkata, 29 November 2010, 15 October 2015, https://www.telegraphindia.com/1101129/jsp/opinion/story_13224735.jsp#.
27. Oliver Mendelsohn and Upendra Baxi, 'Introduction', in *The Rights of Subordinated Peoples*, ed. Oliver Mendelsohn and Upendra Baxi (Delhi: Oxford University Press, 1994), 9.
28. Bhimrao Ramji Ambedkar, 'Untouchables or the Children of India's Ghetto', in *Dr. Babasaheb Ambedkar Writings and Speeches: Unpublished Writings*, ed. Vasant Moon, vol. 5 (Bombay: Education Department, Government of Maharashtra, 1989), 102.

Glossary

avarna	those without a *varna*, the untouchables
bhakti	devotional worship
Brahmin	the highest of the four *varnas*, the category of priests and intellectuals
Dalit	means oppressed, broken to pieces
dharna	peaceful, sit-in protest
Harijan	Gandhi's term for the untouchables, meaning People of God or Children of God
Hindutva	Hinduness; a term to designate Hindu nationalism
jati	sub-caste, often understood as the actual caste
Kshatriya	the second of the *varnas*, meaning high caste and traditionally understood to be rulers, kings
Lok Sabha	the lower house in the Indian parliament
Madiga	a particularly disadvantaged Dalit sub-caste in Andhra Pradesh
Mahar	one of the main Dalit sub-caste in Maharashtra
Mala	a Dalit sub-caste in Andhra Pradesh
Mahasabha	great assembly
mandal	an administrative division (towns and group of villages) and the name of the second Backward Classes Commission of 1980 after its Chairman B. P. Mandal
Naxalite	a generic name for the Maoist movement, named after uprisings in the late 1960s in Naxalbari, an area in West Bengal
palle	a hamlet in Telugu, although the term *palle* can also be used for entire villages
Panchamas	the fifth category, outside the *varna* system
panchayat	administrative unit, village government
Parayars	Dalit sub-caste in Tamil Nadu, also known as Paraiyar
reservation	term used for equal opportunity policy, known as affirmative action and positive discrimination in the United States of America
Shudra	the lowest of the *varnas*, traditionally servants and engaged in manual labour

sibiram	camp in Telugu
swaraj	self-rule, independence for India
Vaishya	the third of the *varna*s, traditionally understood as traders and businessmen
varna	the four categories that the Vedic texts divide society into; literal meaning is colour
wada	a hamlet or settlement in Telegu; it can also be used as a suffix for cities
*zamindar*s	landlords who were instrumental for revenue in the colonial administration

Bibliography

Akhil Bharatiya Vidyarthi Parishad 'History'. Accessed 27 June 2016. http://abvp.org/history.

Ambedkar, B. R. 'Annihilation of Caste'. In *Dr. Babasaheb Ambedkar Writings and Speeches*, edited by Vasant Moon, vol. 1, 23–96. Bombay: Education Department, Government of Maharashtra, 1989.

———. 'Castes in India: Their Mechanism, Genesis and Development, Paper Read before the Anthropology Seminar of Dr. A. A. Goldenwizer at The Columbia University, New York, U. S. A. on 9th May 1916'. In *Dr. Babasaheb Ambedkar Writings and Speeches*, edited by Vasant Moon, vol. 1, 3–22. Bombay: Education Department, Government of Maharashtra, 1989.

———. 'Evidence before the Southborough Committee on Franchise: Examined on 27th 1919'. In *Dr. Babasaheb Ambedkar Writings and Speeches*, edited by Vasant Moon, vol. 1, 243–78. Bombay: Education Department, Government of Maharashtra, 1989.

———. 'Political'. In *Dr. Babasaheb Ambedkar Writings and Speeches: Unpublished Writings*, edited by Vasant Moon, vol. 5, 227–399. Bombay: Education Department, Government of Maharashtra, 1989.

———. 'Untouchables or the Children of India's Ghetto'. In *Dr. Babasaheb Ambedkar Writings and Speeches: Unpublished Writings*, edited by Vasant Moon, vol. 5, 1–124. Bombay: Education Department, Government of Maharashtra, 1989.

———. 'The Untouchables: Who Were They and Why They Became Untouchables?' In *Dr. Babasaheb Ambedkar Writings and Speeches*, edited by Vasant Moon, vol. 7, 231–379. Bombay: Education Department, Government of Maharashtra, 1990.

———. 'What Congress and Gandhi Have Done to the Untouchables: Mr. Gandhi and the Emancipation of the Untouchables'. In *Dr. Babasaheb Ambedkar Writings and Speeches*, edited by Vasant Moon, vol. 9, i–387. Bombay: Education Department, Government of Maharashtra, 1991.

———. *The Buddha and His Dhamma*. Nagpur: Buddha Bhoomi Publication, 1997.

———. 'Dr. Ambedkar at the Round Table Conferences'. In *Dr. Babasaheb Ambedkar Writings and Speeches*, edited by Vasant Moon and Hari Narke, vol. 2, 2nd edn, 503–792. Bombay: Government of Maharashtra, 2005.

———. *Dr. Babasaheb Ambedkar Writings and Speeches*, edited by Vasant Moon, vol. 14, 1. New Delhi: Dr. Ambedkar Foundation, 2014.

———. 'Hindu Code Bill (Clause by Clause Discussion)'. In *Dr. Babasaheb Ambedkar Writings and Speeches*, edited by Vasant Moon, vol. 14, Part 2. New Delhi: Dr. Ambedkar Foundation, 2014. Accessed 8 November 2018. https://www.mea.gov.in/Images/attach/amb/Volume_14_02.pdf.

Anand, S. *Brahmans & Cricket: Lagaan's Millennial Purana and Other Myths*. Pondicherry: Navayana, 2003.

Anderson, Benedict. *Imagined Communities: Reflections on the Origin and Spread of Nationalism*. London: Verso, 1991.

Andhra Pradesh Civil Liberties Committee. *The Chundur Carnage: AP-Civil Liberties Committee Report*. Vijaywada, 1991. Accessed 26 January 2017. http://balagopal.org/wp-content//uploads/2014/04/Tsunduru/THE%20TSUNDURU%20CARNAGE-APCLC%20REPORT-PUBLISHED%20IN%20AUGUST%201991.pdf.

Andhra Pradesh Civil Liberties Committee. *The Karamchedu Massacre: A Report*. Guntur, 22 July 1985. On file with the author.

Anti-Slavery International. 'Slavery in India's Brick Kilns & the Payment System Way Forward in the Fight for Fair Wages, Decent Work and Eradication of Slavery'. September 2017. Accessed 12 November 2017. http://www.antislavery.org/wp-content/uploads/2017/09/Slavery-In-Indias-Brick-Kilns-The-Payment-System.pdf.

Arendt, Hannah. *Between Past and Future: Eight Exercises in Political Thought*. Penguin Classics. New York: Penguin Books, 2006.

Austin, Granville. *The Indian Constitution: Cornerstone of a Nation*. New Delhi: Oxford University Press, 1999.

———. *Working a Democratic Constitution: A History of the Indian Experience*, first published in 1999. 2nd impression. New Delhi: Oxford University Press, 2004.

Ayyathurai, Gajendran. 'Foundations of Anti-Caste Consciousness: Pandit Iyothee Thass, Tamil Buddhism, and the Marginalized in South India'. Unpublished PhD thesis. Columbia University, New York, 2011.

Backward Classes Commission. *Reservations for Backward Classes. Mandal Commission Report of the Backward Classes Commission, 1980: Alongwith Introduction*. Delhi: Akalank Publications, 1991.

Badiou, Alain. *Ethics: An Essay on the Understanding of Evil*. London: Verso, 2002.

———. *Being and Event*. London: Continuum, 2005.

Badiou, Alain and Fabien Tarby. *Philosophy and the Event*. Cambridge: Polity, 2013.

Bajpai, Rochana. *Debating Difference: Group Rights and Liberal Democracy in India*. New Delhi: Oxford University Press, 2011.

Balagopal, K. 'The Karamchedu Killings: The Essence of the NTR Phenomenon'. *Economic and Political Weekly* 20, no. 31 (1985): 1298–300.

———. 'Karamchedu: Second Anniversary'. *Economic and Political Weekly* 22, no. 33 (1987): 1378–81.

———. '"Law and Order" on Lease'. *Economic and Political Weekly* 24, no. 24 (1989): 1322–4. doi:10.2307/4394952.

———. 'Post-Chundur and Other Chundurs'. *Economic and Political Weekly* 26, no. 42 (1991): 2399–405. Accessed 15 October 2015. http://www.epw.in/system/files/pdf/1991_26/42/post_chundur_and_other_chundurs.pdf.

———. *Ear to the Ground: Selected Writings on Class and Caste*. New Delhi: Navayana, 2011.

Baru, Sanjaya. 'Economic Policy and the Development of Capitalism in India: The Role of Regional Capitalists and Political Parties'. In *Transforming India*, edited by Francine R. Frankel et al., 206–30. New Delhi: Oxford University Press, 2000.

Basu, Durga Das. *Shorter Constitution of India*, 13th edn. Nagpur: Wadhwa and Company, 2001.

Baviskar, Amita, and Nandini Sundar. 'Democracy versus Economic Transformation?' *Economic and Political Weekly* 43, no. 46 (2008): 87–9.

Baxi, Upendra. 'Historic New Law: Protecting SC/ST Rights'. *Times of India*, 15 September 1989.

———. 'Emancipation as Justice: Legacy and Vision of Dr. Ambedkar'. In *From Periphery to Centre Stage*, edited by K. C. Yadav, 49–74. New Delhi: Manohar, 2000.

Bayly, Susan. *Caste, Society and Politics in India from the Eighteenth Century to the Modern Age*. Cambridge: Cambridge University Press, 1999.

BBC News. 'Yakub Memon: Mumbai Bomb Plotter's Execution Sparks Death Penalty Debate'. 30 July 2015. Accessed 28 June 2017. http://www.bbc.com/news/world-asia-india-33713805.

Béland, Daniel, and Robert Henry Cox. 'Introduction: Ideas and Politics'. In *Ideas and Politics in Social Science Research*, edited by Daniel Béland and Robert H. Cox, 3–20. Oxford: Oxford University Press, 2011.

Benbabaali, Dalel. 'Caste Dominance and Territory in South India: Understanding Kammas' Socio-Spatial Mobility'. *Modern Asian Studies* 52, no. 6 (2018): 1938–76. doi:10.1017/S0026749X16000755.

Berg, Dag-Erik. 'Sovereignties, the World Conference against Racism 2001 and the Formation of a Dalit Human Rights Campaign'. In *Questions de Recherche/Research in Question*, no. 20. Paris: Centre d'études et de recherches internationals, Sciences Po., 2007. https://www.sciencespo.fr/ceri/sites/sciencespo.fr.ceri/files/qdr20.pdf.

———. 'Dalits and the Constitutional State: Untouchability, Dalit Movements and Legal Approaches to Equality and Social Justice for India's Scheduled Castes'. PhD thesis. Department of Administration and Organization Theory, University of Bergen, Bergen, 2011.

———. 'Scheduled Castes Policies in Interstate Perspective: Constitutional Power, Argumentative Practices, and Governance in India'. *India Review* 13, no. 3 (2014): 235–50. doi:10.1080/14736489.2014.937269.

———. 'Structural Mechanism, Law, and the Dalit Question in India'. *Asian Journal of Law and Society* 2, no. 1 (2015): 21–33. doi:10.1017/als.2014.14.

———. 'Hindu Nationalism and Caste Exclusion in Indian Universities'. *openDemocracy*. 9 April 2016. Accessed 23 May 2016. https://www.opendemocracy.net/openindia/dag-erik-berg/hindu-nationalism-and-caste-exclusion-in-indian-universities.

———. 'Foregrounding Contingency in Caste-Based Dominance: Ambedkar, Hegemony, and the Pariah Concept'. *Philosophy & Social Criticism* 44, no. 8 (2018): 843–64. doi:10.1177/0191453717744007.

———. 'Race as a Political Frontier against Caste: WCAR, Dalits and India's Foreign Policy'. *Journal of International Relations and Development* 21, no. 4 (2018): 990–1013. https://doi.org/10.1057/s41268-017-0091-3.

Béteille, André. *Society and Politics in India: Essays in a Comparative Perspective.* London: Athlone Press, 1991.

———. *Anti-Utopia: Essential Writings of André Béteille.* Oxford: Oxford University Press, 2005.

———. 'Democracy in Bihar: If Caste Is Not an Issue Now, It May Be So Only for a Time'. *Telegraph*, Kolkata, 29 November 2010. Accessed 15 October 2015. https://www.telegraphindia.com/1101129/jsp/opinion/story_13224735.jsp#.

Bhupendra, Yadav. 'Mirchpur: Assertion and Retaliation'. *Economic and Political Weekly* 46, no. 31 (2011): 10–11 .

Bob, Clifford. ''Dalit Rights Are Human Rights': Caste Discrimination, International Activism, and the Construction of a New Human Rights Issue'. *Human Rights Quarterly* 29, no. 1 (2007): 167–93.

Bombay High Court . Criminal Confirmation Case No. 4/2008, in the High Court of Judicature in Bombay, Nagpur Bench, Nagpur. Accessed 10 April 2017. http://online.wsj.com/public/resources/documents/Khairlanji.pdf.

Bose, Sugata and Ayesha Jalal. *Modern South Asia: History, Culture, Political Economy*, 3rd edn. London: Routledge, 2011.

Bourdieu, Pierre. *Outline of a Theory of Practice.* Cambridge: Cambridge University Press, 1977.

———. *Distinction: A Social Critique of the Judgement of Taste.* London: Routledge & Kegan Paul, 1984.

Brass, Paul R. *The Politics of India since Independence*, 2nd edn. Cambridge: Cambridge University Press, 1994.

———. *Theft of an Idol: Text and Context in the Representation of Collective Violence*, Princeton Studies in Culture/Power/History. Princeton, NJ: Princeton University Press, 1997.

Brown, Judith M. *Modern India: the Origins of an Asian Democracy.* Oxford: Oxford University Press, 1994.

———, ed. *Mahatma Gandhi: The Essential Writings.* Oxford World's Classics Oxford: Oxford University Press, 2008.

Capoccia, G. 'When Do Institutions "Bite"? Historical Institutionalism and the Politics of Institutional Change'. *Comparative Political Studies* 49, no. 8 (2016): 1095–127. doi:10.1177/0010414015626449.

Census Organization of India. *Scheduled Castes Population: Census 2011.* New Delhi: Ministry of Home Affairs, Government of India, 2011. Accessed 5 November 2018. https://www.census2011.co.in/scheduled-castes.php.

Chidipudi Srivasava Reddy and Others vs the State of A.P. Rep by the Public Prosecutor, High Court of A.P. (Andhra Pradesh High Court, Criminal Appeal, 22-04-2014). On file with author. Hyderabad: Andhra Pradesh High Court.

Chakraborty, Debashis, D. Shyam Babu and Manashi Chakravorty. 'Atrocities on Dalits: What the District Level Data Say on State-Society Complicity'. *Economic and Political Weekly* 41, no. 24 (2006): 2478–81.

Chatterjee, Partha. 'A Possible India: Essays in Political Criticism'. In *The Partha Chatterjee Omnibus*. New Delhi: Oxford University Press, 1999.

———. *The Politics of the Governed: Reflections on Popular Politics in Most of the World*. New York: Columbia University Press, 2004.

Chowdhry, Prem. '"First Our Jobs Then Our Girls": The Dominant Caste Perceptions on the "Rising" Dalits'. *Modern Asian Studies* 43, no. 1 (2009): 437–79. doi: 10.1017/S0026749X07003010.

Cohn, Bernard S. *An Anthropologist among the Historians and Other Essays*. Delhi and Oxford: Oxford University Press, 1987.

Constituent Assembly of India. 'Constituent Assembly Debates: Volume III. 28th April to 2nd May 1947'. In *Constituent Assembly Debates: Official Report*, vol. 3. 6 vols. New Delhi: Lok Sabha Secretariat, 1946–50.

———. 'Adoption of the Constitution'. In *Dr. Babasaheb Ambedkar Writings and Speeches*, edited by Vasant Moon, vol. 13, 1161–219. New Delhi: Dr. Ambedkar Foundation, 2013. Accessed 7 November 2018. https://www.mea.gov.in/Images/attach/amb/Volume_13.pdf.

———. 'Monday, the 9th December 1946'. Constituent Assembly of India Debates (Proceedings), vol. I. New Delhi: Lok Sabha Secretariat, Government of India. Accessed 11 July 2019. http://164.100.47.194/Loksabha/Debates/cadebatefiles/C09121946.html.

Corbridge, Stuart, and John Harriss. *Reinventing India: Liberalization, Hindu Nationalism and Popular Democracy*. Malden, MA: Polity Press, 2000.

Crehan, Kate A. F. *Gramsci's Common Sense: Inequality and Its Narratives*. Durham: Duke University Press Books, 2016.

Crompton, Rosemary. *Class and Stratification*. Cambridge: Polity Press, 2008.

Dahiwale, S. M. 'Khairlanji: Insensitivity of Mahar Officers'. *Economic and Political Weekly* 44, no. 31 (2009): 29–33.

Daily Mail. 'Modi's India on Britain's Doorstep? An MP and a "Hindutva" Charity Accused of Working Together to "Push into the Long Grass" a Law to Protect British Dalits'. 31 October 2017. Accessed 5 February 2018. http://www.dailymail.co.uk/indiahome/indianews/article-5032729/National-Council-Hindu-Temples-working-repeal-caste.html.

Dalit Camera. 'Advocate Tarakam on Tsundur Judgement of AP High Court'. YouTube, 23 April 2014. Accessed 23 March 2017. https://www.youtube.com/watch?v=BjaazZOVG9Q.

Dalit Voice. 'Karamchedu Massacre Helps Dalit Militancy'. Vol. 5, no. 2. (1985).

Dalton, Dennis. 'The Gandhian View of Caste, and Caste after Gandhi'. In *India and Ceylon: Unity and Diversity*, edited by Philip Mason, 159–81. London: Oxford University Press, 1967.

Damodaran, Harish. *India's New Capitalists: Caste, Business, and Industry in a Modern Nation*. Ranikhet: Permanent Black, 2008.

Das, Bhagwan. *In Pursuit of Ambedkar*. New Delhi: Navayana, 2009.

Dasgupta, Aditya. 'Technological Change and Political Turnover: The Democratizing Effects of the Green Revolution in India'. *American Political Science Review* 112, no. 4 (2018): 918–38. doi:10.1017/S000305541800031X.

Datta, Nonica. 'Jats: Trading Caste Status for Empowerment'. *Economic and Political Weekly* 34 (1999): 3172.

Deliège, Robert. *The Untouchables of India*. Oxford: Berg, 1999.

Department of Social Justice and Empowerment. *List of Scheduled Castes*. New Delhi: Department of Social Justice and Empowerment, Government of India, 2018. Accessed 11 November 2018. http://socialjustice.nic.in/UserView/index?mid=76750.

Department of Social Welfare. *Report of the Committee on Untouchability, Economic and Educational Development of the Scheduled Castes and Connected Documents*, L2 Dept. of SW 69-2. New Delhi: Department of Social Welfare, Government of India, 1969.

Deśapāṇḍe, Govind P., ed. *Selected Writings of Jotirao Phule*. With annotations and introduction by Givind P. Deśapāṇḍe. New Delhi: Leftword, 2002.

Deshpande, Ashwini and Rajesh Ramachandran. 'Dominant or Backward? Political Economy of Demand for Quotas by Jats, Patels, and Marathas'. *Economic and Political Weekly* 52, no. 19 (2017): 81–90.

Deshpande, Satish. 'Caste and Castelessness: Towards a Biography of the "General Category"'. *Economic and Political Weekly* 48 (2013): 32–9. Accessed 24 October 2015. http://www.epw.in/perspectives/caste-and-castelessness.html.

Devarajiah vs B. Padmanna. Karnataka High Court, 10 September 1957. Accessed 26 Feburary 2016. http://indiankanoon.org/doc/337685/.

Dewey, John. 'Moral Judgement and Knowledge: From Ethics (1932)'. In *The Essential Dewey: Vol. 2, Ethics, Logics, Psychology*, edited by Larry A. Hickman and Thomas M. Alexander, 328–54. Bloomington, IN: Indiana University Press, 1998.

———. 'The Place of Habit in Conduct'. In *The Essential Dewey: Vol. 2, Ethics, Logics, Psychology*, edited by Larry A. Hickman and Thomas M. Alexander, 24–49. Bloomington, IN: Indiana University Press, 1998.

Dhavan, Rajeev. *Reserved! How Parliament Debated Reservations, 1995–2007*. New Delhi: Rupa & Co., 2008.

Dirks, Nicholas B. *Castes of Mind: Colonialism and the Making of Modern India*. Princeton, NJ: Princeton University Press, 2001.

Dr. Subhash Kashinath Mahajan versus the State of Maharashtra and Anr. New Delhi: Supreme Court of India, 20 March 2018. Accessed 4 April 2018. Available at http://supremecourtofindia.nic.in/supremecourt/2017/22086/22086_2017_Judgement_20-Mar-2018.pdf.

Dumont, Louis. *Homo Hierarchicus: The Caste System and Its Implications*. Chicago: University of Chicago Press, 1980.

Economist. 'Arguments over Caste Spread from India to Britain'. 1 November 2015. Accessed 17 November 2017. https://www.economist.com/blogs/erasmus/2015/11/hinduism-britain-and-caste.

Editorial Board. 'Suicide on an Indian Campus'. *New York Times*, 27 January 2016. Accessed 1 February 2016. http://www.nytimes.com/2016/01/28/opinion/suicide-on-an-indian-campus.html?_r=0.

Elster, Jon. *Alchemies of the Mind: Rationality and the Emotions*. Cambridge: Cambridge University Press, 1999.

———. *Explaining Social Behavior: More Nuts and Bolts for the Social Sciences*. Cambridge: Cambridge University Press, 2007.

Epp, Charles R. *The Rights Revolution: Lawyers, Activists, and Supreme Courts in Comparative Perspective*. Chicago: University of Chicago Press, 1998.

Figueira, Dorothy Matilda. *Aryans, Jews, Brahmins: Theorizing Authority through Myths of Identity*, SUNY Series, the Margins of Literature. Albany: State University of New York Press, 2002.

Foucault, Michel. *The Archaeology of Knowledge*. London: Routledge, 1989.

———. 'Subject and Power'. In *Power: Essential Works of Foucault, 1954–1984*, edited by James D. Faubion, vol. 3, 326–48. London: Penguin Books, 2002.

———. 'Lemon and Milk'. In *Power: Essential Works of Foucault, 1954–1984*, edited by James D. Faubion, vol. 3, 435–8. London: Penguin Books, 2002.

Frontline. 'Enforcing Silence'. 15 December 2006. Accessed 10 July 2019. http://www.frontline.in/static/html/fl2324/stories/20061215002809800.htm.

Fuller, C. J. 'Anthropologists and Viceroys: Colonial Knowledge and Policy Making in India, 1871–1911'. *Modern Asian Studies* 50, no. 1 (2016): 217–58. doi:10.1017/S0026749X15000037.

———. 'Colonial Anthropology and the Decline of the Raj: Caste, Religion and Political Change in India in the Early Twentieth Century'. *Journal of the Royal Asiatic Society* 26, no. 3 (2016): 463–86. doi:10.1017/S1356186315000486.

Galanter, Marc. 'Temple-Entry and the Untouchability (Offences) Act, 1955'. *Journal of the Indian Law Institute* 6 (1964): 185–95. Accessed 6 February 2016. http://marcgalanter.net/Documents/templeentryandtheuntouchabilityact.pdf.

———. 'Why the "Haves" Come Out Ahead: Speculations on the Limits of Legal Change'. *Law & Society Review* 9, no. 1 (1974): 95–160.

———. *Competing Equalities: Law and the Backward Classes in India*. Berkeley, CA: University of California Press, 1984.

Gandhi, M. K. 'Caste Must Go'. In *Caste and Democratic Politics in India*, edited by Ghanshayam Shah, 80–2. New Delhi: Permanent Black, 2002.

Giddens, Anthony. *The Constitution of Society: Outline of the Theory of Structuration*. Cambridge: Polity Press, 1984.

Gidla, Sujatha. *Ants among Elephants: An Untouchable Family and the Making of Modern India*, paperback edn. New York: Farrar, Straus and Giroux, 2018.

Glynos, Jason. 'The Grip of Ideology: A Lacanian Approach to the Theory of Ideology'. *Journal of Political Ideologies* 6, no. 2 (2001): 191–214.

Glynos, Jason, and David R. Howarth. *Logics of Critical Explanation in Social and Political Theory*. New York: Routledge, 2007.

Gokhale, Jayashree. *From Concessions to Confrontation: The Politics of an Indian Untouchable Community*. Bombay: Popular Prakashan, 1993.

Golder, Ben and Peter Fitzpatrick. *Foucault's Law*. Oxon: Routledge, 2009.

Gordon, Colin. 'Expelled Questions: Foucault, the Left and the Law'. In *Re-reading Foucault: On Law, Power and Rights*, edited by Ben Golder, 13–38. London: Routledge, 2013.

Gorringe, Hugo. *Untouchable Citizens: Dalit Movements and Democratization in Tamil Nadu*. New Delhi: Sage Publications, 2005.

Government Equalities Office. *Caste in Great Britain and Equality Law: A Public Consultation, Government Consultation Response*. London, July 2018. Accessed 5 August 2018. https://assets.publishing.service.gov.uk/government/uploads/system/uploads/attachment_data/file/727790/Caste_in_Great_Britain_and_equality_law-consultation_response.pdf.

Government of India. The Scheduled Castes and the Scheduled Tribes (Prevention of Atrocities) Amendment Bill. 2018. Accessed 10 July 2019. https://www.prsindia.org/billtrack/scheduled-castes-and-scheduled-tribes-prevention-atrocities-amendment-bill-2018.

Gramsci, Antonio. *Selections from the Prison Notebooks of Antonio Gramsci*. London: Lawrence & Wishart Ltd, 1971.

Gudavarthy, Ajay. 'Dalit and Naxalite Movements in AP: Solidarity or Hegemony?' *Economic and Political Weekly* 40, no. 51 (2005): 5410–18.

———. *The Politics of Post-Civil Society: Contemporary History of Political Movements in India*. New Delhi: Sage Publications, 2013.

Gundimeda, Sambaiah. 'Dalits, Praja Rajyam Party and Caste Politics in Andhra Pradesh'. *Economic and Political Weekly* 44, no. 21 (2009): 50–8.

———. 'Dalit Activism in Telugu Country, 1917–30'. *South Asia Research* 36, no. 3 (2016): 322–42. doi:10.1177/0262728016663270.

———. *Dalit Politics in Contemporary India*. Abingdon: Routledge, 2016.

Hacker, Jacob S., Paul Pierson and Kathleen Thelen. 'Drift and Conversion: Hidden Faces of Institutional Change'. In *Advances in Comparative-Historical Analysis*, edited by James Mahoney and Kathleen A. Thelen, 180–208. Strategies for Social Inquiry. New York: Cambridge University Press, 2015.

Hansen, Thomas Blom. *The Saffron Wave: Democracy and Hindu Nationalism in Modern India*. Princeton, NJ: Princeton University Press, 1999.

Hans India. 'MRPS Slams BJP for Trying Dilute SC, ST Act'. 1 June 2018. Accessed 14 September 2018. http://www.thehansindia.com/posts/index/Khammam-Tab/2018-06-01/MRPS-slams-BJP-for-trying-dilute-SC-ST-Act/385744.

———. 'MRPS Leaders to Participate in Meet on SC/ST Act in New Delhi'. 6 August 2018. Accessed 31 October 2018. http://www.thehansindia.com/posts/index/

Telangana/2018-08-06/MRPS-leaders-to-participate-in-meet-on-SCST-Act-in-New-Delhi/403770.

Hardtmann, Eva-Maria. *The Dalit Movement in India: Local Practices, Global Connections*. New Delhi and Oxford: Oxford University Press, 2009.

Haryana Government Gazette. The Haryana Backward Classes (Reservation in Services and Admission in Educational Institutions) Act, 2016. (Haryana Act No. 15 of 2016). 2016. Accessed 2 September 2017. http://haryanascbc.gov.in/writereaddata/Document/1_44_1_Reservtion.pdf.

Hedström, Peter, and Petri Ylikoski. 'Causal Mechanisms in the Social Sciences'. *Annual Review of Sociology* 36 (2010): 49–67. doi:10.2307/25735068.

Herrenschmidt, Olivier. 'Ambedkar and the Hindu Social Order'. In *Reconstructing the World: B. R. Ambedkar and Buddhism in India*, edited by Surendra Jondhale and Johannes Beltz, 37–48. New Delhi: Oxford University Press, 2004.

———. 'The Indians' Impossible Civil Code'. *European Journal of Sociology/Archives Européennes de Sociologie* 50, no. 2 (2009): 309–47. doi:10.1017/S0003975609990154.

Hindu. '1991 Dalit Massacre: Committee to Challenge HC Verdict'. 8 May 2014. Accessed 16 January 2018. http://www.thehindu.com/news/national/andhra-pradesh/1991-dalit-massacre-committee-to-challenge-hc-verdict/article5989321.ece.

———. 'Tsundur Dalit Massacre Case Takes New Turn'. 18 March 2014. Accessed 24 March 2017. http://www.thehindu.com/news/cities/Vijayawada/Tsundur-Dalit-massacre-case-takes-new-turn/article11416977.ece.

———. 'Kandadevi Temple Car Festival Mired in Controversy'. 2 July 2014. Accessed 24 October 2018. https://www.thehindu.com/news/cities/Madurai/kandadevi-temple-car-festival-mired-in-controversy/article6169348.ece.

———. 'Modi Govt. Backs Quota for Jats'. 5 December 2014. Accessed 15 October 2015. http://www.thehindu.com/news/national/other-states/Modi-govt.-backs-quota-for-Jats/article10930280.ece.

———. '"Honour" Killing of Dalit Youth Shankar in Tamil Nadu: Death for Six, Including Father-in-Law'. 12 December 2017. Accessed 12 December 2017. http://www.thehindu.com/news/national/tamil-nadu/shankar-murder-case-father-in-law-gets-death-sentence/article21478790.ece?homepage=true.

———. 'Gaddar for SC/ST Act in 9th Schedule'. 15 May 2018. Accessed 16 May 2018. http://www.thehindu.com/todays-paper/tp-national/tp-andhrapradesh/gaddar-for-scst-act-in-9th-schedule/article23888169.ece.

Hindustan Times. 'Rajasthan Gives Reservation to Jats of Bharatpur-Dholpur under OBC Category'. 23 August 2017. http://www.hindustantimes.com/jaipur/rajasthan-gives-reservation-to-jats-of-bharatpur-dholpur-under-obc-category/story-3EvMasr4OhCqLGiX2NJpsM.html.

———. 'Rohith Vemula Not a Dalit, Says Collector; Andhra Govt to Cancel SC Certificate'. 14 February 2017. Accessed 18 February 2017. http://www.hindustantimes.com/india-news/rohith-vemula-s-mother-asked-to-prove-dalit-status-or-get-declared-as-an-obc/story-kflGppKb0Exg5pEPc9qW3K.html.

———. 'Soaps to Dalits: Congress Demands UPCM Yogi Adityanath Apology, Case against Him'. 28 May 2017. Accessed 21 June 2017. http://www.hindustantimes.com/india-news/soaps-to-dalits-congress-demands-up-cm-yogi-adityanath-apology-case-against-him/story-moCJtxwvG7CtpSJNzG9P9K.html.

———. 'HC Upholds Haryana's Jat Quota Law, Stays Implementation till March 31, 2018'. 1 September 2017. Accessed 2 September 2017. http://www.hindustantimes.com/india-news/hc-upholds-haryana-s-jat-reservation-law-puts-implementation-on-hold-till-quantum-of-quota-is-decided/story-s2IBD2YMNNZbHJ1lIccKtO.html.

Howarth, David R. *Discourse.* Buckingham: Open University Press, 2000.

———. *Poststructuralism and After: Structure, Subjectivity, and Power.* Basingstoke: Palgrave Macmillan, 2013.

Hunt, Lynn. *Inventing Human Rights: A History.* New York: Norton, 2008.

Ilaiah, Kancha. 'Caste or Class or Caste-Class: A Study in Dalitbahujan Consciousness and Struggles in Andhra Pradesh in 1980s'. In *Caste, Class, Gender*, edited by Manoranjan Mohanty, 227–55. New Delhi: Sage Publications, 2004.

Indian Express. 'Law for SCs, STs Could Be Strengthened: PC'. 31 August 2010. Accessed 5 February 2018. http://indianexpress.com/article/news-archive/web/law-for-scs-sts-could-be-strengthened-pc/.

———. 'Cabinet Approval for Panel to Study Quotas within OBC Quota'. 24 August 2017. Accessed 28 August 2017. http://indianexpress.com/article/india/cabinet-approval-for-panel-to-study-quotas-within-obc-quota-4810787/.

———. 'Haryana: Jat Agitation Raises Spectre of Last Year's Violence'. 19 February 2017. Accessed 28 August 2017. http://indianexpress.com/article/india/haryana-jat-agitation-raises-spectre-of-last-years-violence-4532493/.

———. 'Telangana Honour Killing: Son-in-Law Killed, Set Afire by Upper Caste Man'. 28 May 2017. Access 16 June 2017. .

———. 'A Day in the Life of a Manu Statue in the Rajasthan High Court'. 28 October 2018. Accessed 10 July 2019. https://indianexpress.com/article/india/a-day-in-the-life-of-a-manu-statue-in-the-rajasthan-high-court-5421545/.

———. 'After Delhi High Court Verdict: Abandoned Dalit Homes, Tension in Air at Mirchpur'. 26 August 2018. Accessed 24 November 2018. https://indianexpress.com/article/india/after-delhi-high-court-verdict-abandoned-dalit-homes-tension-in-air-at-mirchpur-5325039/.

Supreme Court of India Indian Young Lawyers Association & Ors. v. the State of Kerala & Ors. New Delhi: Supreme Court of India, 28 September 2018. Accessed 30 October 2018. https://www.sci.gov.in/supremecourt/2006/18956/18956_2006_Judgement_28-Sep-2018.pdf.

Indra Sawhney v. Union of India: AIR 1993. New Delhi: Supreme Court of India, 1992.

Jaffrelot, Christophe. *India's Silent Revolution: The Rise of the Lower Castes in North India.* London: Hurst, 2003.

———. *Dr. Ambedkar and Untouchability: Analysing and Fighting Caste.* London: Hurst, 2005.

———. 'The Impact of Affirmative Action in India: More Political than Socioeconomic'. *India Review* 5, no. 2 (2006): 173–89.

———. *Religion, Caste and Politics in India*. London: Hurst, 2011.

———. 'Jats in Wonderlessland'. *Indian Express*, 10 March 2017. Accessed 22 October 2017. http://indianexpress.com/article/opinion/columns/jats-in-wonderlessland-quote-stir-jat-agitation-obc-status-haryana-employment-4562573/.

Jalal, Ayesha. *Democracy and Authoritarianism in South Asia: A Comparative and Historical Perspective*. Cambridge: Cambridge University Press, 1995.

Jangam, Chinnaiah. 'Dilemmas of Dalit Agenda: Political Subjugation and Self-Emancipation in Telugu Country, 1919–1950'. In *Dalit Studies*, edited by Ramnarayan S. Rawat and Kusuma Satyanarayana, 104–30. Durham: Duke University Press, 2016.

———. *Dalits and the Making of Modern India*. 1st edn. New Delhi: Oxford University Press, 2017.

Jayshree, P. M., T. Cynthia, M. Ajai, M. A. Britto and Aloysious Irudayam, eds. *Dalit Human Rights Violations: Atrocities against Dalits in India: Volume 1, Case Papers, Summary & Jury's Interim Observations and Recommendations*. Ahmedabad and Madurai: National Campaign on Dalit Human Rights, 2000.

Jeffrey, Craig, Roger Jeffery and Patricia Jeffery. *Degrees without Freedom? Education, Masculinities, and Unemployment in North India*. Stanford, CA: Stanford University Press, 2008.

Jeffrey, Robin. 'Temple-Entry Movement in Travancore, 1860-1940'. *Social Scientist* 4, no. 8 (1976): 3–27. doi:10.2307/3516377.

Jensenius, Francesca R. 'Mired in Reservations: The Path-Dependent History of Electoral Quotas in India'. *The Journal of Asian Studies* 74, no. 1 (2015): 85–105. doi:10.1017/S0021911814002162.

Jodhka, Surinder S. 'Going Backward'. *Indian Express*, 17 March 2014. Accessed 30 June 2017. http://indianexpress.com/article/opinion/columns/going-backward/.

Jodhka, Surinder S. and Katherine S. Newman. 'In the Name of Globalization. Meritocracy, Productivity, and the Hidden Language of Caste'. In *Blocked by Caste: Economic Discrimination in Modern India*, edited by Sukhadeo Thorat and Katherine S. Newman, 52–87. New Delhi: Oxford University Press, 2010.

Jodhka, Surinder S., and Murli Dhar. 'Cow, Caste and Communal Politics: Dalit Killings in Jhajjar'. *Economic and Political Weekly* 38, no. 3 (2003): 174–6.

Johnson, W. J., trans. *The Bhagavad Gita*. Oxford: Oxford University Press, 2008.

Johri, Ankita Dwivedi. 'In Mirchpur, a Race Leads to Clashes, Many Caste Narratives'. *Indian Express*, 3 February 2017. Accessed 5 February 2018. http://indianexpress.com/article/india/in-mirchpur-a-race-leads-to-clashes-many-caste-narratives-dalit-4505066/.

Jondhale, Surendra, and Johannes Beltz, eds. *Reconstructing the World: B. R. Ambedkar and Buddhism in India*. New Delhi: Oxford University Press, 2004.

Juergensmeyer, Mark. *Religious Rebels in the Punjab: The Ad Dharm Challenge to Caste*. New Delhi: Navayana, 2009.

Kannabiran, Vasanth, and Kalpana Kannabiran. 'Caste and Gender: Understanding Dynamics of Power and Violence'. *Economic and Political Weekly* 26, no. 37 (1991): 2130–3. doi:10.2307/41626993.

Kapur, Devesh, Chandra Bhan Prasad, Lant Pritchett and D. Shyam Babu. 'Rethinking Inequality: Dalits in Uttar Pradesh in the Market Reform Era'. *Economic and Political Weekly* 45, no. 35 (2010): 39–49.

Kapur, Devesh, D. Shyam Babu and Chandra Bhan Prasad. *Defying the Odds: The Rise of Dalit Entrepreneurs*. Gurgaon: Random House India, 2014.

Karthikeyan, D. and Hugo Gorringe. 'Rescuing Ambedkar', *Frontline*, 2012. Accessed 5 July 2019. https://www.frontline.in/static/html/fl2919/stories/20121005291913600.htm.

Kasturi, Charu Sudan. 'Ghetto in Medical Hostel: Quota Students in AIIMS Allege Being Driven into a Corner'. *Telegraph*, Calcutta, 5 July 2006. Accessed 6 February 2018. https://www.telegraphindia.com/india/ghetto-in-medical-hostel-quota-students-in-aiims-allege-being-driven-into-a-corner/cid/785574.

Kaviraj, Sudipta. 'On State, Society and Discourse in India'. In *Rethinking Third World Politics*, edited by James Manor, 72–99. London: Longman, 1991.

———. 'The Imaginary Institution of India'. In *Writings on South Asian History and Society*, edited by Partha Chatterjee and Gyanendra Pandey, 1–39. Subaltern Studies, VII. New Delhi: Oxford University Press, 1992.

Keer, Dhananjay. *Dr. Ambedkar: Life and Mission*. 3rd edn. Bombay: Popular Prakashan, 2003.

Keiko, Yamada. 'Politics and Representation of Caste Identity in Regional Historiography'. *Indian Economic & Social History Review* 45, no. 3 (2008): 353–80. doi:10.1177/001946460804500302.

———. 'Origin and Historical Evolution of the Identity of Modern Telugus'. *Economic and Political Weekly* 45, no. 34 (2010): 57–63.

Khilnani, Sunil. *The Idea of India*. London: Penguin Books, 1998.

Kohli, Atul. 'The NTR Phenomenon in Andhra Pradesh: Political Change in a South Indian State'. *Asian Survey* 28, no. 10 (1988): 991–1017.

Kothari, Rajni. 'Introduction'. In *Caste in Indian Politics*, edited by Rajni Kothari, 3–26. New Delhi: Orient Longman, 1970.

———. 'Rise of the Dalits and the Renewed Debate on Caste'. *Economic and Political Weekly* 29, no. 26 (1994): 1589–94.

Krishnan, P. S. 'Untouchability and Atrocities'. In *The Emerging Dalit Identity: The Re-assertion of the Subalterns*, edited by Walter Fernandes, 122–39. New Delhi: Indian Social Institute, 1996.

———. 'Atrocities against Dalits: Retrospect and Prospect'. *Combat Law: The Human Rights & Law Bimonthly* (2009): 6–17. Accessed 10 July 2019. https://www.yumpu.com/en/document/view/38026162/pdf-437mb-combat-law/2.

———. 'Walls in Minds'. *Frontline* 26, no. 24 (2009). Accessed 1 February 2018. http://www.frontline.in/static/html/fl2624/stories/20091204262402500.htm.

———. 'Scheduled Castes and Scheduled Tribes (Prevention of Atrocities) Amendment Act 2018: Justified by Constitutional Duty to Protect SCs and STs, but Does Not

Pose Any Threat to Really Innocent Persons, Annexure-2'. Letter to chief minister, Madhya Pradesh, unpublished, 26 September 2018.

Krishnaswamy, Sudhir. *Democracy and Constitutionalism in India: A Study of the Basic Structure Doctrine*. New Delhi: Oxford University Press, 2009.

Kumar, Aishwary. *Radical Equality: Ambedkar, Gandhi, and the Risk of Democracy*. Cultural Memory in the Past. Stanford, CA: Stanford University Press, 2015.

Kumar, P. Kesava. 'Popular Culture and Ideology: The Phenomenon of Gaddar'. *Economic and Political Weekly* 45, no. 7 (2010): 61–7.

Kumaraswamy, Nagam. 'Dalits and Autonomy: Towards Construction of Dalit Movement in Andhra Pradesh'. PhD thesis. Department of Political Science, Osmania University, Hyderabad, 2011.

Lacan, Jacques. *The Four Fundamental Concepts of Psychoanalysis*. The Seminar of Jacques Lacan, Book XI, trans. with notes by Bruce Fink. New York: Norton, 1998.

Laclau, Ernesto. *New Reflections on the Revolution of Our Time*. London: Verso, 1990.

———. *On Populist Reason*. London: Verso, 2005.

———. *The Rhetorical Foundations of Society*. London: Verso, 2014.

Laclau, Ernesto, and Chantal Mouffe. *Hegemony and Socialist Strategy: Towards a Radical Democratic Politics*. London: Verso, 2001.

Laxminarayana, K., K. Srinivasulu, Arun K. Patnaik, K. Y. Ratnam and Timma Reddy. 'Laxmipet Dalit Killings'. *Economic and Political Weekly* 47, nos. 47–8 (2012): 26–8.

Lieberman, Robert C. 'Ideas, Institutions, and Political Order: Explaining Political Change'. *American Political Science Review* 96, no. 4 (2002): 697–712. doi:10.1017/S0003055402000394.

Little, Daniel. 'The Heterogeneous Social: New Thinking about the Foundations of the Social Sciences'. In *Philosophy of the Social Sciences: Philosophical Theory and Scientific Practice*, edited by C. Mantzavinos, 154–78. Cambridge: Cambridge University Press, 2009.

Lourduswamy, S. 'Christian or Hindu, a Dalit Is a Dalit, Reservation Is His Right'. *Times of India*, 11 October 1998.

Manor, James. 'Prologue: Caste and Politics in Recent Times'. In *Caste in Indian Politics*, edited by Rajni Kothari and James Manor, 2nd edn, xi–lxi. Hyderabad: Orient BlackSwan, 2010.

Manu. *The Laws of Manu: With an Introduction and Notes*, trans. Wendy Doniger with Brian K. Smith. New Delhi: Penguin Books, 1991.

Marchart, Oliver. *Post-Foundational Political Thought: Political Difference in Nancy, Lefort, Badiou and Laclau*. Edinburgh: Edinburgh University Press, 2007.

Marmor, Andrei. *Interpretation and Legal Theory*. Oxford: Hart, 2005.

Mendelsohn, Oliver, and Marika Vicziany. *The Untouchables: Subordination, Poverty and the State in Modern India*. Cambridge: Cambridge University Press, 1998.

Mendelsohn, Oliver, and Upendra Baxi. 'Introduction'. In *The Rights of Subordinated Peoples*, edited by Oliver Mendelsohn and Upendra Baxi, 1–18. Delhi: Oxford University Press, 1994.

Mhaskar, Sumeet. 'Maratha Unrest and Its Linkages with Mumbai's Political Economy'. *Wire*, 5 December 2016. Accessed 7 December 2016. http://thewire.in/84198/maratha-unrest-linkages-mumbai-political-economy/.

Ministry of Labour & Employment. The Bonded Labour System (Abolition) Act, 1976 (Act No. 19 of 1976). New Delhi: Ministry of Labour & Employment, Government of India, 9 February 1976. Accessed 11 November 2017. http://labour.gov.in/sites/default/files/TheBondedLabourSystem(Abolition)Act1976.pdf.

Ministry of Law and Justice. The Protection of Civil Rights Act, 1955. Act No. 22 of 1955. 8 May 1955. Government of India, New Delhi: Ministry of Law and Justice, Government of India, 1955. Accessed 1 December 2016. http://lawmin.nic.in/ld/P-ACT/1955/A1955-22.pdf.

———. *The Institutes of Technology Act, 1961.* New Delhi: Ministry of Law and Justice, Government of India, 19 December 1961. Accessed 24 November 2018. http://legislative.gov.in/actsofparliamentfromtheyear/institutes-technology-act-1961.

———. The Scheduled Castes and the Scheduled Tribes (Prevention of Atrocities) Act. New Delhi: Ministry of Law and Justice, Government of India, 1989. Accessed 11 December 2017. http://lawmin.nic.in/ld/P-ACT/1989/The%20Scheduled%20Castes%20And%20the%20Scheduled%20Tribes%20%20(Prevention%20of%20Atrocities)%20Act,%201989.pdf.

Mitchel, Lise. *Language, Emotion, and Politics in South India: The Making of a Mother Tongue*. Bloomington, IN: Indiana University Press, 2009.

Mitta, Manoj. 'From Bihar to Maharashtra via Telangana: Brutal Reminders of Systemic Bias against Dalits'. *Scroll.in*, 26 January 2017. Accessed 27 January 2017. https://scroll.in/article/827674/from-bihar-to-maharashtra-via-telangana-brutal-reminders-of-systemic-bias-against-dalits.

Mohan, P. Sanal. *Modernity of Slavery: Struggles against Caste Inequality in Colonial Kerala*. New Delhi: Oxford University Press, 2015.

Mohanty, Manoranjan. 'Kilvenmani, Karamchedu to Khairlanji: Why Atrocities on Dalits Persist?' Unpublished paper. Institute for Human Development, New Delhi, July 2007. http://www.boell-india.org/download_en/mohanty_ amrita_corrected.pdf.

Mondal, Sudipto. 'Rohith Vemula: An Unfinished Portrait'. *Hindustan Times*, February 2017. Accessed 21 February 2017. http://www.hindustantimes.com/static/rohith-vemula-an-unfinished-portrait/index.html.

Montagu, Edwin Samuel, and Frederic John Napier Thesiger Chelmsford. *Report on Indian Constitutional Reforms*. East India (Constitutional Reforms), presented to both houses of parliament by command of His Majesty. London: H. M. S. O., 1918.

Moon, Vasant. *Dr. Babasaheb Ambedkar*, in Marathi, 1991. Trans. Asha Damle. New Delhi: National Book Trust, 2002.

Morris, Aldon D. *The Scholar Denied: W.E.B. Du Bois and the Birth of Modern Sociology*. Oakland, CA: University of California Press, 2015.

Mosse, David. 'Caste and Development: Contemporary Perspectives on a Structure of Discrimination and Advantage'. *World Development* 110 (2018): 422–36. doi:10.1016/j.worlddev.2018.06.003.

Mouffe, Chantal. *On the Political*. Abingdon: Routledge, 2005.

———. *Agonistics: Thinking the World Politically*. London: Verso, 2013.

Moyn, Samuel. *The Last Utopia: Human Rights in History*, vol. 1, paperback edn. Cambridge, MA: Belknap Press of Harvard University Press, 2012.

Murthy, N. Chandra Bhanu. 'Identity, Autonomy and Emancipation: The Agendas of the Adi-Andhra Movement in South India, 1917–30'. *The Indian Economic & Social History Review* 53, no. 2 (2016): 225–48. doi:10.1177/0019464616634841.

Muruli, K. 'Upper Caste Violence on Dalits: Case Studies of Karamchedu and Chundur Massacres'. MPhil dissertation, unpublished. Department of Political Science, University of Hyderabad, 1995.

Muthaiah, P. 'Dandora: The Madiga Movement for Equal Identity and Social Justice in A.P'. *Social Action* 54 (2004): 184–209.

Nag, Kingshuk. *Battleground Telangana: Chronicle of an Agitation*. New Delhi: Harper Collins Publishers India, 2011.

Narayana, G. 'Rule Making for Scheduled Castes: Analysis of Lok Sabha Debates, 1962-71'. *Economic and Political Weekly* 15, no. 8 (1980): 433–40.

Narayana, P. S. *Commentary on The Scheduled Castes and The Scheduled Tribes (Prevention of Atrocities) Act, 1989 & Rules, 1995 and Protection of Civil Rights Act, 1955 & Rules, 1977*, 5th edn. Hyderabad: Gogia Law Agency, 2006.

National Crime Records Bureau. *Crime in India 2016: Statistics*. New Delhi: Ministry of Home Affairs, Government of India, 2017. Accessed 7 December 2018. http://ncrb.gov.in/StatPublications/CII/CII2016/pdfs/NEWPDFs/Crime%20in%20India%20-%202016%20Complete%20PDF%20291117.pdf.

Navsarjan Trust and Robert F. Kennedy Center for Justice & Human Rights. *Understanding Untouchability: A Comprehensive Study of Practices and Conditions in 1589 Villages*. 2010.

NDTV. 'Caste Fine, Not Casteism, Says BJP's Yogi Adityanath'. 5 March 2017. Accessed 21 May 2017. https://www.youtube.com/watch?v=gE4RONcQIUA&feature=youtu.be.

———. 'Student Suicide: Congress Demands Probe against Smriti Irani'. 20 January 2016. Accessed 20 June 2017. http://www.ndtv.com/india-news/student-suicide-congress-demands-probe-against-smriti-irani-1268087.

———. 'They Did Namaz for Yakub Memon: BJP Student Leader about Rohith Vemula'. 21 January 2016. Accessed 21 June 2016. http://www.ndtv.com/hyderabad-news/hyderabad-suicide-have-proof-of-my-assault-says-abvp-man-1268275.

Nehru, Jawaharlal. *An Autobiography*. New Delhi: Jawaharlal Nehru Memorial Fund, 1980.

Nietzsche, Friedrich. 'Homer's Contest'. In *On the Genealogy of Morality*, edited by Keith Ansell-Pearson, rev. student edn, 174–81. Cambridge Texts in the History of Political Thought. Cambridge: Cambridge University Press, 2007.

O'Hanlon, Rosalind. *Caste Conflict and Ideology: Mahatma Jotirao Phule and Low Caste Protest in Nineteenth-Century Western India*. Cambridge: Cambridge University Press, 1985.

Omvedt, Gail. *Dalits and the Democratic Revolution: Dr. Ambedkar and the Dalit Movement in Colonial India*. New Delhi: Sage Publications, 1994.

———. *Buddhism in India: Challenging Brahmanism and Caste*. New Delhi: Sage Publications, 2003.

———. *Seeking Begumpura: The Social Vision of Anticaste Intellectuals*. New Delhi: Navayana, 2008.

Pai, Sudha. *Dalit Assertion and the Unfinished Democratic Revolution: The Bahujan Samaj Party in Uttar Pradesh*. New Delhi: Sage Publications, 2002.

Pandey, Sidharth. 'Quota Wrangle: Caste War Divides AIIMS'. *NDTV*, 16 September 2007.

Pandian, M. S. S. *Brahmin & Non-Brahmin: Genealogies of the Tamil Political Present*. Delhi: Permanent Black, 2007.

Parliament of India, Lok Sabha Debates. 'Re. Brutal Killing of Harijans in Tsundur Village of Guntur District'. 1991. Accessed 15 January 2018. http://parliamentofindia.nic.in/ls/lsdeb/ls10/ses1/0409089101.htm.

Parliament of India. 'Monday, the 9th December 1946'. In *Constituent Assembly of India*, vol. 1. New Delhi. http://parliamentofindia.nic.in/ls/debates/vol1p1.htm.

Pettit, Philip. *Just Freedom: A Moral Compass for a Complex World*. New York: W. W. Norton & Company, 2014.

Philipose, Pamela. 'Khairlanji to Kanpur'. *Indian Express*, 2 December 2006. Accessed 10 July 2019. http://archive.indianexpress.com/news/khairlanji-to-kanpur/17707/.

Picherit, David. 'Rural Youth and Circulating Labour in South India: The Tortuous Paths towards Respect for Madigas'. *Journal of Agrarian Change* 37, no. 43 (2018): 178–95. doi:10.1111/joac.12196.

Price, Gregory N., William A. Darity and Alvin E. Headen. 'Does the Stigma of Slavery Explain the Maltreatment of Blacks by Whites? The Case of Lynchings'. *The Journal of Socio-Economics* 37, no. 1 (2008): 167–93. doi:10.1016/j.socec.2007.06.001.

PUCL. 'Suppressing the Voice of the Oppressed: State Terror on Protests against the Khairlanji Massacre: A Report to the Nation by an All Indian Team'. 2007. Accessed 10 April 2017. http://www.pucl.org/major_reports/Report%20on%20Khairlanji%20Massacre,%202007-2.pdf.

Radhakrishnan, P. 'Mandal Commission Report: A Sociological Critique'. In *Caste: Its Twentieth Century Avatar*, edited by M. N.Srinivas, 203–20. New Delhi: Penguin Books, 1996.

———. 'Backward Classes in Tamil Nadu 1872–1988'. *Economic and Political Weekly* 25, no. 10 (1990). Accessed 26 February 2016. http://www.epw.in/journal/1990/10/special-articles/backward-classes-tamil-nadu-1872-1988.html.

Raj, Jayaseelan. 'Alienated Enclaves: Economic Crisis and Neo-bondage in a South Indian Plantation Belt'. *Forum for Development Studies* 40, no. 3 (2013): 465–90. doi:10.1080/08039410.2013.799098.

Ramaswamy, Uma. 'The Belief System of the Non-Brahmin Movement in India: The Andhra Case'. *Asian Survey* 18, no. 3 (1978): 290–300. doi:10.2307/2643221.

Rani, Challapalli Swaroopa. 'Dalit Women's Writing in Telugu'. *Economic and Political Weekly* 33, no. 17 (1998): 21–4. doi:10.2307/4406697.

Rao, Anupama. *The Caste Question: Dalits and the Politics of Modern India*. Berkeley, CA: University of California Press, 2009.

———. 'Who is the Dalit? The Emergence of a New Political Subject'. In *Claiming Power from Below: Dalits and the Subaltern Question in India*, edited by Manu Bhagavan and Anne Feldhaus, 11–27. New Delhi: Oxford University Press, 2009.

Rao, Katti Padma. *Caste and Alternative Culture*. Chennai: The Gurukul Lutheran Theological College & Research Institute, 1998.

Rao, M. S. A. 'Some Conceptual Issues in the Study of Caste, Class, Ethnicity and Dominance'. In *Dominance and State Power in Modern India: Decline of a Social Order*, edited by Francine R. Frankel and M. S. A. Rao. vol. 1, 21–45, 2 vols. Delhi: Oxford University Press, 1989.

Rao, Yagati Chinna. *Dalits Struggle for Identity: Andhra and Hyderabad 1900-1950*. New Delhi: Kanishka, 2003.

———. 'Introduction'. In *Dividing Dalits: Writings on Sub-Categorisation of Scheduled Castes*, edited by Yagati C. Rao, 1–50. Jaipur: Rawat Publications, 2009.

Ratnam, K. Y. 'The Dalit Movement in Andhra Pradesh: A Study of Political Consciousness and Identity'. PhD thesis. Centre for Political Studies, School of Social Sciences, University of Jawaharlal Nehru, New Delhi, 2014.

———. 'The Dalit Movement and Democratization in Andhra Pradesh'. Working Paper No. 13. East-West Center, Washington, DC, 1 January 2008. Accessed 10 July 2019. https://www.eastwestcenter.org/fileadmin/stored/pdfs/ewcwwp013.pdf.

Reddy, D. Narasimha. 'Karamchedu: A Dialectic without Development'. *Economic and Political Weekly* 20 (1985): 1546–9.

Reddy, G. Ram. 'The Politics of Accommodation: Caste, Class and Dominance in Andhra Pradesh'. In *Dominance and State Power in Modern India*, edited by Francine R. Frankel and M. S. A. Rao. 265–321. Delhi: Oxford University Press, 1989.

Rediff. 'Damaged Ambedkar Statue Sparks Protests in Kanpur'. 29 November 2006. Accessed 5 February 2018. http://www.rediff.com/news/2006/nov/29statue.htm.

Risley, Herbert. *The People of India,1915*, 2nd edn. New Delhi: Munshiram Manoharlal, 1991.

Roberts, Nathaniel. *To be Cared For: The Power of Conversion and Foreignness of Belonging in an Indian Slum*. Oakland, CA: University of California Press, 2016.

Roskamm, Nikolai. 'On the other Side of "Agonism": "The Enemy," the "Outside," and the Role of Antagonism'. *Planning Theory* 14, no. 4 (2015): 384–403. doi:10.1177/1473095214533959.

Round Table India. 'Tsunduru Trial: Judge Drops Contempt Charges against Bojja Tharakam', 27 March 2014. Accessed 24 March 2017. https://roundtableindia.co.in/index.php?option=com_content&view=article&id=7314:tsunduru-trial-judge-drops-contempt-charges-against-bojja-tharakam&catid=129:events-and-activism&Itemid=195.

———. 'The Doctor and the Saint'. In *The Annihilation of Caste: The Annotated Critical Edition, B. R. Ambedkar*, edited by S. Anand, 15–179. London: Verso.

Rudolph, Lloyd I. and Susanne Hoeber Rudolph. *The Modernity of Tradition: Political Development in India*. Bombay: Orient Longman, 1969.

———. *Postmodern Gandhi and other Essays: Gandhi in the World and at Home*, rev. edn. Chicago and London: University of Chicago Press, 2006.

Sahay, Gaurang R. 'Dominance of Jats Is Unabated: Caste and Dominance in the Villages of Western Uttar Pradesh'. *Contributions to Indian Sociology* 49, no. 2 (2015): 216–49. doi:10.1177/0971945815575448.

Salaha. *Karamchedu: Report by Fact Finding Team*. Hyderabad: Hyderabad Book Trust, 1985.

Sankaran, S. R. 'Social Exclusion and Criminal Law'. In *Challenging the Rule(s) of Law: Colonialism, Criminology and Human Rights in India*, edited by Kalpana Kannabirān and Ranbir Singh, 121–41. Los Angeles and London: Sage Publications, 2008.

Satyanarayana, A. 'Caste and Class in Rural Andhra'. In *Caste and Class in India*, edited by Kanhaiya Lal Sharma, 367–91. Jaipur: Rawat Publishers, 1994.

———. 'Dalit Protest Literature in Telugu: A Historical Perspective'. *Economic and Political Weekly* 30, no. 3 (1995): 171–5.

Schmitt, Carl. *The Concept of the Political*. Chicago, London: University of Chicago Press, 1996.

Scheduled Caste Welfare Department. The Constitution (Scheduled Castes) Order, 1950. New Delhi: Ministry of Social Welfare and Empowerment. Accessed 10 July 2019. http://socialjustice.nic.in/writereaddata/UploadFile/scorders-updated-30062016.pdf.

Scott, James C. *Seeing like a State: How Certain Schemes to Improve the Human Condition Have Failed*. New Haven, CT: Yale University Press, 1998.

Scroll.in. 'Bharat Bandh: Nine Killed, Hundreds Detained as Protests Turn Violent in Several States'. 2 April 2018. Accessed 2 November 2018. https://scroll.in/latest/874124/bharat-bandh-dalit-protestors-block-trains-in-bihar-odisha-against-scs-order-on-sc-st-act.

Searle, John R. 'Social Ontology: Some Basic Principles'. *Anthropological Theory* 6, no. 1 (2006): 12–29. doi:10.1177/1463499606061731.

Selznick, Philip. *Leadership in Administration: A Sociological Interpretation*. Berkeley, CA, and London: University of California Press, 1957 and 1984.

Seshadri, K. 'The Telengana Agitation and the Politics of Andhra Pradesh'. *The Indian Journal of Political Science* 31, no. 1 (1970): 60–81. doi:10.2307/41854361.

Sharma, Smriti. 'Caste-Based Crimes and Economic Status: Evidence from India'. *Journal of Comparative Economics* 43, no. 1 (2015): 204–26. doi:10.1016/j.jce.2014.10.005.

Singh, Gurharpal. 'Religious Transnationalism and Development Initiatives: The Dera Sachkhand Ballan'. *Economic and Political Weekly* 47, no. 1 (2012): 53–60. Accessed 3 October 2018. https://www.epw.in/journal/2012/01/religion-and-citizenship-special-issues/religious-transnationalism-and-development.

Singh, Jagpal. 'Ambedkarisation and Assertion of Dalit Identity: Socio-Cultural Protest in Meerut District of Western Uttar Pradesh'. *Economic and Political Weekly* 33, no. 40 (1998): 2611–18. doi:10.2307/4407245.

Singh, K. S. *The Scheduled Castes*, Anthropological Survey of India. Delhi: Oxford University Press, 1995.

Singh, Manmohan. *PM's Speech at the Chief Minister's Meet on Naxalism*. New Delhi: Prime Minister's Office, 2006.

Sivaramakrishnan, Arvind. 'Caste Out by the Law'. *Hindu*, 1 August 2013.

Skinner, Quentin. *Visions of Politics: Regarding Method*, vol. 1. Cambridge: Cambridge University Press, 2002.

Smith, A. T. H., ed. *Glanville Williams: Learning the Law*, 15th edn. London: Sweet & Maxwell, 2013.

Som, Reba. 'Jawaharlal Nehru and the Hindu Code: A Victory of Symbol over Substance?' *Modern Asian Studies* 28, no. 1 (1994): 165–94. http://dx.doi.org/10.1017/S0026749X00011732.

Sommers, Samuel R., and Phoebe C. Ellsworth. 'White Juror Bias: An Investigation of Prejudice against Black Defendants in the American Courtroom'. *Psychology, Public Policy, and Law* 7, no. 1 (2001): 201–29. doi:10.1037/1076-8971.7.1.201.

Sorabjee, Soli J. 'The Official Position'. *Seminar – India*, December, no. 508 (2001). Accessed 25 February 2016. http://www.india-seminar.com/2001/508/508%20soli%20j.%20sorabjee.htm.

Special public prosecutor. 'Written Arguments in SC no. 36/1993. In the Court of the Special Session Judge under the SCs & STs (PoA) Act, 1989 (IV ASJ) Guntur. Camp: Tsundur. SC No. 36/91', unpublished, July 2007.

Srinivas, M. N. 'A Note on Sanskritization and Westernization'. *The Far Eastern Quarterly* 15, no. 4 (1956): 481–96. doi:10.2307/2941919.

———. 'Caste in Modern India'. *The Journal of Asian Studies* 16, no. 4 (1957): 529–48.

———. 'The Dominant Caste in Rampura'. *American Anthropologist* 61, no. 1 (1959): 1–16.

———. *Social Change in Modern India (1966)*. New Delhi: Orient Longman, 1995.

———. *The Remembered Village*, 2nd edn. New Delhi: Oxford University Press, 2012.

Srinivasulu, K. 'Caste, Class and Social Articulation in Andhra Pradesh: Mapping Differential Regional Trajectories'. Working Paper 179. Overseas Development Institute, London, 2002. Accessed 10 July 2019. https://www.odi.org/sites/odi.org.uk/files/odi-assets/publications-opinion-files/2692.pdf.

———. 'The Caste Question in the Naxalite Movement'. *Economic and Political Weekly* 52, no. 21 (2017): 47–52. http://www.epw.in/journal/2017/21/naxalbari-and-after/naxalbari-chhattisgarh.html.

State of Andhra Pradesh. 2014. Special Leave Petition (CRL). No. 5353-5361/2014. In the Supreme Court of India (Order XXI Rule 4). Criminal Appellate Jurisdiction (Under Article 136 of the Constitution of India). New Delhi, 30 June. On file with the author.'*Sub-Divisional Police Officer, Tenali* (Crime Nos. 65 to 73 and 89 and 90/91 of Tsundur P.S. and Crime No. 64/91 of Amarthaluru P.S.) *vs Accused 1* (Modugula Sami Reddy - 219). Tsundur court, 31 August 2007.

Subramanian, Ajantha. 'Making Merit: The Indian Institutes of Technology and the Social Life of Caste'. *Comparative Studies in Society and History* 57, no. 2 (2015): 291–322. doi:10.1017/S0010417515000043.

Subramanian, K. S. *Political Violence and the Police in India*. New Delhi: Sage Publications, 2007.

Supreme Court of India. *E.V. Chinnaiah v. State of Andhra Pradesh and Ors*. Civil Appeal No. 6758 of 2000. 5 November 2004. http://www.judis.openarchive.in/.

Suri, K. C. 'Telugu Desam Party: Rise and Prospects for Future'. *Economic and Political Weekly* 39, nos. 14–15 (2004): 1481–90.

Tarrow, Sidney. *Power in Movement: Social Movements and Contentious Politics*. Cambridge: Cambridge University Press, 2011.

Tartakov, Gary Michael. 'The Navayāna Creation of the Buddha Image'. In *Reconstructing the World: B. R. Ambedkar and Buddhism in India*, edited by Surendra Jondhale and Johannes Beltz, 151–85. New Delhi: Oxford University Press, 2004.

Teltumbde, Anand. *Khairlanji: A Strange and Bitter Crop*. New Delhi: Navayana, 2008.

———. 'High Court's Verdict on Khairlanji: Justice Diminished'. *Economic and Political Weekly* 45, no. 32 (2010): 10–11.

———. *The Persistence of Caste: The Khairlanji Murders and India's Hidden Apartheid*. New Delhi: Navayana, 2010.

———. '10 Years of Khairlanji: What Do We See?' *Economic and Political Weekly* 51, no. 36 (2016): 10–11 .

Tharakam, Bojja. 'Laxmipeta: Deadly Combination of Caste and Political Power'. *Economic and Political Weekly* 47, no. 28 (2012). Accessed 11 July 2019. http://www.epw.in/journal/2012/28/web-exclusives/laxmipeta-deadly-combination-caste-and-political-power.html.

The Central Educational Institutions (Reservation in Admission) Bill, 2006. Bill No. 76 of 2006.

Thelen, Kathleen. 'How Institutions Evolve: Insights from Comparative Historical Analysis'. In *Comparative Historical Analysis in the Social Sciences*, edited by James Mahoney and Dietrich Rueschemeyer, 208–40. Cambridge Studies in Comparative Politics. Cambridge: Cambridge University Press, 2003.

Thorat, Sukhadeo and Umakant, eds. *Caste, Race and Discrimination: Discourses in International Context*. New Delhi: Indian Institute of Dalit Studies, 2004.

Thorat, Sukhadeo, K. M. Shyamprasad and R. K. Srivastava. *Report of the Committee to Enquire into the Allegation of Differential Treatment of SC/ST Students in All India Institute of Medical Science, Delhi*. New Delhi: University Grant Commission, 2005.

Times of India. 'The Burning of Manu'. 30 January 1928. Accessed 15 March 2016. https://search.proquest.com/docview/346271176?accountid=11144.

———. 'Right of Entry to Poona Parvati Temple'. 17 October 1929. Accessed 21 September 2018. https://search.proquest.com/docview/613812370?accountid=9735.

———. 'Untouchables Win'. 17 October 1931. Accessed 20 September 2018. https://search.proquest.com/docview/325523999?accountid=11144.

———. 'Huge Crowds Welcome Mr. Gandhi: Depressed Classes' Counter-Demonstration, Impressions of Second Round Table Conference'. 29 December 1931. Accessed 20 September 2018. https://search.proquest.com/docview/325423172?accountid=9735.

———. 'Untouchability and Temple Entry: Important Movement'. 18 November 1932. Accessed 20 September 2018.https://search.proquest.com/docview/324543375?accountid=9735.

———. 'Surprise for Dr. Ambedkar: Attack on Caste and Its Sequel'. 19 May 1936. Accessed 20 September 2018. http://search.proquest.com/docview/608398064?accountid=11144.

———. 'Right of Using Tank'. 18 March 1937. Accessed 14 March 2016. https://search.proquest.com/docview/325343193?accountid=11144.

———. 'Eyewitness Account Given: Burning of Harijan Boy'. 3 May 1968. Accessed 25 April 2016. http://search.proquest.com/docview/614027427/fulltextPDF/97566C7EEE244A2PQ/2?accountid=11144.

———. 'Use MISA to End Atrocities on Harijans'. 1 December 1974. Accessed 20 September 2018. https://search.proquest.com/docview/750801793?accountid=9735.

———. 'NTR Demands Delhi Rule in AP'. 12 August 1991.

———. 'SC Convicts 31 in Karamchedu Dalit Massacre'. 20 December 2008. Accessed 10 July 2019. https://timesofindia.indiatimes.com/city/hyderabad/SC-convicts-31-in-Karamchedu-Dalit-massacre/articleshow/3864622.cms?referral=PM.

———. 'My Cabinet Colleagues Are Vegetarians, Yet Not Weak: Adityanath Yogi'. 1 May 2017. Accessed 23 June 2017. http://timesofindia.indiatimes.com/city/lucknow/my-cabinet-colleagues-are-vegetarian-yet-not-weak-adityanath-yogi/articleshow/58463422.cms.

———. 'Parliament Passes Bill to Restore Original SC_ST Atrocity Law'. 9 August 2018. Accessed 29 October 2018. https://timesofindia.indiatimes.com/india/parliament-okays-bill-to-restore-original-sc/st-atrocity-law/articleshow/65340768.cms.

Upadhya, Carol. 'Amaravati and the New Andhra: Reterritorialization of a Region'. *Journal of South Asian Development* 12, no. 2 (2017): 177–202. doi:10.1177/0973174117712324.

Upadhya, Carol Boyak. 'The Farmer-Capitalists of Coastal Andhra Pradesh'. *Economic and Political Weekly* 23, no. 28 (1988): 1433–42.

Vemula, Rohith. 'My Birth is My Fatal Accident: Full Text of Dalit Student Rohith's Suicide Letter'. *Indian Express*, 19 January 2016. Accessed 20 June 2016. http://indianexpress.com/article/india/india-news-india/dalit-student-suicide-full-text-of-suicide-letter-hyderabad/?utm_content=buffer0c986&utm_medium=social&utm_source=facebook.com&utm_campaign=buffer.

Villa, Dana Richard. *Politics, Philosophy, Terror: Essays on the Thought of Hannah Arendt*. Princeton, NJ: Princeton University Press, 1999.

Viswanath, Rupa. *The Pariah Problem: Caste, Religion, and the Social in Modern India*. New York: Columbia University Press, 2014.

———. 'Commissioning Representation: The Misra Report, Deliberation and the Government of the People in Modern India'. *South Asia: Journal of South Asian Studies* 38, no. 3 (2015): 495–511. doi:10.1080/00856401.2015.1049773.

Viswanathan, S. *Dalits in Dravidian Land: Frontline Reports on Anti-Dalit Violence in Tamil Nadu (1995-2004)*. Pondicherry: Navayana, 2005.

Washbrook, D. A. *The Emergence of Provincial Politics: The Madras Presidency, 1870–1920*. Cambridge: Cambridge University Press, 1976.

———. 'Law, State and Agrarian Society in Colonial India'. *Modern Asian Studies* 15, no. 3 (1981): 649–721.

Weber, Max. *Economy and Society: An Outline of Interpretive Sociology*. Berkeley, CA: University of California Press, 1978.

Weiner, Myron. 'The Struggle for Equality: Caste in Indian Politics'. In *The Success of India's Democracy*, edited by Atul Kohli, vol. 6, 193–225. Contemporary South Asia. Cambridge: Cambridge University Press, 2001.

Weisskopf, Thomas E. *Affirmative Action in the United States and India: A Comparative Perspective*. London: Routledge, 2004.

Wenman, Mark. *Agonistic Democracy: Constituent Power in the Era of Globalisation*. Cambridge: Cambridge University Press, 2013.

Wilkinson, Steven I. 'Communal Riots in India'. *Economic and Political Weekly* 40, nos. 44–5 (2005): 4768–70. doi:10.2307/4417364.

Wire. 'Letter Trail Shows HRD Ministry's Keen Interest in "Anti-National" Activities in Hyderabad University'. 20 January 2016. Accessed 26 June 2017. https://thewire.in/19757/letter-trail-shows-hrd-ministrys-keen-interest-in-anti-national-activities-in-hyderabad-university/.

———. 'Shivraj Chouhan's Legally Untenable Promise on SC/ST Act Betrays BJP's Desperation in MP'. 22 September 2018. Accessed 8 Novemebr 2018. https://thewire.in/politics/shivraj-chouhan-madhya-pradesh-bjp-sc-st-act.

Yadav, Kripal Chandra, ed. *From Periphery to Centre Stage*. New Delhi: Manohar Publishers, 2000.

Yanow, Dvora. *Constructing 'Race' and 'Ethnicity' in America: Category-Making in Public Policy and Administration*. Armonk, NY: M.E. Sharpe, 2003.

Zelliot, Eleanor. 'Learning the Use of Political Means: The Mahars of Maharasthra'. In *Caste in Indian Politics*, edited by Rajni Kothari, 27–65. New Delhi: Orient Longman, 1970.

———. *From Untouchable to Dalit: Essays on the Ambedkar Movement*. New Delhi: Manohar Publishers, 2001.

———. 'Dr. Babasaheb Ambedkar and the Untouchable Movement'. PhD thesis. University of Pennsylvania, 1969. New Delhi: Blumoon Books, 2004.

Index

For EU product safety concerns, contact us at Calle de José Abascal, 56–1°, 28003 Madrid, Spain or eugpsr@cambridge.org.

www.ingramcontent.com/pod-product-compliance
Lightning Source LLC
LaVergne TN
LVHW011522200926
848484LV00001B/118
9781108489874